LEONARDO DA VINCI

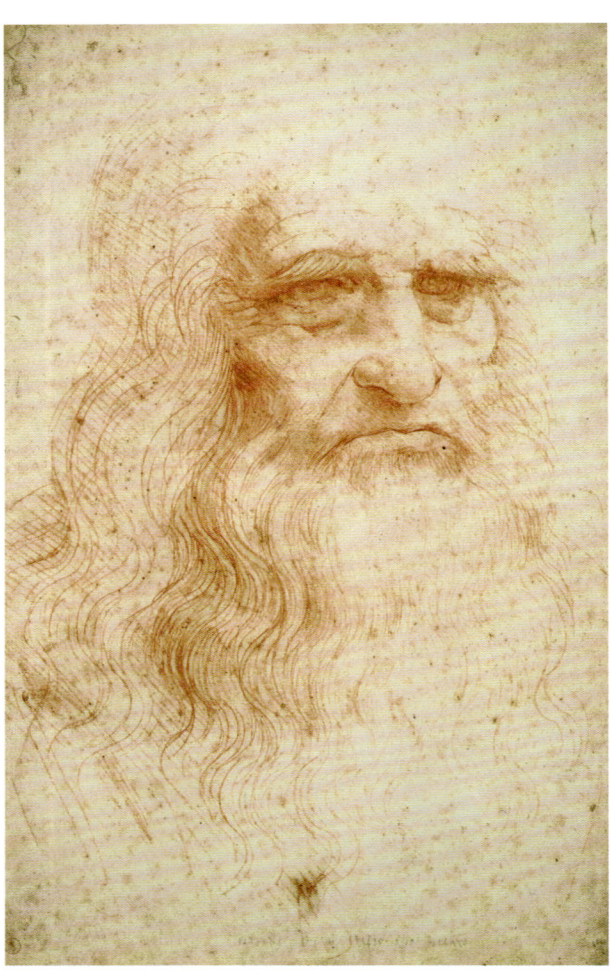

LEONARDO DA VINCI

DANIEL KIECOL

p. 2

Self portrait

Autoportrait

Selbstporträt

Autorretrato

Autoritratto

Zelfportret

c. 1512, Red chalk on paper/Sanguine sur papier, 33,3 × 21,3 cm, Biblioteca Reale, Torino

KÖNEMANN
© 2017 koenemann.com GmbH
www.koenemann.com

© Éditions Place des Victoires
6, rue du Mail – 75002 Paris
www.victoires.com
ISBN: 978-2-8099-1376-7
Dépôt légal: 1er trimestre 2017

Concept, Project Management: koenemann.com GmbH
Text: Dr. Daniel Kiecol
Editing: Ruth Dangelmaier

Translations into English: David Nash
Translations into French: Denis-Armand Canal

Spanish, Italian, Dutch translations:

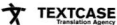

info@textcase.nl
textcase.de   textcase.eu

Layout: Christoph Eiden
Picture credits: Bridgeman Images, akg-images gmbh (p. 18)

ISBN: 978-3-95588-115-3 (international)

Printed in China by Shenzhen Hua Xin Colour-printing & Platemaking Co., Ltd

Contents   Sommaire   Inhalt   Índice   Indice   Inhoud

À propos

Leonardo da Vinci—
Renaissance artist par excellence
Although Leonardo da Vinci appears to us today as the embodiment of a Renaissance artist, he actually towers above even the most respected of his contemporaries. He was not only a pioneer of painting and drawing —stylistically, technically, and in his choice of subjects—but also in the sciences, and he was able to set out his ideas in theoretical form and, with his

Léonard de Vinci –
Un pur artiste de la Renaissance
Autant Léonard de Vinci fait aujourd'hui figure de symbole par excellence de l'artiste Renaissance, autant il a dépassé, de son temps, les plus considérés de ses contemporains. Non seulement il fut un pionnier dans l'art de la peinture et du dessin (en matière de style, de technique et de thématique) comme dans les sciences, mais il a également su consigner ses pensées sous forme

Leonardo da Vinci –
Renaissancekünstler schlechthin
So sehr Leonardo da Vinci heute als Renaissancekünstler schlechthin erscheint, so sehr überragte er doch selbst die angesehensten seiner Zeitgenossen. So war er eben nicht nur ein Pionier der Malerei und Zeichenkunst – in Bezug auf Stilistik, Technik und Thematik – und der Wissenschaften, sondern verstand es auch, seine Gedanken in

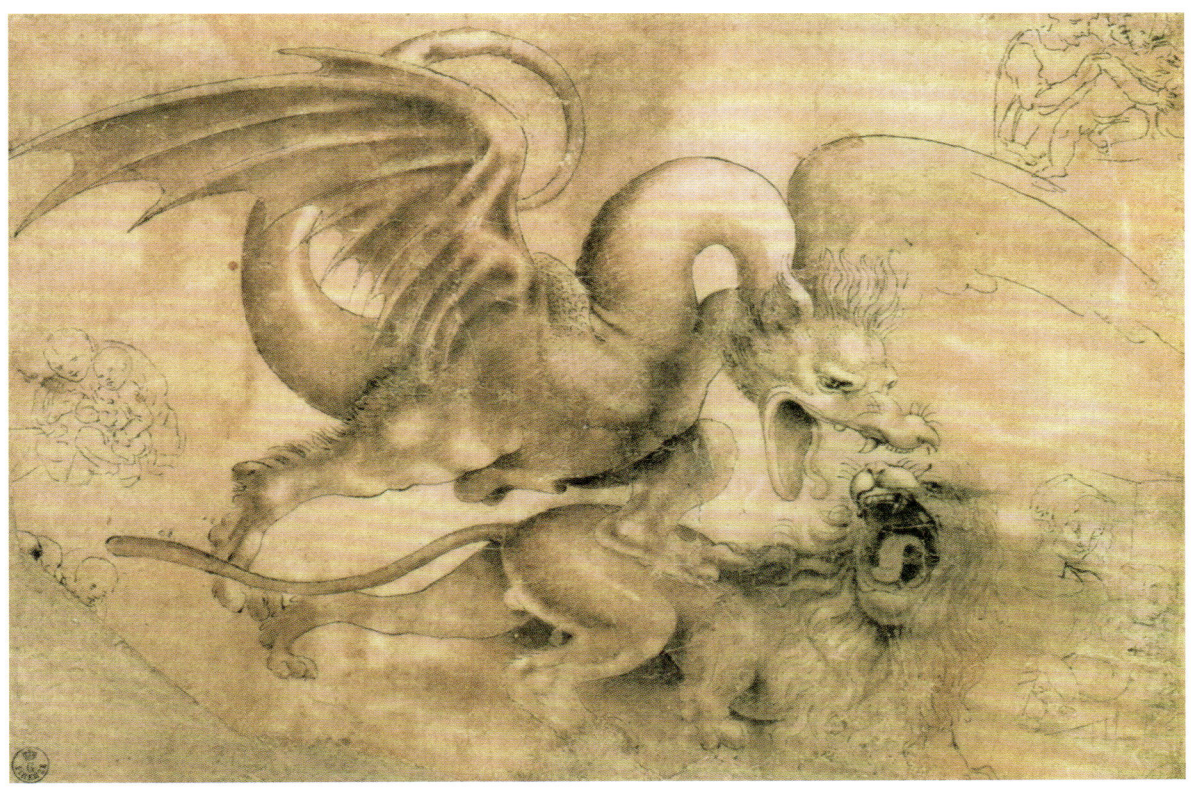

Leonardo da Vinci – Artista del renacimiento por antonomasia

Aunque actualmente Leonardo da Vinci parezca ser el artista del renacimiento por antonomasia, cabe destacar que ya en su época era uno de los artistas más admirados. No sólo fue pionero en la pintura y el dibujo con su estilo, en técnica y temática, también lo fue en la ciencia. Supo darle forma teórica a sus pensamientos en sus códigos, que llegaron a tener una tremenda

Leonardo da Vinci – l'artista del Rinascimento per eccellenza

Così come oggi Leonardo da Vinci è considerato l'artista per eccellenza del Rinascimento, allo stesso modo fu di gran lunga superiore ai suoi contemporanei più stimati. Infatti non fu solo un pioniere della pittura, dell'arte del disegno, per quanto riguarda stilistica, tecnica e tematica, e delle scienze, ma comprese anche come mettere per iscritto i suoi pensieri

Leonardo da Vinci – renaissancekunstenaar *par excellence*

Hoezeer Leonardo da Vinci tegenwoordig als schoolvoorbeeld van de renaissancekunstenaar wordt gezien, hij torent toch ver uit boven de meest vermaarde van zijn tijdgenoten. Niet alleen was hij een pionier in de schilder- en tekenkunst – in stijl, techniek en thematiek – en in de wetenschappen, maar hij wist zijn ideeën ook in theoretische vorm vast te leggen en

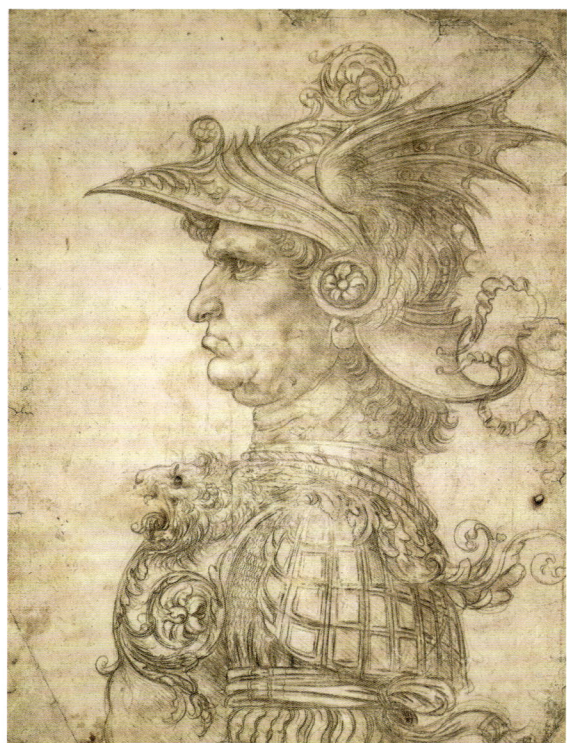

codices, exercise immense influence upon future generations. This holistic claim, the indissoluble connection between art and science, as well as to Christian traditions, and with reference to antiquity, made Leonardo a Renaissance polymath.

Leonardo da Vinci was born on 15 April 1452 in Vinci, near Florence, as the illegitimate son of the notary Piero da Vinci and a peasant girl, Caterina. In spite of his unpromising family circumstances, he seemed to have

théorique et exercer, par ses manuscrits, une immense influence sur la postérité. Cette exigence de globalité fondée sur l'union indissoluble de l'art et de la science, mais aussi de la tradition chrétienne et du retour à l'Antiquité, Léonard en a presque fait le phénotype de l'homme de la Renaissance.

Léonard de Vinci, né le 14 avril 1452 à Vinci, petite ville toscane proche de Florence, est le fils naturel d'un notaire de la République, Maître Piero, et d'une paysanne. Malgré les difficultés de la

theoretischer Form niederzulegen und mit seinen Codizes immensen Einfluss auf die Nachwelt auszuüben. Dieser ganzheitliche Anspruch, die unauflösliche Verbindung aus Kunst und Wissenschaft sowie aus christlicher Tradition und Rückbesinnung auf die Antike ließ Leonardo geradezu zum Phänotyp des Renaissancemenschen werden.

Leonardo da Vinci kam am 15. April 1452 als unehelicher Sohn des Notars Piero da Vinci und des Bauernmädchens

Leonardo da Vinci's handwriting
Écriture manuscrite de Léonard de Vinci
Handschrift Leonardo da Vincis
Manuscrito de Leonardo da Vinci
Grafia di Leonardo da Vinci
Handschrift van Leonardo da Vinci

Pen and ink on paper/Encre et plume sur papier,
Private collection

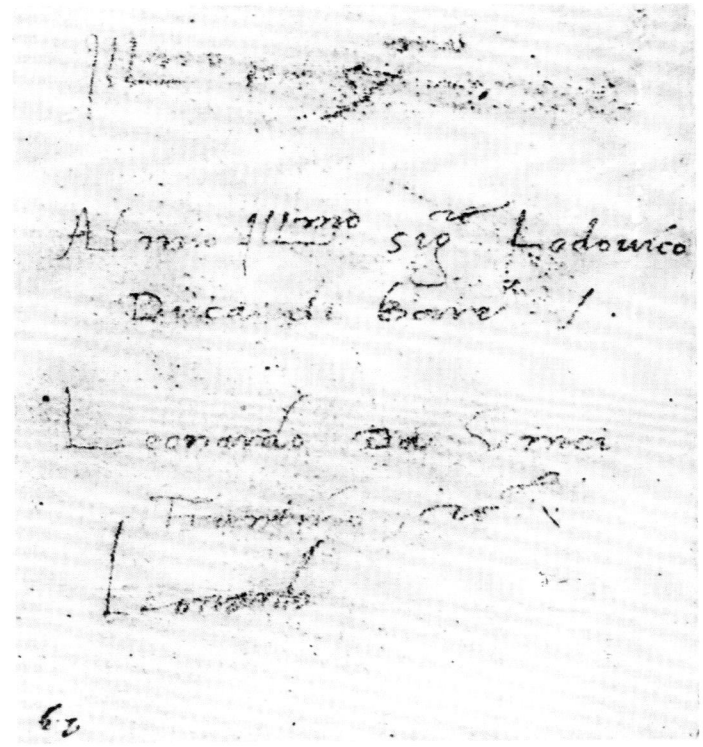

repercusión para la posteridad. Esta visión totalitaria, la unión indisoluble entre el arte y la ciencia, de la tradición cristiana y la antigüedad clásica, es lo que realmente convirtió a Leonardo en el fenotipo del hombre renacentista.

Leonardo da Vinci vino al mundo el 15 de abril de 1452 como hijo ilegítimo del notario Piero da Vinci y la campesina Caterina in Vinci, cerca de Florencia. A pesar de sus difíciles circunstancias familiares disfrutó de una educación exigente, pero afectuosa, que con tan

in forma teoretica esercitando un influsso enorme sui posteri con i suoi codici. Questa esigenza complessiva, l'unione indissolubile tra arte e scienza e tra la tradizione cristiana e il ritorno all'antichità permise a Leonardo di diventare un fenotipo dell'uomo del Rinascimento.

Leonardo da Vinci venne alla luce il 15 aprile 1452 a Vinci, nei dintorni di Firenze, come figlio naturale del notaio Piero da Vinci e della giovane contadina Catarina. Nonostante le

had met zijn codices een enorme invloed op latere generaties. Door deze aanspraak op de totale beheersing van de menselijke kennis en op het verband tussen kunst en wetenschap, en tussen christelijke en klassieke tradities, werd Leonardo hét voorbeeld van de 'renaissancemens'.

Leonardo da Vinci werd op 15 april 1452 als onechtelijk kind van de notaris Piero da Vinci en het boerenmeisje Catarina geboren in het dorpje Vinci, in de buurt van Florence. Ondanks deze

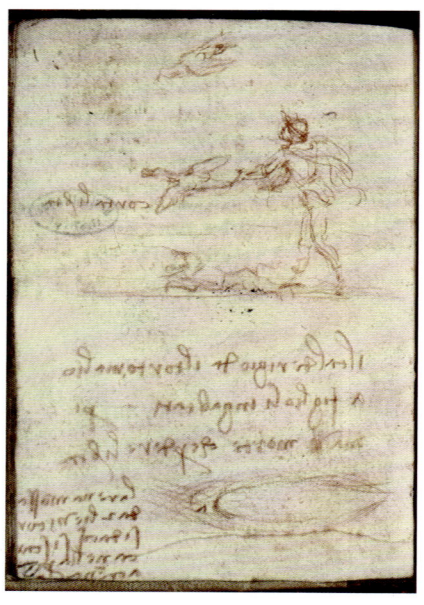

enjoyed a considerate and supportive upbringing, which eventually led him to Florence at the age of 17 where he became a pupil of Andrea del Verrocchio, the most sought-after painter and sculptor of the time. His entry into the Guild of St. Luke, around 1472, marked the formal completion of his training. However, Leonardo stayed on for another ten years in Florence.

At the instigation of the Medici, Leonardo recommended himself, in a letter, to Ludovico Sforza, the mighty Duke of Milan and consequently went to Lombardy at the beginning of the 1480s. His time in Milan produced not only masterpieces such as *The Last Supper* and *The Virgin of the Rocks,* but also his intensive study of scientific

situation familiale, il semble avoir reçu une éducation relativement soignée qui le conduit pour finir à Florence, à l'âge de dix-sept ans, où il entre comme élève dans l'atelier d'Andrea del Verrocchio, peintre et sculpteur alors très demandé. Après son admission dans la Guilde de Saint-Luc, vers 1472, qui marque la fin « officielle » de sa formation, il reste une dizaine d'années à Florence.

À l'instigation des Médicis, Léonard se recommande ensuite lui-même auprès de Ludovic Sforza, le puissant duc de Milan, et s'installe en Lombardie au début des années 1480. À Milan naissent des chefs-d'œuvre comme *La Cène* et *La Vierge aux rochers.* Dans le même temps, l'artiste s'intéresse activement aux phénomènes étudiés par les sciences de

Catarina in Vinci, in der Nähe von Florenz zur Welt. Trotz der schwierigen Familienverhältnisse schien er eine fürsorgliche und fördernde Erziehung genossen zu haben, die schließlich dazu führte, dass er im Alter von 17 Jahren nach Florenz ging, wo er Schüler Andrea del Verrocchios wurde, dem damals gefragtesten Maler und Bildhauer. Der Eintritt in die St. Lukas-Gilde etwa 1472 markierte den formalen Abschluss der Ausbildung, doch blieb Leonardo noch etwa weitere zehn Jahre in Florenz.

Auf Betreiben der Medici hin empfahl sich Leonardo selbst in einem Brief dem mächtigen Herzog von Mailand, Ludovico Sforza und ging zu Beginn der 1480er-Jahre in die Lombardei. In Mailand entstanden nicht nur

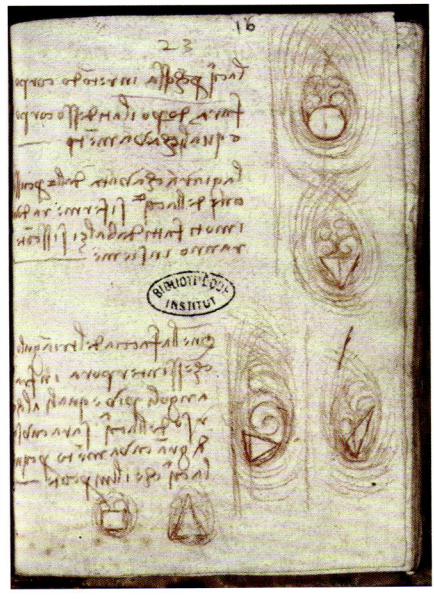

sólo 17 años, lo empujó a mudarse a Florencia, dónde se convirtió en discípulo de Andrea del Verrocchio, el pintor y escultor más renombrado del momento. Su aceptación en el Gremio de San Lucas, alrededor de 1472, marcó la etapa final de sus estudios, aunque permanecería otros diez años más en Florencia.

Leonardo se encomendó, por iniciativa de los Medici, en una carta al poderoso Duque de Milán, Ludovico Sforza. A principios de 1480 partiría hacia Lombardía. En Milán no sólo compuso la mayoría de sus obras maestras como *La Última Cena* o *La Virgen de las Rocas,* en esta época se dedicó a estudiar de forma intensiva los fenómenos de la naturaleza y a resolver problemas

difficili circostanze familiari, sembra che abbia goduto di un'educazione attenta e stimolante, che alla fine lo condusse a Firenze all'età di 17 anni, dove divenne allievo di Andrea del Verrocchio, il pittore e scultore più richiesto dell'epoca. L'ingresso nella corporazione di San Luca nel 1472 segnò la conclusione formale della sua istruzione, ma Leonardo rimase ancora altri dieci anni a Firenze.

Su iniziativa dei Medici, lo stesso Leonardo si raccomanda in una lettera al potente duca di Milano, Ludovico Sforza, e all'inizio degli anni Ottanta del 1400 si trasferisce in Lombardia. A Milano realizzò non soltanto capolavori come *L'Ultima Cena* e la *Vergine delle Rocce,* ma in questo periodo svolse anche un'intensa attività con i fenomeni

lastige gezinssituatie lijkt Leonardo een zorgzame en stimulerende opvoeding te hebben genoten, die er toe leidde dat hij op 17-jarige leeftijd naar Florence trok om in de leer te gaan bij Andrea del Verrocchio, destijds de meest gevraagde kunstschilder en beeldhouwer. Leonardo's toelating tot het Gilde van Sint-Lucas in 1472 betekende de formele afsluiting van zijn scholing, maar hij bleef daarna nog tien jaar in Florence.

Op instigatie van de Medici beval Leonardo zichzelf aan bij de machtige Hertog van Milaan, Ludovico Sforza, en verhuisde in 1482 naar de Lombardijnse hoofdstad. Daar ontstonden meesterwerken als *Het Laatste Avondmaal* en *De Madonna op de Rotsen,* maar het was ook de tijd waarin

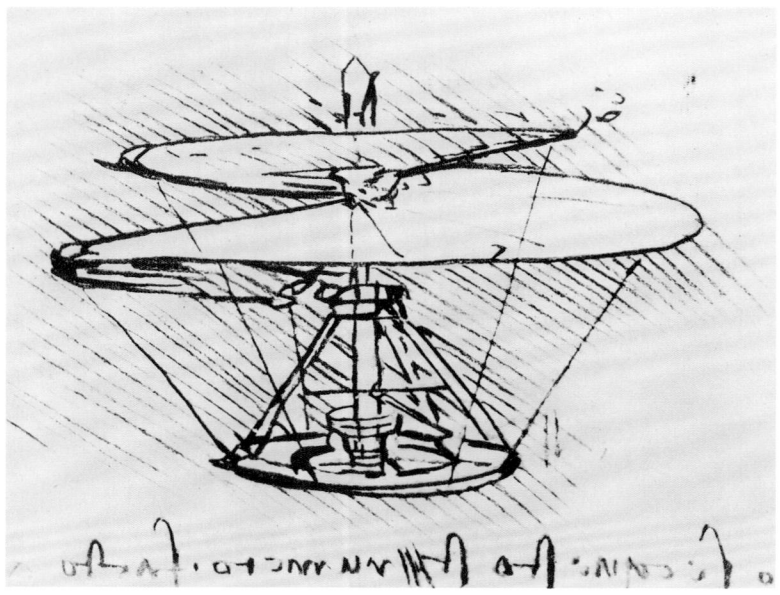

Detail of a design for a flying machine
Détail d'un projet pour une machine volante
Detail eines Entwurfs für eine Flugmaschine
Detalle de un boceto para una avioneta
Dettaglio di un disegno per macchina volante
Detail van een ontwerp voor een vliegmachine

c. 1488, Pen and ink on paper/Encre et plume sur papier, Bibliothèque de l'Institut de France, Paris

phenomena and technical problems, which was reflected in countless records and sketches. When his patron was overthrown in 1499, Leonardo had to leave the city and spent some years as an itinerant, living in Mantua and Venice amongst other towns and then, after 1503, again in Florence. His most famous work, the *Mona Lisa,* was created during this period. The year 1508 saw him begin his second stay in Milan, this time at the request of the French king's governor, Charles d'Amboise. In 1513, following the death of this influential patron, Leonardo transferred to Rome at the invitation of Giuliano di Lorenzo de' Medici, the younger brother of the new Pope, Leo X. Here, he moved into the Belvedere in the

la nature et aux problèmes techniques les plus divers – recherches qu'il consigne dans de nombreux dessins et esquisses très fréquemment annotés.

Lorsque son protecteur est chassé par les Français victorieux en 1499, Léonard doit quitter la ville. Commence alors pour lui une assez longue période de voyages, avec des séjours à Mantoue et Venise (entre autres), puis de nouveau à Florence à partir de 1503. C'est pendant ces années qu'il réalise la plus célèbre de ses œuvres : le *Portrait de Lisa Gherardini, épouse de Francesco del Giocondo,* dite *Monna Lisa* ou *La Joconde.* En 1508 débute son deuxième séjour milanais, à l'invitation de Charles d'Amboise, gouverneur français de la ville occupée. En 1513, après la mort

Meisterwerke wie das *Abendmahl* und die *Felsgrottenmadonna,* in diese Zeit fiel auch die intensive Beschäftigung mit naturwissenschaftlichen Phänomenen und technischen Problemen, die sich in unzähligen Aufzeichnungen und Skizzen niederschlug.

Als sein Mäzen 1499 gestürzt wurde, musste Leonardo die Stadt verlassen und es begann eine lange Zeit der Wanderschaft, in der er unter anderem in Mantua und Venedig lebte, aber ab 1503 auch wieder in Florenz. Während dieser Zeit entstand sein berühmtestes Werk, die *Mona Lisa.* 1508 begann sein zweiter Aufenthalt in Mailand, nachdem der dortige Statthalter des französischen Königs, Charles d'Amboise, ihn dorthin gebeten hatte. 1513, nachdem auch dieser

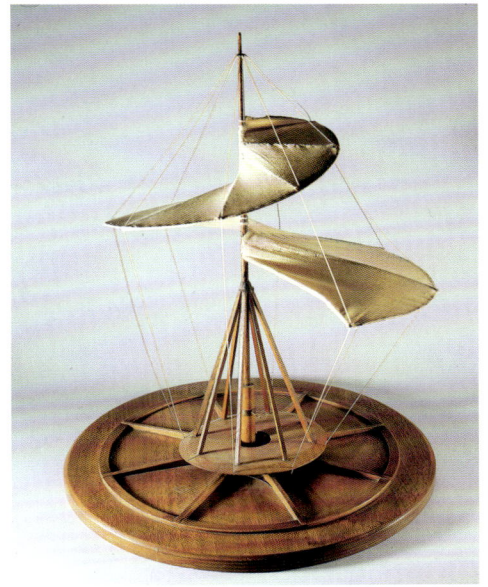

técnicos plasmados en numerosos de sus dibujos y esbozos.

Cuando en 1499 su mecenas fue abatido, Leonardo se vio obligado a abandonar la ciudad. Para él empezó entonces un largo recorrido, en el que vivió en Mantua y Venecia, entre otras localidades, aunque en 1503 regresó a Florencia. Durante esta época se gestó su obra más conocida, *La Mona Lisa*. En 1508 empezó su segunda etapa en Milán, cuando el gobernador del rey francés, Charles d'Amboise, le solicitó que volviese a la ciudad. En 1513, tras la muerte de este también influyente mecenas, Leonardo se trasladaría, por invitación de Giuliano di Lorenzo de' Medici, el joven hermano del nuevo Papa Leo X, a Roma. Allí se encargaría de

scientifico-naturali e i problemi tecnici, che trovano espressione in innumerevoli disegni e schizzi.

Quando nel 1499 il suo mecenate fu deposto, Leonardo dovette lasciare la città e cominciò un lungo periodo di vagabondaggio, nel quale visse tra l'altro a Mantova e Venezia, finché nel 1503 tornò a Firenze. In questo periodo realizzò la sua opera più celebre, la *Monna Lisa*. Nel 1508 iniziò il suo secondo soggiorno a Milano, dopo che fu invitato dal governatore locale del re francese, Charles d'Amboise. Nel 1513, dopo la morte di questo influente promotore, Leonardo si trasferì a Roma su invito di Giuliano di Lorenzo de' Medici, il fratello minore del nuovo Papa Leone X. Qui trovò alloggio

Leonardo zich intensief bezighield met natuurwetenschappelijke fenomenen en technische kwesties, zoals blijkt uit de enorme hoeveelheid schetsen die hij hiervan maakte.

Toen zijn mecenas in 1499 ten val werd gebracht, moest Leonardo de stad verlaten en begon hij aan een periode van rondzwervingen, waarin hij onder andere in Mantua en Venetië woonde, en vanaf 1503 opnieuw in Florence. In deze tijd ontstond ook zijn beroemdste werk, de *Mona Lisa*. In 1508 begon hij aan zijn tweede verblijf in Milaan, nadat de stadhouder van de Franse koning, Charles d'Amboise, hem naar de stad had ontboden. Toen ook deze invloedrijke schutspatroon in 1513 overleed, verhuisde Leonardo op uitnodiging

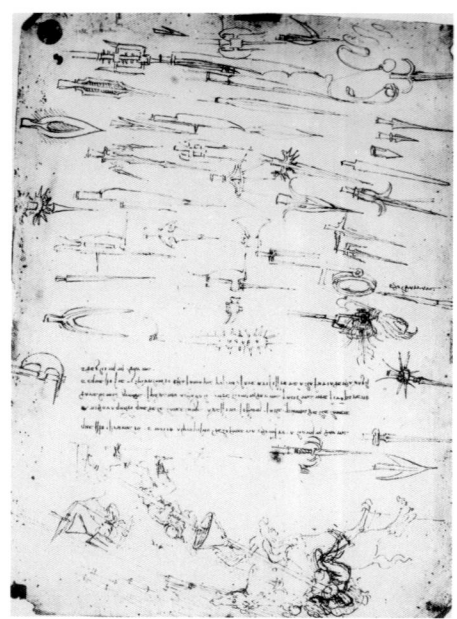

Vatican and met again with old friends, including Bramante and Luca Pacioli.

In 1516, Leonardo, accompanied by at least three of his most important paintings (the *Mona Lisa,* the *Virgin and Child with St. Anne,* and *St. John the Baptist*), went on his last great journey, following an invitation from King Francis I, to Cloux Castle, near Amboise in the Loire Valley. He lived there for three more years, until his death on 2 May 1519.

de ce mécène influent, Léonard part pour Rome à l'invitation de Julien de Médicis, frère cadet du nouveau pape Léon X. Il est logé au palais du Belvédère, au Vatican, où il retrouve de vieux amis comme le peintre Bramante et le mathématicien Luca Pacioli.

En 1516, à l'invitation du roi François Ier, il part pour la France – son dernier voyage – en emportant trois de ses plus importants tableaux : *La Joconde, La Vierge à l'Enfant avec sainte Anne* et *Saint Jean-Baptiste*. Il réside pendant trois ans au château du Clos Lucé, tout près d'Amboise, dans le Val de Loire, et c'est là qu'il meurt, le 2 mai 1519.

einflussreiche Förderer verstorben war, übersiedelte Leonardo auf Einladung Giuliano di Lorenzo de' Medicis, des jüngeren Bruders des neuen Papstes Leo X., nach Rom. Hier bezog er im Belvedere des Vatikans Logis und traf wieder mit alten Freunden wie Bramante oder Luca Pacioli zusammen.

1516 schließlich begab sich Leonardo mit mindestens dreien seiner wichtigsten Gemälde im Gepäck (*Mona Lisa, Anna selbdritt* und *Johannes der Täufer*) auf seine letzte große Reise, nachdem ihn König Franz I. eingeladen hatte, auf Schloss Cloux in der Nähe von Amboise im Loiretal zu residieren. Noch drei Jahre lebte er dort, bis er am 2. Mai 1519 starb.

Codex Altanticus

Mortars firing stones over a wall into a fort

Mortiers tirant des boulets de pierre sur un rempart

Mörser feuern Steine über eine Festungsmauer

Los lanzagranadas lanzan piedras hacia el muro de la fortaleza

Mortai che sparano pietre oltre il muro di una fortezza

Met mortieren worden stenen over een vestingmuur geschoten

Pen and ink on paper/Plume et encre sur papier,
Biblioteca Ambrosiana, Milano

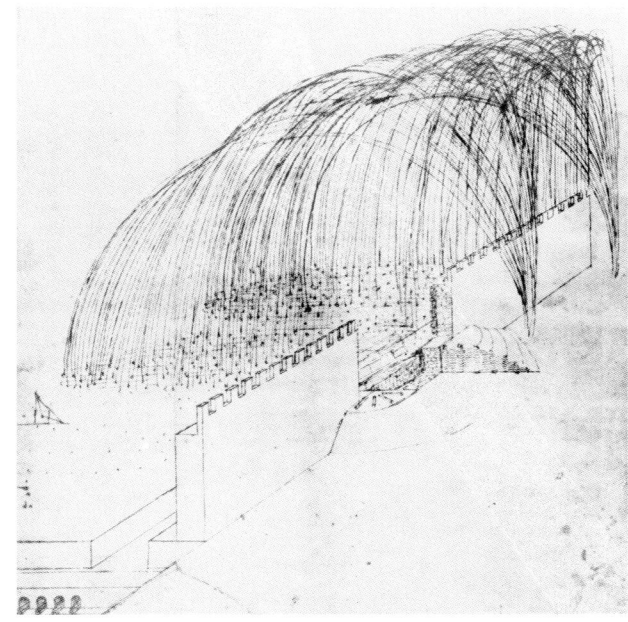

tapizar las logias y se reencontraría con amigos como Bramante o Luca Pacioli.

Finalmente en 1516, Leonardo emprendió con al menos tres de sus obras más importantes en el equipaje (*Mona Lisa, Ana trinitaria* y *San Juan Bautista*), su último gran viaje, después de haber sido invitado por el Rey Francisco I a vivir en el Castillo de Cloux, cerca de Amboise, en el Valle del Loira. Allí vivió tres años más hasta su muerte el 2 de mayo de 1519.

nel Belvedere del Vaticano, dove si incontrava con vecchi amici come il Bramante e Luca Pacioli.

Infine nel 1516 Leonardo intraprese il suo ultimo grande viaggio portando con sé almeno tre dei suoi dipinti più importanti (la *Monna Lisa, Sant'Anna con la Vergine e il Bambino* e *San Giovanni Battista*), dopo aver ricevuto l'invito di re Francesco I a stabilirsi al castello di Cloux, vicino ad Amboise nella Valle della Loira. Lì visse per altri tre anni, finché morì il 2 maggio 1519.

van Giuliano di Lorenzo de' Medici, de jongere broer van de nieuwe paus Leo X, naar Rome. Hier betrok hij een woonatelier in de Belvedere van het Vaticaan en ontmoette hij oude vrienden, onder wie Bramante en Luca Pacioli.

In 1516 ondernam Leonardo – met minstens drie van zijn meesterwerken in zijn bagage (de *Mona Lisa, Anna te Drieën* en *Johannes de Doper*) – zijn laatste grote reis, nadat de Franse koning Frans I hem had uitgenodigd naar het Manoir du Clos Lucé bij Amboise in het Loiredal te verhuizen. Daar woonde hij nog drie jaar, tot aan zijn dood op 2 mei 1519.

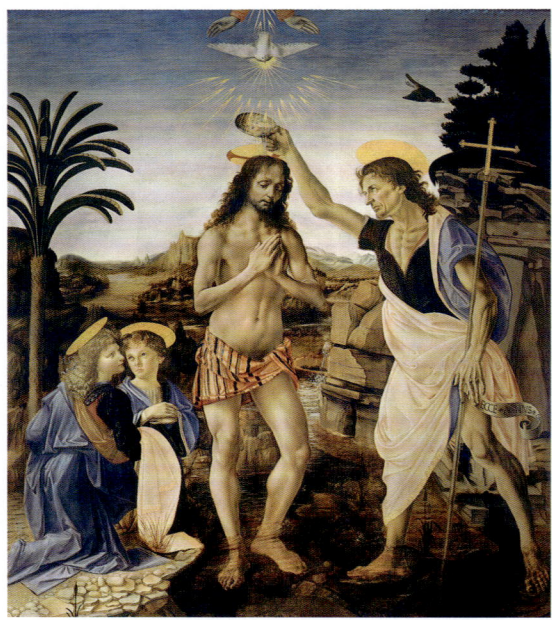

Andrea del Verrocchio (1435–88), Leonardo da Vinci (1452–1519)

The Baptism of Christ by John the Baptist

Le Baptême du Christ

Die Taufe Christi

El Bautismo de Cristo

Battesimo di Cristo

De doop van Christus

c. 1475, Oil on panel/Huile sur bois, 177 × 151 cm, Galleria degli Uffizi, Firenze

Detail
Détail
Detail
Detalle
Detttaglio
Detail

Paintings

In his treatise on painting, the *Trattato della Pittura,* which was posthumously assembled from 18 of his notebooks, Leonardo expounded his theory of the primacy of painting over sculpture and, above all, over poetry. He drew attention to the more differentiated possibilities of expression which were available to the painter, as opposed to the sculptor, whom he argued had to take much less into account in terms of the natural representation of an object than would a painter, and which in turn, therefore, constituted less exertion for the mind.

Even if there are only a little more than a dozen paintings to which, according to the current research, Leonardo can

Les tableaux

Dans son *Trattato della Pittura* (« Traité de la peinture »), compilé après sa mort à partir de dix-huit de ses carnets, il s'agit pour Léonard d'expliquer la primauté de la peinture sur la sculpture, mais avant tout sur la poésie. Il met en lumière les possibilités d'expression différenciées dont dispose selon lui la peinture et – en défaveur de la sculpture – le fait que le sculpteur, pour représenter un objet de façon réaliste, aurait beaucoup moins de choses à prendre en considération que le peintre, ce qui représenterait un effort moindre pour l'esprit.

Même s'il n'y a finalement qu'un peu plus d'une douzaine de tableaux que les chercheurs actuels peuvent attribuer

Gemälde

In seinem aus 18 seiner Notizbücher posthum zusammengestellten *Trattato della Pittura,* dem Traktat über die Malerei, ging es Leonardo darum, den Vorrang der Malerei vor der Bildhauerei, vor allem aber vor der Dichtkunst darzulegen. Er verwies auf die differenzierteren Ausdrucksmöglichkeiten, die der Malerei zur Verfügung stünden und – gegenüber der Bildhauerei – darauf, dass der Bildhauer bei der naturgetreuen Darstellung eines Objektes ja viel weniger zu berücksichtigen hätte als der Maler, was wiederum eine wesentlich geringere Anstrengung für den Geist darstelle.

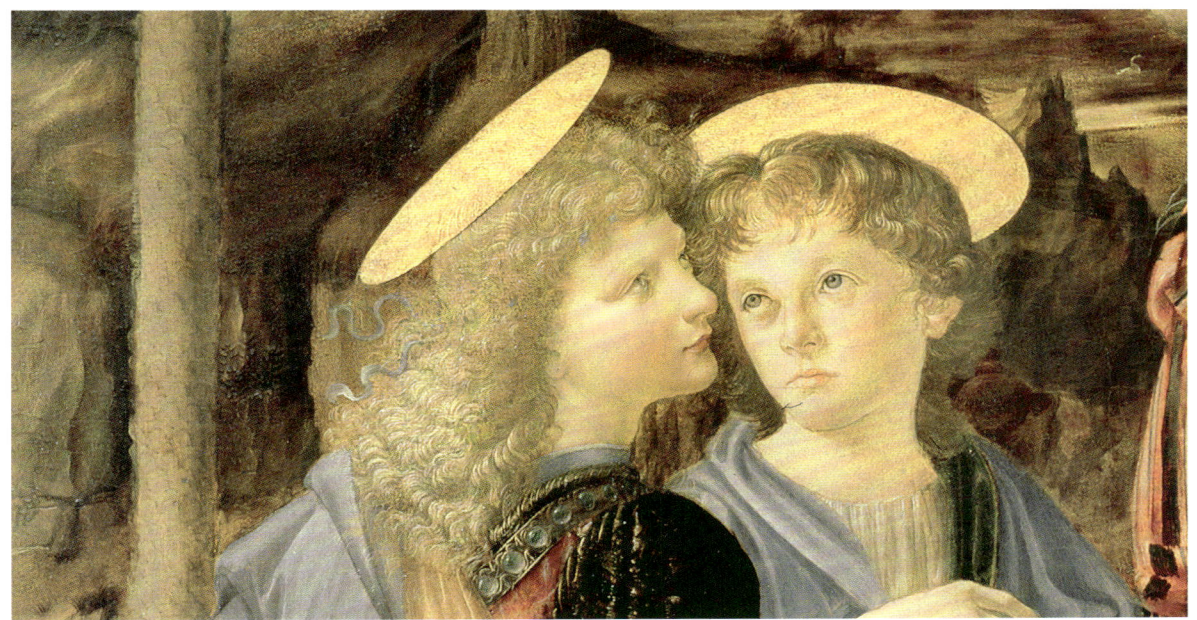

Pinturas

En su *Trattato della Pittura* (Tratado
sobre la Pintura), en el que se recogen
18 de sus libretas de forma póstuma,
Leonardo pretendía demostrar la
primacía de la pintura sobre la escultura,
pero principalmente sobre la poesía.
En él habla de las diferentes formas de
expresión de la pintura en comparación
con la escultura. Afirma además que un
escultor tiene que tener menos detalles
en cuenta que un pintor, a la hora de
realizar una representación fiel de un
objeto, lo que implicaría un menor
esfuerzo intelectual para el escultor.

Aunque finalmente no se le puedan
atribuir a ciencia cierta algo más que una
docena de pinturas, merece la pena ver

Dipinti

Nel suo *Trattato della Pittura*, redatto
dopo la sua morte e composto da
18 taccuini, Leonardo espone il concetto
della priorità della pittura sulla scultura,
ma soprattutto sull'arte poetica. Egli
rimanda alle possibilità espressive
differenziate che sono a disposizione
della pittura e, al contrario nella scultura,
lo scultore ha molto meno da considerare
rispetto al pittore nella rappresentazione
fedele alla natura di un oggetto, cosa che
comunque rappresenta un piccolo sforzo
per lo spirito.

Anche se alla fine si tratta di non più
di una dozzina di quadri, che secondo lo
stato attuale delle ricerche si possono
attribuire con certezza a Leonardo, vale

Schilderijen

In zijn *Trattato della Pittura* (Traktaat
over de schilderkunst), dat na zijn dood
uit achttien van zijn notitieboeken
werd samengesteld, ging het Leonardo
erom te bewijzen dat de schilderkunst
een voornamere plaats innam dan
de beeldhouwkunst en vooral de
dichtkunst. Hij wees op de zeer
veelzijdige uitdrukkingsmogelijkheden
die de kunstschilder, anders dan
de beeldhouwer, ter beschikking
stonden; de beeldhouwer zou in de
natuurgetrouwe weergave van zijn
objecten met veel minder aspecten
rekening hoeven te houden dan de
kunstschilder, waardoor hij een minder
zware geestelijke inspanning zou leveren.

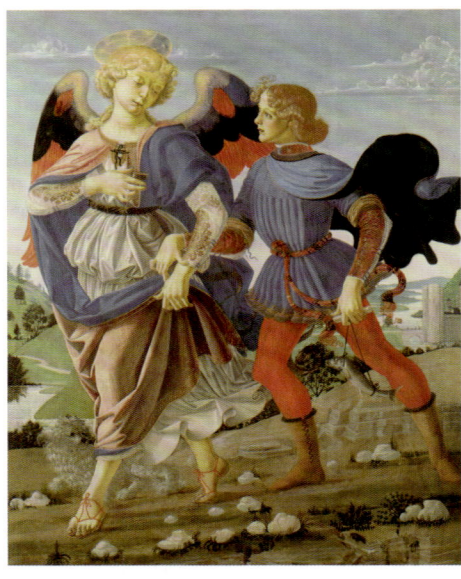

Andrea del Verrocchio, Leonardo da Vinci

Tobias and the Angel

Tobie et l'Ange

Tobias und der Engel

Tobías y el Ángel

Tobiolo e l'angelo

Tobias en de Engel

c. 1470–75, Tempera on panel/Tempera sur bois, 83,6 × 66 cm, National Gallery, London

with certainty be attributed, it is worth examining the development which he carried out, in a painterly way, throughout his entire artistic life in order to satisfy, as far as possible his ideal of the representation of nature.

We may consider his beginnings as a painter if we look at the first pictures on which he was allowed to collaborate, in the workshop of his teacher, Andrea del Verrocchio (*Tobias and the Angel,* as well as *The Baptism of Christ by John the Baptist*). Here we see idiosyncratic technical features which illustrate the contrast of his work from the style of his teacher, for instance as in the case of his color application, where he allowed the colored surfaces to merge into one another. This is known as *Sfumato* (soft, or blurred), which later became one of

avec certitude à Léonard, il vaut toutefois la peine d'observer l'évolution que l'artiste a suivie du point de vue pictural tout au long de sa vie créatrice, afin de s'approcher au plus près de son idéal : l'appropriation la plus complète possible de la nature et de ses phénomènes.

Lorsqu'on regarde ses débuts de peintre, c'est-à-dire les premiers tableaux auxquels il a pu collaborer dans l'atelier de Verrochio (*Tobie et l'Ange* ou encore *Le Baptême du Christ*), on discerne déjà des spécificités techniques qui le distinguent du style de son maître, telle par exemple l'application de la couleur qui fond les glacis superposés l'un dans l'autre. Le *sfumato* (« nuancé », « flou »), qui deviendra par la suite une des marques de fabrique de Léonard, est déjà perceptible dans ses débuts.

Wenn es auch letztlich nur etwas mehr als ein Dutzend Gemälde sind, die Leonardo nach aktueller Forschungslage sicher zugeschrieben werden können, so lohnt es doch, sich die Entwicklung anzuschauen, die er in malerischer Hinsicht während seines gesamten künstlerischen Lebens vollzogen hat, um seinem Ideal einer möglichst weitgehenden Anverwandlung der Natur nahezukommen.

Betrachten wir seine Anfänge als Maler, also die ersten Bilder, an denen er wohl in der Werkstatt seines Lehrers Andrea del Verrocchio mitarbeiten durfte (*Tobias und der Engel* sowie *Die Taufe Christi*), dann sehen wir bereits technische Eigenheiten, die ihn vom Stil seines Lehrers abheben; so etwa beim Farbauftrag, der die farbigen Flächen ineinander übergehen lässt: das

Andrea del Verrocchio

Madonna and Child

Vierge à l'Enfant

Maria mit dem Kind

Virgen con el niño

Madonna col Bambino

Madonna met kind

c. 1470, Tempera on wood/Tempera sur bois, 75,5 × 54,8 cm, Gemäldegalerie, Berlin

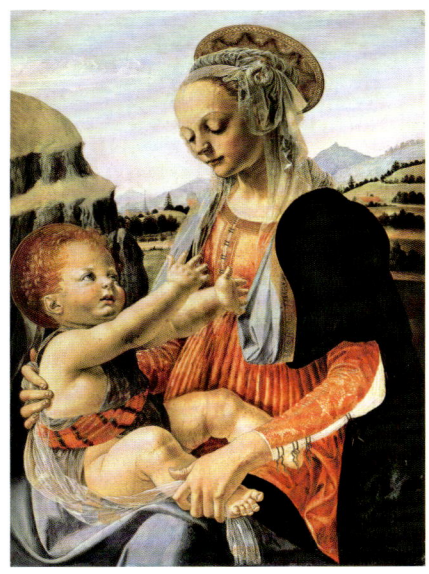

la evolución de sus pinturas a lo largo de su vida como artista, para acercarse todo lo posible a su ideal de asimilación de la naturaleza.

Si observamos sus comienzos como pintor, es decir, las primeras imágenes, en las que probablemente haya podido colaborar en el taller de su maestro Andrea del Verrocchio (*Tobías y el ángel* y *El bautismo de Cristo*), podemos apreciar ciertas características técnicas, que lo desmarcan del estilo de su maestro: la aplicación del color, donde deja que las superficies de colores se sobrepongan, dando lugar a la llamada técnica del *sfumato* (ital. difuso), que posteriormente se convertiría en el sello de identidad inequívoco de Leonardo. Estas características se pueden reconocer en varios puntos de las imágenes.

tuttavia la pena di osservare lo sviluppo che egli eseguì dal punto di vista pittorico durante la sua intera vita artistica, allo scopo di avvicinarsi al suo ideale di un adattamento della natura il più ampio possibile.

Considerando i suoi inizi come pittore, quindi i primi quadri ai quali egli collaborò nel laboratorio del suo maestro Andrea del Verrocchio (*Tobiolo e l'angelo* e il *Battesimo di Cristo*), possiamo già notare delle caratteristiche tecniche che lo differenziano dallo stile del suo insegnante; per esempio l'applicazione del colore che gli permette di sovrapporre le superfici colorate: è già visibile la tecnica dello sfumato, che in seguito sarebbe diventata uno dei tratti distintivi di Leonardo.

Mentre il primo dipinto realizzato probabilmente sotto la sua regia

Hoewel volgens de laatste stand van het onderzoek slechts een dozijn schilderijen met absolute zekerheid aan Leonardo kunnen worden toegeschreven, is het zeer de moeite waard stil te staan bij Leonardo's schilderkunstige ontwikkeling, waarin hij zijn hele leven lang naar de ideale weergave van de natuur streefde.

Als we kijken naar Leonardo's beginjaren en dus naar zijn vroegste werken, waaraan hij in de werkplaats van zijn leermeester Andrea del Verrocchio moet hebben gewerkt (*Tobias en de engel* en *De doop van Christus*), dan zien we al technische kenmerken die hem van zijn leermeester onderscheidden; zo is al te herkennen dat Leonardo een opbrengingstechniek gebruikte waarbij hij kleurvlakken in elkaar laat overvloeien,

19

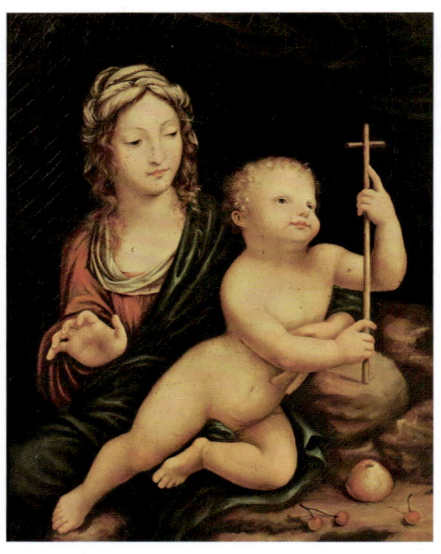

Unknown artist/
Artiste inconnu

Madonna of the Yarnwinder

Madone aux fuseaux

Madonna mit der Spindel

Virgen de la rueca

Madonna dei Fusi

Madonna met kind en spintol

Oil on canvas/Huile sur toile,
45,5 × 34 cm, Private collection

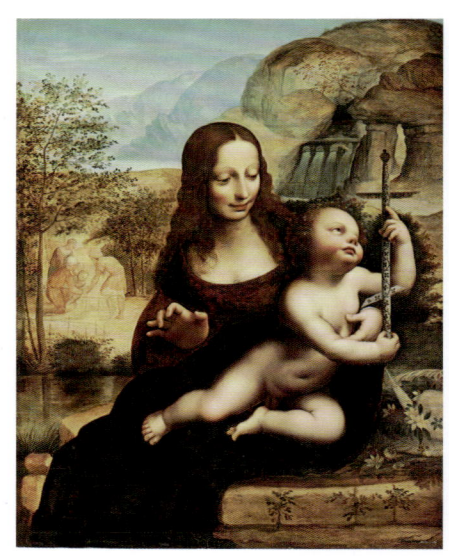

Leonardo's trademarks and is already visible here in its beginnings.

Whilst his painting, *Annunciation,* supposedly the first produced alone, dating from 1472 to 1475, still bears witness in some respects to an uncertainty in the perspective used, his first single portrait, that of *Ginevra de' Benci,* reveals that he is ready to venture into new terrain. The inscrutability and equanimity of the women he portrayed fascinated the audience as well as his painter colleagues, even if his portraits in particular only reached a maturity in Milan when he painted *The Lady with the Ermine* and *Portrait of a Lady from the Court of Milan,* better known as *La belle ferronière.*

Whilst one may talk about his success as a portraitist, on the other hand one should not be silent about his failures,

Tandis que *L'Annonciation* des années 1472–1475 – probablement son premier tableau entièrement autographe – témoigne encore d'une certaine incertitude dans l'utilisation de la perspective, son premier portrait consacré à *Ginevra de' Benci* (v. 1474–1476) montre déjà qu'il est prêt à entrer dans de nouvelles voies. La profondeur mystérieuse et la sérénité impassible des femmes qu'il représente fascinent alors le public autant que ses collègues peintres – même s'il n'atteint la maturité dans l'art du portrait qu'à l'époque de Milan, avec *La Dame à l'hermine* (1488–1490) et *La Belle Ferronnière* (1495–1499).

Si l'on parle de ses succès comme portraitiste, ses échecs ne doivent pas être passés sous silence. On pense ici surtout à la monumentale fresque murale avec laquelle Léonard voulait

Sfumato (ital. verschwommen), das später zu einem der Markenzeichen Leonardos werden sollte, ist bereits in Ansätzen sichtbar.

Während das vermutlich erste in alleiniger Regie entstandene Gemälde, *Die Verkündigung,* aus den Jahren 1472 bis 1475, noch von einer gewissen Unsicherheit in Bezug auf die verwendete Perspektive zeugt, verrät bereits sein erstes Einzelporträt, das *Bildnis der Ginevra de' Benci,* dass er bereit ist, neues Terrain zu betreten. Die Unergründlichkeit und der Gleichmut der von ihm dargestellten Frauen faszinierte das Publikum ebenso wie seine Malerkollegen, auch wenn das Reifestudium vor allem seiner Porträts wohl erst in seine Mailänder Zeit fiel, als er die *Dame mit dem Hermelin* und die *Belle Ferronière* malte.

Unknown artist/Artiste inconnu

Madonna of the Yarnwinder

Madone aux fuseaux

Madonna mit der Spindel

Virgen de la rueca

Madonna dei Fusi

Madonna met kind en spintol

Oil on canvas/Huile sur toile, 62,2 × 48,6 cm, Private collection

Unknown artist/Artiste inconnu

Madonna of the Yarnwinder

Madone aux fuseaux

Madonna mit der Spindel

Virgen de la rueca

Madonna dei Fusi

Madonna met kind en spintol

Oil on canvas/Huile sur toile, 48 × 35 cm, Private collection

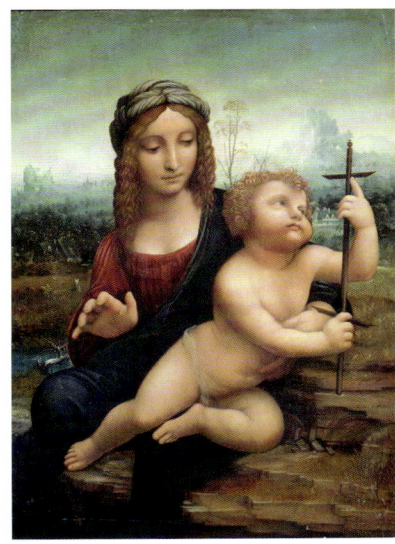

Aunque la primera pintura supuestamente creada bajo su dirección, *La Anunciación* (1472 a 1475), muestra todavía una cierta inseguridad en la perspectiva utilizada; su primer retrato, el de *Ginebra de Benci,* confirma que el artista ya está preparado para pisar nuevos terrenos. La impenetrabilidad e impasibilidad de las mujeres que retrata, fascinan tanto al público como a sus compañeros, a pesar de que el estudio de la madurez, sobre todo en sus retratos, no se desarrollaría hasta su época en Milán en la *Dama y el armiño* y *Belle Ferronière.*

Si hablamos de sus éxitos como retratista, no deberíamos ocultar sus fracasos. Pensamos sobre todo en la colosal pintura mural en la que Leonardo quería representar en el Salón del Gran Consejo del Palazzo Vecchio en Florencia

esclusiva dal 1472 al 1475, *L'Annunciazione,* mostra ancora una certa insicurezza in relazione alla prospettiva utilizzata, il suo primo ritratto individuale, il *Ritratto di Ginevra de' Benci,* rivela che il pittore era già pronto ad entrare in un nuovo campo. L'imperscrutabilità e imperturbabilità delle donne da lui raffigurate affascinarono il pubblico tanto quanto i suoi colleghi pittori, anche se lo studio della maturità avvenne soprattutto con i ritratti del suo periodo milanese, quando dipinse la *Dama con l'ermellino* e la *Belle Ferronière.*

Quando si parla dei suoi successi come ritrattista, non si deve tacere dei suoi fallimenti. Qui non si può fare a meno di pensare alla monumentale pittura murale sulla quale Leonardo volle raffigurare la Battaglia di Anghiari, nella Sala del Gran Consiglio di Palazzo Vecchio

een techniek die *sfumato* (Italiaans voor 'verdampt') wordt genoemd en later hét handelsmerk van zijn schilderwerk zou worden.

Het eerste schilderij dat Leonardo waarschijnlijk zelfstandig heeft vervaardigd, *De Annunciatie* van 1472–1475, getuigt nog van tweeslachtigheid met betrekking tot het gekozen perspectief, maar in zijn eerste zelfstandige portret, dat van *Ginevra de'Benci,* is al te zien met hoeveel zelfvertrouwen hij zich op dit nieuwe terrein bewoog. De ondoorgrondelijkheid en kalmte van de door hem uitgebeelde vrouwen fascineerden het publiek en collega-schilders, ook al zouden zijn rijpere en beste portretten in Milaan ontstaan, waar hij *De dame met de hermelijn* en de *Belle Ferronière* schilderde.

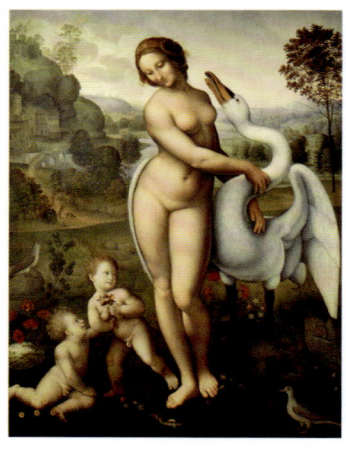

Unknown artist/Artiste inconnu

Leda and the Swan
Léda et le cygne
Leda mit dem Schwan
Leda y el cisne
Leda col cigno
Leda en de zwaan

Oil on canvas/Huile sur toile,
Galleria Borghese, Roma

Unknown artist/Artiste inconnu

Leda and the Swan, preparatory drawing
Léda et le cygne, esquisse préparatoire
Leda mit dem Schwan, Skizze
Leda y el cisne, esbozo
Leda col cigno, schizzo
Leda en de zwaan, schets

Pen and brown ink over black chalk on paper/Plume et encre brune
sur pierre noire, sur papier, 16 × 13,7 cm, Chatsworth House, Bakewell

foremost amongst these being the monumental mural in the recently redesigned hall of the Grand Council in the Florentine Palazzo Vecchio, with which Leonardo wanted to represent the battle of Anghiari. The reasons for the failure of this enterprise can only be speculated upon, but reference to some of the still-existing sketches, in addition to contemporary reports, show that Leonardo had planned something pioneering in the field of combat painting.

So, in addition to *The Last Supper* and the *Mona Lisa,* we have *The Virgin and Child with St. Anne* and the *Head of a Woman (La Scapigliata),* upon which is founded the immortality of Leonardo in the field of painting. Many painters would be grateful if they succeeded in producing a single such masterpiece in their lifetime.

décorer la salle du Grand Conseil, réaménagée dans le Palazzo Vecchio de Florence. On en est réduit aux spéculations sur les raisons de l'échec de cette entreprise, mais les quelques esquisses conservées et des témoignages de contemporains sur les travaux préparatoires effectués montrent bien que, dans le domaine de la peinture d'histoire aussi, Léonard aurait pu être un pionnier.

À côté de *La Cène* et de *La Joconde,* il ne nous reste essentiellement que *La Vierge à l'Enfant avec sainte Anne* et *La Scapigliata* (« *L'Ébouriffée* ») ou *Tête de jeune fille* pour fonder l'immortalité de Léonard dans le domaine de la peinture. Bien des peintres seraient heureux d'avoir réussi un seul chef-d'œuvre de cette classe dans leur vie d'artiste...

Wenn man über seine Erfolge als Porträtist spricht, darf man über seine Misserfolge nicht schweigen. Hier ist natürlich vor allem an das monumentale Wandgemälde gedacht, auf dem Leonardo im gerade erst neu gestalteten Saal des Großen Rats im florentinischen Palazzo Vecchio die Schlacht von Anghiari darstellen wollte. Über die Gründe für das Scheitern dieser Unternehmung lässt sich nur spekulieren, doch machen einige noch erhaltene Skizzen sowie Zeitzeugenberichte zu bereits geleisteten Vorarbeiten deutlich, dass Leonardo sich auch auf dem Gebiet der Schlachtengemälde etwas Bahnbrechendes vorgenommen hatte.

So bleiben uns neben dem *Abendmahl* und der *Mona Lisa* vor allem auch noch die *Anna selbdritt* und die *Scapigliata,* die die Unsterblichkeit Leonardos auf dem Gebiet der Malerei begründeten. Viele Maler wären dankbar, gelänge ihnen auch nur ein einziges solches Meisterwerk im Leben.

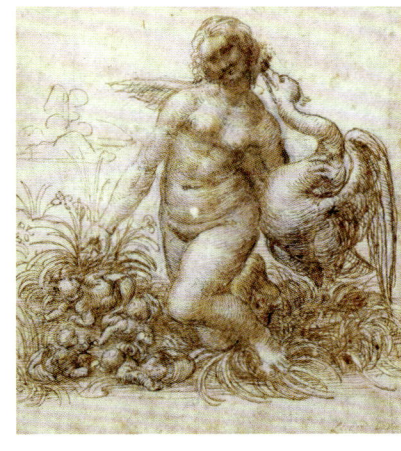

pp. 24/25
Annunciation
L'Annonciation
Die Verkündigung
La Anunciación
L'Annunciazione
De annunciatie
1472–75, Oil on panel/Huile sur bois, 98 × 217 cm, Galleria degli Uffizi, Firenze

la Batalla de Anghiari. Sobre los motivos de este proyecto fallido sólo se puede especular, aunque algunos de los esbozos conservados, así como informes con testimonios de la época sobre los trabajos previos realizados, evidencian que Leonardo también se había propuesto realizar en este campo, el de la pintura de batallas, algo rompedor.

Finalmente, además de *La Última Cena* y la *Mona Lisa,* nos quedan sobre todo la *Ana trinitaria* y la *Scapigliata* para reafirmar la inmortalidad del artista en el campo de la pintura. Muchos pintores estarían agradecidos, si lograsen crear tan sólo una de las obra maestras de Leonardo a lo largo de su vida.

a Firenze che era appena stata realizzata. Sulle ragioni del fallimento di questa impresa si può solo speculare, anche se alcuni schizzi ancora conservati e racconti di testimoni dell'epoca sui lavori preparatori già eseguiti fanno capire che Leonardo aveva in programma qualcosa di pionieristico nel settore dei quadri di battaglie.

Così a noi rimangono, oltre all'*Ultima Cena* e alla *Monna Lisa* soprattutto anche *Sant'Anna con la Vergine e il Bambino* e la *Scapigliata,* che giustificano l'immortalità di Leonardo nel campo della pittura. Molti pittori sarebbero soddisfatti se potessero realizzare anche solo uno di questi capolavori unici durante la loro vita.

Wanneer we het over Leonardo's successen als portrettist hebben, dan mogen we andere, mislukte, werken niet over het hoofd zien. Het gaat dan vooral om de monumentale wandschildering in de pas heringerichte raadszaal (Salone dei Cinquecento) van het Florentijnse Palazzo Vecchio, waar hij de Slag bij Anghiari wilde uitbeelden. Waarom de onderneming mislukte, is nog altijd niet duidelijk, maar uit bewaard gebleven schetsen en uit berichten van tijdgenoten over werkzaamheden zie al aan de schildering waren uitgevoerd, komt naar voren dat Leonardo zich iets geheel nieuws op het gebied van de uitbeelding van veldslagen had voorgenomen.

Daarmee is Leonardo's onsterfelijkheid als kunstschilder vooral gebaseerd op de *Het Laatste Avondmaal* en de *Mona Lisa,* maar zeker ook op de *Anna te Drieën* en *La Scapigliata*. Veel schilders zouden dankbaar zijn als ze in hun leven één zo'n meesterwerk zouden creëren.

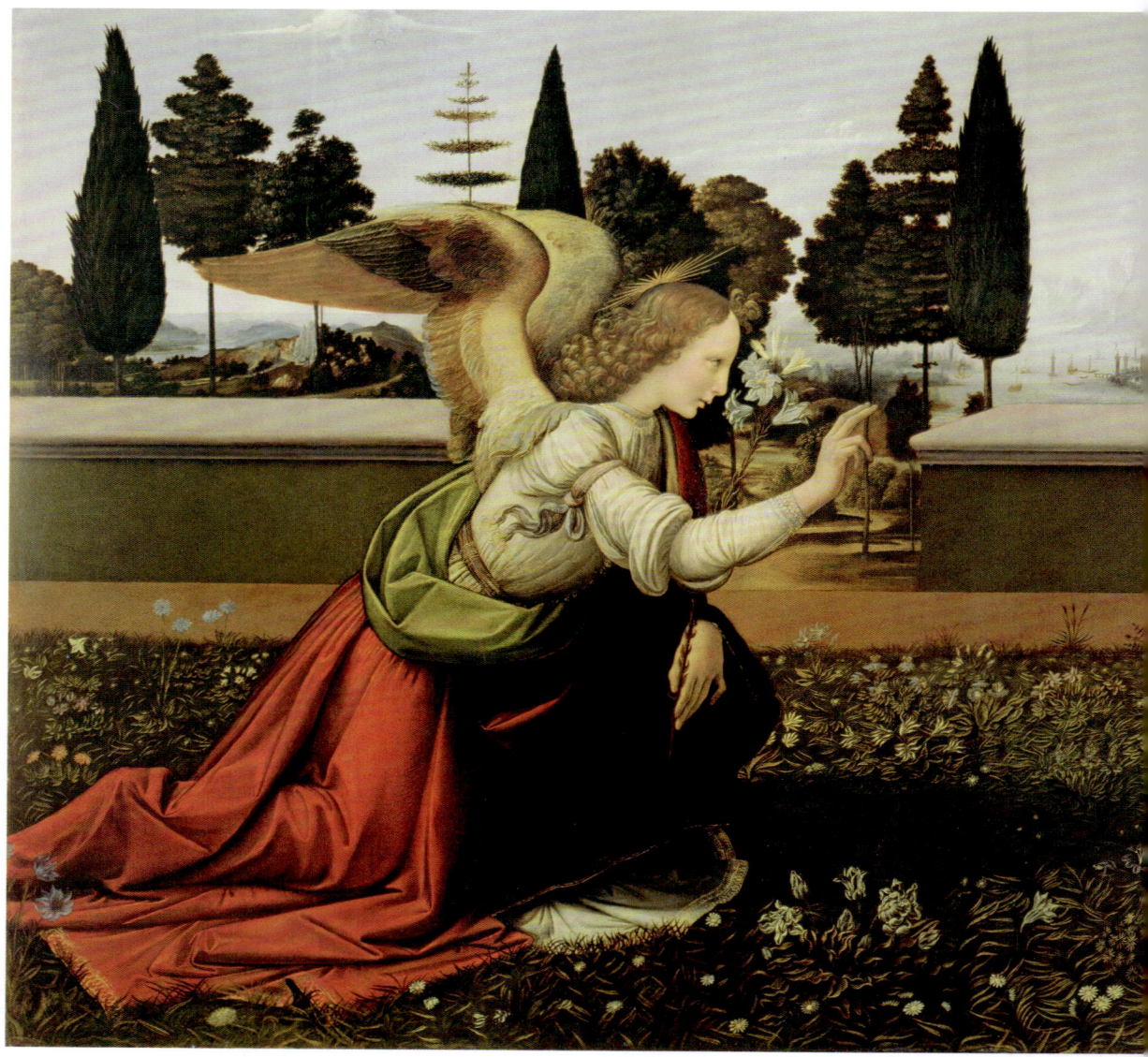

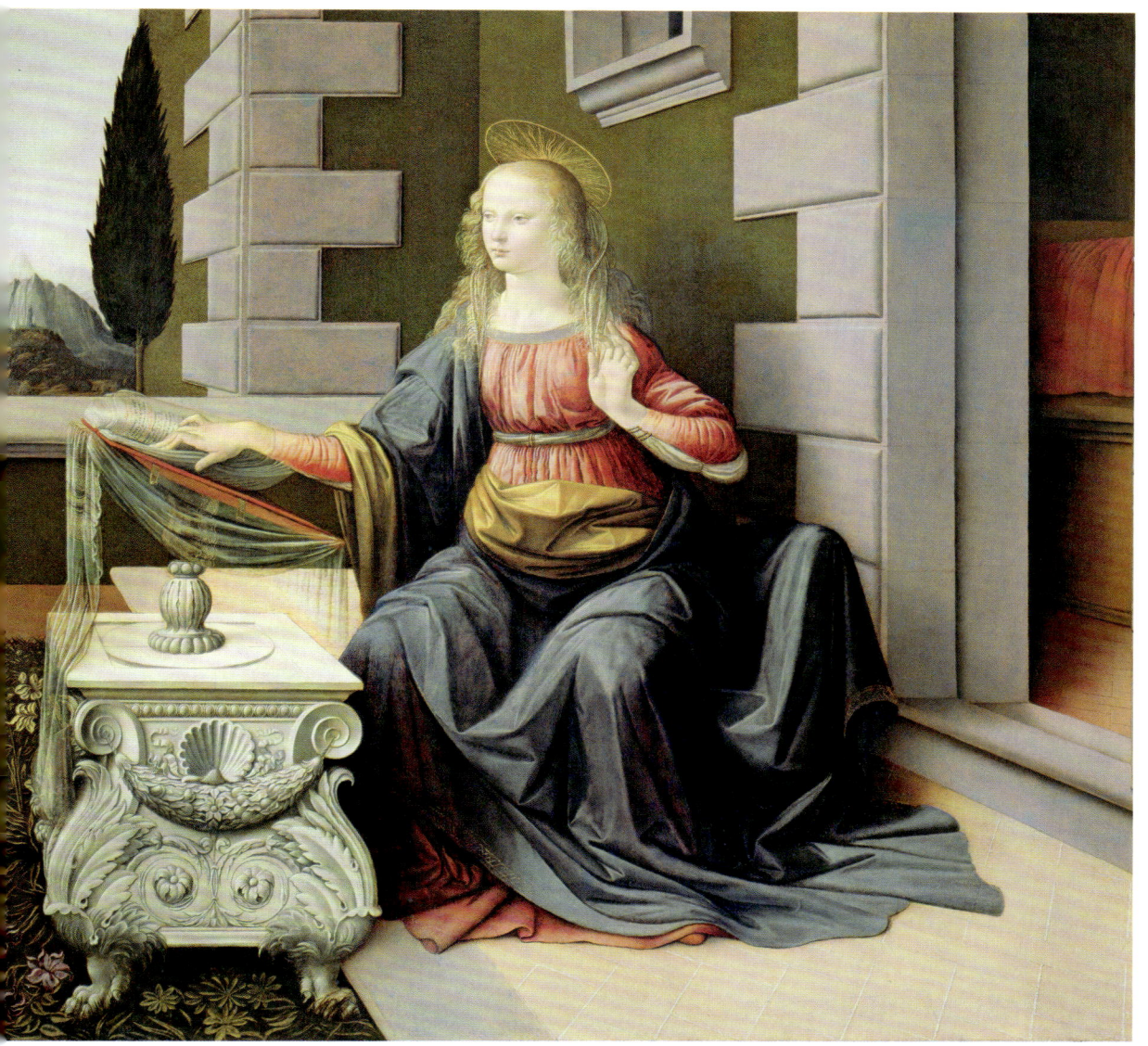

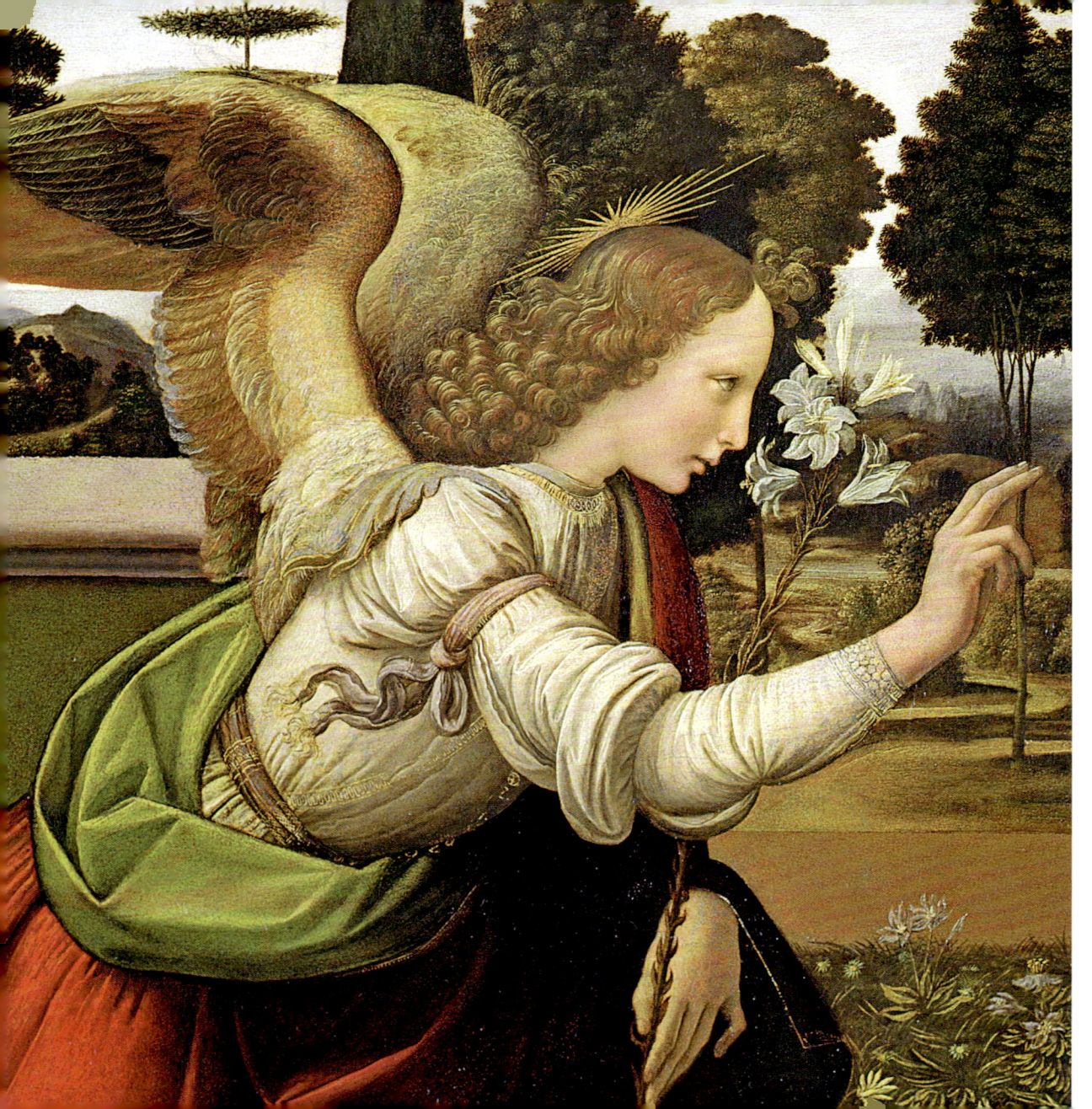

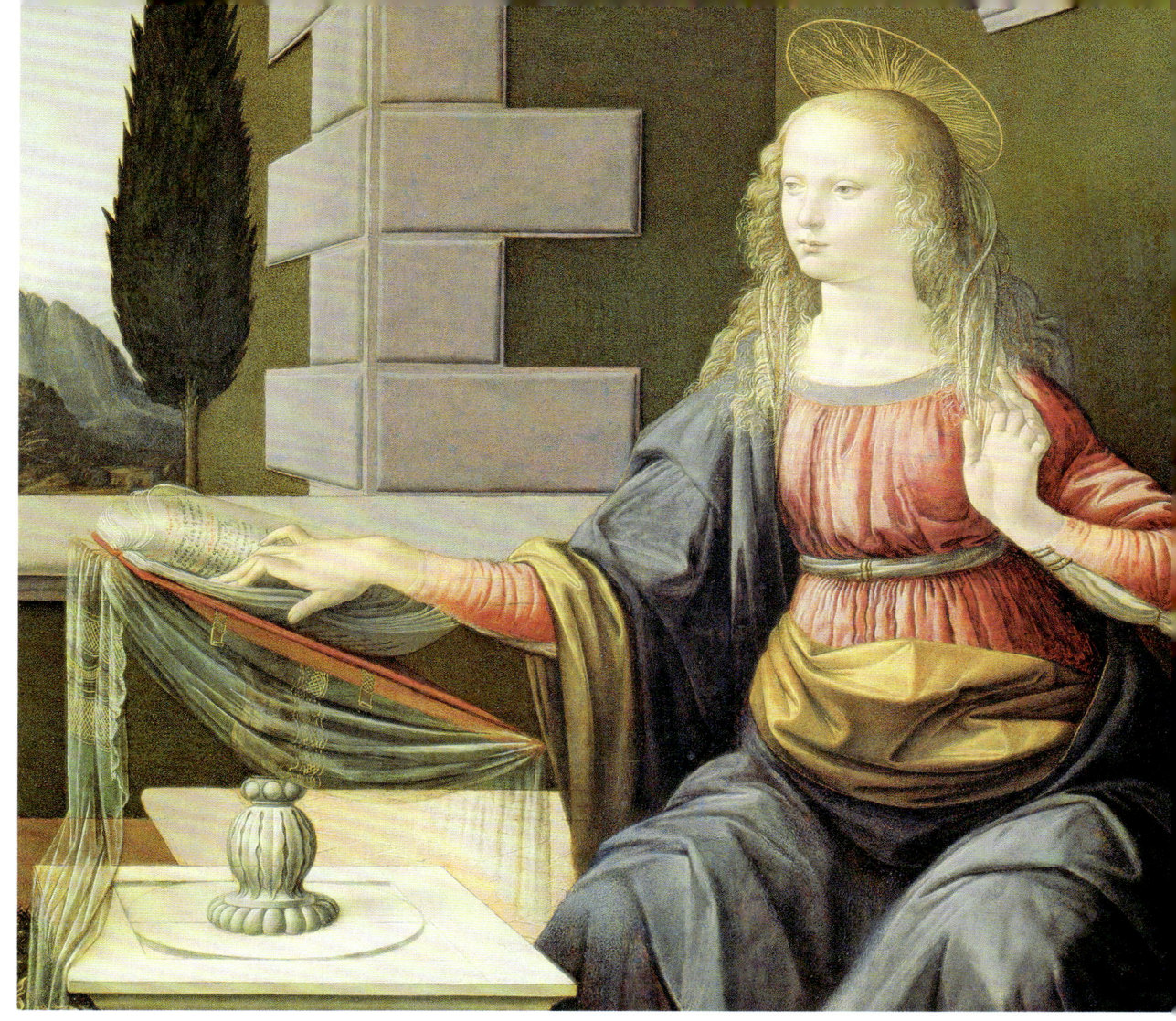

Annunciation, details   *Die Verkündigung*, Details   *L'Annunciazione*, dettaglie

L'Annonciation, détails   *La Anunciación*, detalles   *De annunciatie*, details

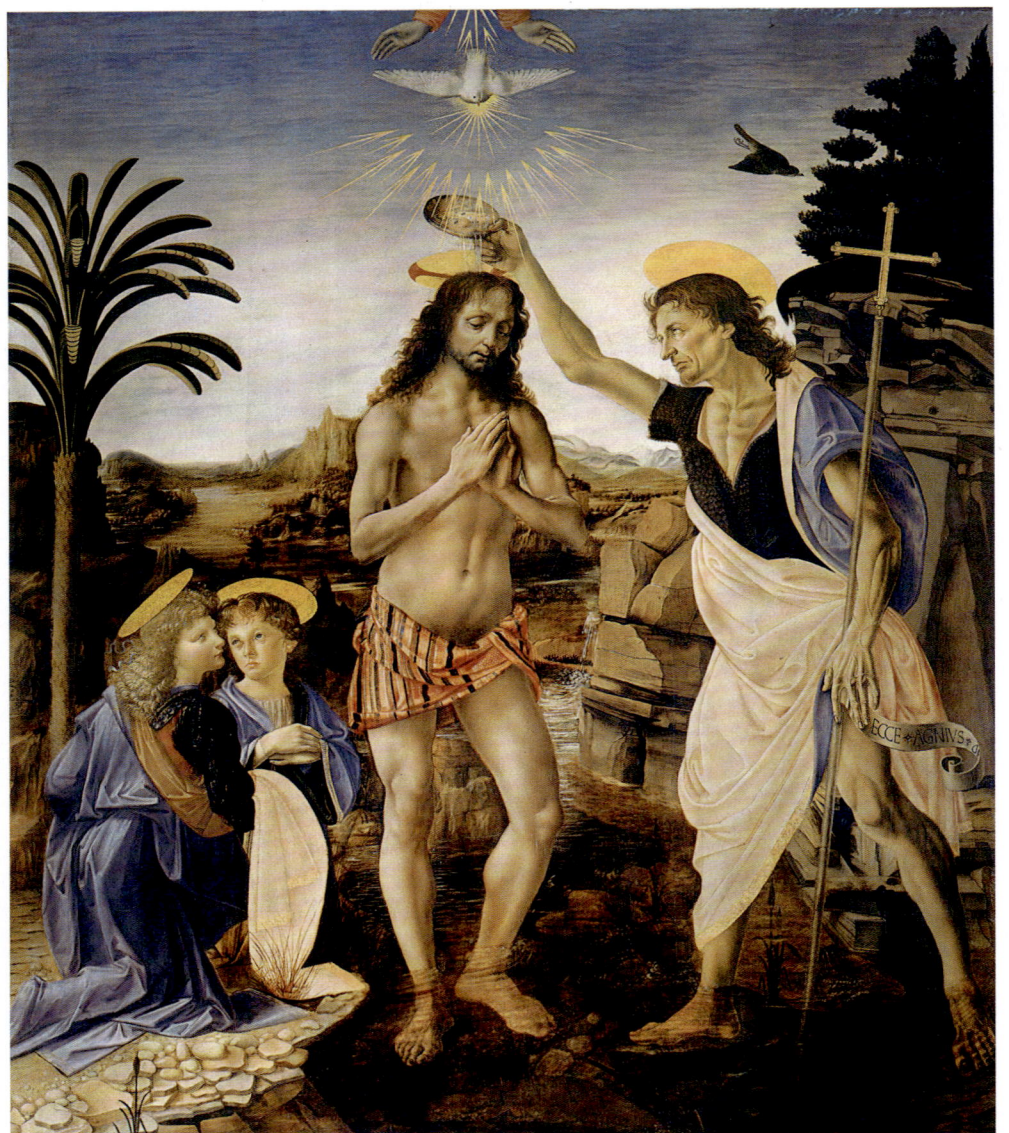

Andrea del Verrocchio, Leonardo da Vinci

The Baptism of Christ by John the Baptist

Le Baptême du Christ

Die Taufe Christi

El Bautismo de Cristo

Battesimo di Cristo

De doop van Christus

c. 1475, Oil on panel/ Huile sur bois, 177 × 151 cm, Galleria degli Uffizi, Firenze

Detail

Détail

Detail

Detalle

Detttaglio

Detail

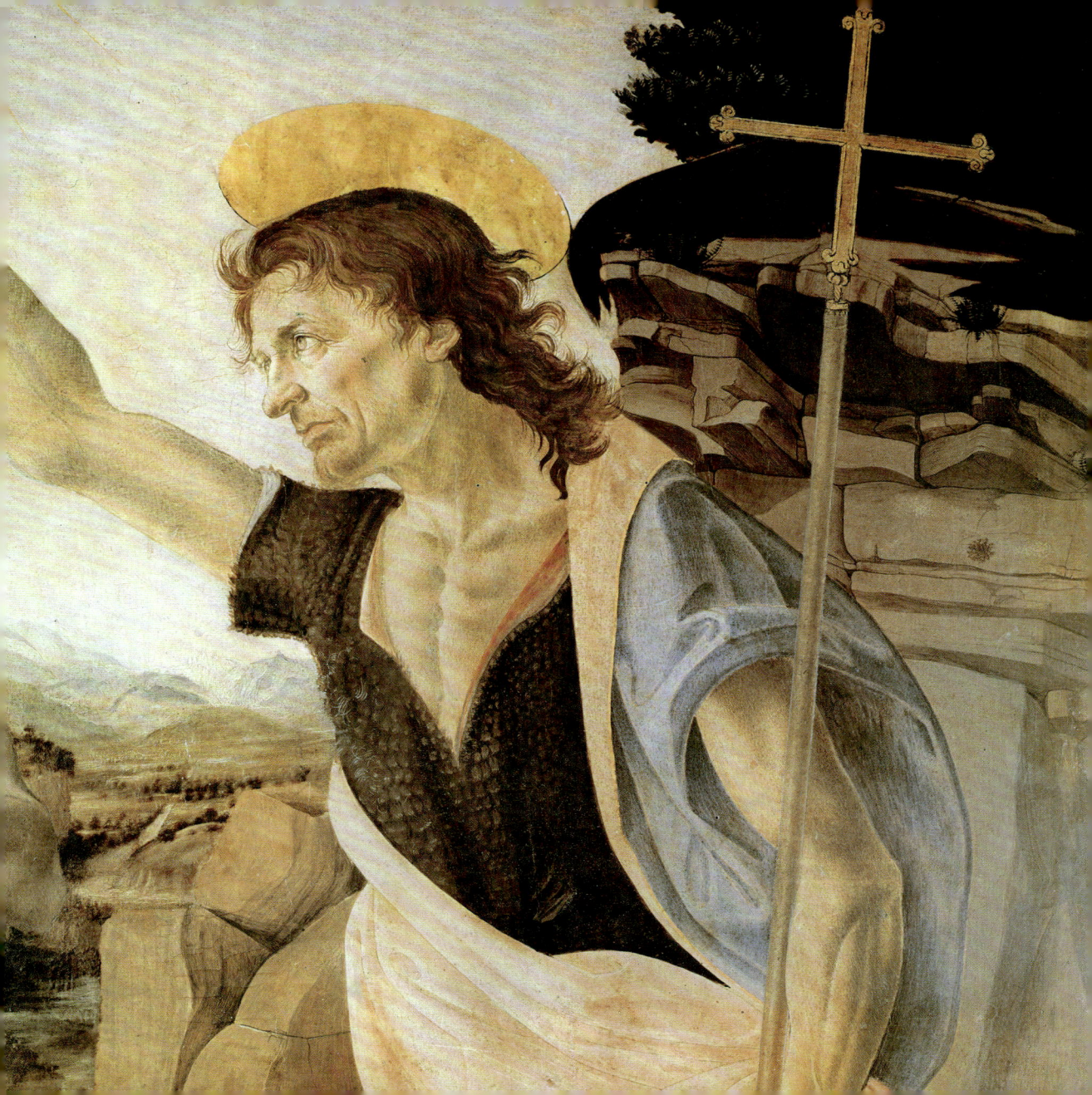

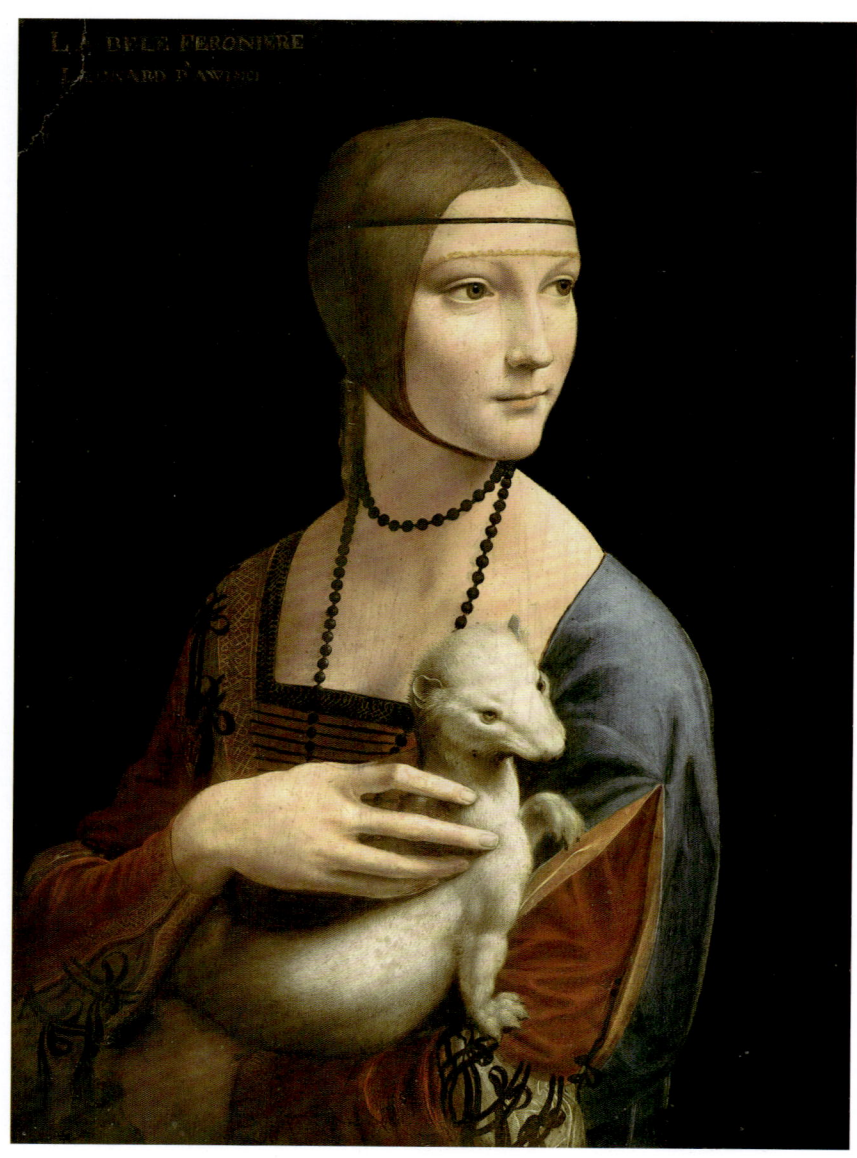

The Lady with the Ermine
La Dame à l'hermine
Die Dame mit dem Hermelin
La dama del armiño
La dama con l'ermellino
De dame met de hermelijn

1496, Oil on walnut panel/Huile sur bois de noyer, 53,4 × 39,3 cm, Muzeum Narodowe, Kraków

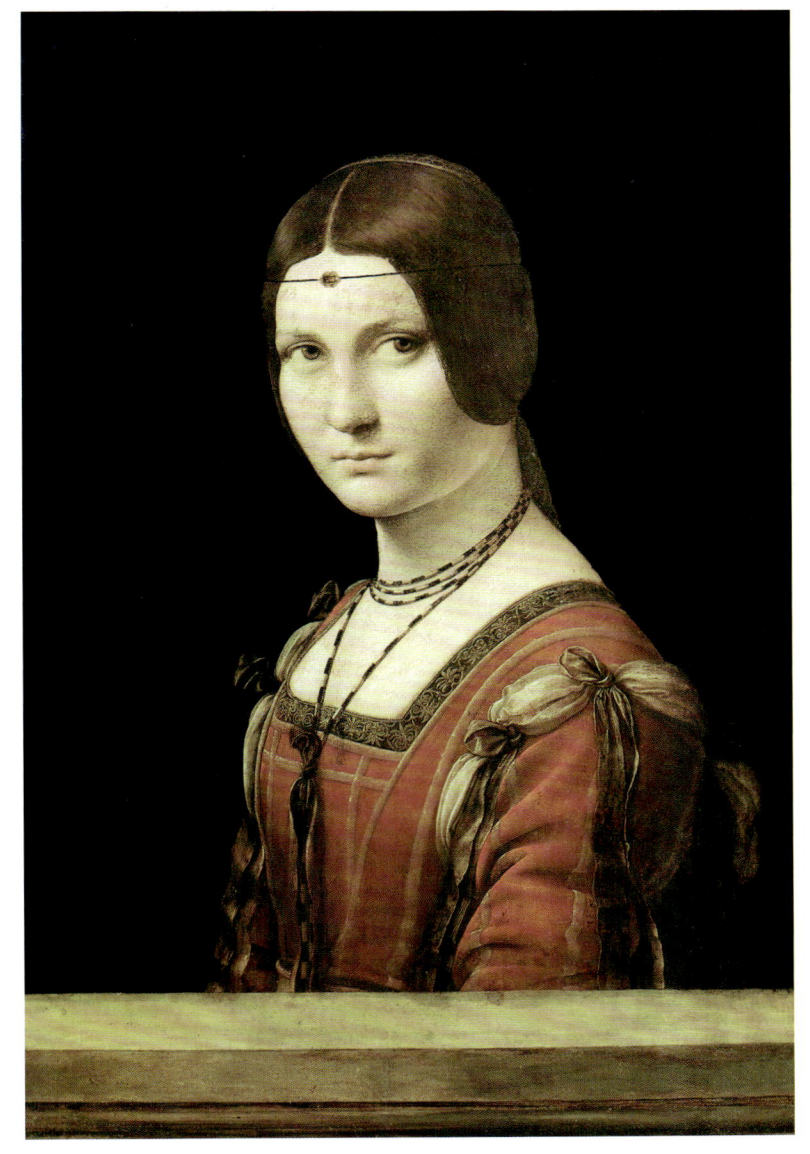

La Belle Ferronière

1490–95, Oil on panel/Huile sur bois, 63 × 45 cm,
Musée du Louvre, Paris

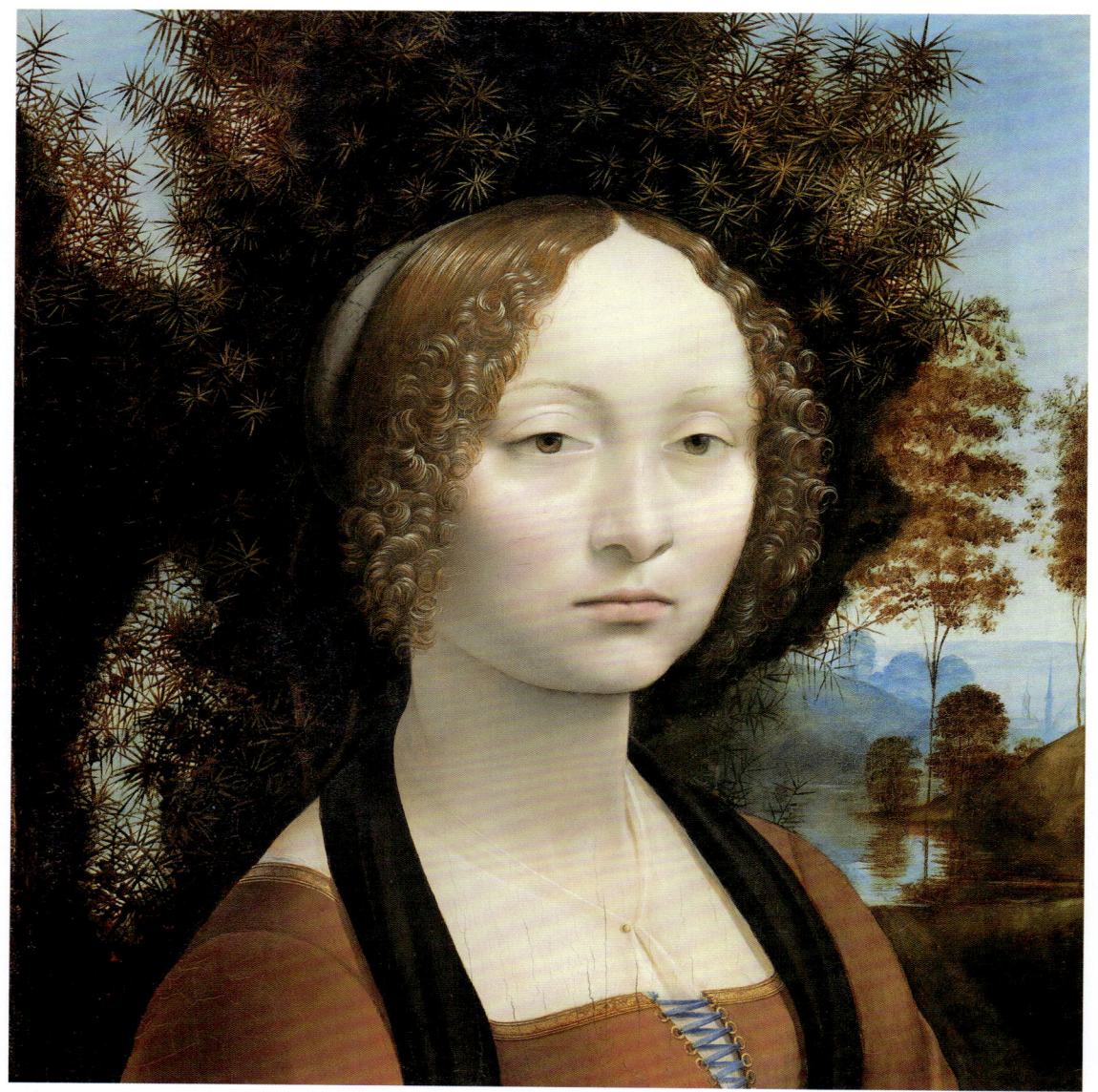

Ginevra de' Benci

1474–78, Oil on panel/Huile sur bois, 38,1 × 37 cm, National Gallery of Art, Washington

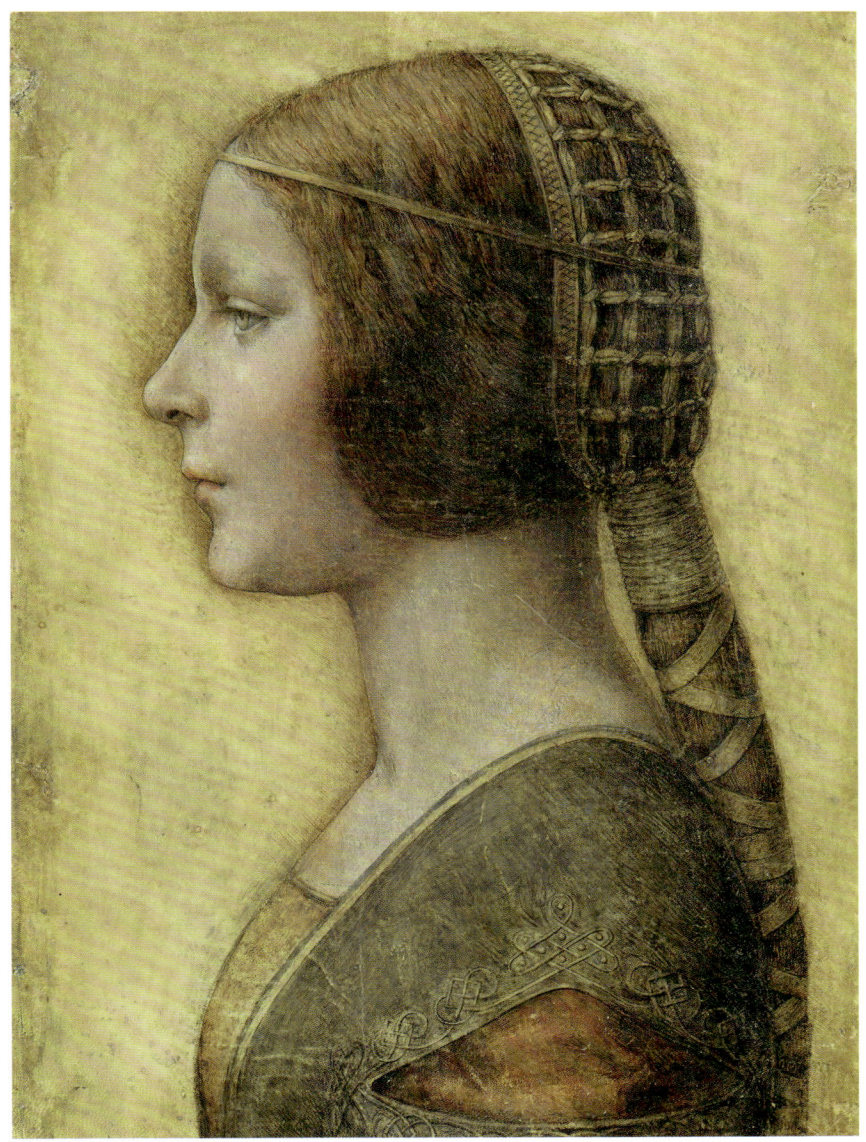

La Belle Princesse

La Bella Principessa

Chalk and ink on vellum/Craie et encre de Chine sur vélin, 33 × 22 cm, Private collection

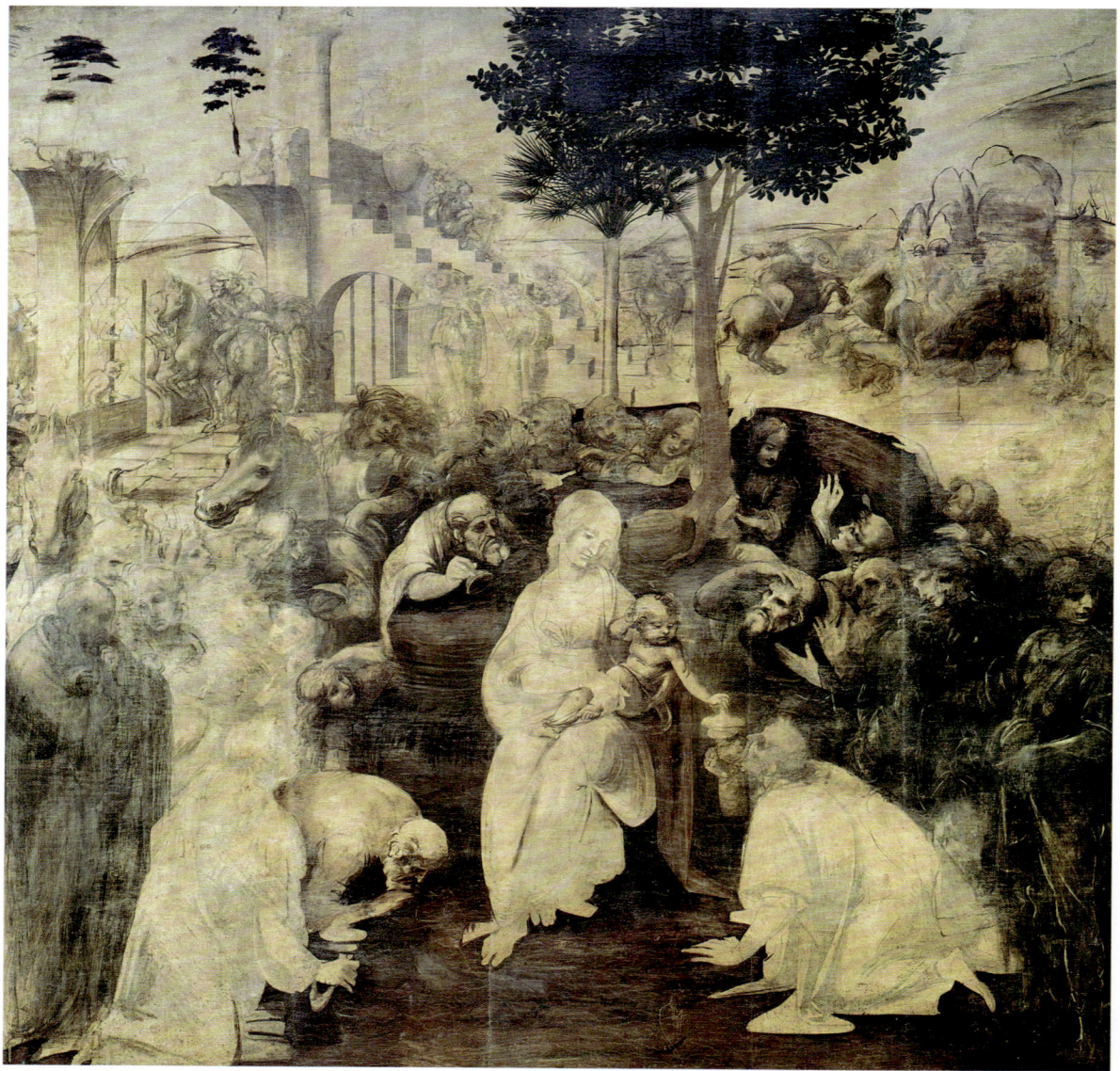

The Adoration of the Magi

L'Adoration des mages

Die Anbetung der Könige aus dem Morgenland

La Adoración de los Magos

L'Adorazione dei Magi

De aanbidding door de Wijzen uit het Morgenland

1481/82, Oil on panel/Huile sur bois, 246 × 243 cm, Galleria degli Uffizi, Firenze

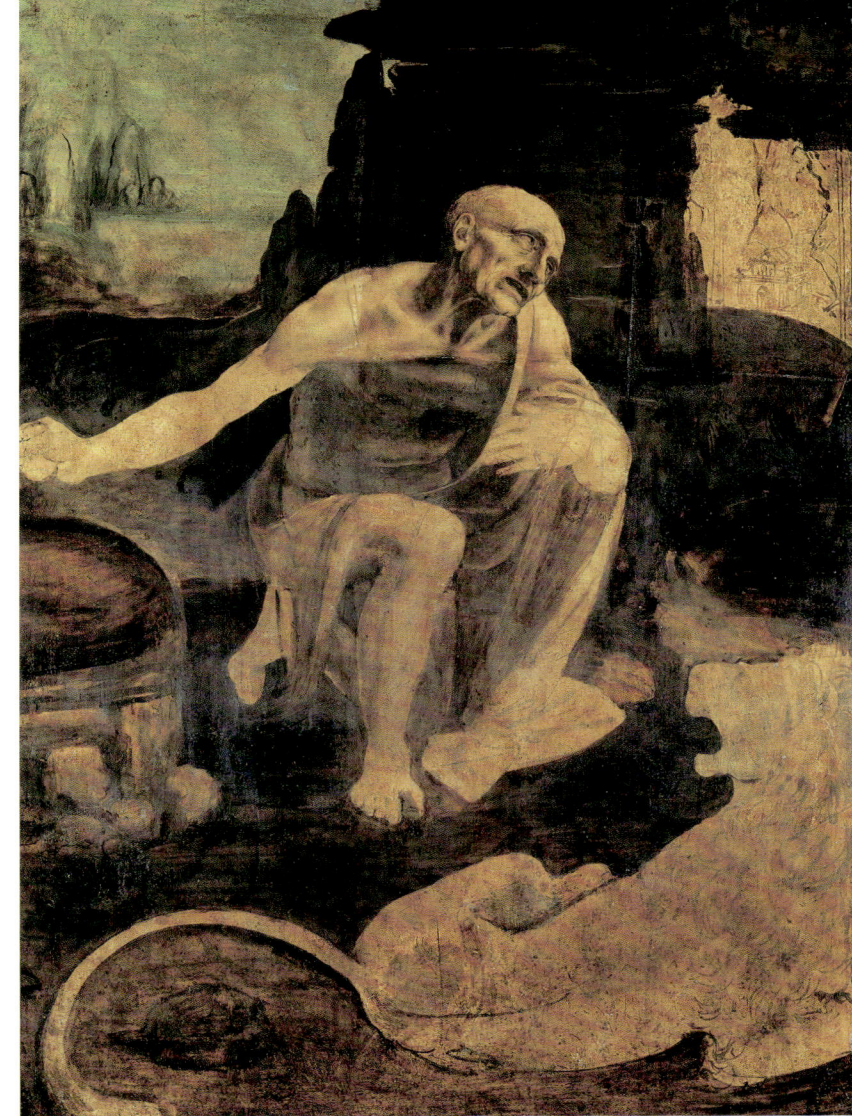

St. Jerome

Saint Jérôme

Der hl. Hieronymus

San Jerónimo

San Girolamo

De Heilige Hiëronymus

c. 1480–82, Oil and tempera on walnut/ Huile et détrempe sur bois, 103 × 73,5 cm, Musei Vaticani, Città del Vaticano

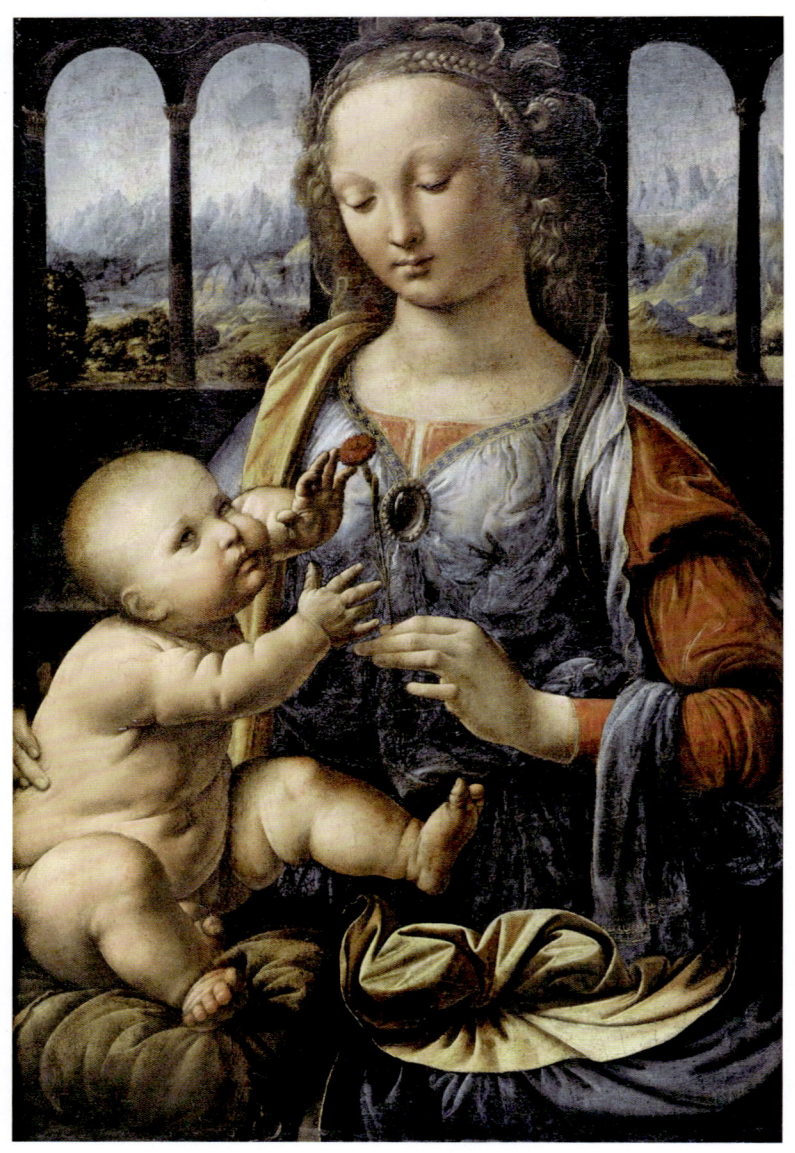

The Madonna of the Carnation
Madone à l'œillet
Madonna mit der Nelke
Virgen del clavel
Madonna del Garofano
Madonna met de anjer

*1478–80, Oil on panel/Huile sur bois, 47,5 × 62 cm,
Alte Pinakothek, München*

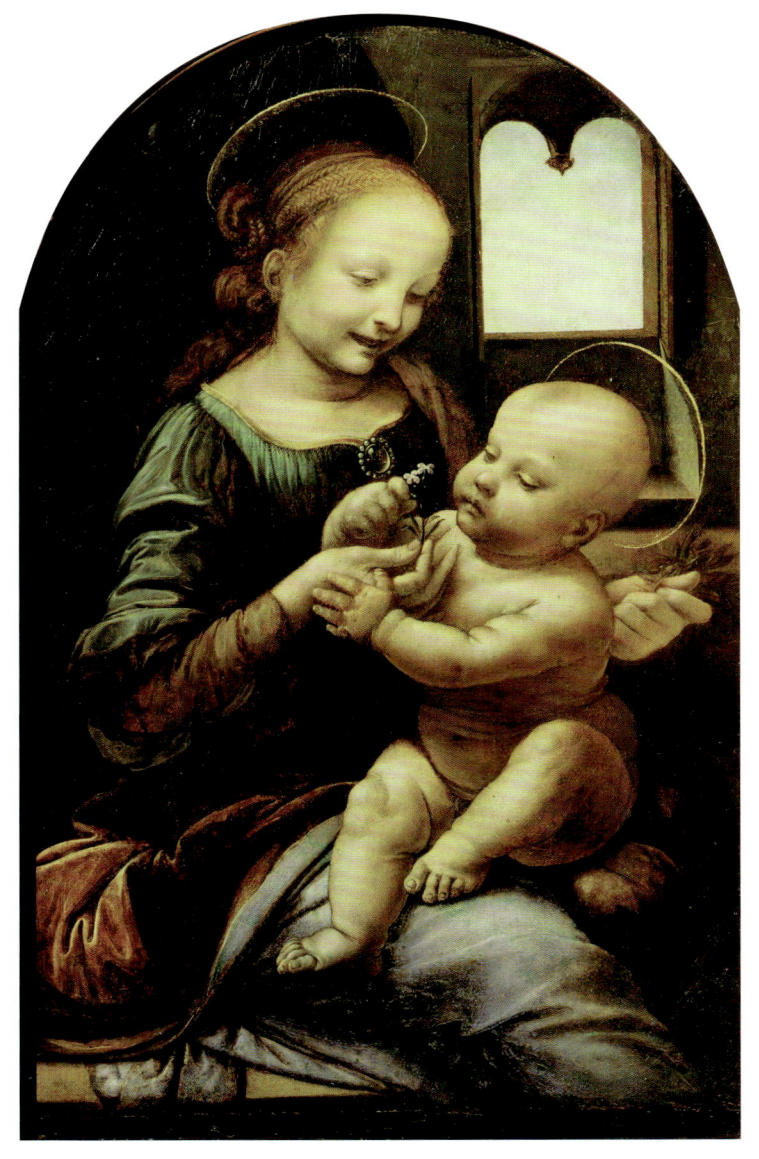

Madonna Benois

*c. 1478, Oil on canvas/Huile sur toile, 49,5 × 33 cm,
State Hermitage Museum, St. Petersburg*

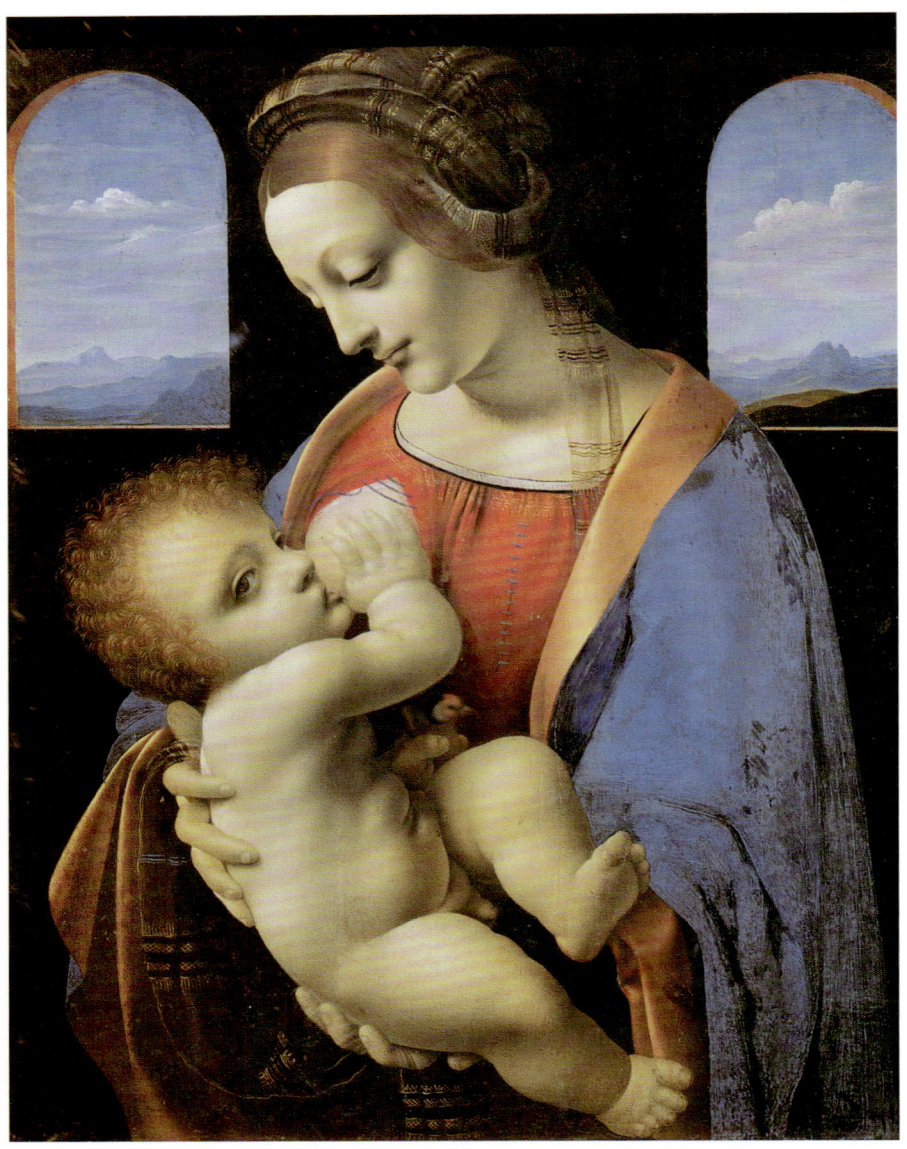

The Litta Madonna

Madone Litta

Madonna Litta

Madonna Litta

Madonna Litta

**Madonna lactans
(Madonna litta)**

*1490, Oil and tempera on canvas/
Huile et détrempe sur toile,
42 × 33 cm, State Hermitage
Museum, St Petersburg*

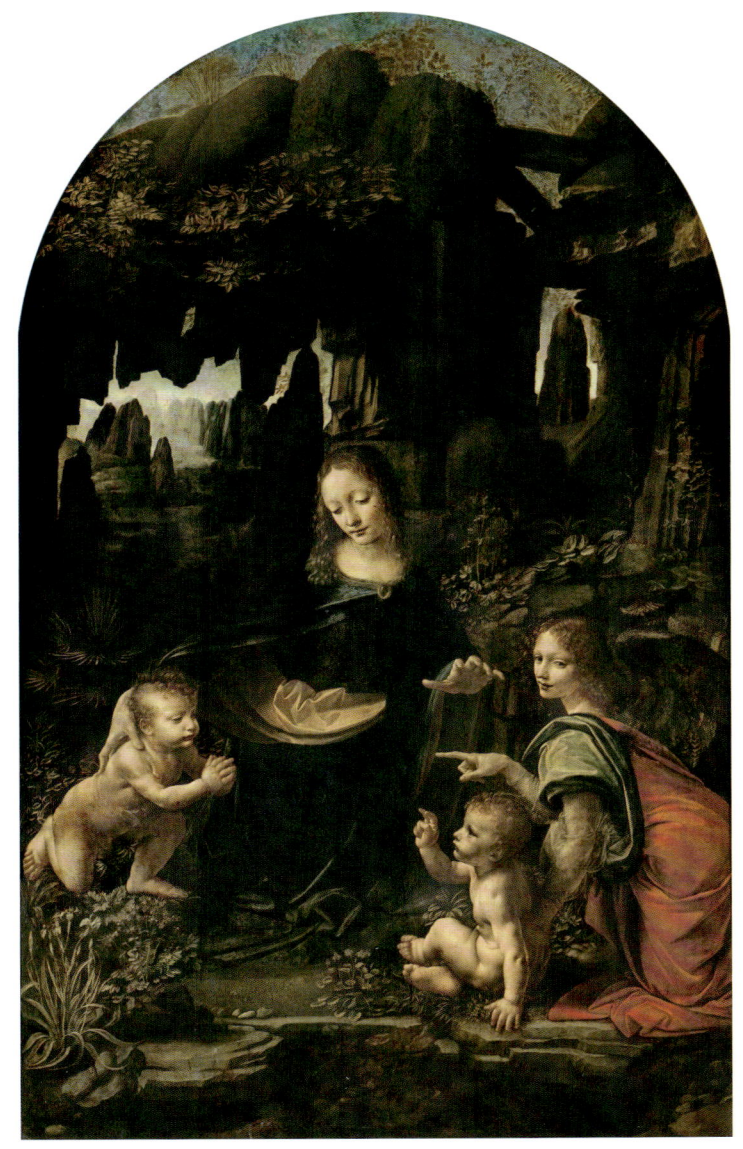

The Virgin of the Rocks, 1st version
La Vierge aux rochers, 1ʳᵉ version
Felsgrottenmadonna, 1. Version
La Virgen de las Rocas, 1ª versión
Vergine delle Rocce, 1° versione
De Maagd op de Rotsen, 1ᵉ versie

c. 1478, Oil on panel, transferred to canvas/Huile sur bois,
199 × 122 cm, Musée du Louvre, Paris

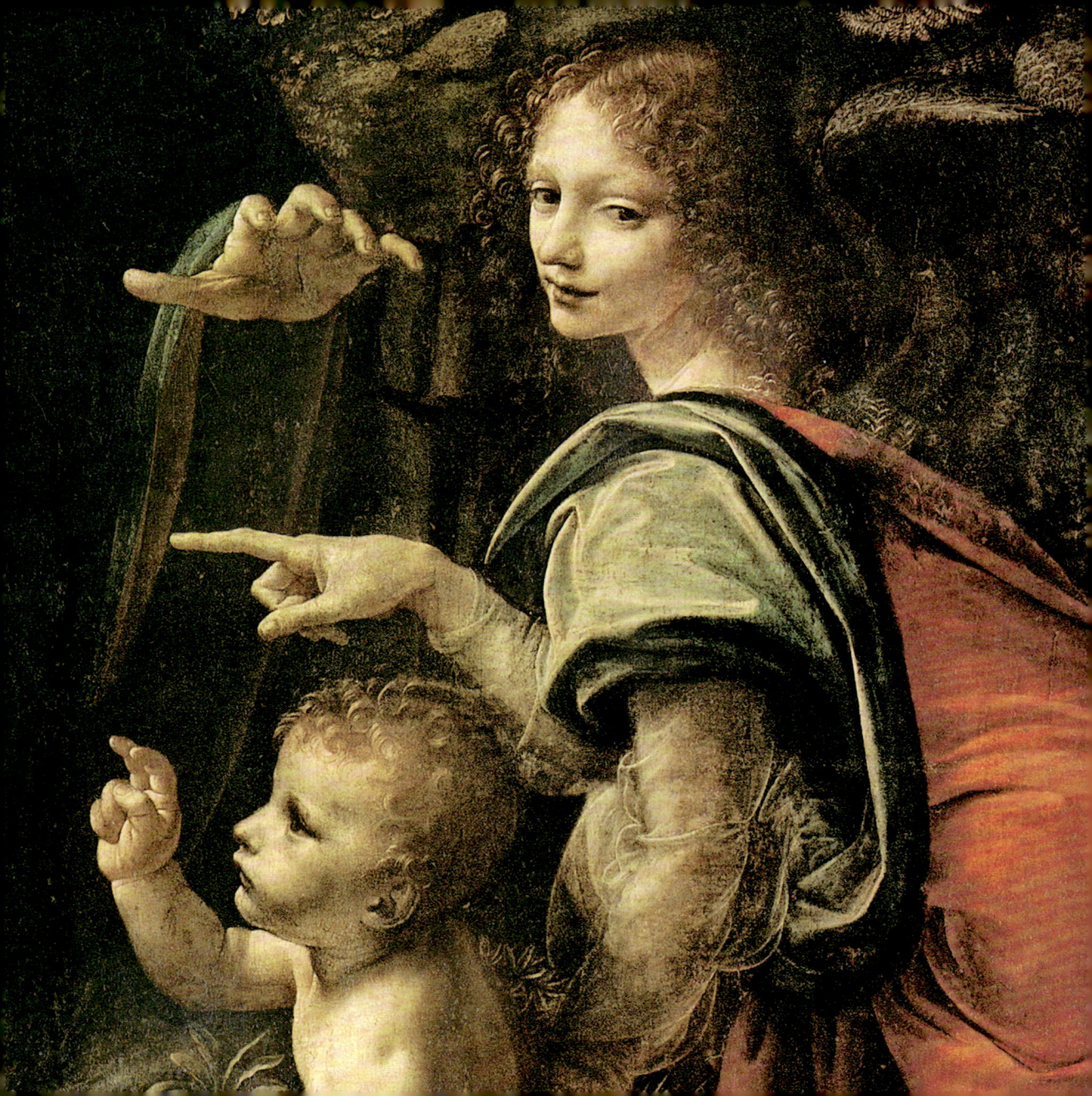

The Virgin of the Rocks, 1st version, detail
La Vierge aux rochers, 1ʳᵉ version, détail
Felsgrottenmadonna, 1. Version, Detail
La Virgen de las Rocas, 1ª versión, detalle
Vergine delle Rocce,
1° versione, dettaglio
De Maagd op de Rotsen, 1e versie, detail

1483–86, Oil on canvas/Huile sur toile, 199 × 122 cm,
Musée du Louvre, Paris

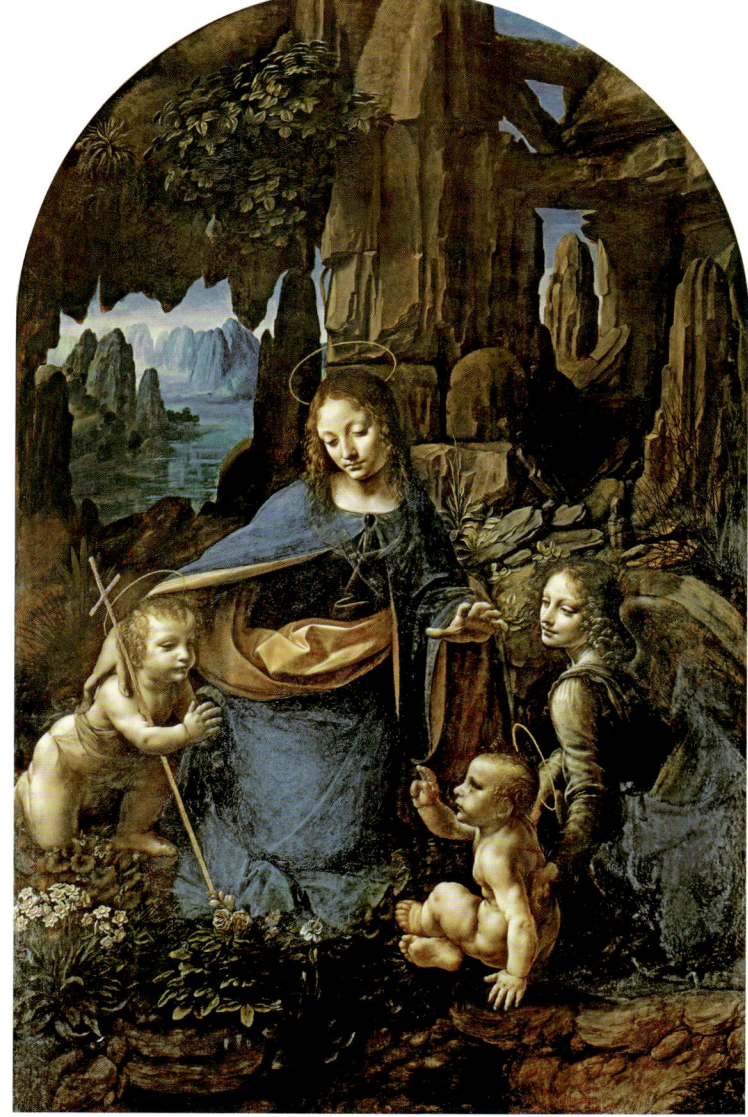

The Virgin of the Rocks, 2nd version
La Vierge aux rochers, 2ᵉ version
Felsgrottenmadonna, 2. Version
La Virgen de las Rocas, 2ª versión
Vergine delle Rocce, 2° versione
De Maagd op de Rotsen, 2e versie

c. 1508, Oil on panel/Huile sur bois, 189,5 × 120 cm,
National Gallery, London

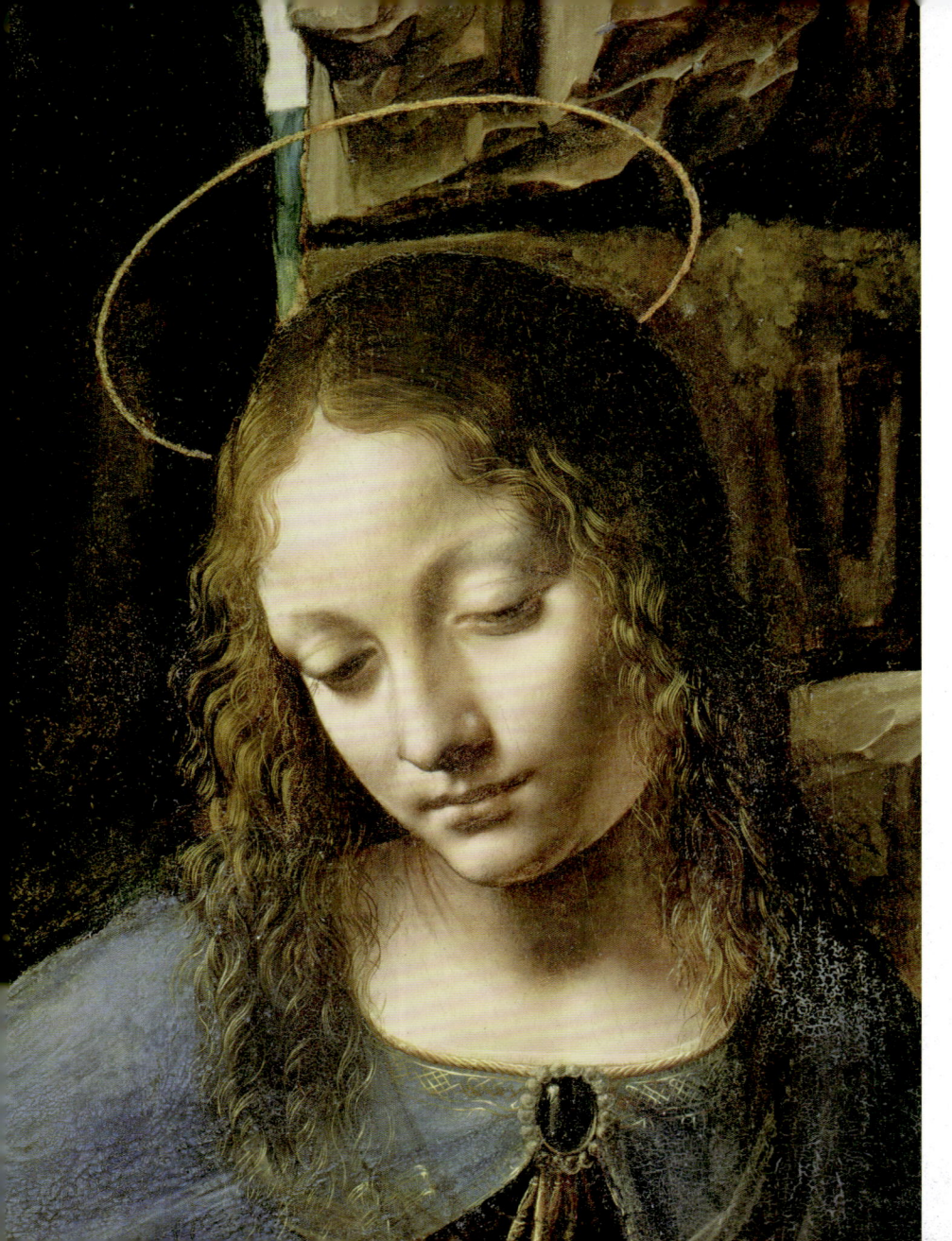

The Virgin of the Rocks,
2nd version, details

La Vierge aux rochers,
2e version, détails

Felsgrottenmadonna,
2. Version, Details

La Virgen de las Rocas,
2ª versión, detalles

Vergine delle Rocce,
2° versione, dettaglie

De Maagd op de Rotsen,
2e versie, details

c. 1508, Oil on panel/Huile sur bois,
189,5 × 120 cm, National Gallery,
London

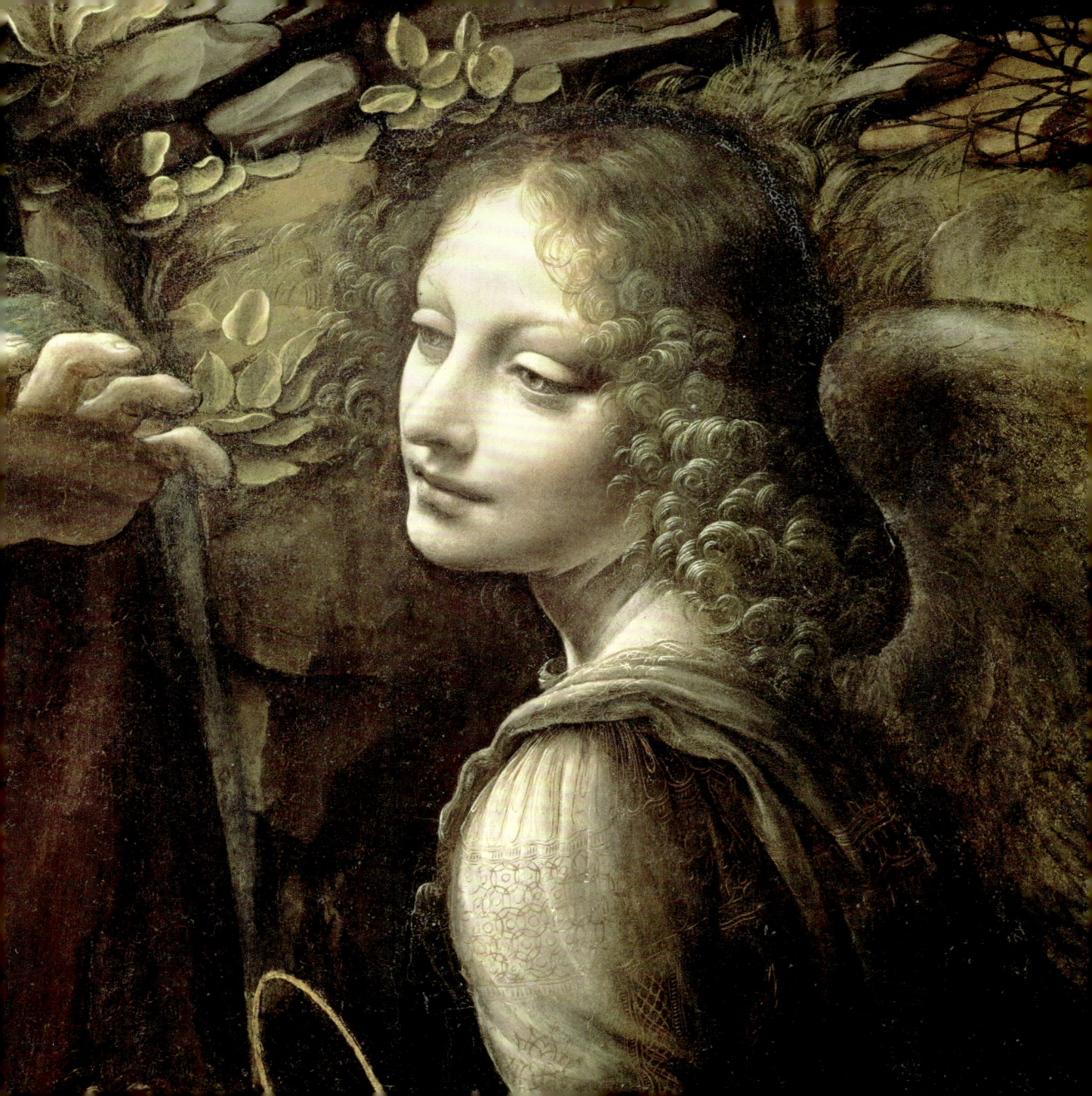

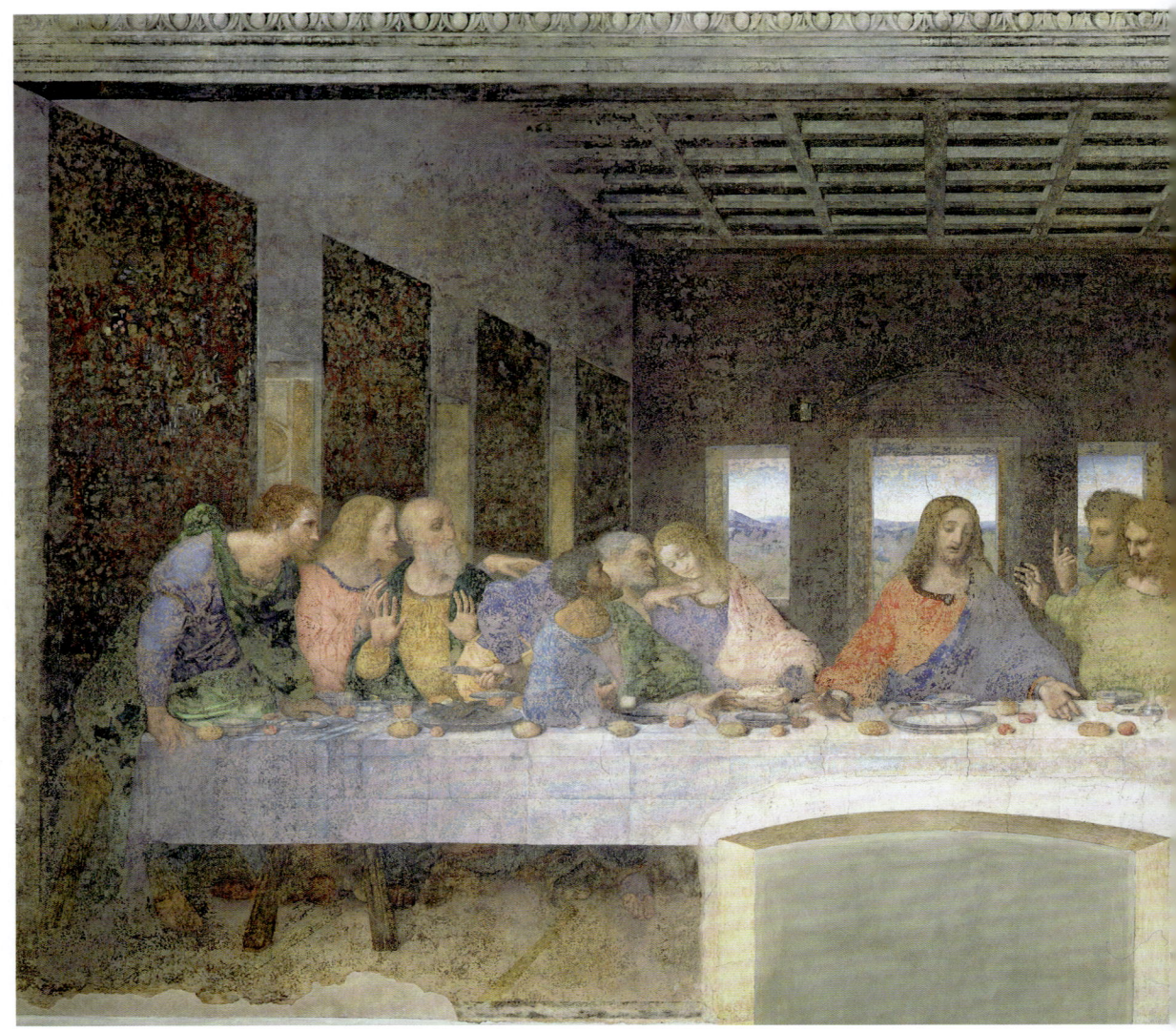

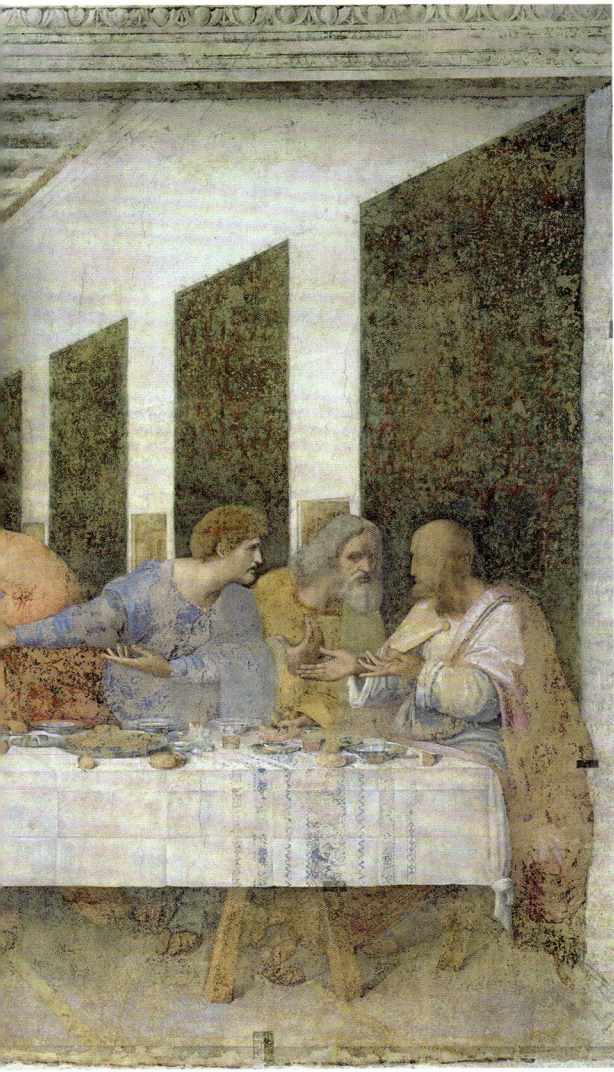

The Last Supper

La Cène

Das letzte Abendmahl

La Última Cena

L'Ultima Cena

Het Laatste Avondmaal

1495–97, Fresco/Fresque, 460 × 880 cm, Santa Maria della Grazie, Milano

This wall painting, which has become an icon of Western art, and which decorates the refectory of the convent of Santa Maria delle Grazie in Milan, shows Jesus with his disciples at the moment when he informs them that one of his followers will betray him. We see the reactions of each individual, ranging from disbelief and shock to incomprehension. Only Judas Iscariot, who is leaning on the table to the left of center, is conspicuously reserved.

Cette fresque murale devenue icône de l'art occidental et qui orne toujours le réfectoire du couvent de Santa Maria delle Grazie à Milan, représente Jésus avec ses disciples lors de leur dernier repas avant la Passion, au moment où il leur annonce que l'un d'entre eux va le trahir. On voit les réactions contrastées des apôtres, de l'incrédulité choquée à l'incompréhension totale ; seul Judas Iscariote, appuyé sur la table, à gauche du milieu de la table, se recule d'un air étonné.

Dieses zur Ikone der abendländischen Kunst gewordene Wandbild, das das Refektorium des Klosters Santa Maria delle Grazie in Mailand schmückt, zeigt Jesus mit seinen Jüngern in dem Augenblick, als er ihnen mitteilt, dass einer der ihren ihn verraten wird. Wir sehen die Reaktionen jedes einzelnen, die von Ungläubigkeit und Schock bis zu Unverständnis reichen. Nur der sich links der Bildmitte auf den Tisch stützende Judas Ischariot hält sich auffallend zurück.

Esta pintura mural convertida en icono del arte occidental decora el refectorio del Convento de Santa Maria delle Grazie en Milán. Muestra a Jesús con sus discípulos en el momento en el que les anuncia que uno de ellos lo va a traicionar. Podemos ver la reacción de cada uno de ellos, desde la incredulidad y el asombro hasta la falta de comprensión. Sólo Judas Iscariote, al que vemos apoyado a la izquierda del centro de la pintura, parce ocultarse de manera llamativa.

Questa pittura murale diventata un'icona dell'arte occidentale, che adorna il refettorio del convento di Santa Maria delle Grazie a Milano, mostra Gesù con i suoi apostoli nel momento in cui comunica che verrà tradito da uno di loro. Possiamo osservare le reazioni di ognuno, che vanno dall'incredulità allo shock fino all'incomprensione. Solo Giuda Iscariota, che siede alla sinistra del centro del quadro, si tiene chiaramente in disparte.

Dit fresco behoort tot de hoogtepunten van de westerse kunst en is aangebracht in de refter (eetzaal) van het klooster Santa Maria delle Grazie in Milaan. Het werk toont Jezus en zijn discipelen op het moment dat hij hen meedeelt dat hij door een van hen zal worden verraden. We zien de reacties van de discipelen, variërend van ongeloof tot ontsteltenis. Alleen Judas Ischariot, die links van het midden van het schilderij op de tafel leunt, reageert kalm.

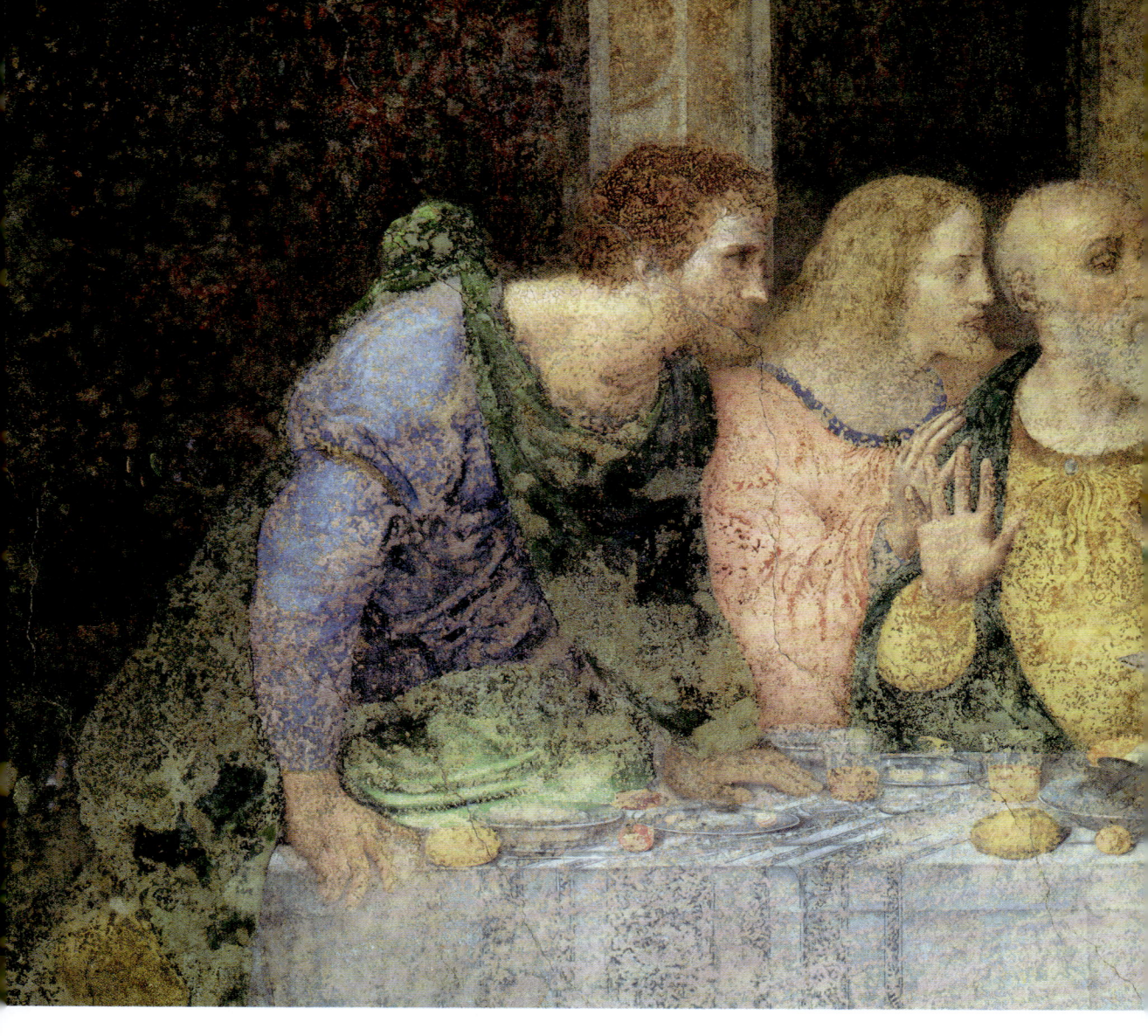

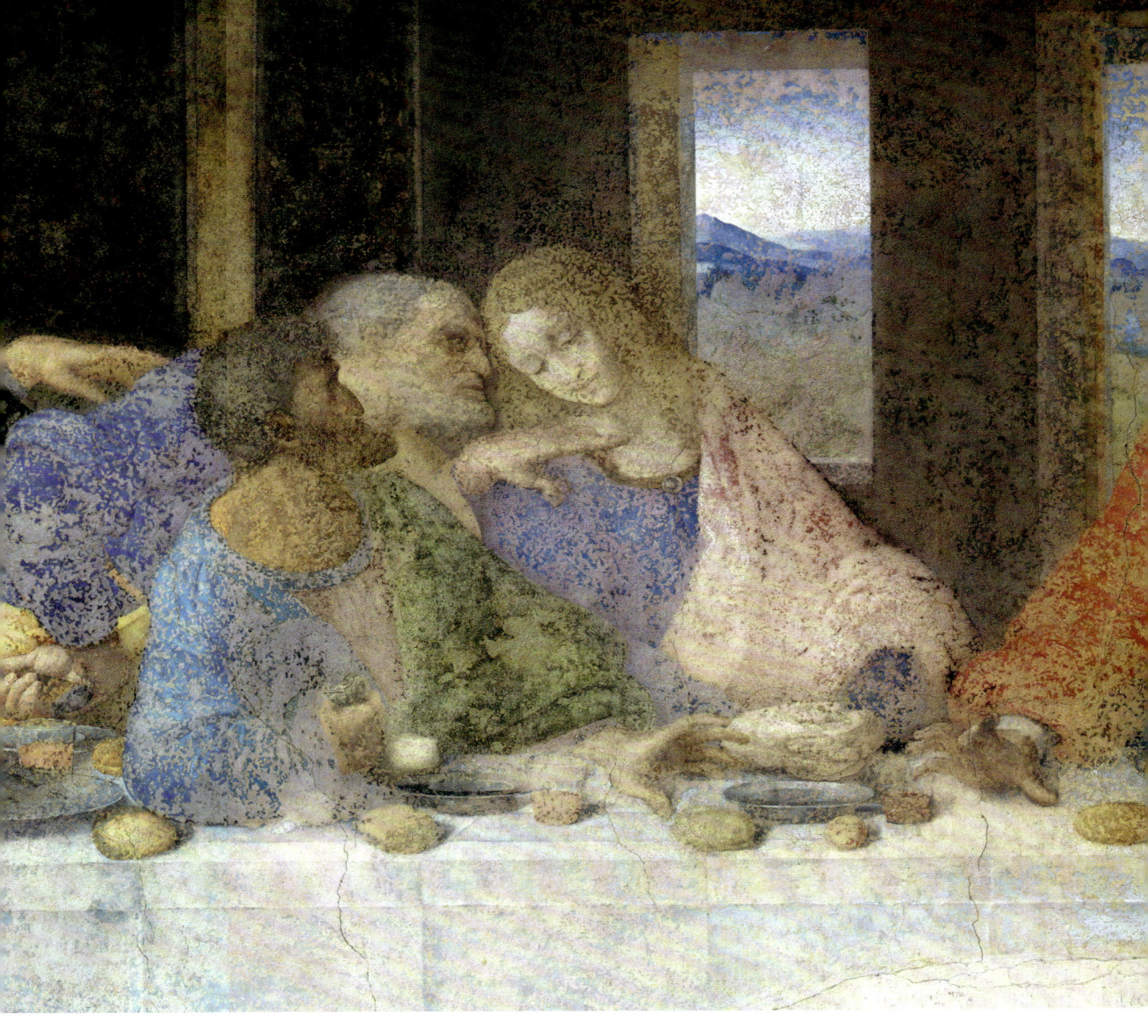

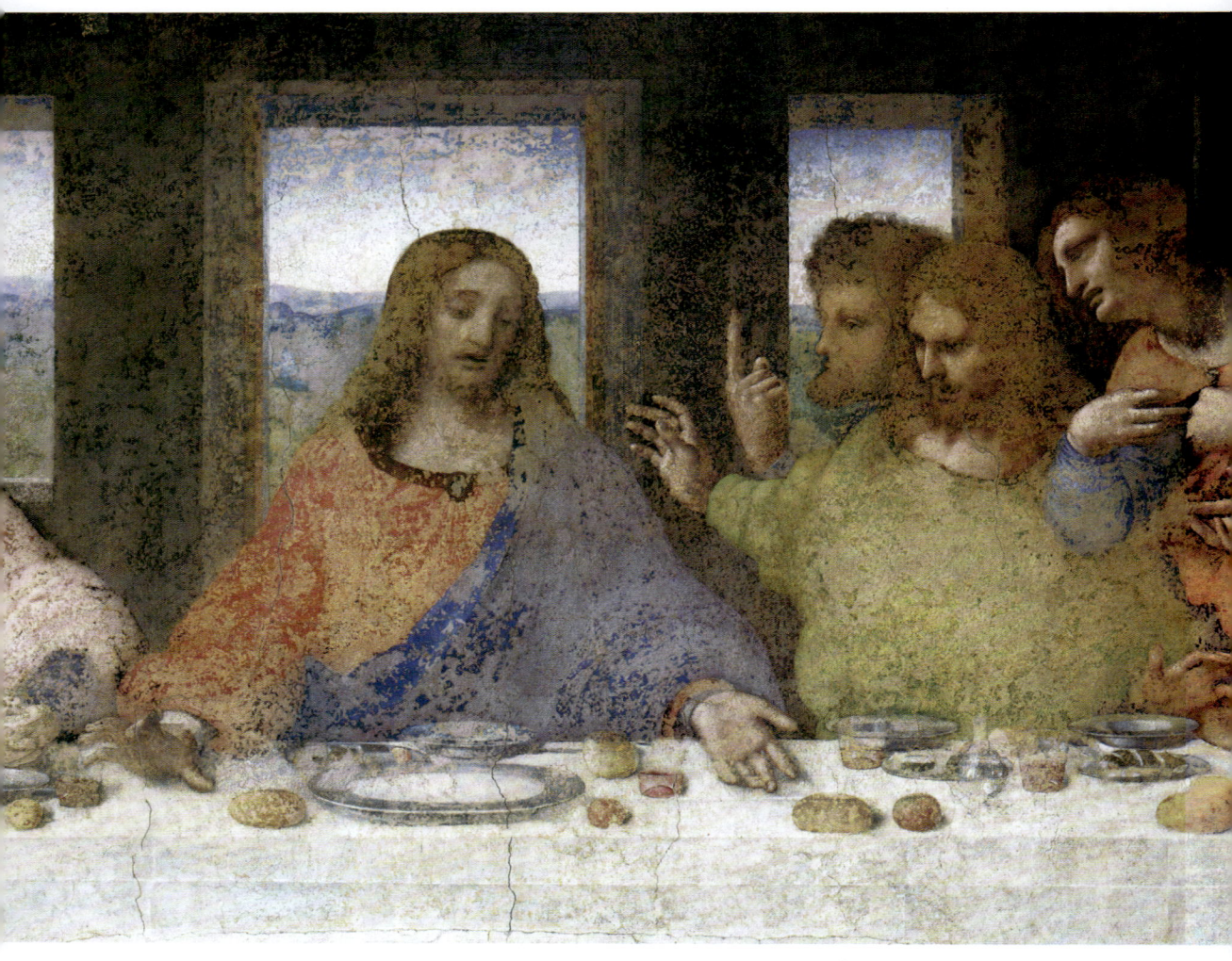

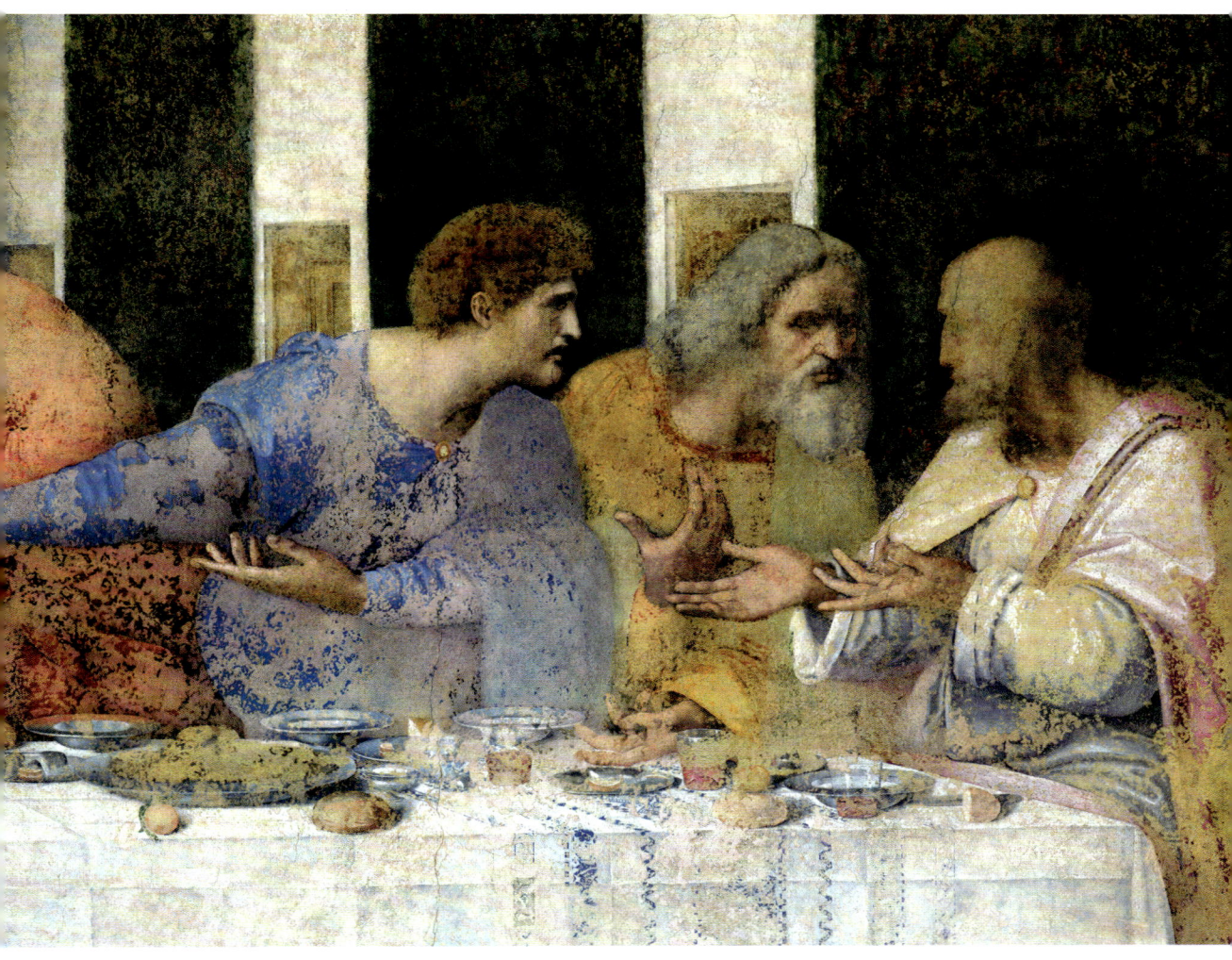

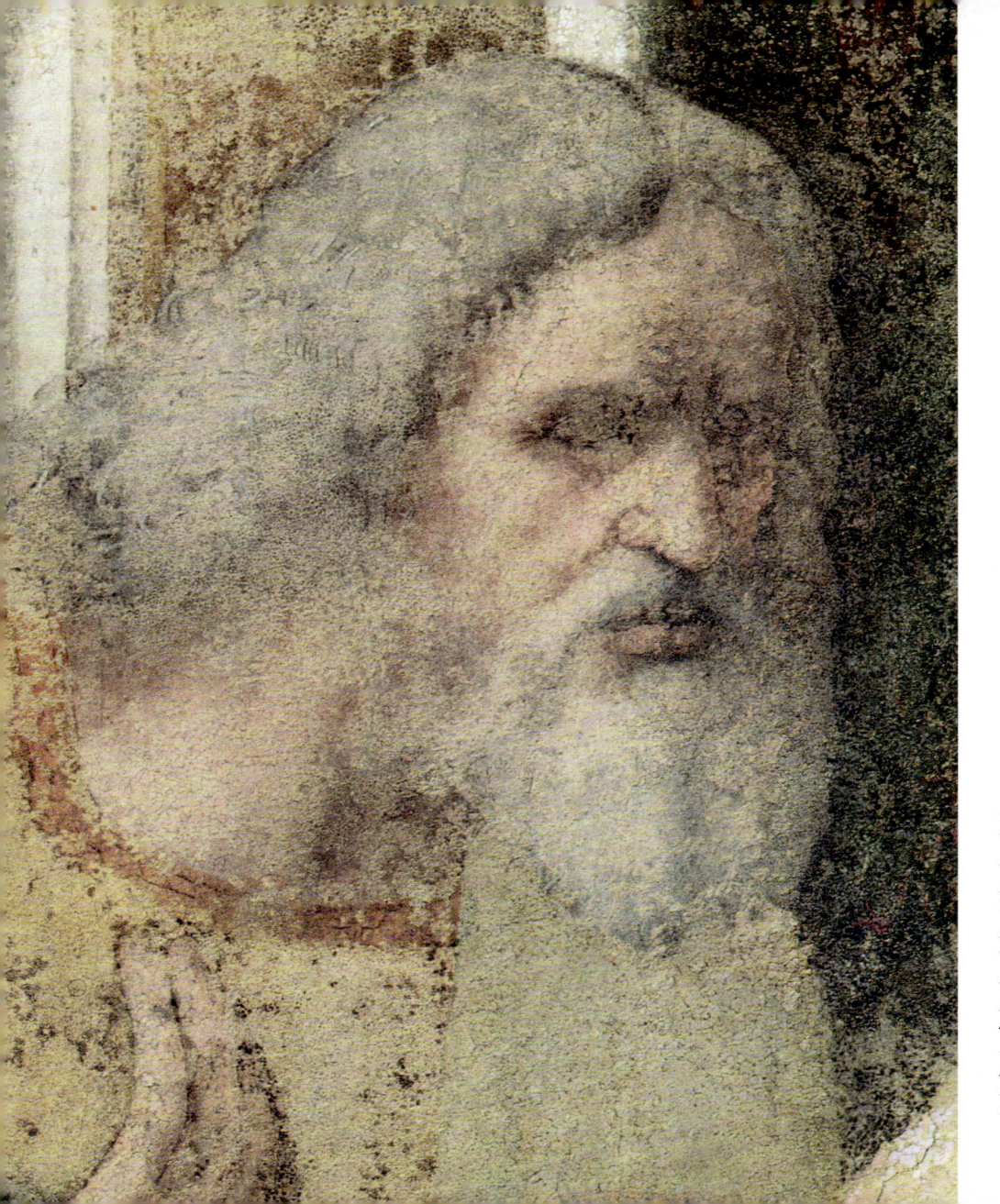

The Last Supper,
details

La Cène, détails

Das letzte Abendmahl,
Details

La Última Cena,
detalles

L'Ultima Cena, dettagli

*Het Laatste
Avondmaal,* details

*1495–97, Fresco/Fresque,
460 × 880 cm, Santa
Maria della Grazie,
Milano*

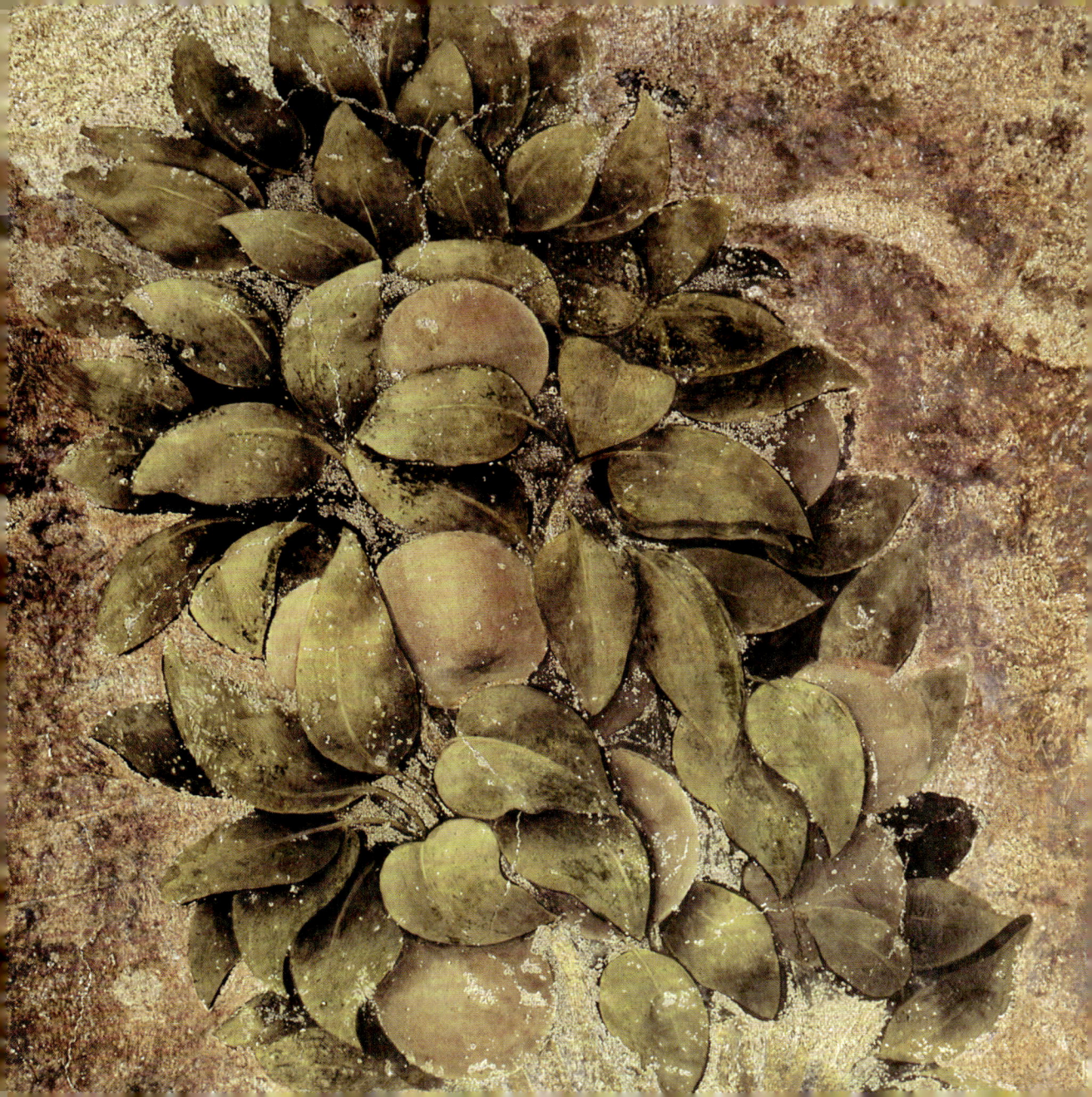

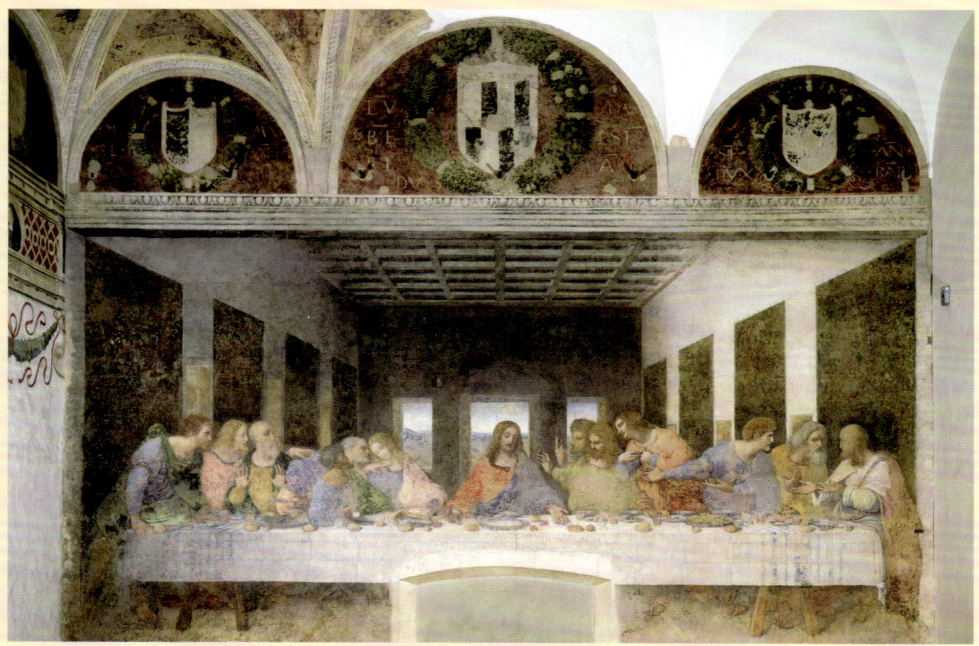

Central perspective

Leonardo's name is often mentioned when the story of central perspective is concerned, which is mainly due to the fact that although this had already been understood theoretically and practically in fifteenth century architecture and painting by others (Brunelleschi, Alberti, Masaccio, et al.), he was able to supplement this and formulate further findings from his study of optics and geometry. If one looks for a textbook example of central perspective then, along with Raphael's *The School of Athens,* Leonardo's *Last Supper* is able to convey this.

Perspective centrale

Le nom de Léonard est souvent mentionné lorsqu'il est question de l'histoire de la perspective centrale. Cela tient au fait qu'il a complété et formulé de façon globale, en les étendant à d'autres connaissances d'optique et de géométrie, ce qui avait été déjà réalisé au XVᵉ siècle par d'autres dans l'architecture et dans la peinture, en théorie comme en pratique (Brunelleschi, Alberti, Masaccio...). Et cela tient naturellement aussi au fait que seule *L'École d'Athènes* du Vatican peut se mesurer à *La Cène* de Milan, pour la parfaite application de la perspective centrale.

Zentralperspektive

Leonardos Name wird häufig genannt, wenn von der Geschichte der Zentralperspektive die Rede ist, was vor allem daran liegt, dass er das, was im 15. Jahrhundert von anderen in der Architektur und Malerei theoretisch wie praktisch bereits geleistet worden war (Brunelleschi, Alberti, Masaccio u. a.), um weitere Erkenntnisse aus der Optik und Geometrie ergänzte und umfassend formulierte. Und natürlich auch daran, dass höchstens Raffaels *Schule von Athen* es mit seinem *Abendmahl* aufnehmen kann, suche man nach einem Schulbeispiel für die perfekte Anwendung der Zentralperspektive.

Raphael (Raffaello
Sanzio of Urbino)
(1483–1520)

The School of Athens

L'École d'Athènes

Die Schule von Athen

La escuela de Atenas

Scuola di Atene

De school van Athene

*1510–11, Fresco/Fresque,
500 × 770 cm, Stanza
della Segnatura, Roma,
Città del Vaticano*

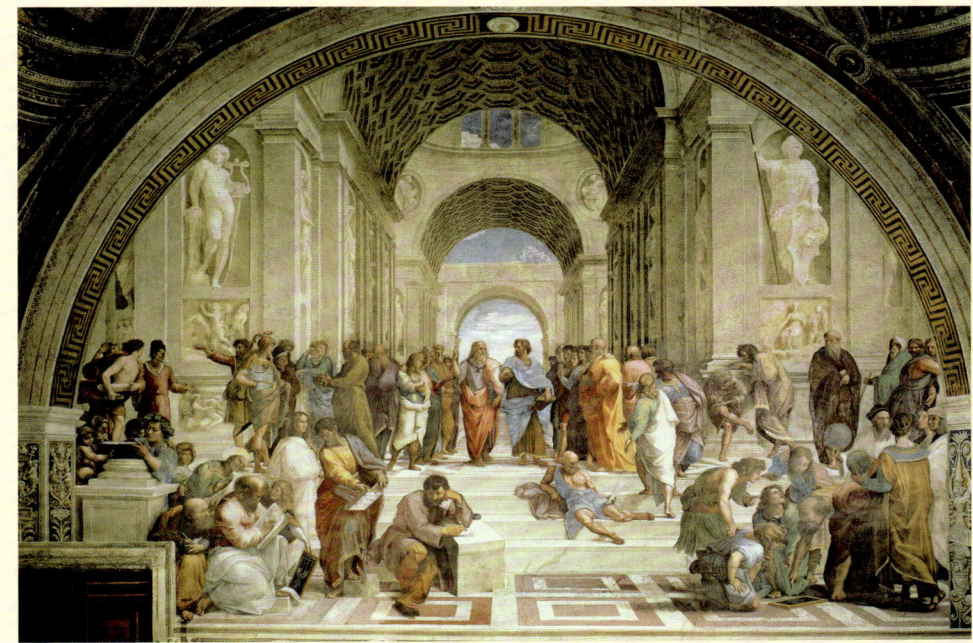

Perspectiva central

Habitualmente su nombre aparece
cuando hablamos de la historia de la
perspectiva central, puesto que formuló
lo que otros ya habían hecho en el
siglo XV en la arquitectura y pintura de
manera teórica y práctica (Brunelleschi,
Alberti, Masaccio, entre otros) y lo
completó con nuevos conocimientos
sobre la óptica y geometría. Si buscamos
un ejemplo clásico del perfecto uso
de la perspectiva central, únicamente
La escuela de Atenas de Rafael puede
medirse con *La Última Cena* del artista.

Prospettiva centrale

Il nome di Leonardo viene spesso citato
quando il discorso cade sulla storia
della prospettiva centrale, soprattutto
per il motivo che egli aggiunse ulteriori
conoscenze nel campo dell'ottica e della
geometria e le formulò completamente,
cosa che nel XV secolo era già stata
effettuata da altri in architettura e
pittura, sia in teoria che in pratica
(Brunelleschi, Alberti, Masaccio etc.).
E naturalmente anche il fatto che tutt'al
più la *Scuola di Atene* di Raffaello si può
assimilare alla sua *Ultima Cena;* in base
ad un esempio classico si cerca un uso
perfetto della prospettiva centrale.

Eenpuntsperspectief

Leonardo's naam wordt ook vaak
genoemd in de geschiedenis van het
eenpuntsperspectief, vooral omdat
hij deze natuurwetenschappelijke
benadering – die eerder in de vijftiende
eeuw door anderen (Brunelleschi, Alberti,
Masaccio) zowel theoretisch als praktisch
in de architectuur en schilderkunst was
geïntroduceerd – aanvulde en verbeterde,
met nieuwe inzichten in de optica en de
geometrie, en alomvattend beschreef.
Wie een perfect voorbeeld van de
toepassing van het eenpuntsperspectief
zoekt, zal naast Rafaëls *School van Athene*
uiteraard bij Leonardo's *Het Laatste
Avondmaal* uitkomen.

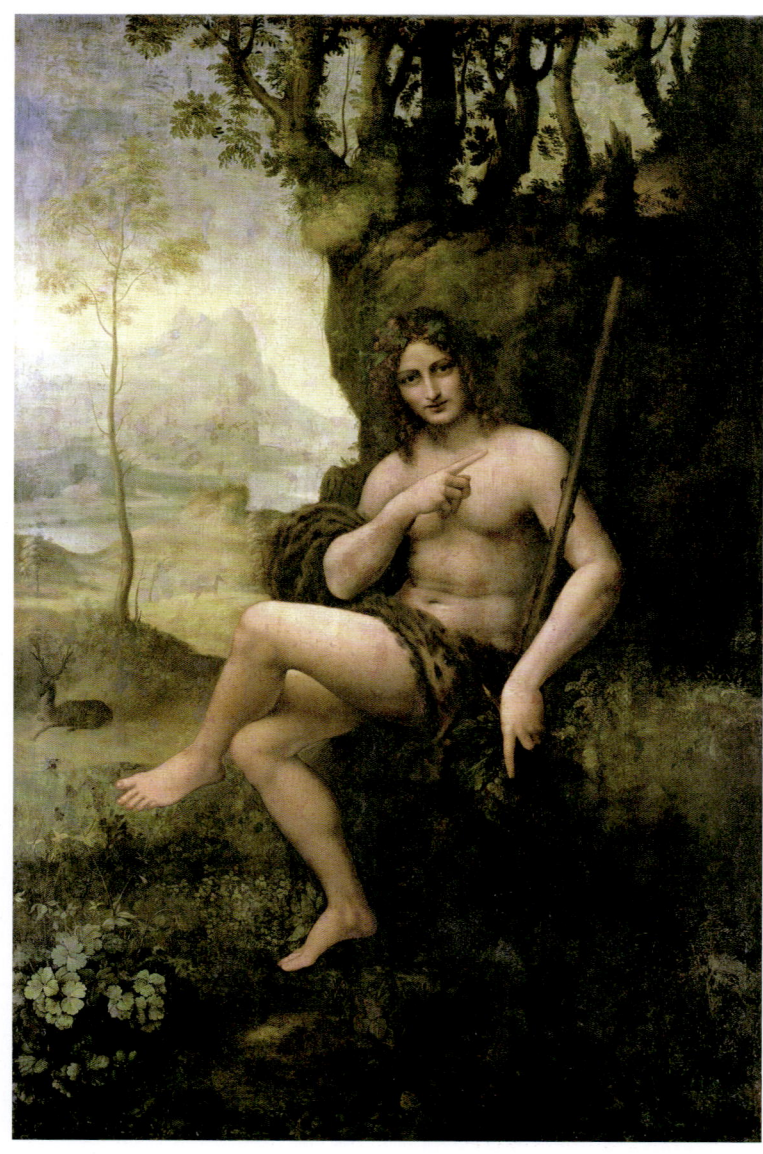

Unknown artist/Artiste inconnu

Bacchus

Bacchus

Bacchus

Baco

Bacco

Bacchus

c. 1695, Oil on canvas/Huile sur toile, 177 × 115 cm,
Musée du Louvre, Paris

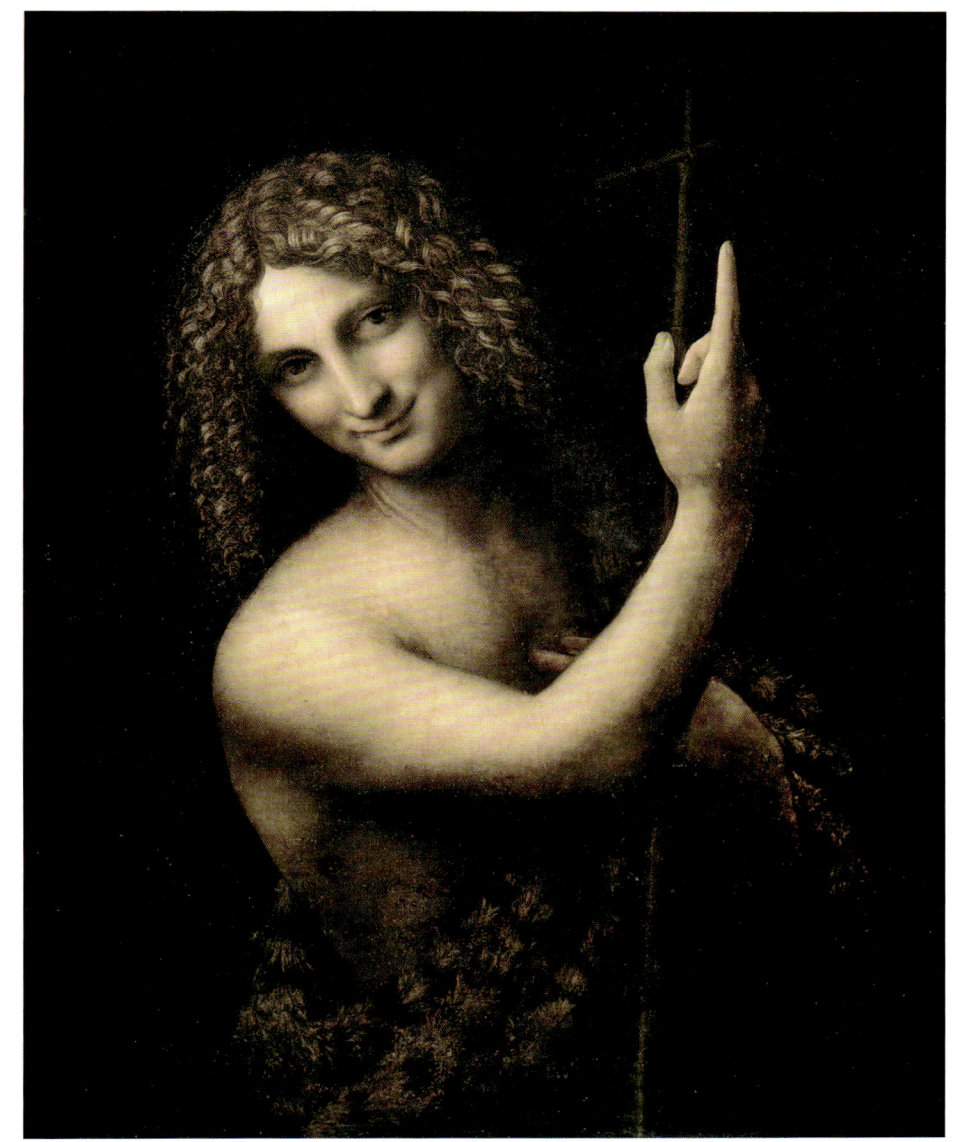

St. John the Baptist
Saint Jean-Baptiste
Johannes der Täufer
San Juan bautista
San Giovanni Battista
Johannes de Doper

1513–16, Oil on canvas/Huile sur toile, 69 × 57 cm, Musée du Louvre, Paris

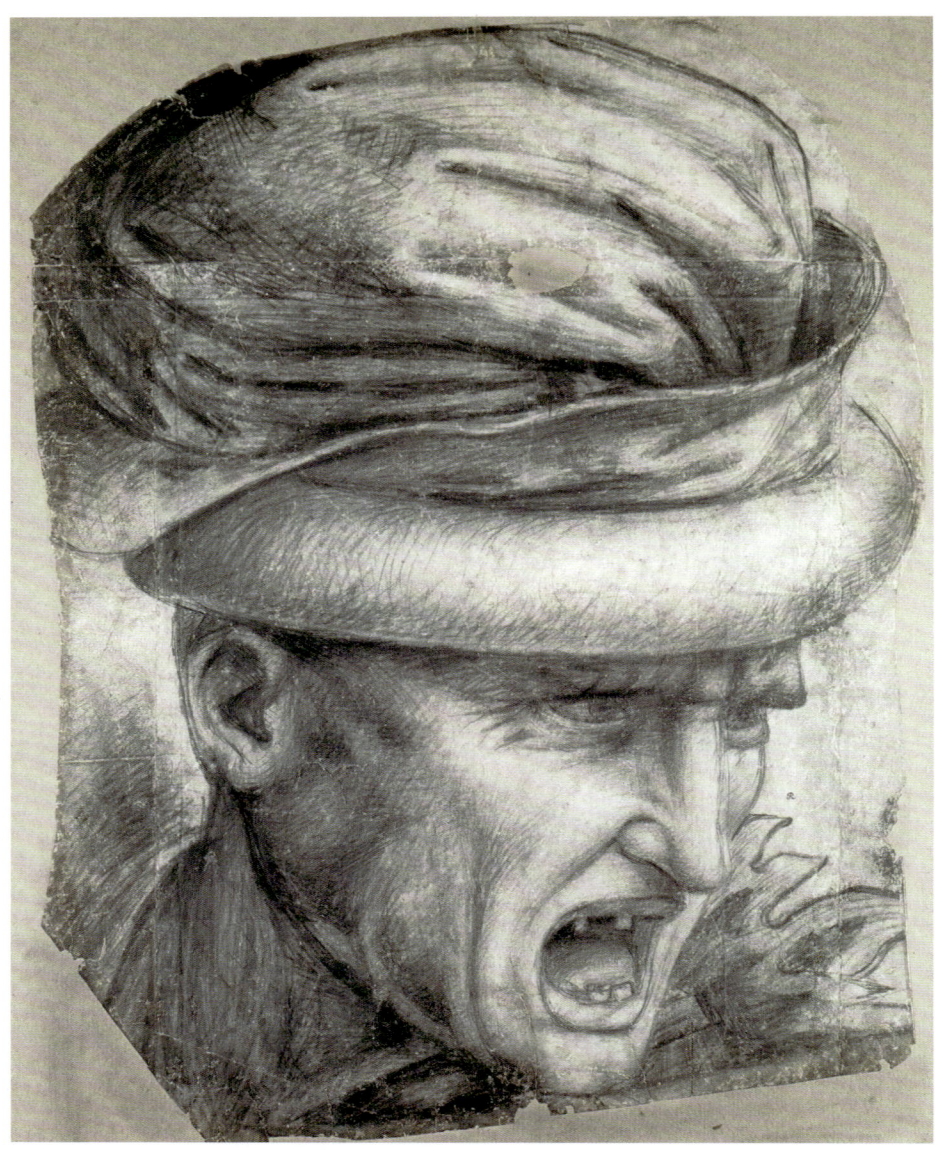

Study for the head
of a soldier in
The Battle of Anghiari

Tête de guerrier, esquisse
pour la *Bataille d'Anghiari*

Kopf eines Kriegers
aus der Skizze zur
Schlacht von Anghiari

Cabeza de un guerrero
del esbozo para
La batalla de Anghiari

Testa di guerriero
dallo schizzo della
Battaglia di Anghiari

Studie van soldatenkop
uit de schets voor
De Slag bij Anghiari

*c. 1504–05, Black chalk on
paper/Pierre noire sur papier,
50,5 × 37,5 cm, Ashmolean
Museum, Oxford*

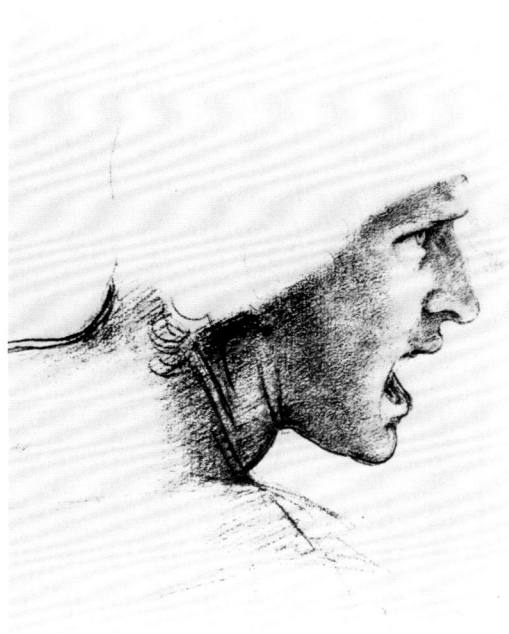

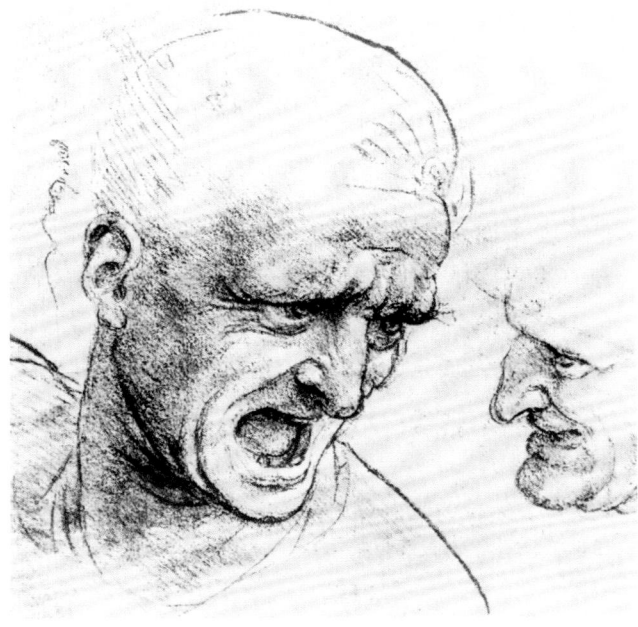

Study for the head of a soldier in *The Battle of Anghiari*

Tête de guerrier, esquisse pour la *Bataille d'Anghiari*

Kopf eines Kriegers aus der Skizze zur *Schlacht von Anghiari*

Cabeza de un guerrero del esbozo para *La batalla de Anghiari*

Testa di guerriero dallo schizzo della *Battaglia di Anghiari*

Studie van soldatenkop uit de schets voor *De Slag bij Anghiari*

c. 1504–05, Red chalk on paper/Sanguine sur papier, 22,6 × 18,6 cm,
Szépművészeti Múzeum, Budapest

Studies for the heads of two soldiers in *The Battle of Anghiari*

Études pour les têtes de deux soldats, esquisse pour la *Bataille d'Anghiari*

Studien für die Köpfe zweier Soldaten in der *Schlacht von Anghiari*

Estudios para las cabezas de dos soldados en *La batalla de Anghiari*

Studi per le teste di due soldati nella *Battaglia di Anghiari*

Studie van twee soldatenhoofden voor *De Slag bij Anghiari*

c. 1504–05, Black chalk or charcoal on paper/Pierre noire ou fusain sur papier,
19,1 × 18,8 cm, Szépművészeti Múzeum, Budapest

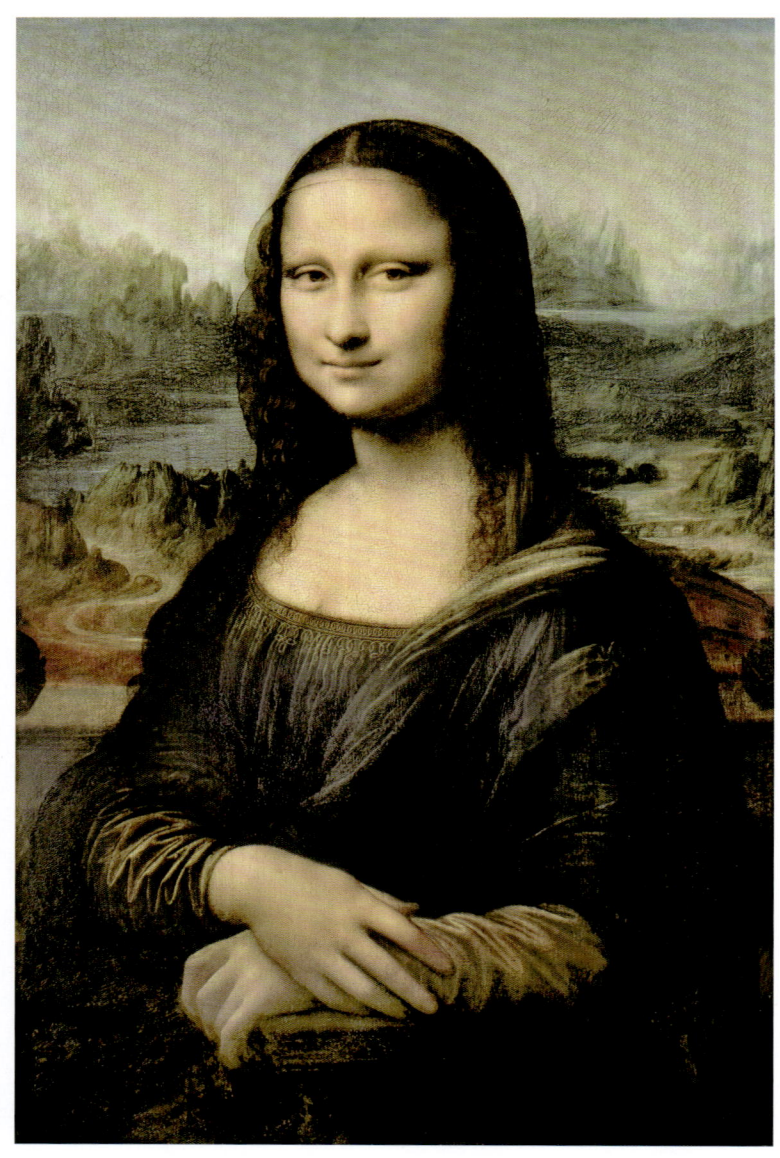

Mona Lisa
La Joconde
Mona Lisa
La Gioconda
La Gioconda
Mona Lisa

c. 1503–06, Oil on panel/Huile sur bois, 77 × 53 cm,
Musée du Louvre, Paris

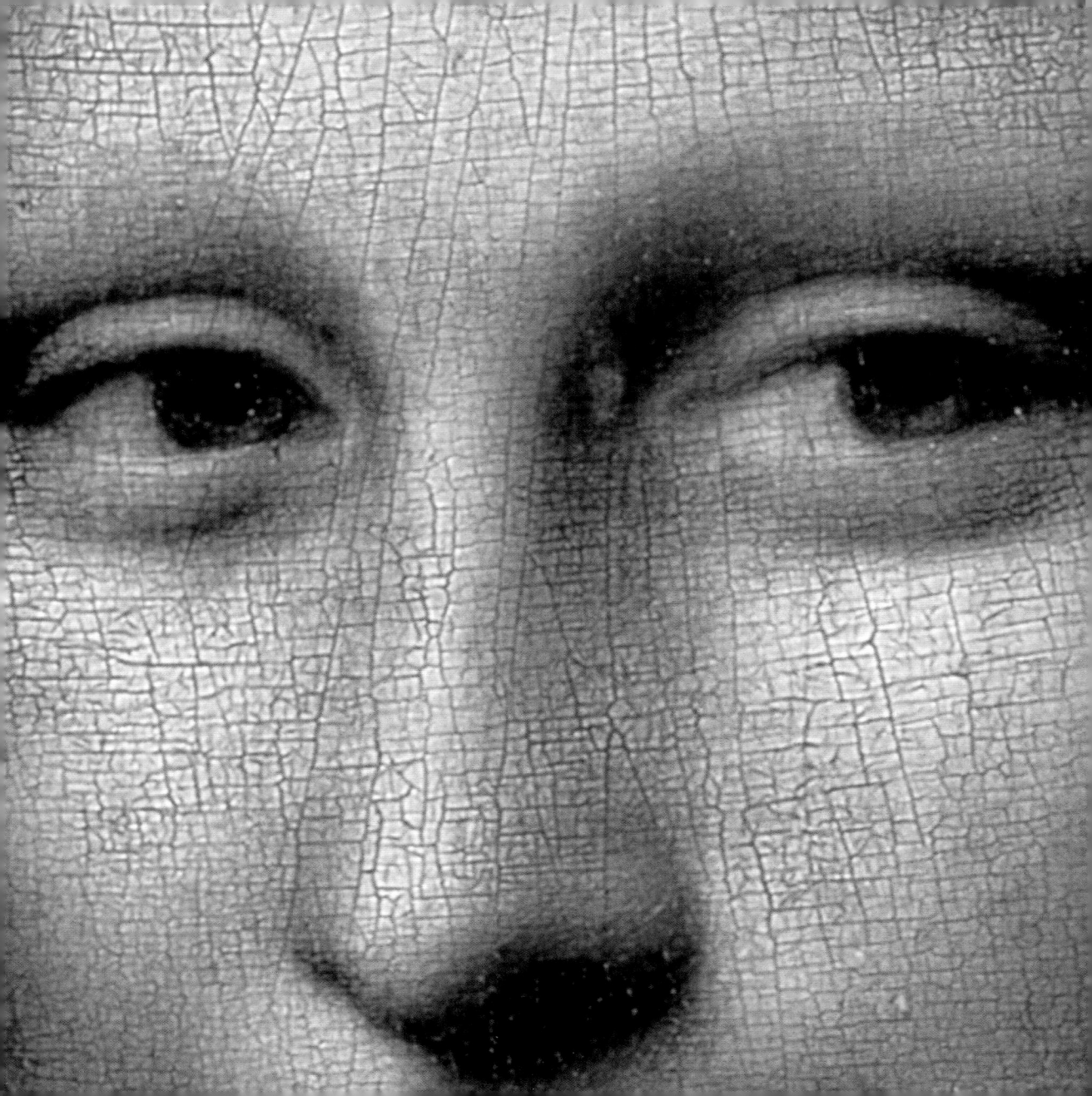

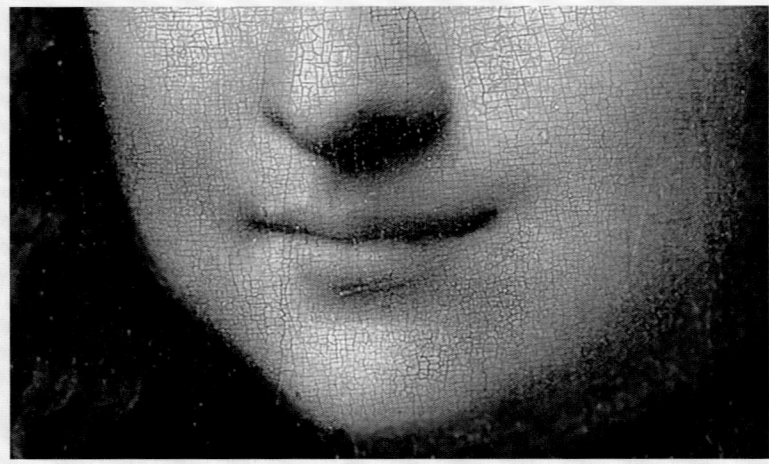

Color theory

Important innovations came from Leonardo's study of color theory. He was particularly interested in the effect of complementary colors on human perception. Centuries before the Bauhaus professor Johannes Itten formulated his color circle and theories of color contrasts, Leonardo had recognized the effect of simultaneous contrast on the human eye. This involves the interaction of adjacent color areas and the subjectively perceived amplification or reduction of the objectively present contrast.

This is also connected to his thoughts on light and shadow in painting. A glance at the mouth of the *Mona Lisa,* which appears as if modeled by a sculptor, suffices to see how fruitfully he was able to translate his theoretical reflections into his painting. But also, in other works, we can admire his ability to convey fabrics and other materials as

Théorie des couleurs

Innovations importantes de Léonard sont venues de ses recherches sur la théorie des couleurs. Il s'est intéressé avant tout à l'effet des couleurs complémentaires sur la perception humaine. Plusieurs siècles avant que Johannes Itten, professeur au Bauhaus, ne conçût son cercle chromatique et ne formulât sa théorie sur les contrastes de couleurs, Léonard a identifié les effets des contrastes simultanés sur l'œil humain. Il s'agit ici de l'interaction réciproque de surfaces colorées juxtaposées, et de l'affaiblissement ou du renforcement ressentis subjectivement en présence d'un contraste objectivement présent.

Les pensées de Léonard sur la lumière et l'ombre dans la peinture sont également en relation. Un regard sur la bouche de *La Joconde* – comme modelée par un sculpteur – suffira pour reconnaître avec quelle fécondité il a réussi à transposer dans sa peinture

Farbenlehre

Wesentliche Innovationen entsprangen Leonardos Beschäftigung mit der Farbenlehre. Er interessierte sich vor allem für die Wirkung der Komplementärfarben auf die menschliche Wahrnehmung. Jahrhunderte bevor der Bauhaus-Professor Johannes Itten seinen Farbkreis konzipierte und Lehren zu den Farbkontrasten formulierte, erkannte Leonardo so etwa die Wirkung des Simultankontrastes auf das menschliche Auge. Hierbei geht es um die Wechselwirkung nebeneinanderliegender Farbflächen und die subjektiv empfundene Verstärkung oder Verminderung des objektiv vorhandenen Kontrastes.

Hiermit im Zusammenhang stehen auch seine Gedanken zu Licht und Schatten in der Malerei. Ein Blick auf die wie von einem Bildhauer modelliert wirkende Mundpartie der *Mona Lisa*

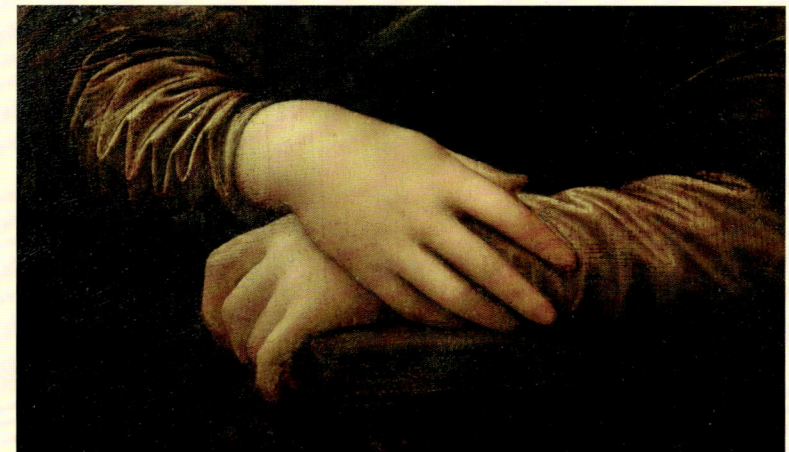

Estudio del color

Innovaciones sustanciales de Leonardo fueron producto de su estudio del color. Se interesó sobre todo por el efecto de los colores complementarios desde la percepción humana. Siglos antes de que el profesor Johannes Itten de la Escuela de la Bauhaus concibiera su círculo del color y de que formulase teorías sobre los contrastes, Leonardo ya había reconocido los efectos del contraste simultáneo sobre el ojo humano. Se trata de la interacción de los colores de dos superficies colindantes y la impresión subjetiva de que el contraste objetivamente existente se ve reforzado o disminuido dependiendo de la tonalidad elegida.

El color está intrínsecamente ligado a su línea de pensamiento sobre las luces y las sombras en la pintura. Una mirada hacia la boca de la *Mona Lisa,* que el artista modeló como si se tratase de una escultura, basta para reconocer

Teoria dei colori

Innovazioni essenziali di Leonardo nacquero dal suo studio della teoria dei colori. Egli si interessò soprattutto all'effetto dei colori complementari sulla percezione umana. Secoli prima che il professore del Bauhaus Johannes Itten concepisse il suo cerchio cromatico e formulasse le teorie dei contrasti cromatici, Leonardo riconobbe l'effetto del contrasto simultaneo sull'occhio umano. In questo caso si tratta dell'interazione delle superfici cromatiche poste l'una accanto all'altra e del potenziamento o la diminuzione percepita soggettivamente del contrasto oggettivamente esistente.

A questo proposito vi sono anche le sue idee sulla luce e l'ombra nella pittura. Uno sguardo sulla zona della bocca della *Monna Lisa,* che sembra come modellata da uno scultore, è sufficiente a riconoscere come egli fu in grado di tradurre in modo fruttuoso le

Kleurenleer

Belangrijke vernieuwingen ontsproten aan Leonardo's interesse in de kleurenleer. Hij hield zich vooral bezig met de effecten van complementaire kleuren op de menselijke waarneming: eeuwen voordat Bauhaus-professor Johannes Itten zijn kleurencirkel bedacht en een leer van kleurcontrasten formuleerde, herkende Leonardo al de uitwerking van simultane contrasten op het menselijk gezichtsvermogen. Daarbij gaat het om de wisselwerking tussen naast elkaar gelegen kleurvlakken en de waargenomen versterking of afzwakking van de daadwerkelijk aanwezige kleurcontrasten.

In verband daarmee onderzocht Leonardo ook de werking van licht en schaduw in de schilderkunst. Eén blik op de mondpartij van de *Mona Lisa,* dat als door een beeldhouwer gemodelleerd lijkt, toont aan hoe effectief hij zijn theoretische inzichten

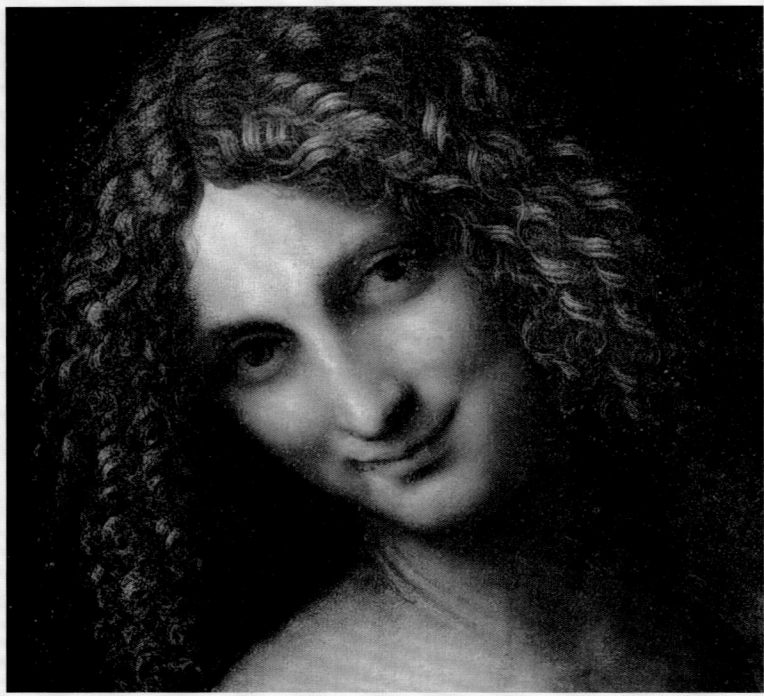

St. John the Baptist, detail
Saint Jean-Baptiste, détail
Johannes der Täufer, Detail
San Juan bautista, detalle
San Giovanni Battista, dettaglio
Johannes de Doper, detail

*1513–16, Oil on canvas/Huile sur toile, 69 × 57 cm,
Musée du Louvre, Paris*

Gerard van Honthorst (1592–1656)
The Procuress
L'Entremetteuse
Die Kupplerin
La alcahueta
La sensale
De koppelaarster

*1625, Oil on canvas/Huile sur toile, 71 × 104 cm,
Centraal Museum, Utrecht*

they actually are, which is to say, in all their density, weight, and plasticity. This was also the result of his study of light phenomena and their effect on different materials. Leonardo was one of the first artists to masterfully use the effect of *chiaroscuro*, or light-dark technique, in his paintings.

ses réflexions théoriques. Mais nous pouvons admirer aussi dans d'autres œuvres sa capacité à nous rapprocher des étoffes et des autres matières telles qu'elles sont réellement, c'est-à-dire dans toute leur densité, leur rigueur et leur plasticité. Cela résulte aussi de ses travaux sur le phénomène de la lumière et son effet sur les matières. Léonard a été l'un des premiers artistes à maîtriser dans ses tableaux les effets de la technique du *chiaroscuro* (« clair-obscur »).

genügt, um zu erkennen, wie fruchtbar er seine theoretischen Überlegungen in seiner Malerei umzusetzen vermochte. Aber auch in anderen Werken können wir seine Fähigkeit bewundern, uns Stoffe und andere Materialien so nahezubringen wie sie tatsächlich sind, das heißt, in ihrer ganzen Dichte, Schwere und Plastizität. Auch dies ist ein Resultat seiner Beschäftigung mit Lichtphänomen und ihrer Wirkung auf Stoffe. Leonardo war einer der ersten Künstler, der den Effekt des *Chiaroscuro*, der Helldunkel-Malerei, in seinen Gemälden meisterlich nutzte.

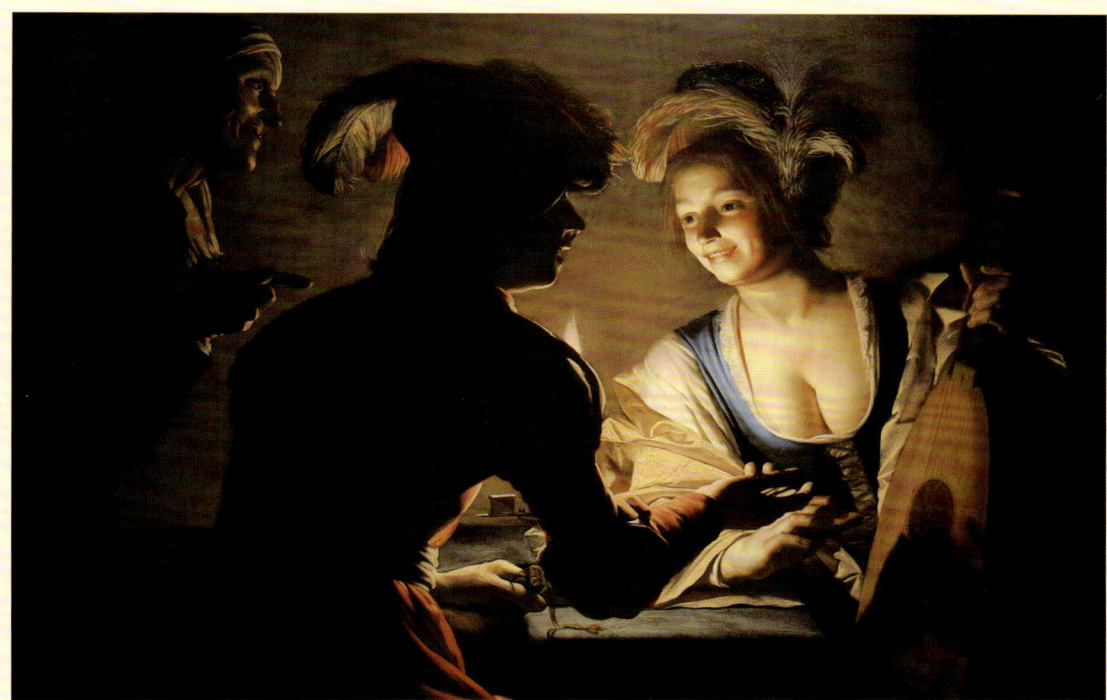

lo fructíferos que sus planteamientos teóricos fueron para sus pinturas. Aunque también podemos admirar sus habilidades en otras obras, en las que nos muestra telas u otros materiales tal como son, es decir, con su densidad, peso y plasticidad real. Estos efectos también son el resultado de su estudio de los fenómenos de la luz y sus reflejos sobre las telas. Leonardo fue uno de los primeros artistas en utilizar el efecto del *claroscuro* de manera magistral.

sue riflessioni teoretiche nella pittura. Ma anche in altre opere possiamo ammirare la sua capacità di raffigurare tessuti e altri materiali così come sono in realtà, il che significa in tutta la loro densità, intensità e plasticità. Anche questo è un risultato dei suoi studi sul fenomeno della luce e del suo effetto sulla materia. Leonardo fu uno dei primi artisti ad utilizzare con maestria l'effetto del *chiaroscuro* nei suoi dipinti.

in zijn schilderwerk wist uit te werken. Maar ook in andere werken kunnen we de gave bewonderen waarmee hij de dichtheid, massiviteit en plasticiteit van stoffen en andere materialen wist uit te beelden. Ook dit was het resultaat van zijn inzichten in de optica en de uitwerking van licht op diverse materialen. Leonardo was een van de eerste kunstenaars die het effect van het *chiaroscuro,* het licht-donkereffect in de schilderkunst, op meesterlijke wijze in zijn schilderijen uitwerkte.

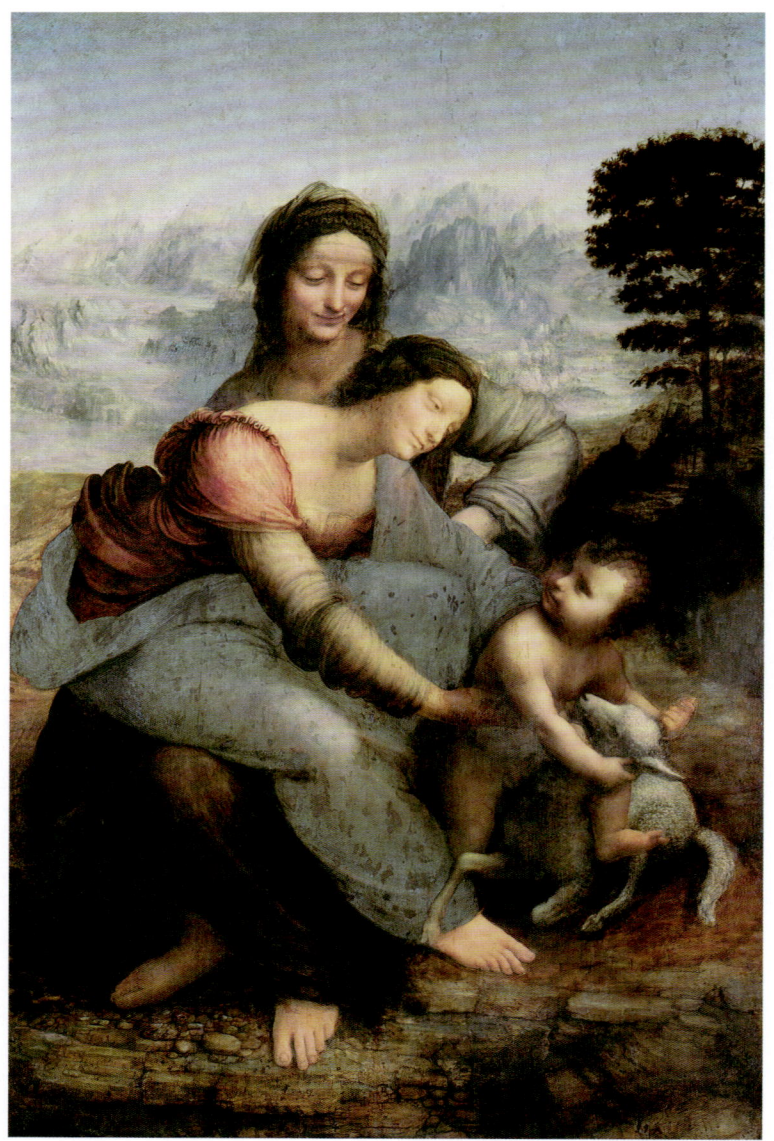

Virgin and Child with St. Anne

La Vierge à l'Enfant avec sainte Anne

Anna selbdritt

Ana trinitaria

Sant'Anna, la Vergine e il Bambino

Anna te Drieën

*c. 1510, Oil on panel/Huile sur bois, 168 × 130 cm,
Musée du Louvre, Paris*

In this work, which simultaneously radiates a great
deal of calmness but, on closer inspection, also
confusion, we see the Virgin caring for the child
Jesus. She sits on the lap of her mother, St. Anne,
whilst the child plays with a lamb. Some parts of
the painting indicate that it was not finished and
this can be seen most clearly in the landscape,
which can be seen in the background. Some
interpretations of the picture see the Christian
church depicted in Anna and the embodiment of
motherly love in Mary.

Cette œuvre rayonne d'une grande paix, mais
elle est en même temps assez troublante si on la
regarde de plus près. On y voit la Vierge veiller sur
l'Enfant (qui joue avec un agneau), alors qu'elle-
même est assise sur les genoux de sa mère, sainte
Anne. Des endroits du tableau révèlent qu'il n'a
pas été terminé : cela se voit surtout dans le
paysage montagneux assez tourmenté de l'arrière-
plan. Certains exégètes voient dans sainte Anne la
personnification de l'Église, la Vierge symbolisant
de son côté l'amour maternel.

In diesem zugleich viel Ruhe ausstrahlenden, bei
näherer Betrachtung aber auch verwirrenden
Werk Leonardos sehen wir die Jungfrau sich
um das Jesuskind kümmernd. Dabei sitzt sie
auf dem Schoß ihrer Mutter, der hl. Anna. Das
Kind spielt mit einem Lamm. Einige Stellen des
Gemäldes verraten, dass es nicht vollendet wurde;
am deutlichsten ist dies an der Landschaft im
Hintergrund abzulesen. Einige Deutungen des
Bildes sehen in Anna die christliche Kirche und in
Maria die Mutterliebe verkörpert.

En esta obra de Leonardo, que nos irradia de paz, confundiéndonos al mismo tiempo al mirarla de cerca, vemos a la Virgen María vigilando al niño Jesús. Está sentada sobre el regazo de su madre Santa Ana. El niño juega con un cordero. En algunos puntos de la pintura se revela que se trata de una obra inacabada. Con mayor claridad se percibe en el paisaje en el segundo plano. Algunas interpretaciones de la imagen ven en Santa Ana la encarnación de la Iglesia Católica y en la Virgen María la del amor de madre.

In quest'opera di Leonardo che da una parte irradia molta pace, ma dall'altra ad un esame più attento è anche sconcertante, vediamo la Vergine Maria che si prende cura di Gesù Bambino. Siede in grembo a sua madre, Sant'Anna, mentre il Bambino gioca con un agnello. In alcuni punti si nota che il quadro non fu terminato; questo è più evidente nel paesaggio sullo sfondo. Secondo alcune interpretazioni del dipinto, Anna personifica la Chiesa Cristiana e Maria l'amore materno.

In dit werk, dat op het eerste gezicht een grote rust uitstraalt maar ook verwarring oproept, zien we de zorgzame Maria zich voorover buigen naar het Jezuskind. Maria zit op schoot bij haar moeder, de heilige Anna, terwijl het kind met een lam speelt. Sommige gedeelten van het schilderij zijn onvoltooid gebleven, wat vooral goed is te zien in het landschap op de achtergrond. Volgens sommige duidingen wordt Anna als belichaming van de christelijke kerk gezien, en Maria als die van de moederliefde.

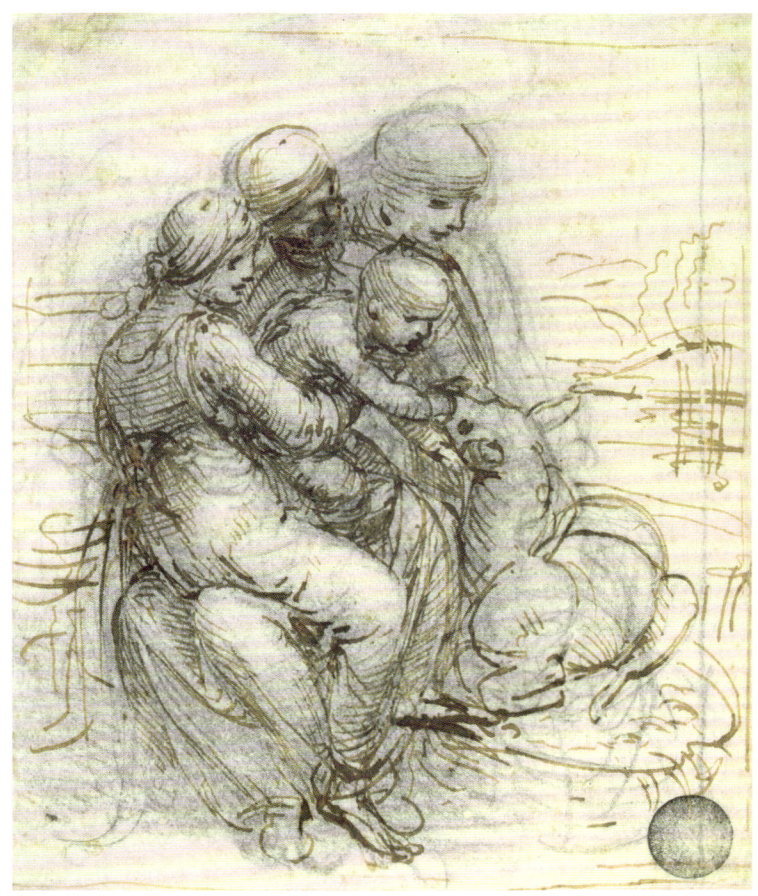

Study	Studie	Studio
Esquisse	Estudio	Studie

c. 1501–10, Pen and ink on paper/Plume et encre sur papier, Galleria dell'Accademia, Venezia

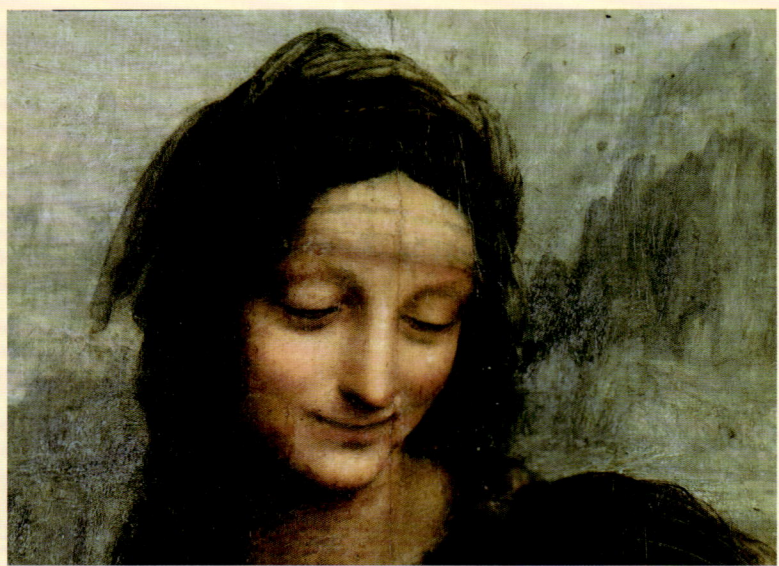

Style of painting

The basis for Leonardo's innovative and distinctive style was influenced by his willingness to utilise varied new techniques with which to apply color to the painting background, thus achieving unorthodox effects.

The *Sfumato* technique is the best known of these today, in which thin layers of color are applied over a dark background in such a way that the individual colors shimmer through, creating a blurred, "smoky" effect. In this way, he imitated the impression that comes to a person when they see something in the landscape from a distance, or from above. Namely, things and surfaces then appear paler and brighter than when viewed from close up.

Style pictoral

Le fondement de style pictural novateur et inimitable de Léonard réside dans sa capacité à appliquer des techniques toujours nouvelles, par exemple pour appliquer la couleur de façon différenciée sur le fond préparé. Il obtenait ainsi des effets novateurs.

La technique dite du *sfumato* est aujourd'hui parfaitement connue : sur un fond de préparation sombre sont appliqués de minces glacis colorés, lisses et transparents, afin de créer un effet vaporeux qui donne au sujet des contours imprécis, un peu flous. Le sfumato crée ainsi l'impression ressentie quand on regarde un paysage d'un peu loin ou de haut : les objets et les surfaces paraissent alors plus pâles et moins précis que quand on les regarde de plus près.

Malstil

Grundlage für Leonardos innovativen und unverwechselbaren Malstil war seine Fähigkeit, immer neue Techniken anzuwenden, mit denen er Farbe in unterschiedlicher Weise auf den Maluntergrund auftrug. Damit erreichte er innovative Effekte.

Am bekanntesten dürfte heute die *Sfumato* genannte Technik sein, bei der über einem dunklen Malgrund dünne Farbschichten so aufgetragen werden, dass die einzelnen Farbtöne durchschimmern, wodurch ein verschwommener, „verrauchter" Effekt entsteht. Damit ahmte er einen Eindruck nach, der beim Menschen entsteht, wenn er in der Landschaft etwas aus weiter Entfernung oder von oben sieht: Dinge und Flächen erscheinen dann blasser und heller als aus der Nähe betrachtet.

Head of a young woman with tousled hair or *Leda*

La Scapigliata ou *L'Ébouriffée*

La Scapigliata

Cabeza de muchacha

La Scapigliata

La Scapigliata

Gouache on wood/Gouache sur bois, 24,7 × 36,2 cm,
Galleria Nazionale, Parma

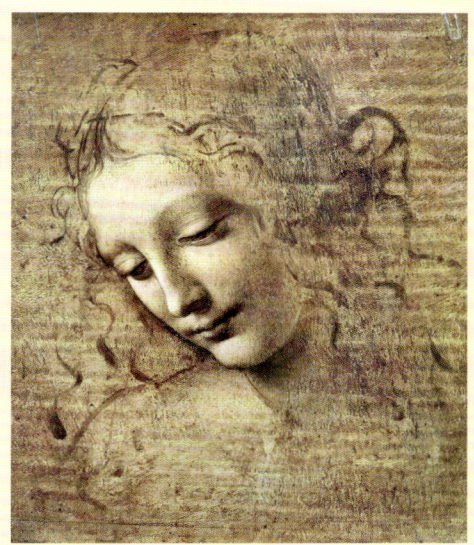

Estilo pintura

La base de innovaciones y estilo inequívoco de Leonardo fue su facultad para utilizar siempre nuevas técnicas con las que aplicar el color en diferentes formas sobre la base de sus pinturas. De esta manera alcanzó efectos innovadores.

El más conocido podría ser la técnica hoy conocida como *sfumato,* en la que sobre un fondo oscuro se aplican finas capas de color, de manera que las diferentes tonalidades translucen, creando un efecto difuso, como si se estuviese dentro de una „nube de humo". Con ello quería replicar el efecto que se genera en el ser humano, cuando en un paisaje, al observar algo desde lo lejos o desde lo alto: Los objetos y las superficies parecen ser más pálidas y más claras de lejos que de cerca.

Stile pittorico

Il fondamento del innovativo e inconfondibile stile pittorico di Leonardo era anche la sua capacità di utilizzare tecniche sempre nuove, grazie alle quali applicava il colore in modo diverso sulla superficie. In questo modo ottenne effetti innovativi.

Oggi la tecnica più conosciuta è quella chiamata lo *sfumato,* per mezzo della quale si potevano applicare su uno sfondo scuro sottili gradazioni di colore che lasciavano intravedere le singole sfumature, attraverso cui nasceva un effetto sfocato e sfumato. In questo modo egli imitava l'impressione che hanno le persone quando in un paesaggio si vede qualcosa da una grande distanza o dall'alto: oggetti e luoghi sembrano quindi più sbiaditi e luminosi di quando vengono osservati da vicino.

Schilderstijl

Het fundament van Leonardo's vernieuwende en onmiskenbaar eigen schilderstijl was zijn gave om telkens nieuwe technieken uit te proberen, waarbij hij kleuren op verschillende manieren opbracht en zo verrassende effecten bereikte.

Zijn bekendste techniek was het *sfumato,* waarbij hij op een donkere ondergrond meerdere verflaagjes over elkaar heen schilderde, zodat de afzonderlijke kleuren doorschemerden en tegelijkertijd een 'nevelachtige' (sfumato) effect creëerden. Zo bootste hij de indruk na die ontstaat als iemand van afstand of van grote hoogte een landschap bekijkt: objecten en vlakken doen zich afwisselend doffer en helderder voor dan wanneer ze van dichtbij worden bekeken.

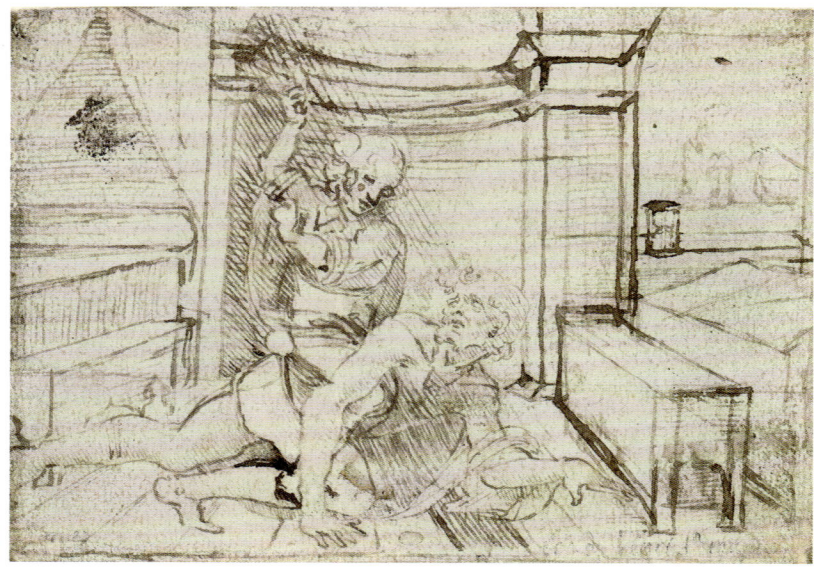

Drawings

Leonardo's fame stems mainly from his paintings, although in recent decades he has been increasingly recognised due to the rediscovery of his technical developments and scientific studies. Despite this, he cannot be underestimated as a draftsman. Drawings served him primarily as a method of investigation. It was only by drawing human beings that it was possible for him to understand them properly and to represent them. This, in turn, was the basis for his ability to portray people in his paintings in such a way as to create the impression that one knows them better than they know themselves.

He commented extensively on many of his drawings, such as some of the

Les dessins

Même si Léonard doit essentiellement sa renommée à ses peintures et – de plus en plus, ces dernières années – à la redécouverte de ses innovations techniques et de ses recherches en sciences de la nature, son talent de dessinateur ne doit certainement pas être oublié. C'était avant tout un moyen de recherche. En dessinant des êtres humains, il lui était possible de bien les saisir de l'intérieur, de s'identifier à eux. Et lorsqu'il les peignait, ce principe de base lui permettait de faire naître chez le spectateur l'impression qu'il connaissait mieux les personnages que lui-même.

Léonard a commenté abondamment beaucoup de ses dessins, comme ses croquis anatomiques ou ses études pour la statue équestre de Francesco Sforza.

Zeichnungen

Auch wenn Leonardos Ruhm vor allem von seinen Gemälden stammt, und in den letzten Jahrzehnten auch zunehmend von der Wiederentdeckung seiner technischen Entwicklungen und naturwissenschaftlichen Studien, darf er als Zeichner keinesfalls vergessen werden. Zeichnungen dienten ihm in erster Linie als Untersuchungsmethode. Erst indem er Menschen zeichnete, war es ihm möglich, sie richtig zu begreifen, sich ihnen anzuverwandeln. Dies wiederum war die Grundlage für seine Fähigkeit, die Menschen in seinen Gemälden derart darzustellen, dass der Eindruck entsteht, man kenne sie besser, als sie sich selbst.

Viele seiner Zeichnungen kommentierte er ausgiebig, so etwa

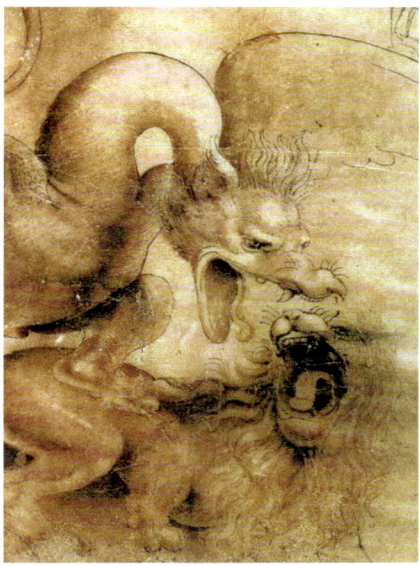

Dibujos

Aunque la fama de Leonardo se debe sobre todo a sus pinturas y, en las últimas décadas también al redescubrimiento de sus desarrollos técnicos y estudios científicos, no debemos olvidar su faceta de dibujante. Los dibujos le sirvieron en primer lugar como método de análisis. Tenía que dibujar al ser humano para poder entenderlo y llevarlo a sus pinturas. Por otra parte, esto fue la base de sus cualidades como artista, representar a las personas en sus pinturas, de manera que nos parezca conocerlas mejor de lo que ellas se conocen a sí mismas.

Comentó muchos de sus dibujos, algunos esbozos de anatomía o también el estudio de la estatua ecuestre de Francesco Sforza y detalle. Pero se

Disegni

Sebbene la fama di Leonardo sia dovuta soprattutto ai suoi dipinti, e negli ultimi decenni in maniera crescente anche grazie alla riscoperta dei suoi sviluppi tecnici e studi di scienze naturali, non può essere assolutamente dimenticato come disegnatore. In primo luogo egli considerava i disegni come un metodo di studio. Solo disegnando l'uomo gli fu possibile comprendere esattamente come poteva imitarlo. D'altronde questa era la base della sua capacità di rappresentare l'uomo nei suoi dipinti in modo che suscitasse l'impressione che lo conosceva meglio di se stesso.

Leonardo commentò profusamente molti dei suoi disegni, come alcuni schizzi anatomici o anche gli studi per la statua del cavaliere Francesco Sforza. Eppure

Tekeningen

Hoewel Leonardo's faam vooral berust op zijn schilderwerk, en in de afgelopen tijd vooral ook op de toenemende herontdekking van zijn technische prestaties en natuurwetenschappelijke studies, mogen zijn tekeningen niet over het hoofd worden gezien. Het nauwkeurig tekenen van mensen was voor Leonardo in de eerste plaats een vorm van onderzoek. En dit vormde weer de basis voor zijn gave om mensen in zijn schilderijen op zeer persoonlijke en vertrouwde wijze uit te beelden.

Bij veel van zijn tekeningen maakte Leonardo uitgebreide aantekeningen, bijvoorbeeld bij zijn anatomische schetsen of zijn studies voor het ruiterstandbeeld dat hij voor Francesco Sforza ontwierp. Toch zou het te

69

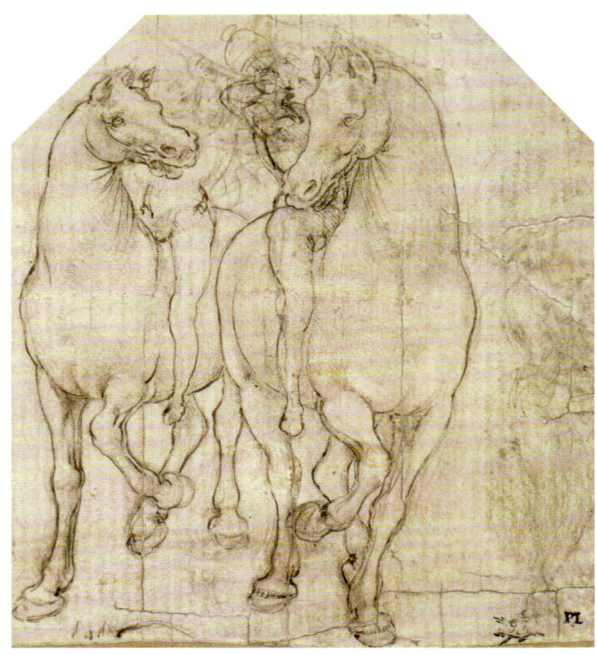

Study of horses and riders

Étude de cavaliers et de chevaux

Studie mit Reitern und Pferden

Estudio con jinetes y caballos

Studio con cavalieri e cavalli

Studie van ruiters en paarden

c. 1480–82, Metalpoint on paper/Pointe métallique sur papier,
14,3 × 12,8 cm, Fitzwilliam Museum, Cambridge

anatomical sketches, or the studies for
the equestrian sculpture of Francesco
Sforza. Nevertheless, it is too easy to see
Leonardo's drawings as only a means to
an end. When one looks at how much
care and refinement he used in many
of his drawings, utilising several pencil
colors, or using entirely different media
such as charcoal, chalk, sanguine and
ink, the claim, that it was used only for
exercise purposes does not stand up.
We see, for example, his many studies of
the flow and folds of cloth, which reveal
his own aesthetic and go far beyond the
primary purpose of practice.

This may also be illustrated by his
drawing of a landscape with a river

Mais il est insuffisant de ne voir dans
ses dessins que le moyen d'atteindre
un but. Si l'on considère avec quel soin
et quel raffinement il a employé pour
beaucoup de ceux-ci plusieurs crayons de
couleur et/ou des techniques totalement
différentes telles que le fusain, la craie
blanche, la sanguine et l'encre de Chine,
il est impossible de maintenir qu'il ne
s'agissait que d'exercices préalables. Ses
multiples études de plis, par exemple,
révèlent une esthétique particulière
qui va bien au-delà du but primaire de
l'étude.

Le dessin daté du 5 août 1473,
représentant un paysage avec un fleuve
(longtemps considéré comme l'Arno),

einige anatomische Skizzen oder auch
die Studien für das Reiterstandbild
Francesco Sforzas. Dennoch griffe es
zu kurz, in Leonardos Zeichnungen
einzig das Mittel zum Zweck zu sehen.
Schaut man sich etwa an, mit wieviel
Sorgfalt und Raffinesse er bei vielen
seiner Zeichnungen mehrere Stiftfarben
einsetzte oder gänzlich unterschiedliche
Medien wie Kohle, Kreide, Rötel und
Tusche nutze, kann die Behauptung nicht
standhalten, es wäre ihm nur um den
Übungszweck gegangen. So offenbaren
etwa die vielen von ihm angefertigten
Faltenwurfstudien eine eigene Ästhetik,
die weit über den primären Zweck des
Einübens hinausgeht.

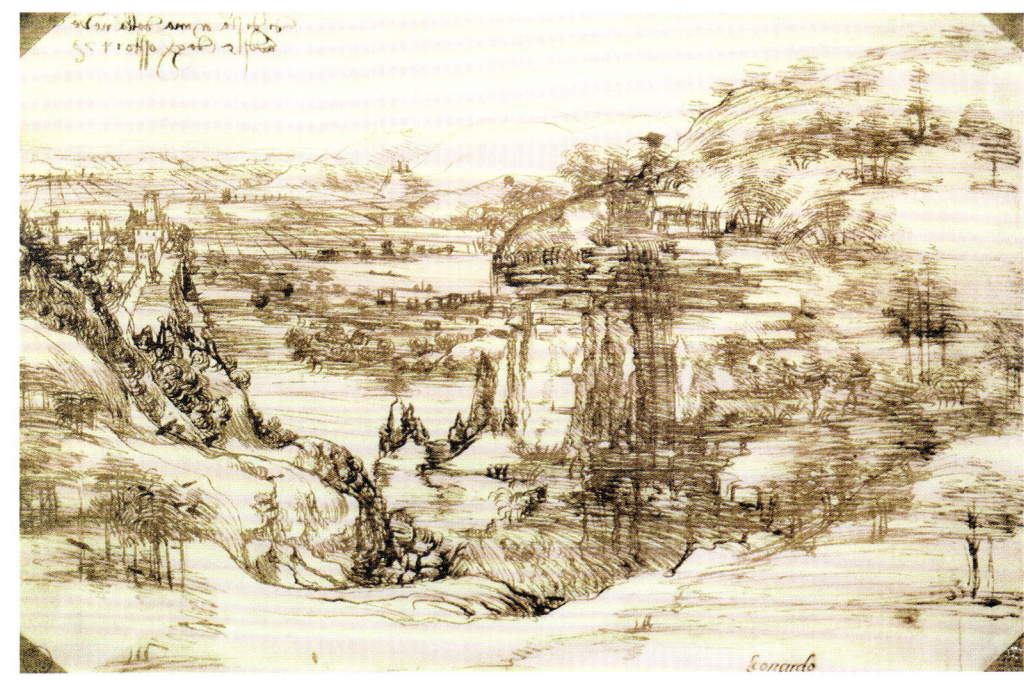

**Arno
Landscape**

**Paysage de la
vallée de l'Arno**

**Landschaft
mit Fluss**

Paisaje con río

**Paesaggio
con fiume**

**Landschap
met rivier**

*1473, Pen and ink
on paper/Plume
et encre sur
papier, Galleria
degli Uffizi,
Firenze*

quedó corto al ver en sus dibujos un mero medio para llegar a su fin. Si analizamos con qué delicadeza y detalle utilizaba los lápices de diferentes colores para sus dibujos o incluso otros artilugios totalmente distintos como el carbón, la tiza, el almagre y la tinta, la afirmación de que sólo se trataba de un medio para practicar, no se sostiene. Muchos de los estudios de pliegues muestran una estética propia, que sobrepasan la finalidad primaria de la práctica.

Su dibujo de un paisaje con río (durante mucho tiempo se creía que era el río Arno) fechado en el 5 de agosto 1473 nos lo confirma. Claro que estudió la naturaleza con este dibujo,

non basta vedere nei disegni di Leonardo solo il mezzo per raggiungere lo scopo. Se si considera anche che in molti dei suoi disegni utilizzò con grande cura e raffinatezza diversi pastelli colorati o mezzi completamente differenti come il carboncino, il gesso, la sanguigna e la china, non può reggere l'affermazione che si trattasse per lui solo di un'attività a scopo di esercizio. Quindi i molti studi di drappeggi da lui realizzati rivelano un'estetica caratteristica, che va ben oltre lo scopo primario dell'esercitazione.

Questo rappresenta anche il suo disegno di un paesaggio con un fiume, da tempo identificato con l'Arno, datato 5 agosto 1473. Naturalmente con questo

eenvoudig zijn om Leonardo's tekeningen slechts als middel tot een hoger doel te zien. Wie de tekeningen goed bekijkt, ziet met hoeveel nauwkeurigheid en finesse Leonardo deze werkjes benaderde: het feit dat hij vaak verschillende pensoorten en zeer uiteenlopende media gebruikte, waaronder houtskool, krijt, roodkrijt (sanguine) en inkt, wijst erop dat Leonardo het tekenen niet alleen als onderzoeksmiddel zag. Uit veel van zijn schetsen van de val van gewaden en vouwen komt een geheel eigen esthetiek naar voren, die het pure doel van onderzoek verre overstijgt.

Dat blijkt ook uit een tekening die op 5 augustus 1473 ontstond en een

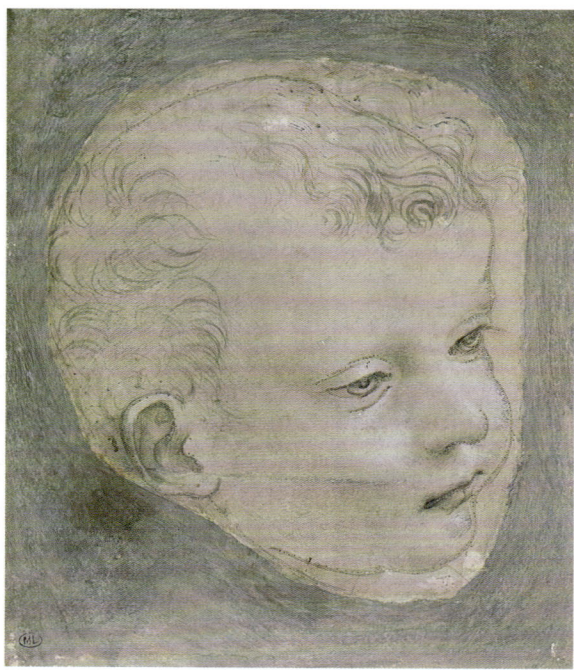

Head of a child

Tête d'enfant

Kopf eines Kindes

Cabeza de niño

Testa di bambino

Kinderhoofd

Pencil on paper/Crayon sur papier,
17 × 14 cm, Kunsthalle, Hamburg

(long thought to be the Arno) and dated 5 August 1473. Characteristically, he explores nature with this drawing, but he also creates a wonderful, independent portrait of a landscape on a summer day. Already, at the age of just 21, he seems to have assigned to the genre of drawing the part which would in the future continue to occupy all his artistic work, which was that he would always be concerned with grasping reality through direct experience and portraying it graphically.

One particular episode from his life may well illustrate that he himself did not regard the art of drawing as lightly as

témoigne aussi de ce fait. L'artiste explore ici évidemment la nature, mais il crée dans le même temps la magnifique image autonome d'un paysage vu par un jour d'été brumeux. À tout juste vingt et un ans, il semble avoir déjà assigné au genre du dessin le rôle qu'il aura désormais tout au long de sa carrière artistique : il s'agira toujours pour lui de saisir la réalité par aperception directe et de la fixer par le dessin.

Un autre épisode authentique de sa vie permet de montrer qu'il tenait en haute estime l'art du dessin, à l'inverse de ce que paraissent signifier ses remarques sur la peinture dans le *Trattato della*

Hierfür spricht etwa auch seine auf den 5. August 1473 datierte Zeichnung einer Landschaft mit Fluss (lange als Arno gedeutet). Natürlich erforscht er mit dieser Zeichnung die Natur, doch schafft er eben auch ein wundervolles, eigenständiges Bildnis einer Landschaft an einem diesigen Sommertag. Mit gerade erst 21 Jahren scheint er hier dem Genre der Zeichnung bereits die Rolle zugewiesen zu haben, die es innerhalb seines künstlerischen Schaffens nun fortan einnehmen wird: Immer wird es ihm darum gehen, die Realität durch die direkte Anschauung zu erfassen und zeichnerisch festzuhalten.

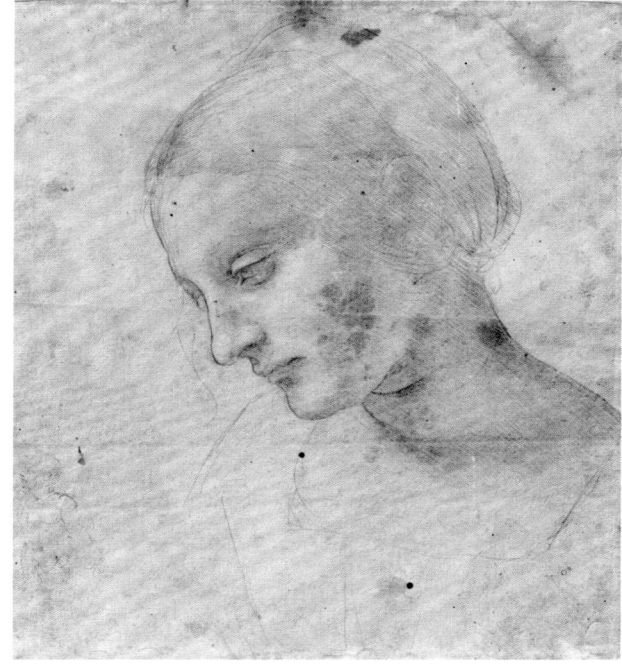

pero también creó una maravillosa imagen independiente de un paisaje de un calimoso día de verano. Con tan sólo 21 años parece haber asignado al género de la pintura su papel, lo que lo ocuparía de ahora en adelante a lo largo de su creación artística: Siempre trataría de comprender la realidad por medio de la observación directa y plasmarla en sus dibujos.

Aunque un desconocido episodio de su vida puede ilustrar que en realidad no prestaba tan poca atención al arte de dibujar como parecían sugerir sus *Trattato della pittura*: Cuando alrededor de 1500 vuelve a Florencia

disegno voleva esplorare la natura, ma creò anche un ritratto meraviglioso e autonomo di un paesaggio in un giorno d'estate pervaso dalla foschia. All'età di soli 21 anni sembra che al genere del disegno fu già assegnato il ruolo che da quel momento in poi avrebbe conquistato all'interno della sua produzione artistica: per Leonardo si tratta sempre di comprendere la realtà attraverso l'osservazione diretta e fissarla graficamente.

E un altro episodio autentico della sua vita può dimostrare che egli stesso diede molto peso all'arte del disegno, come lasciano supporre le sue *Trattato della*

landschap met een rivier (lange tijd geduid als de Arno) weergeeft. Natuurlijk onderzocht Leonardo in deze tekening de natuur, maar hij creëerde tegelijkertijd een prachtig en op zichzelf staand beeld van een zomerse dag. Op slechts 21-jarige leeftijd leek hij al de rol op zich te hebben genomen die hij voortaan in het artistieke landschap zou innemen: steeds weer zou het erom gaan de natuurgetrouwe werkelijkheid door directe waarneming te doorgronden en op papier vast te leggen.

Ook uit een andere, vrij onbekende periode uit zijn leven mag duidelijk worden dat hij de tekenkunst allerminst als ondergeschikt aan de schilderkunst

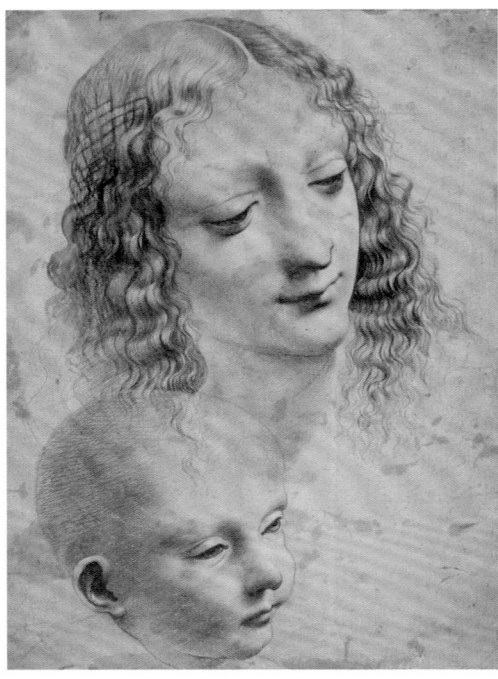

Unknown artist/Artiste inconnu

Heads of a woman and a child

Têtes d'une femme et d'un enfant

Kopf einer Frau und eines Kindes

Cabeza de mujer y de niño

Testa di una donna e un bambino

Hoofd van een vrouw of kind

Metalpoint on grey prepared paper/Pointe métallique sur papier teinté en bleu, 29,7 × 22 cm, Chatsworth House, Bakewell

his *Trattato della pittura* seem to suggest. When he returned to Florence, around 1500, after a long absence, he exhibited a drawing of St. Anne, on cardboard, which was a novelty, as a way for him to demonstrate his drawing skills to the public in Florence and to show them what they had been missing in recent years.

pittura. Lorsqu'il séjourne de nouveau à Florence en 1500, après une longue absence, il y expose – ce qui est une nouveauté absolue – un carton montrant La Vierge à l'enfant avec sainte Anne. Il veut ainsi, très clairement, signifier au public de Florence ses talents de dessinateur – comme pour lui montrer ce dont il a été privé par son absence, les années précédentes.

Und noch eine verbürgte Episode aus seinem Leben mag veranschaulichen, dass er selbst die Zeichenkunst keineswegs so gering achtete, wie seine *Bemerkungen zur Malerei* es nahezulegen scheinen: Als er um das Jahr 1500 nach längerer Abwesenheit wieder in Florenz weilte, stellte er– was ein absolutes Novum war – einen Karton mit der hl. Anna selbdritt aus. Ganz offensichtlich war ihm daran gelegen, seine zeichnerischen Fähigkeiten der Öffentlichkeit in Florenz zu demonstrieren, wie um ihr zu zeigen, worauf sie die Jahre zuvor verzichten musste.

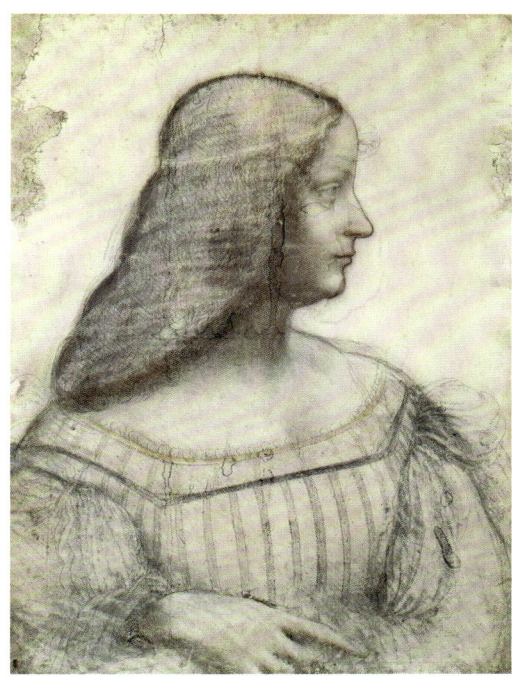

tras haberse ausentado durante años de la ciudad, expuso algo que sería una novedad absoluta, un cartón con Santa Ana trinitaria. Evidentemente quería enseñarle al público de Florencia sus habilidades como dibujante para demostrarle a lo que había tenido que renunciar en años anteriores.

pittura: quando intorno al 1500 ritornò a Firenze dopo una lunga assenza, espose un cartone con il ritratto di Sant'Anna, cosa che era un'assoluta novità. Era piuttosto evidente che gli importava di dimostrare le sue abilità di disegnatore al pubblico di Firenze, come per indicare quello a cui aveva dovuto rinunciare negli anni precedenti.

beschouwde: toen hij in 1500 na een lange afwezigheid in Florence terugkeerde, schetste hij een ontwerp voor de Heilige Anna te Driëen – een volstrekt nieuw concept. Het was duidelijk dat hij zijn tekenaarskwaliteiten aan het Florentijnse publiek wilde tonen, alsof hij zijn stadgenoten wilde laten zien wat zij in de voorgaande jaren hadden gemist.

The Vitruvian Man

L'homme de Vitruve

Der vitruvianische Mensch

El hombre de Vitruvio

L'Uomo vitruviano

De vitruviaanse mens

c. 1492, Pen and ink on paper/Plume, encre et aquarelle sur pointe métallique,
34,3 × 24,5 cm, Galleria dell'Accademia, Venezia

This drawing refers to the ancient architect Vitruvius and his conviction that the proportions of the human figure must be regarded as the basic measure of any architecture of worth. At the same time, it embodies the fusion of art and mathematics in the culture of the Renaissance and demonstrates the great importance which Leonardo attached to human proportions. The text on the sides of the image was written, as was usual for Leonardo, in the form of mirror writing and records what was seen as the ideal dimensions of the human body.

Ce dessin de Léonard communément connu sous ce nom est intitulé en réalité *Études des proportions du corps humain selon Vitruve.* Il se réfère à l'architecte et ingénieur romain Vitruve (Iᵉʳ siècle av. J.-C.), qui était convaincu que les proportions naturelles du corps humain doivent être la mesure de toute belle architecture. Du même coup, il symbolise la fusion de l'art et des mathématiques dans la culture de la Renaissance, et témoigne de la grande importance accordée par Léonard à la structure du corps humain. Le texte qui figure à côté du dessin – dans l'écriture spéculaire habituelle à l'artiste – énumère aussi les mesures idéales des différentes parties de ce corps.

Diese Zeichnung nimmt Bezug auf den antiken Architekten Vitruv und dessen Überzeugung, dass der Mensch als grundlegendes Maß jeder Architektur zu gelten habe. Zugleich verkörpert sie die Verschmelzung von Kunst und Mathematik in der Kultur der Renaissance und zeugt von der hohen Bedeutung, die Leonardo den menschlichen Proportionen beimaß. Der wie bei Leonardo üblich in Spiegelschrift verfasste Text an den Seiten des Bildes zählt die jeweils als ideal angesehenen Maße des menschlichen Körpers auf.

Este dibujo hace referencia al arquitecto Vitruvio de la Antigüedad y a su convencimiento de que el ser humano debe tomarse como patrón para cualquier tipo de obra arquitectónica. Al mismo tiempo representa la unión entre el arte y las matemáticas en la cultura renacentista, atestiguando la gran relevancia que Leonardo atribuía a las proporcionas del ser humano. El texto redactado como de costumbre por Leonardo con letras invertidas en los bordes de la imagen enumera las medidas consideradas como ideales en el cuerpo del ser humano.

Questo disegno si riferisce all'architetto dell'antichità Vitruvio e la sua convinzione che l'uomo è da considerare come la misura fondamentale di ogni architettura. Allo stesso tempo personifica la fusione di arte e matematica nella cultura del Rinascimento e testimonia il grande significato che Leonardo attribuiva alle proporzioni umane. Il testo redatto nella scrittura speculare tipica di Leonardo ai lati del disegno indica le misure del corpo umano considerate ideali.

Deze tekening verwijst naar de klassieke architect Vitruvius en zijn opvatting dat de mens de maat voor alle architectuur zou moeten zijn. Tegelijkertijd belichaamt ze de versmelting van kunst en wiskunde in de cultuur van de Renaissance en getuigt van het grote belang dat Leonardo aan de menselijke proporties hechtte. In de kanttekeningen bij de schets, zoals gebruikelijk bij Leonardo in spiegelschrift, gaat de kunstenaar in op de als ideaal beschouwde verhoudingen van het menselijk lichaam.

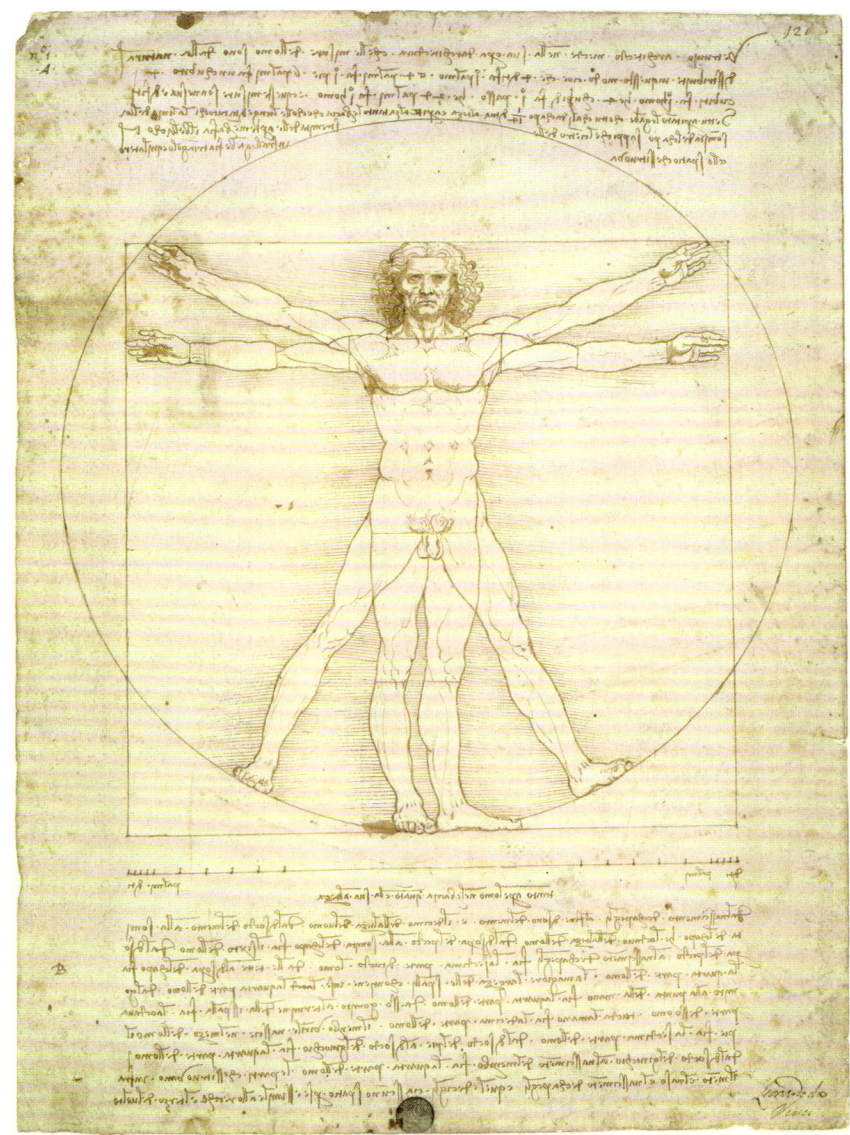

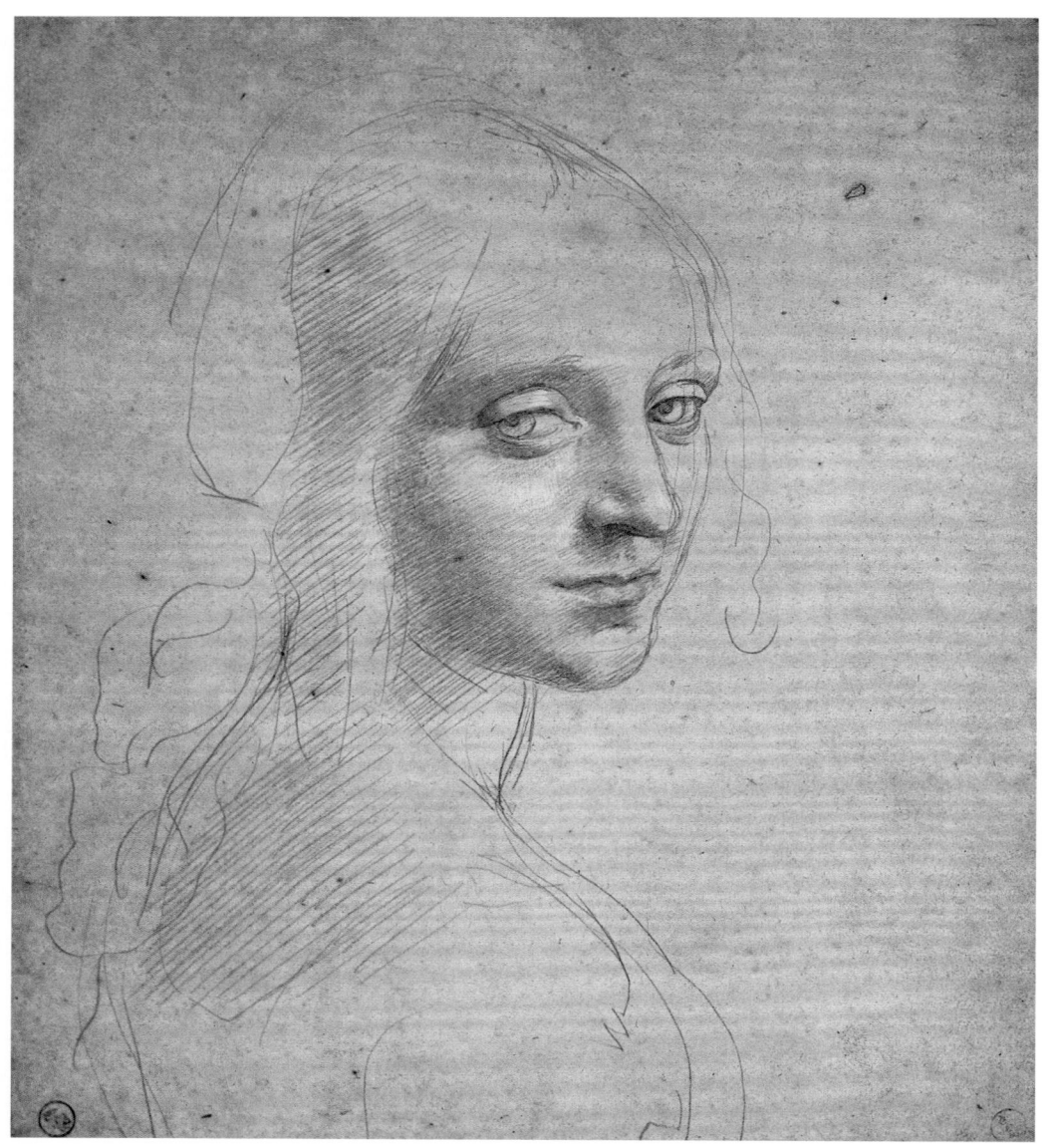

***Portrait
of a girl***

***Portrait d'une
jeune fille***

***Porträt eines
Mädchens***

***Retrato de
una chica***

***Ritratto di
fanciulla***

***Portret van
een meisje***

*1483/84,
Metalpoint
(gold?)
with white
heightening on
paper/Pointe
métallique
(or?) et
rehauts
de blanc
sur papier,
Biblioteca
Reale, Torino*

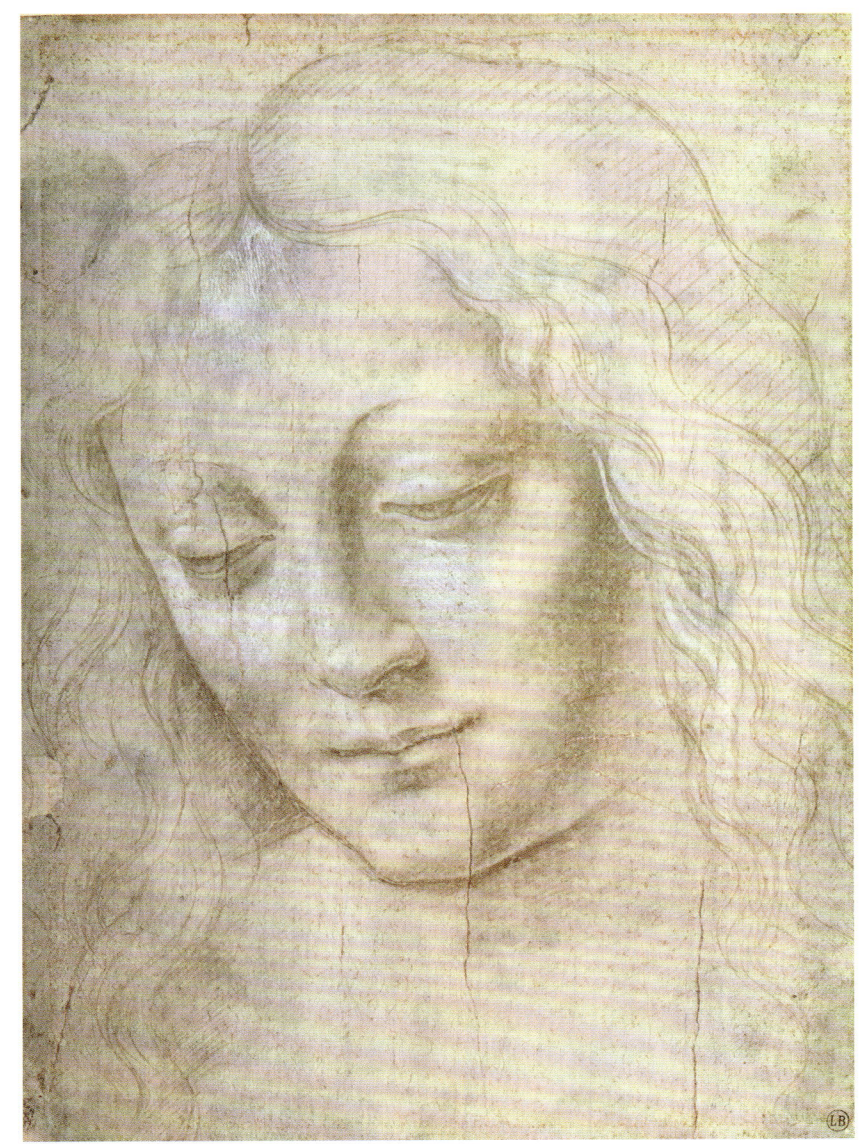

Head of a woman

Tête de femme

Kopf einer Frau

Cabeza de mujer

Testa di donna

Hoofd van een vrouw

*Metalpoint heightened with gouache/
Pointe métallique avec rehauts de
gouache, 19,2 × 13,9 cm, Musée Bonnat,
Bayonne*

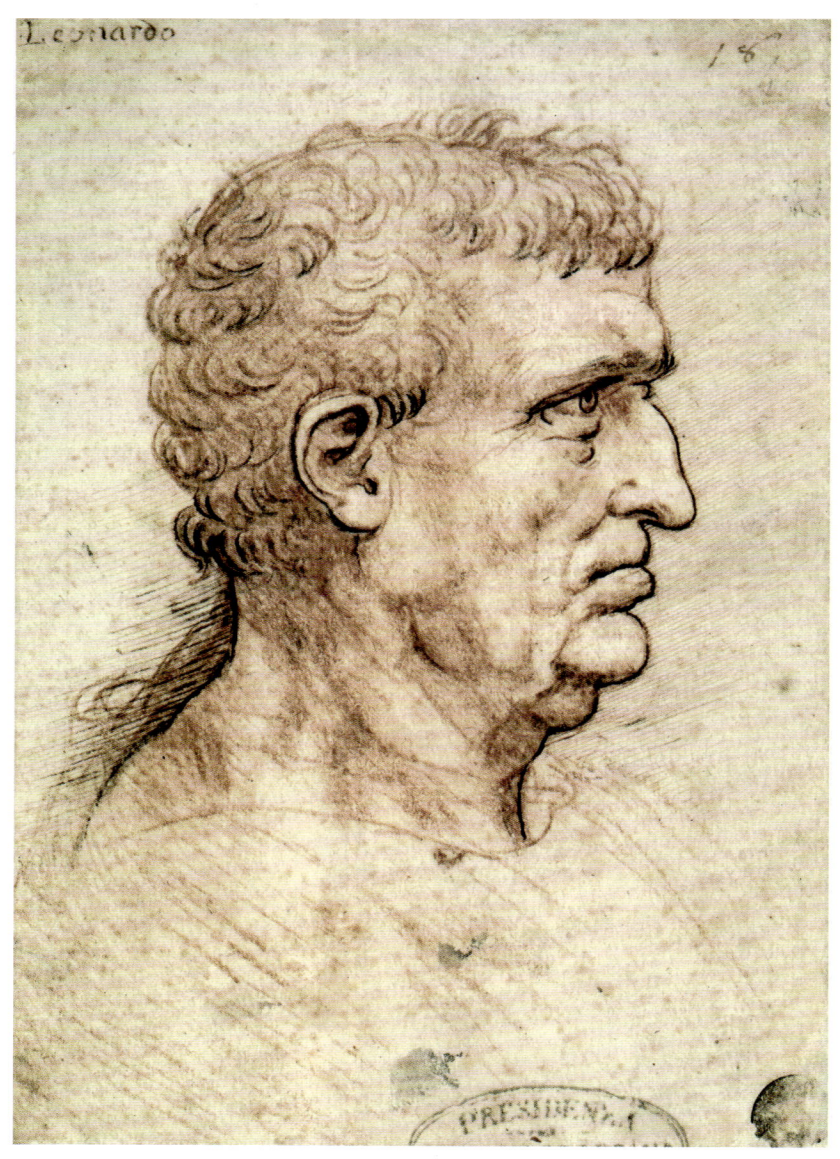

Head of a man in profile
Tête d'homme vu de profil
Kopf eines Mannes im Profil
Cabeza de un hombre de perfil
Testa di un uomo di profilo
Mannenhoofd en profil

c. 1506–08, Pencil and red chalk on paper/
Mine de plomb et sanguine sur papier,
Galleria dell' Accademia, Venezia

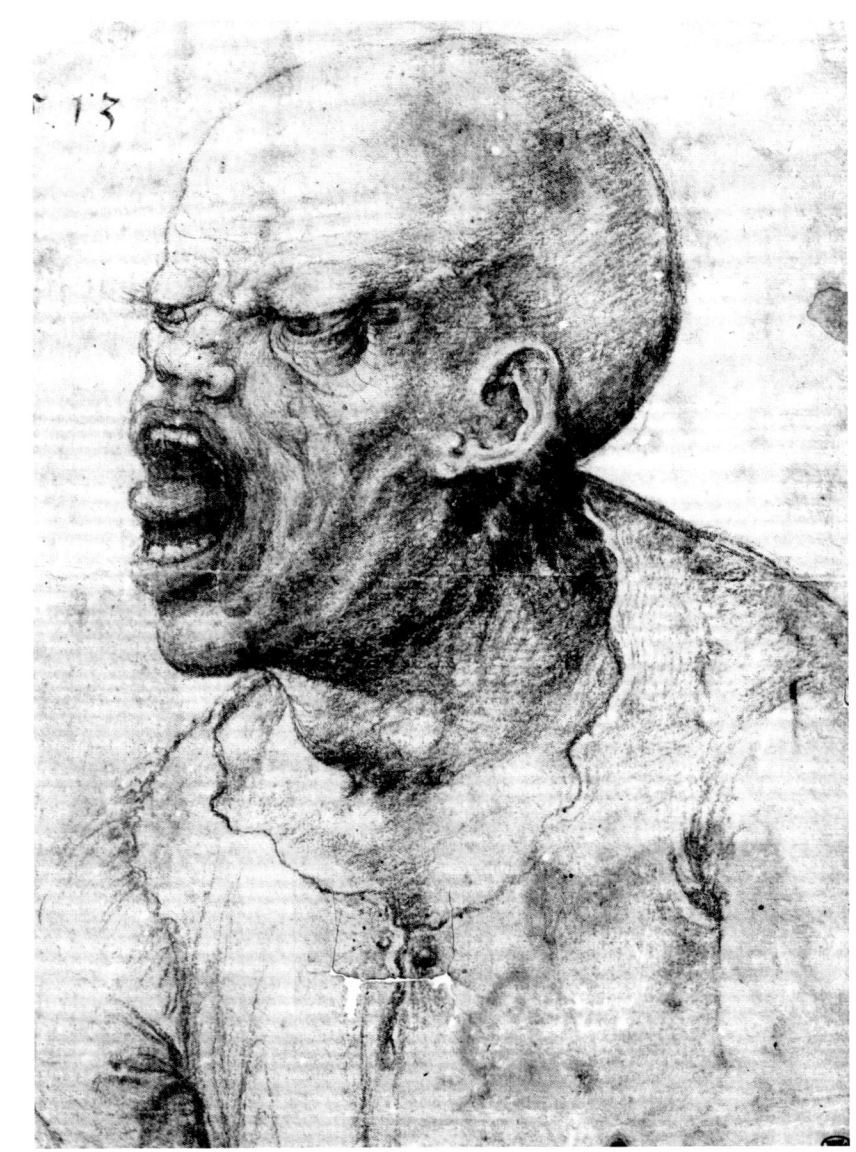

Portrait of a man shouting
Tête d'homme criant
Porträt eines schreienden Mannes
Retrato de un hombre gritando
Ritratto di un uomo urlante
Portret van een schreeuwende man

c. 1507, Charcoal on paper/Fusain sur papier,
Musée du Louvre, Paris

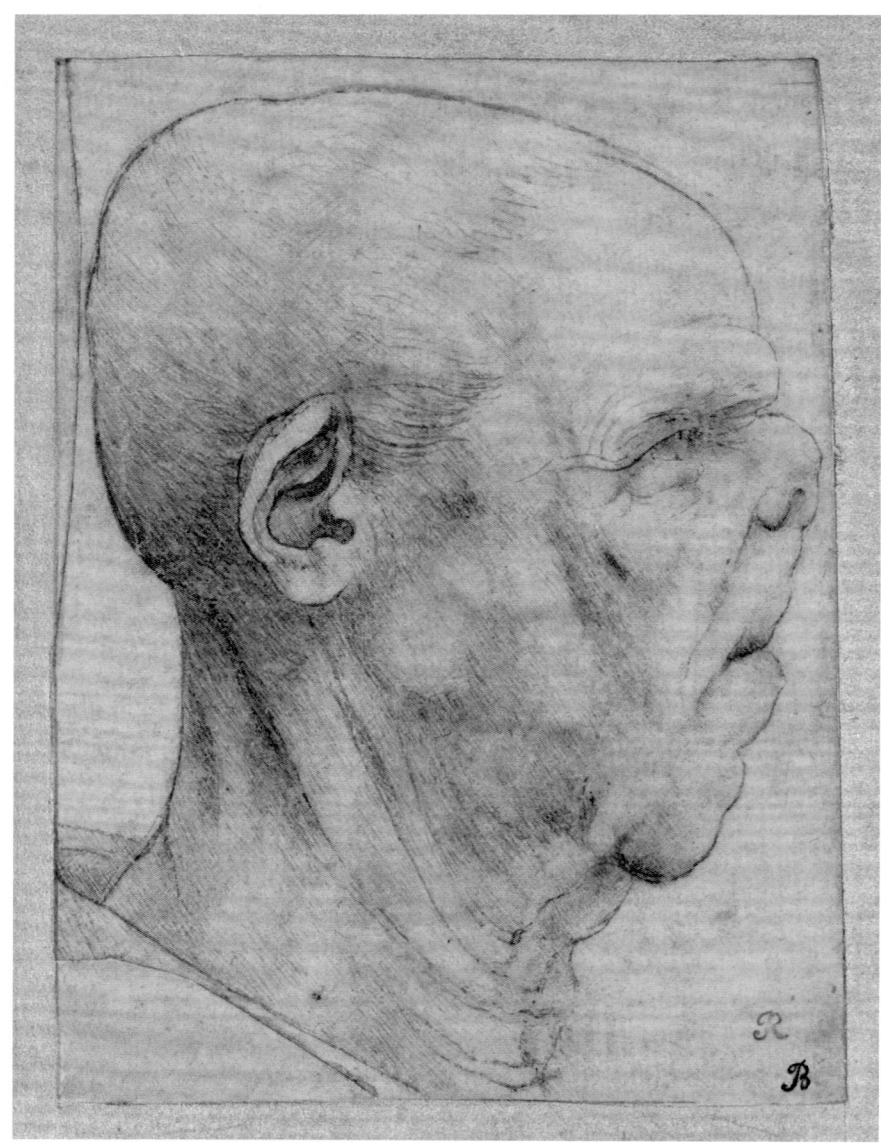

*Caricature of an old man,
in profile to the right*

*Caricature de vieil
homme, profil droit*

*Karikatur eines alten Mannes,
im Profil nach rechts*

*Caricatura de un hombre
mayor, perfil izquierdo*

*Caricatura di un vecchio
di profilo verso destra*

*Karikatuur van oude
man, rechterprofiel*

c. 1507, Pen and brown ink/Plume
et encre brune, 110 × 80 cm, Private
collection

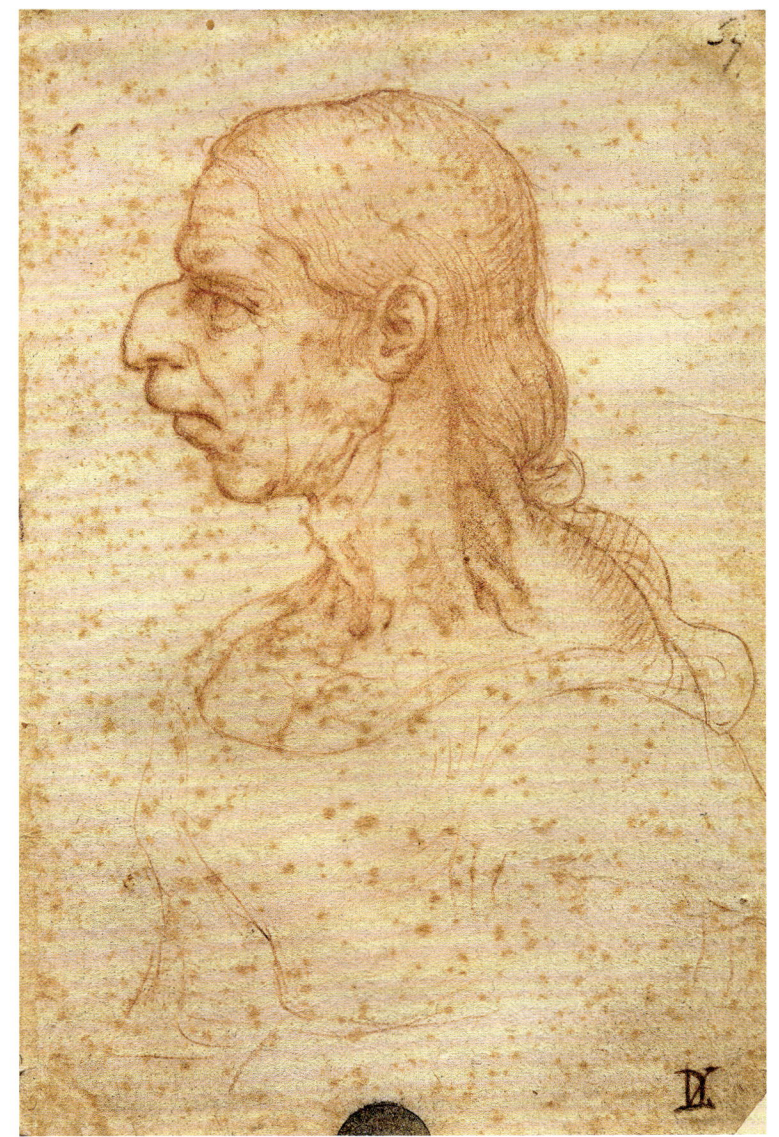

Unknown artist/Artiste inconnu

Caricature of an old woman

Caricature de vieille femme

Karikatur einer alten Frau

Caricatura de una mujer mayor

Caricatura di una donna anziana

Karikatuur van oude vrouw

Red chalk on paper/Sanguine sur papier,
Galleria dell' Accademia, Venezia

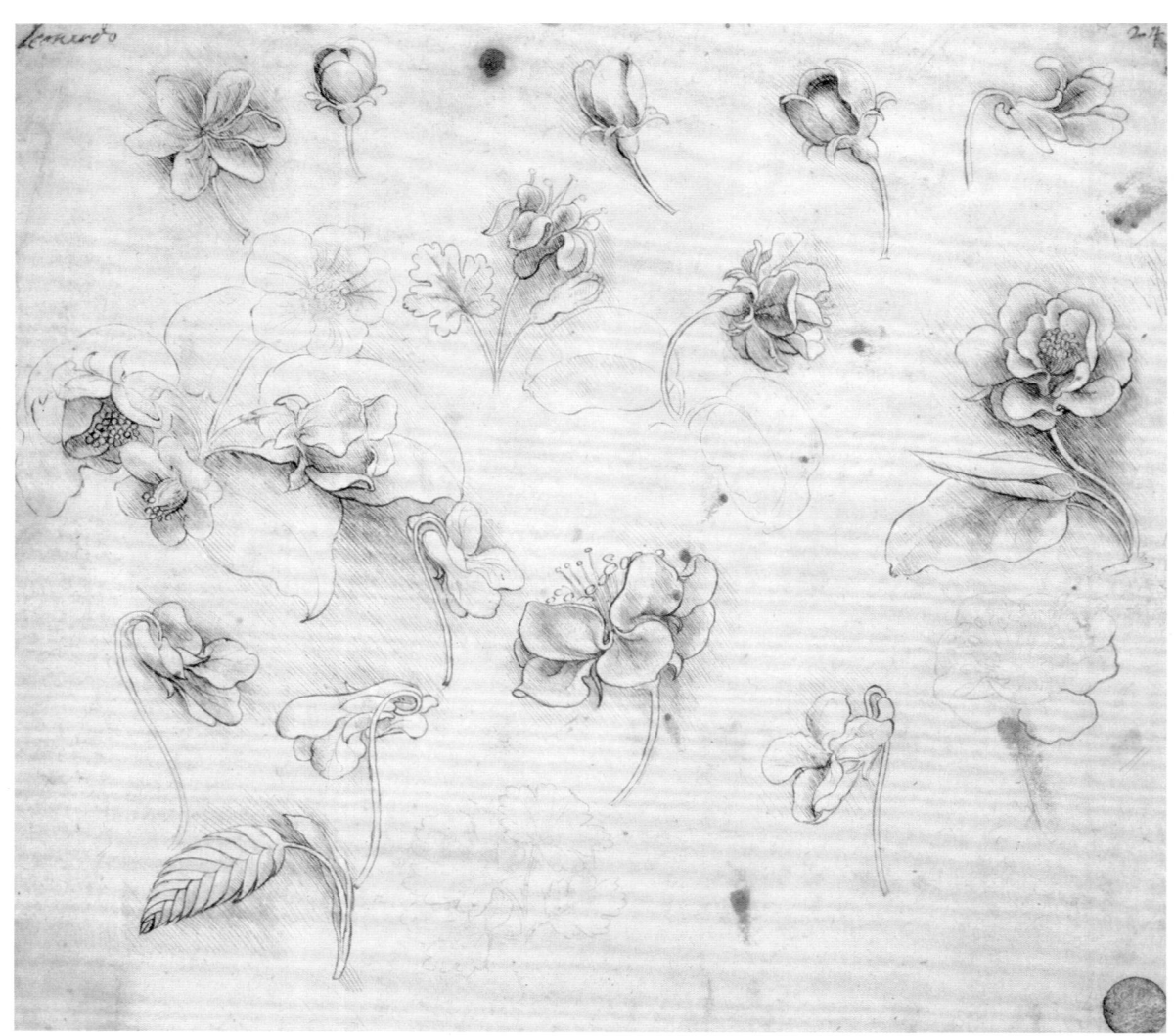

84

Study of the flowers of grass-like plants

Feuille d'étude avec les fleurs d'une plante aux allures de graminée

Studienblatt mit Blüten einer gras-ähnlichen Pflanze

Hoja de estudios con flores de una planta parecida a la hierba

Foglio di studio con fiori di una pianta erbosa

Schetsblad met bloempjes van grasplanten

c. 1481–83, Pencil on paper/ Mine de plomb sur papier, Galleria dell' Accademia, Venezia

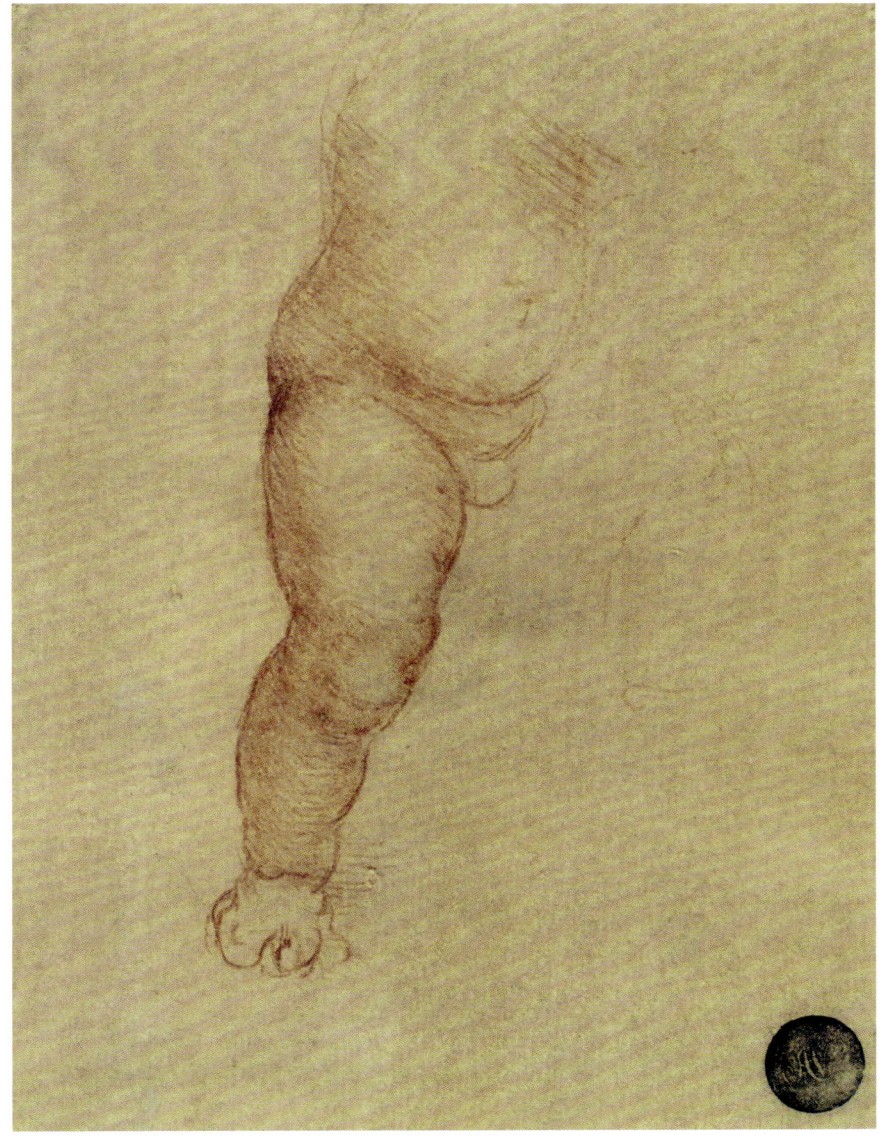

Study of a putto

Étude de putto

Studie einer Putte

Estudio de un angelote

Studio di un putto

Studie van een putto

Red chalk on tinted paper/ Sanguine sur papier teinté, Galleria dell' Accademia, Venezia

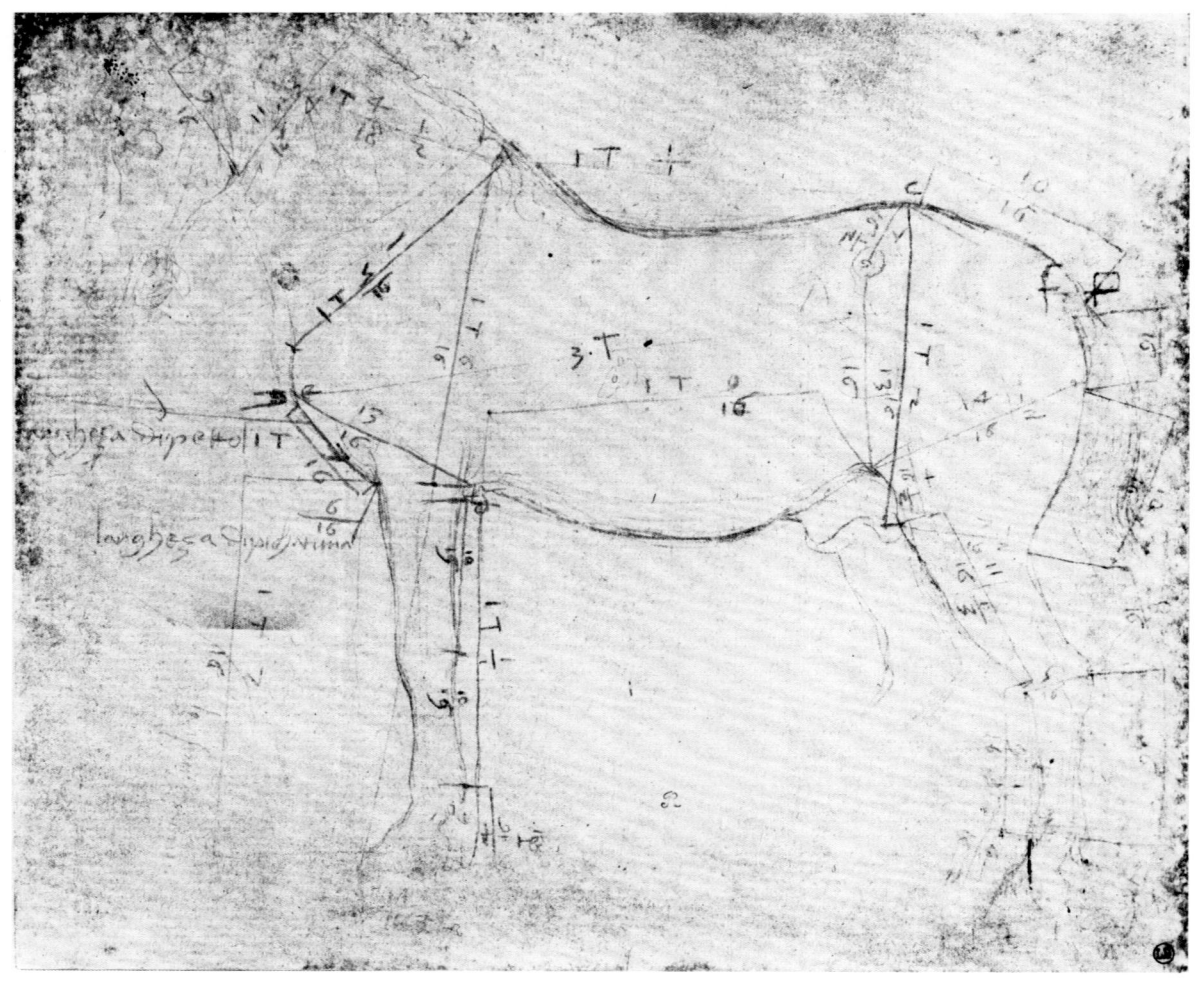

Study of a horse **Studie eines Pferdes** **Studio di un cavallo**

Étude de cheval **Estudio de un caballo** **Studie van een paard**

Metalpoint on paper/Pointe métallique sur papier, 17,5 × 20,7 cm, Musée Bonnat, Bayonne

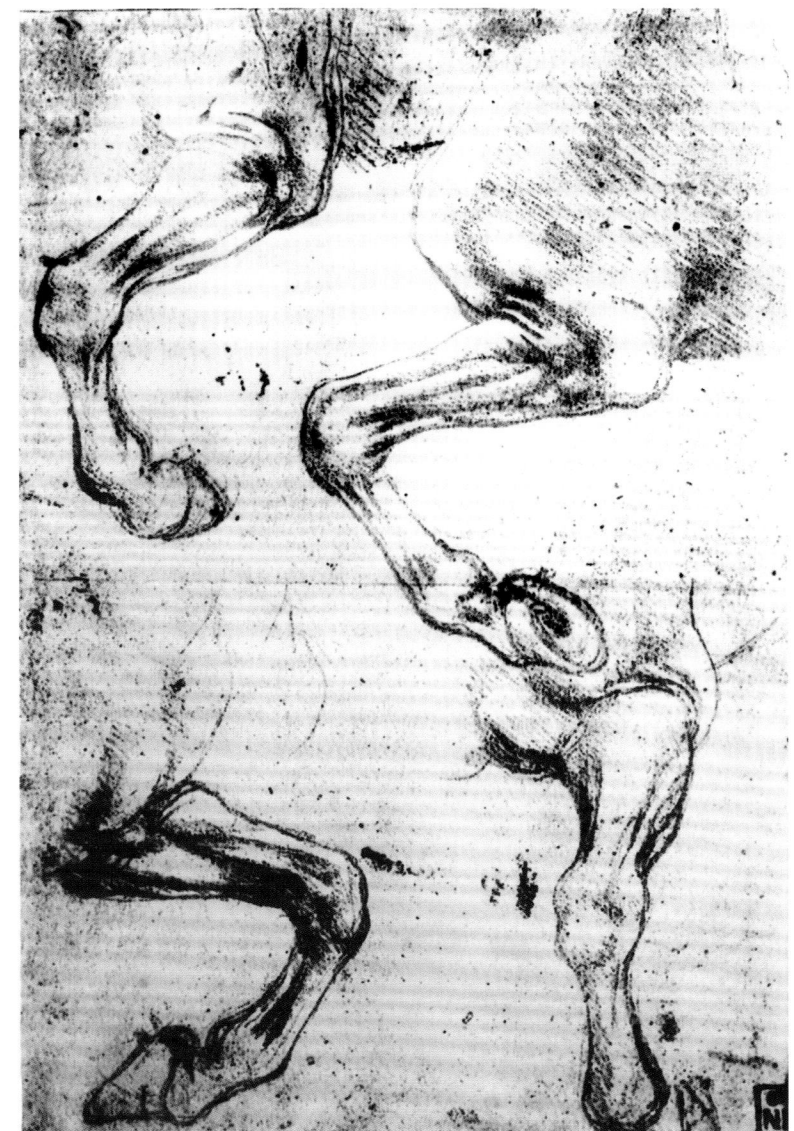

Study of the legs of horses
Étude avec les jambes d'un cheval
Studie mit den Beinen eines Pferdes
Estudio de las patas de un caballo
Studio delle zampe di un cavallo
Studie van paardenbenen

Pen and ink on paper/Plume et encre sur papier,
Szépművészeti Múzeum, Budapest

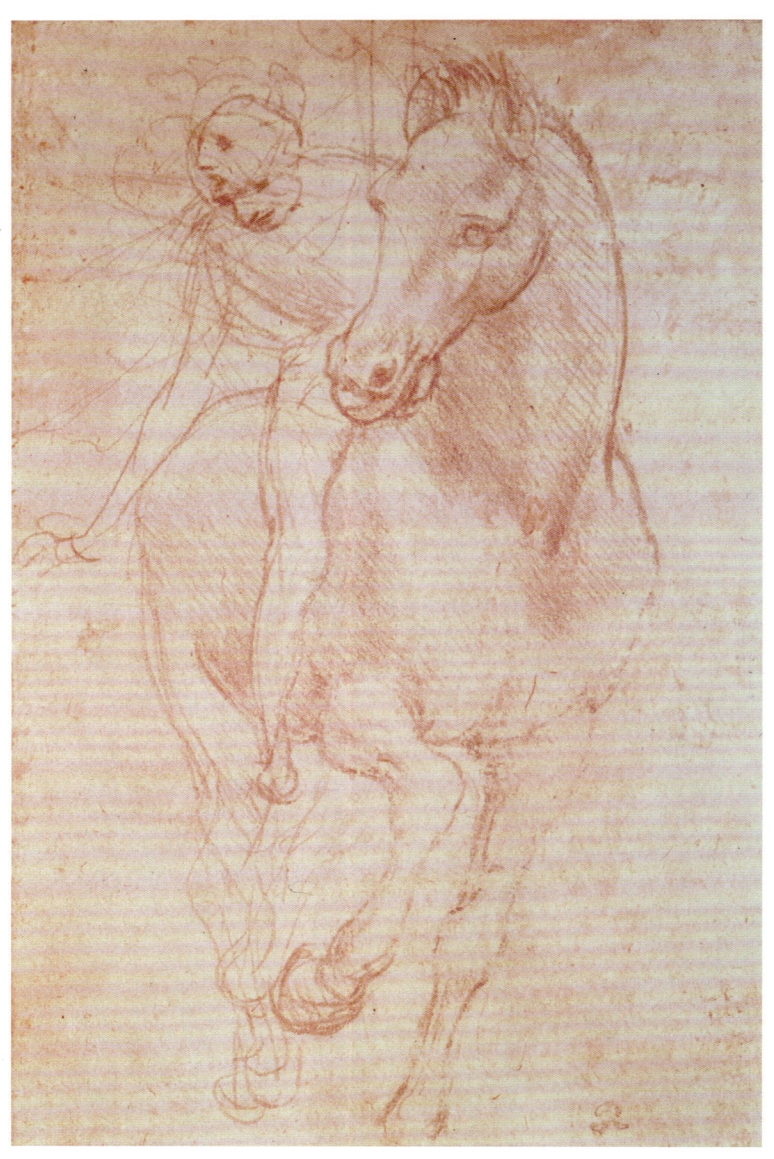

Study of horse and rider

Étude de cheval et de cavalier

Studie von Pferd und Reiter

Estudio de un caballo y su jinete

Studio di cavallo e cavaliere

Studie van paard en ruiter

c. 1481, Metalpoint on paper/Pointe métallique sur papier, 12 × 7,8 cm, Private collection

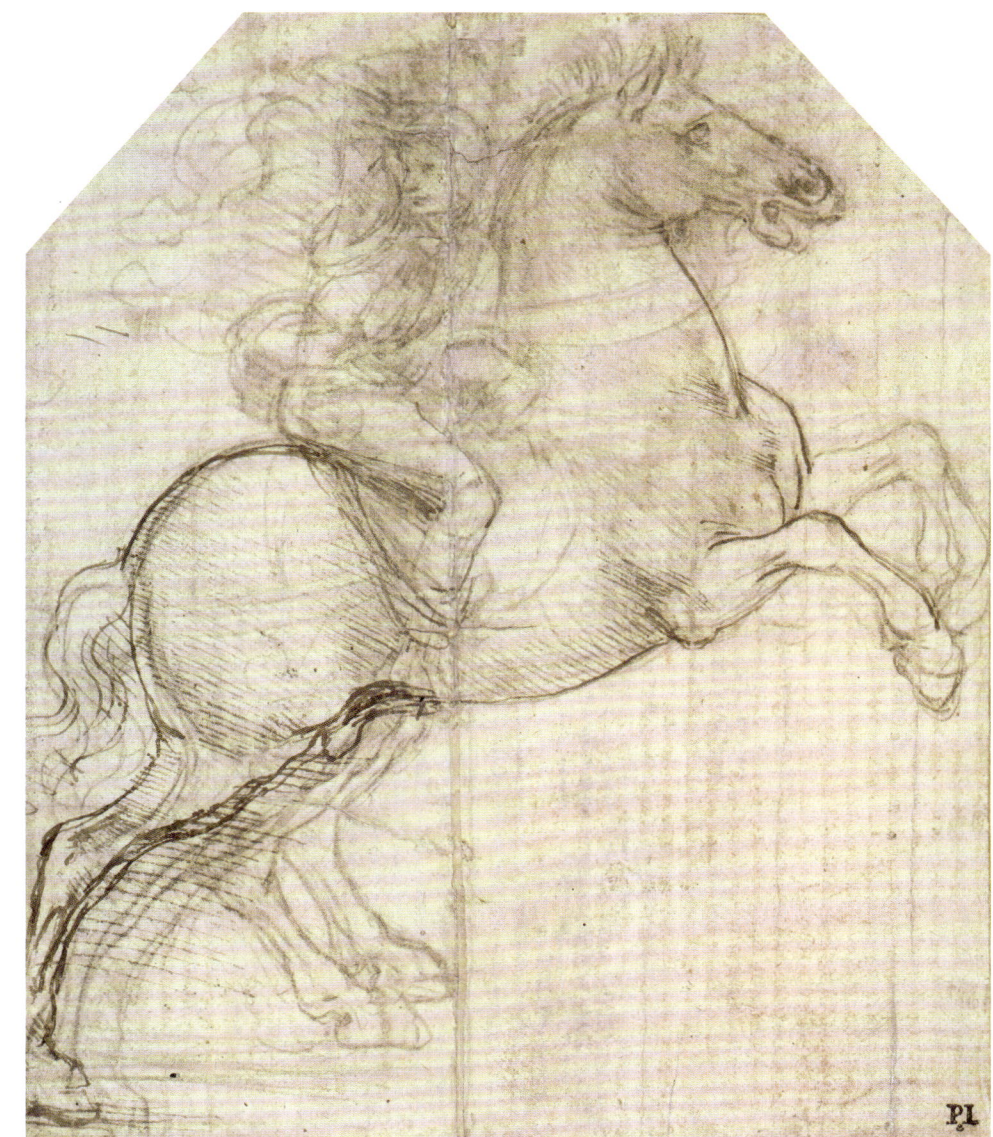

Rider on rearing horse

Cavalier sur un cheval se cabrant

Reiter auf einem sich aufbäumenden Pferd

Jinete sobre un caballo rebelado

Cavaliere su un cavallo imbizzarrito

Ruiter op steigerend paard

c. 1481/82, Silverpoint, pen and brown ink on paper/Pointe d'argent, plume et encre brune sur papier teinté, 14,1 × 11,9 cm, Fitzwilliam Museum, Cambridge

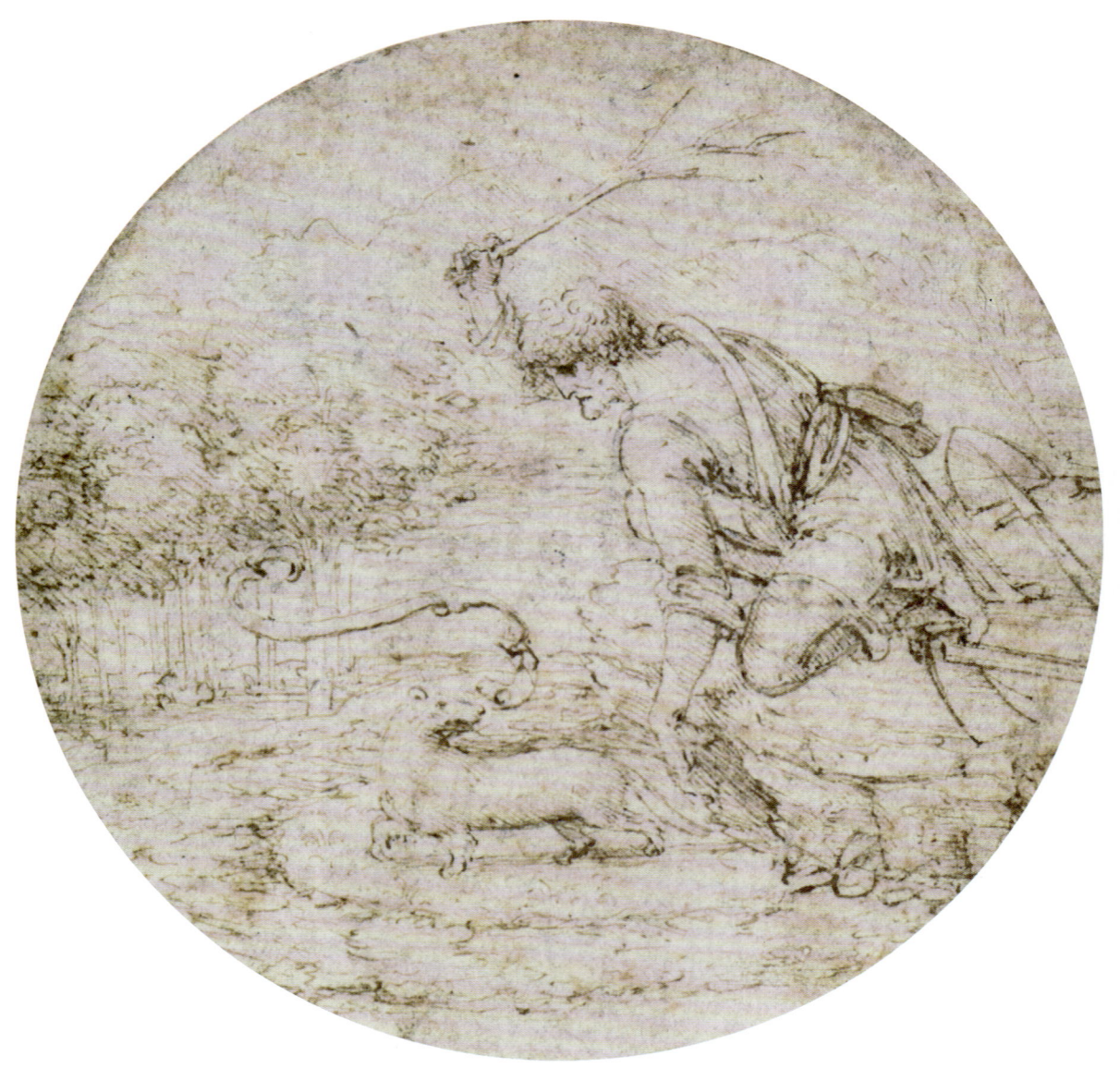

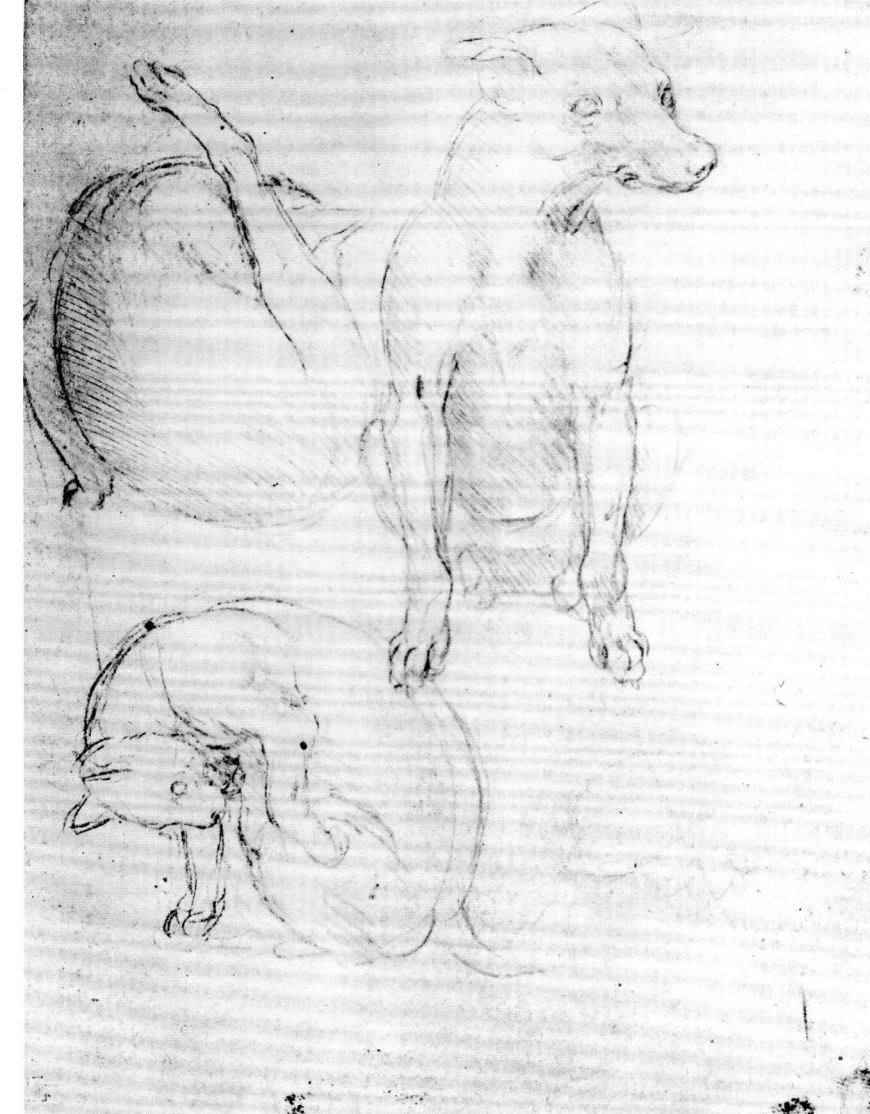

The ermine as a symbol of purity
L'hermine symbole de pureté
**Das Hermelin als Symbol
der Reinheit**
El armiño como símbolo de la pureza
L'ermellino simbolo di purezza
**Das hermelijn als symbool
van puurheid**

*c. 1494, Pen and brown ink over black
on paper/Plume et encre brune sur
pierre noire, sur papier, Fitzwilliam
Museum, Cambridge*

Study of a dog and a cat
Étude d'un chien et d'un chat
**Studie eines Hundes
und einer Katze**
Estudio de un perro y un gato
Studio di un cane e un gatto
Studie van een hond en een kat

*c. 1480, Metalpoint on paper/Pointe
métallique sur papier, British Museum,
London*

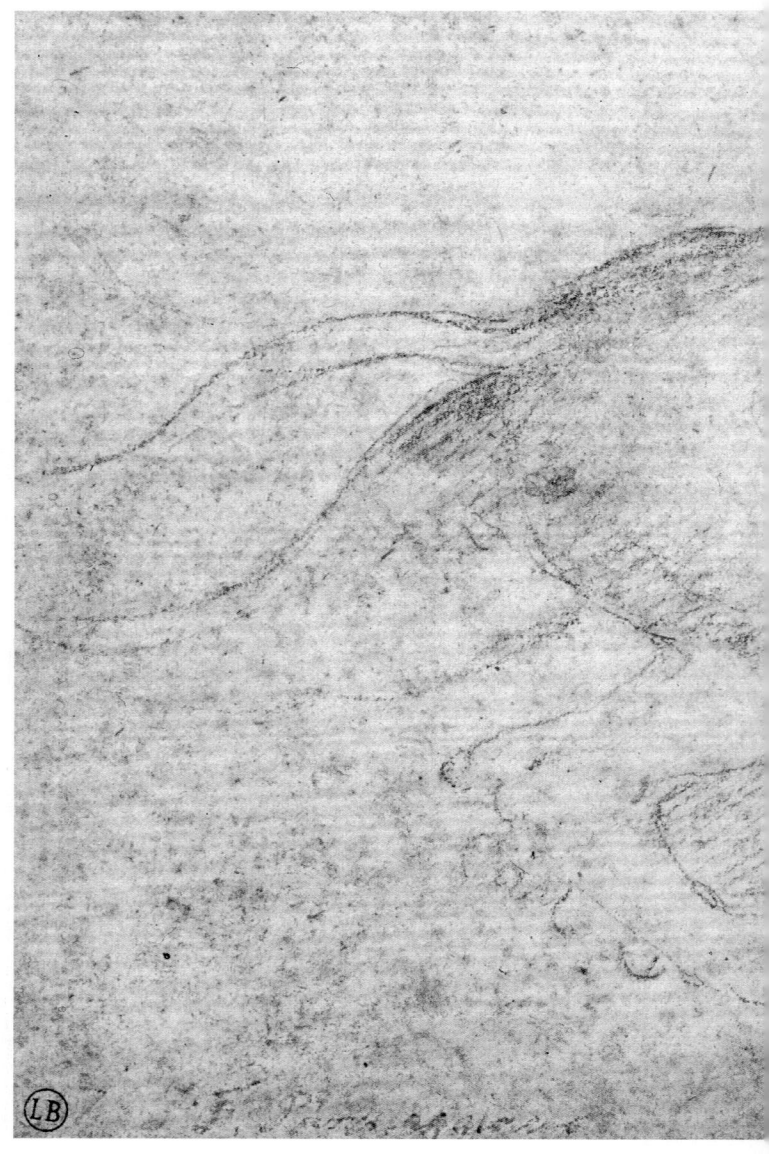

Sketch of a roaring lion

Esquisse de lion rugissant

Skizze eines brüllenden Löwen

Esbozo de un león rugiendo

Schizzo di un leone ruggente

Schets van een brullende leeuw

Red chalk on paper/Sanguine sur papier, 10 × 17,7 cm,
Musée Bonnat, Bayonne

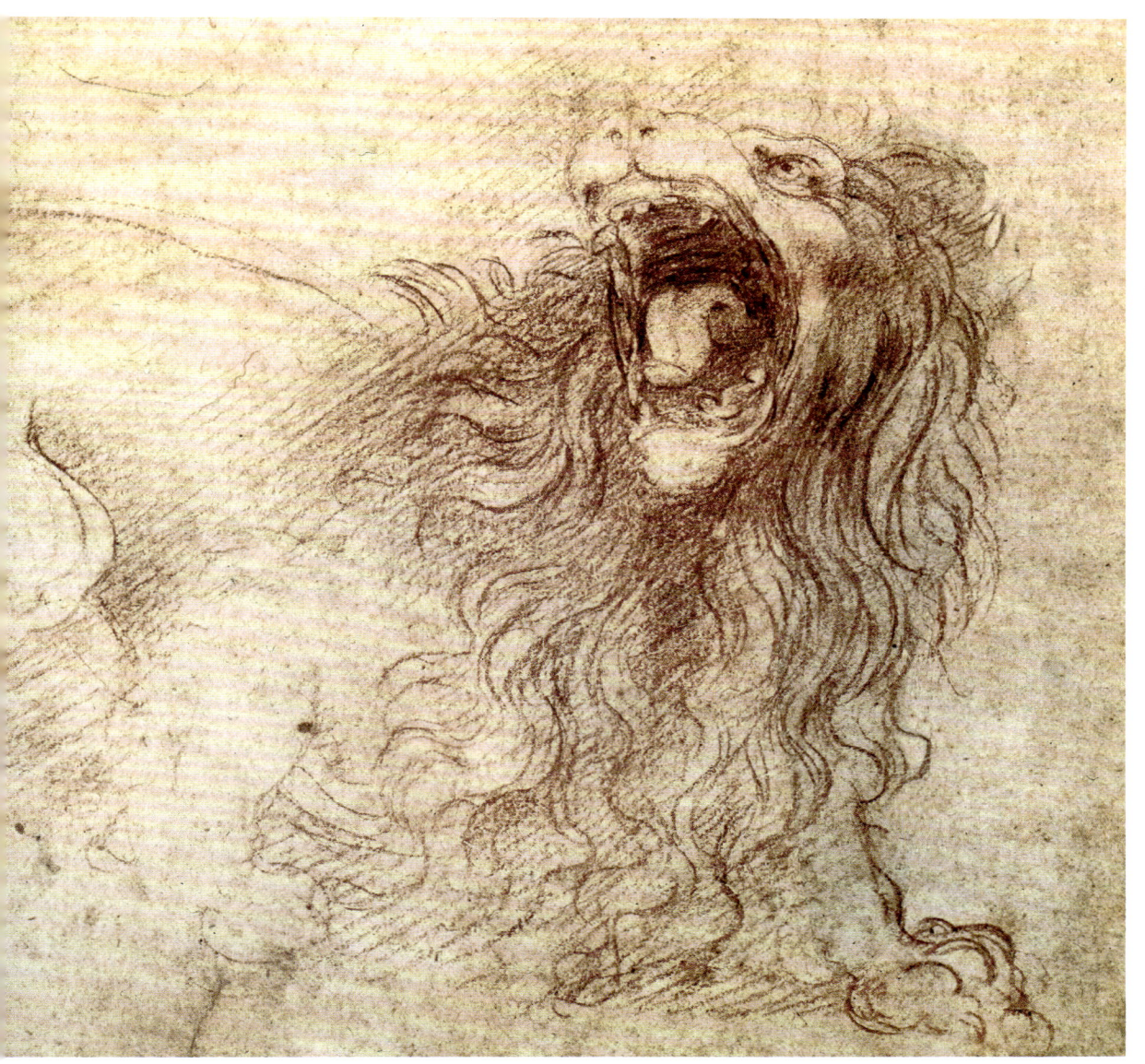

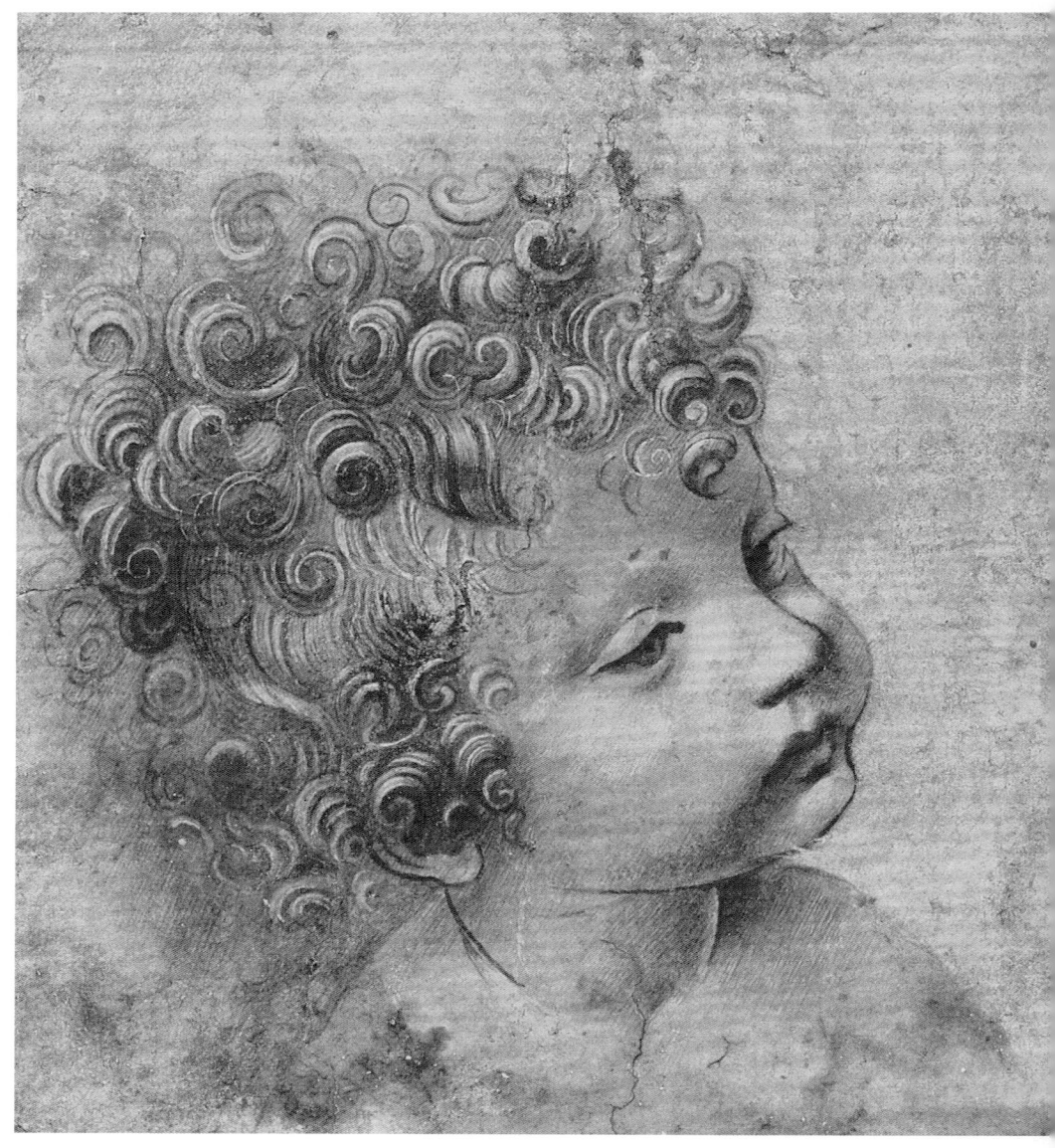

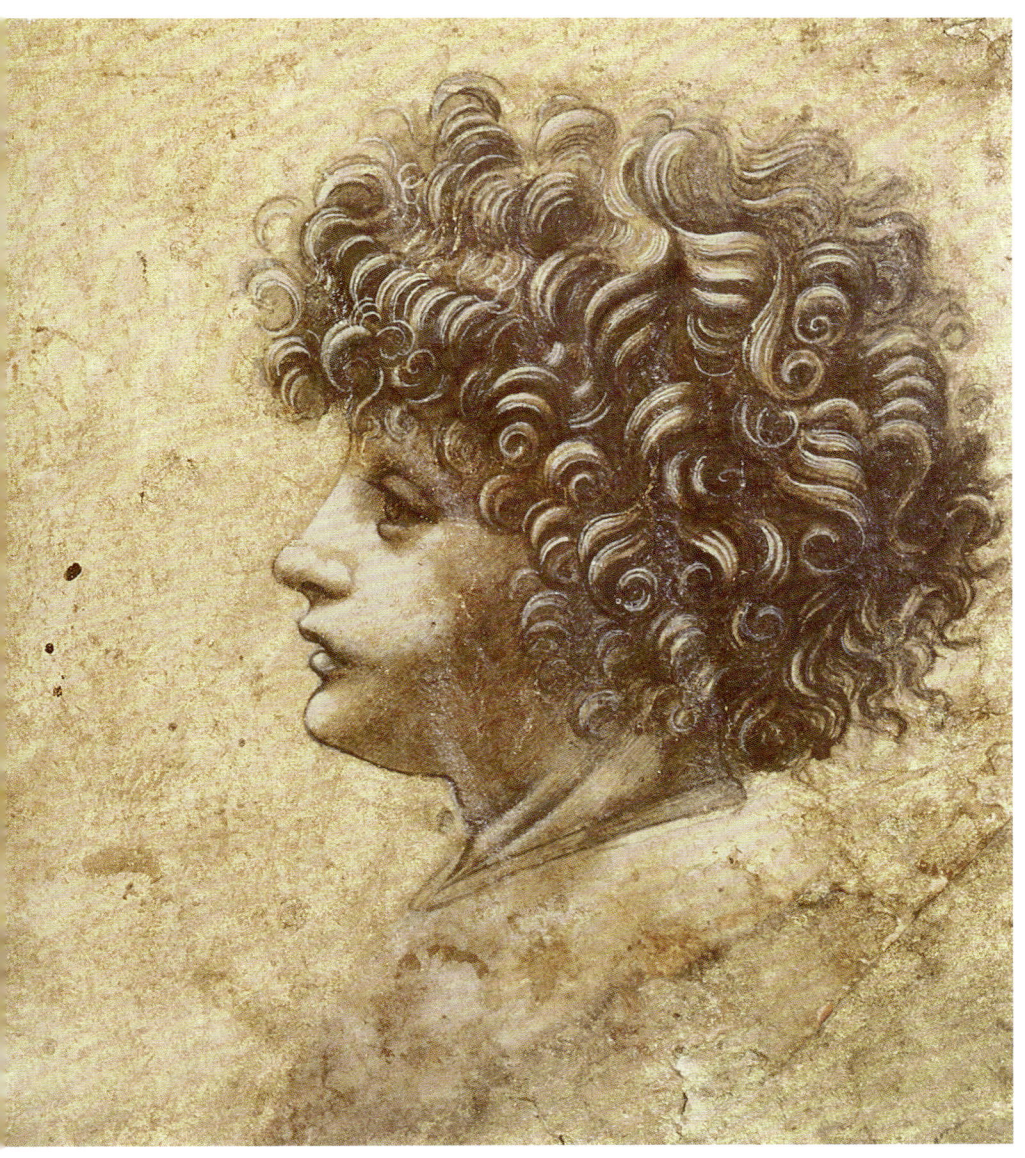

Study of a child's head

Étude avec tête d'enfant

Studie mit Kopf eines Kindes

Estudio con la cabeza de un niño

Studio di una testa di bambino

Studie met kinderhoofdje

Red chalk heightened with white on paper/ Sanguine et rehauts de blanc sur papier, Musée des Beaux-Arts, Caen

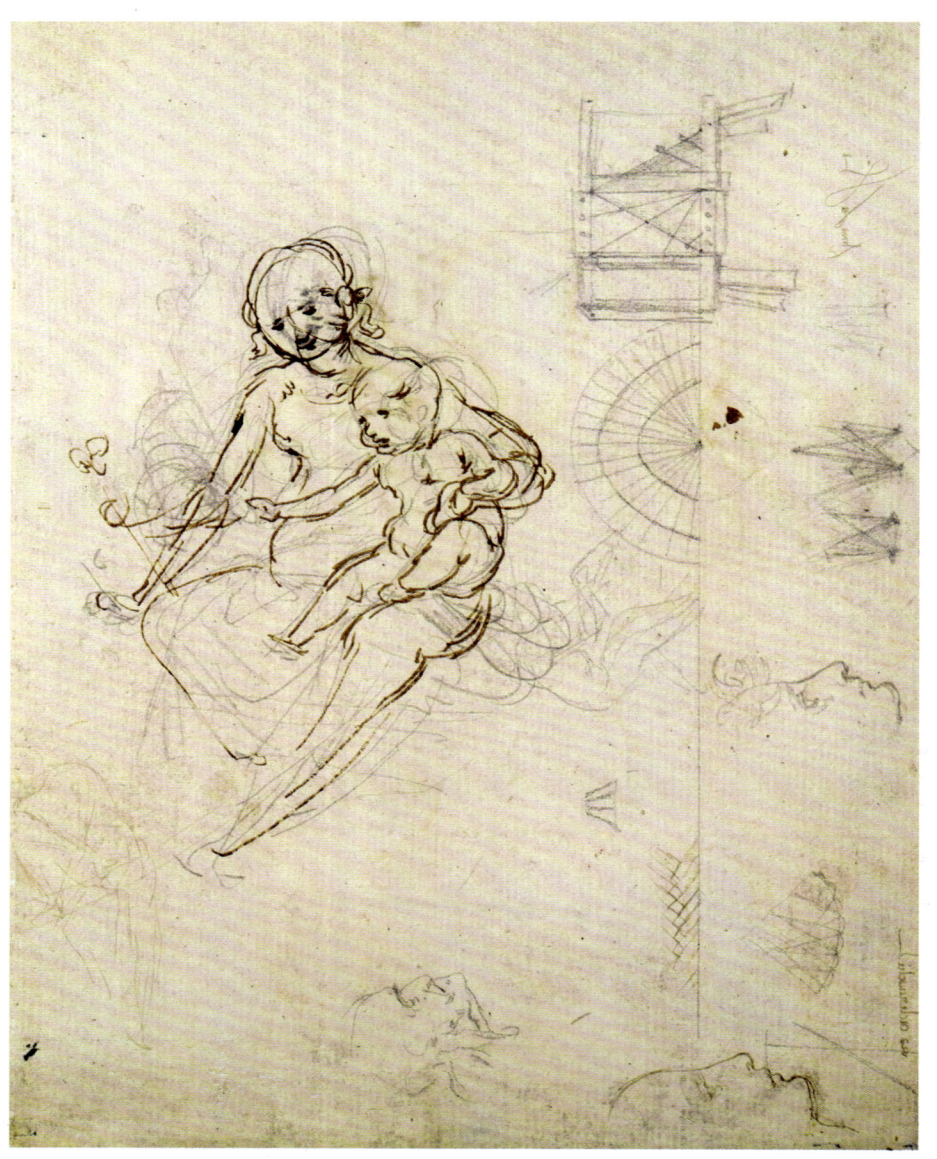

Study for a Virgin and Child in profile

Étude de la Vierge et d'un enfant, de profil

Studie der Heiligen Jungfrau und eines Kindes im Profil

Estudio de la Virgen María y un niño de perfil

Studio della Vergine e del Bambino di profilo

Studie van de Heilige Maagd met kind, en profil

ca. 1478–80, Pencil and ink on paper/Mine de plomb et encre sur papier, British Museum, London

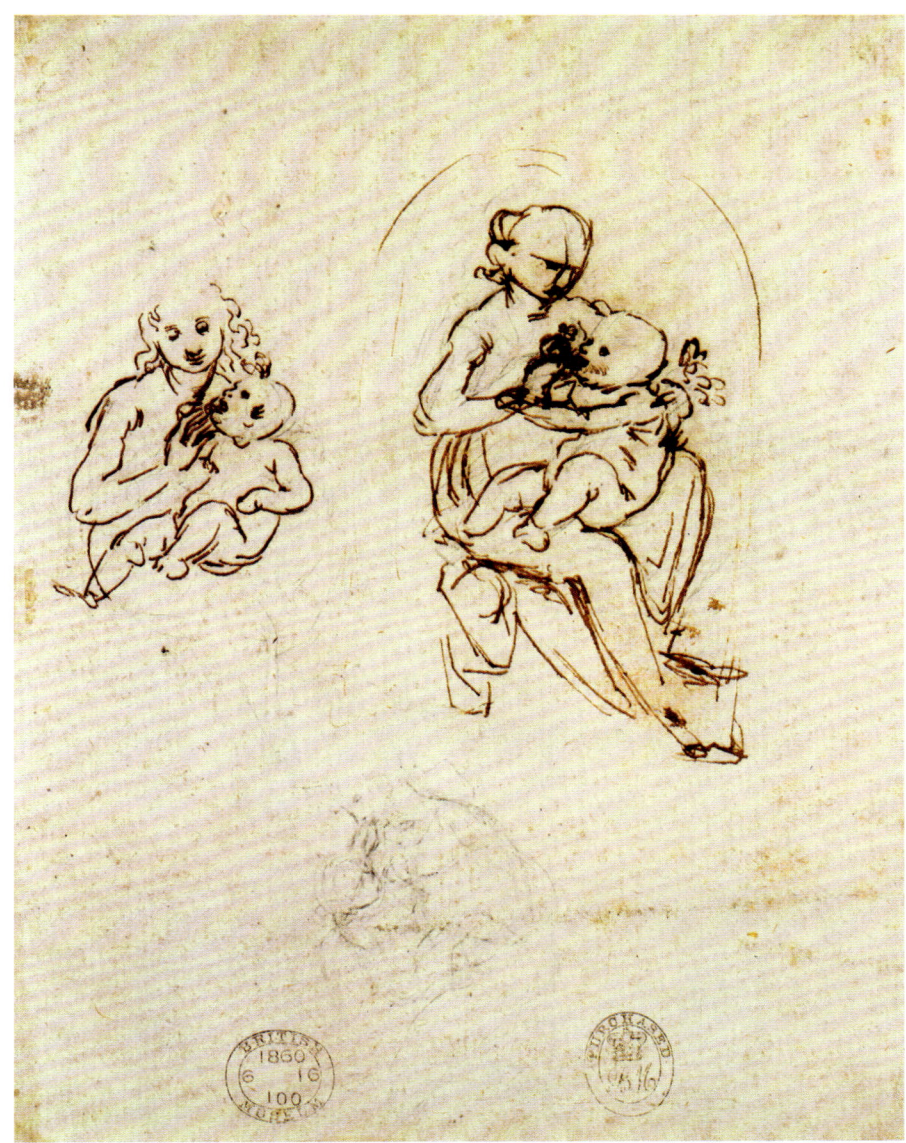

Study for a Virgin and Child

**Étude de la Vierge
et d'un enfant**

**Studie der Heiligen Jungfrau
und eines Kindes**

**Estudio de la Virgen
María y un niño**

**Studio della Vergine
e del Bambino**

**Studie van de Heilige
Maagd met kind**

*c. 1478–80, Pencil and ink on
paper/Mine de plomb et encre sur
papier, British Museum, London*

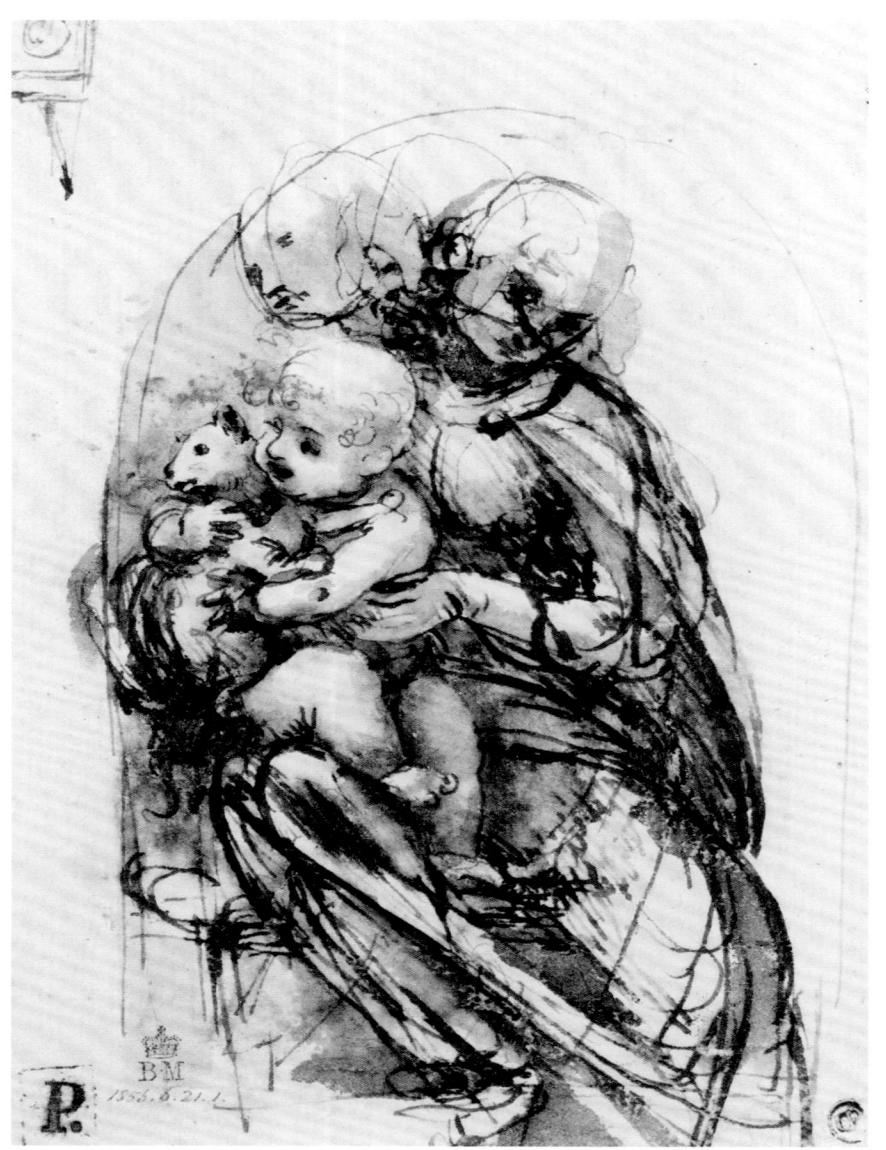

Study for a Madonna with a cat

Étude de Madone avec un chat

Studie einer Madonna mit Katze

Estudio de una Virgen con un gato

Studio della Madonna con gatto

Studie van een madonna met een kat

c. 1478–80, Pen and ink over stylus underdrawing on paper/Plume et lavis d'encre brune sur mine de plomb, sur papier, 13,2 × 9,5 cm, British Museum, London

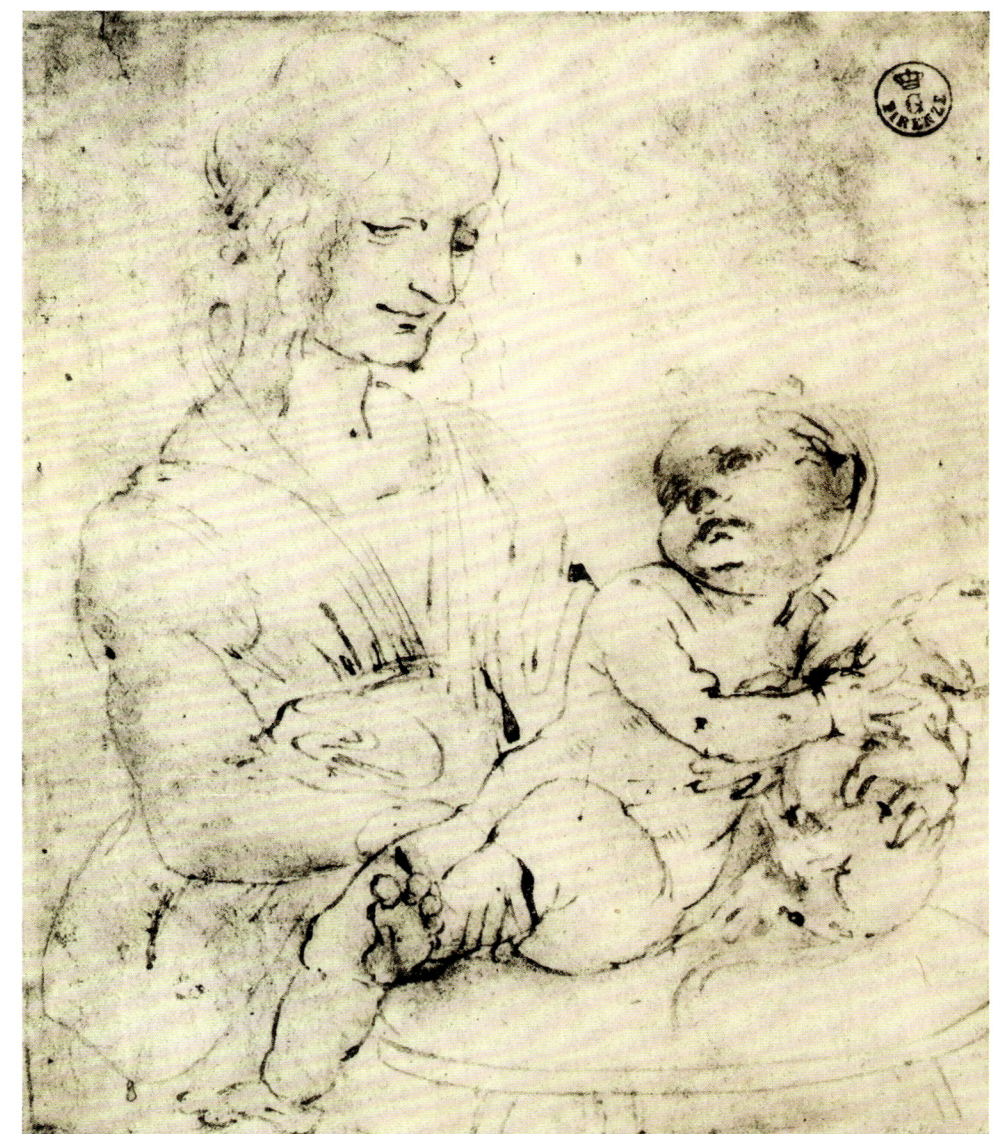

Study for a Madonna with a child

Étude d'une Madone avec un enfant

Studie einer Madonna mit Kind

Estudio de una Virgen con niño

Studio della Madonna con Bambino

Studie van Madonna met kind

Black ink on paper/ Encre noire sur papier, Gabinetto dei Disegni e Stampe, Galleria degli Uffizi, Firenze

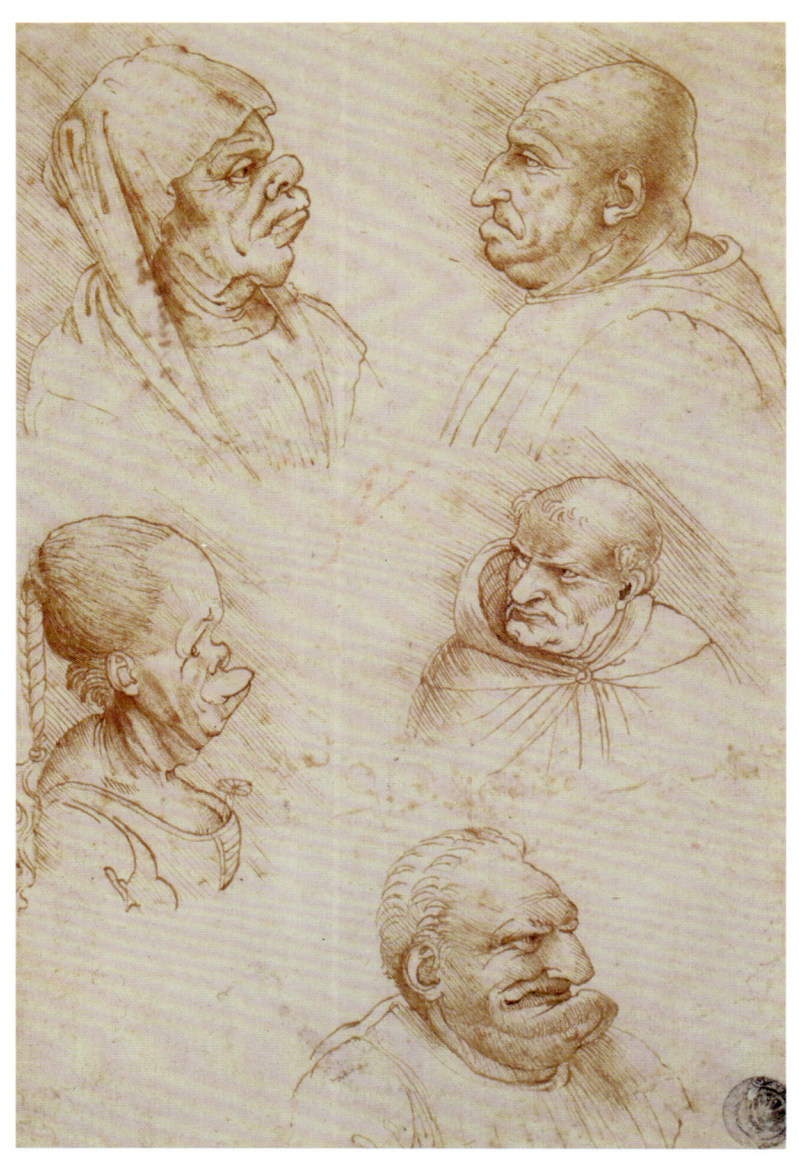

Five studies of grotesque faces

Cinq études de visages grotesques

Fünf Studien mit grotesken Gesichtern

Cinco estudios de caras grotescas

Cinque studi con visi grotteschi

Vijf studies met groteske gezichten

Red chalk on paper/Sanguine sur papier,
Galleria dell' Accademia, Venezia

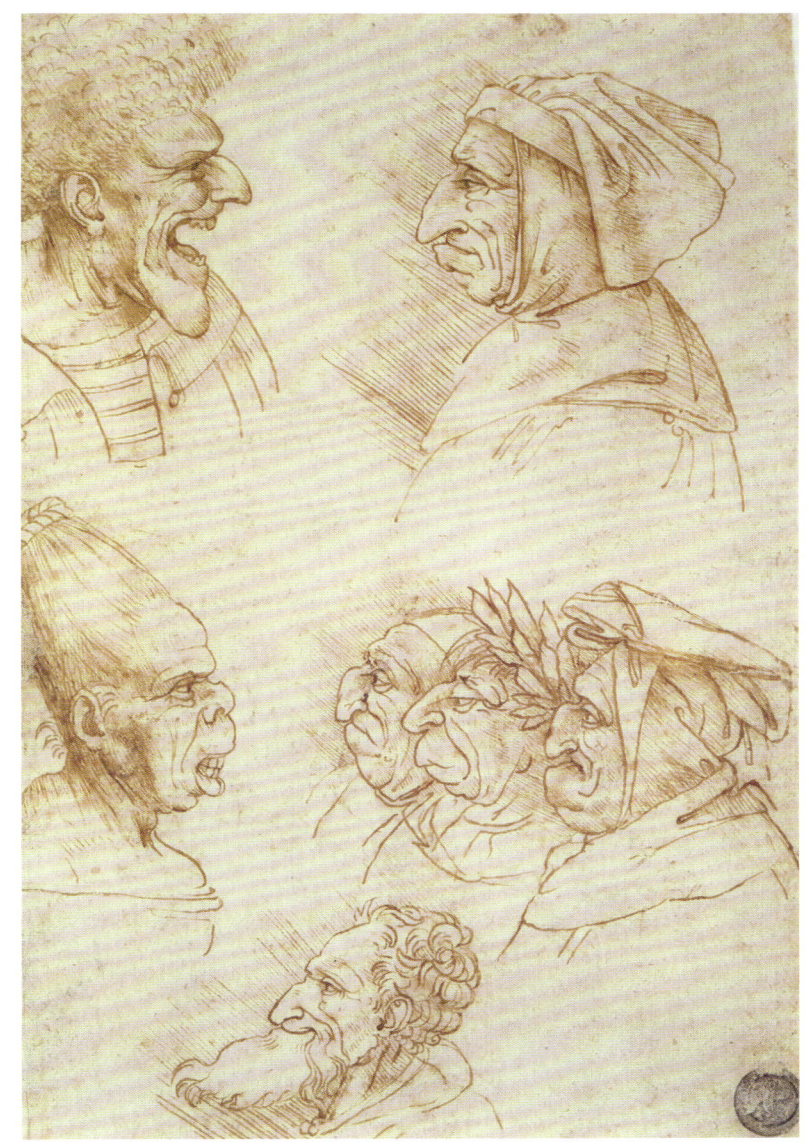

Seven studies of grotesque faces
Sept études de visages grotesques
Sieben Studien mit grotesken Gesichtern
Siete estudios de caras grotescas
Sette studi con visi grotteschi
Zeven studies met groteske gezichten

Red chalk on paper/Sanguine sur papier,
Galleria dell' Accademia, Venezia

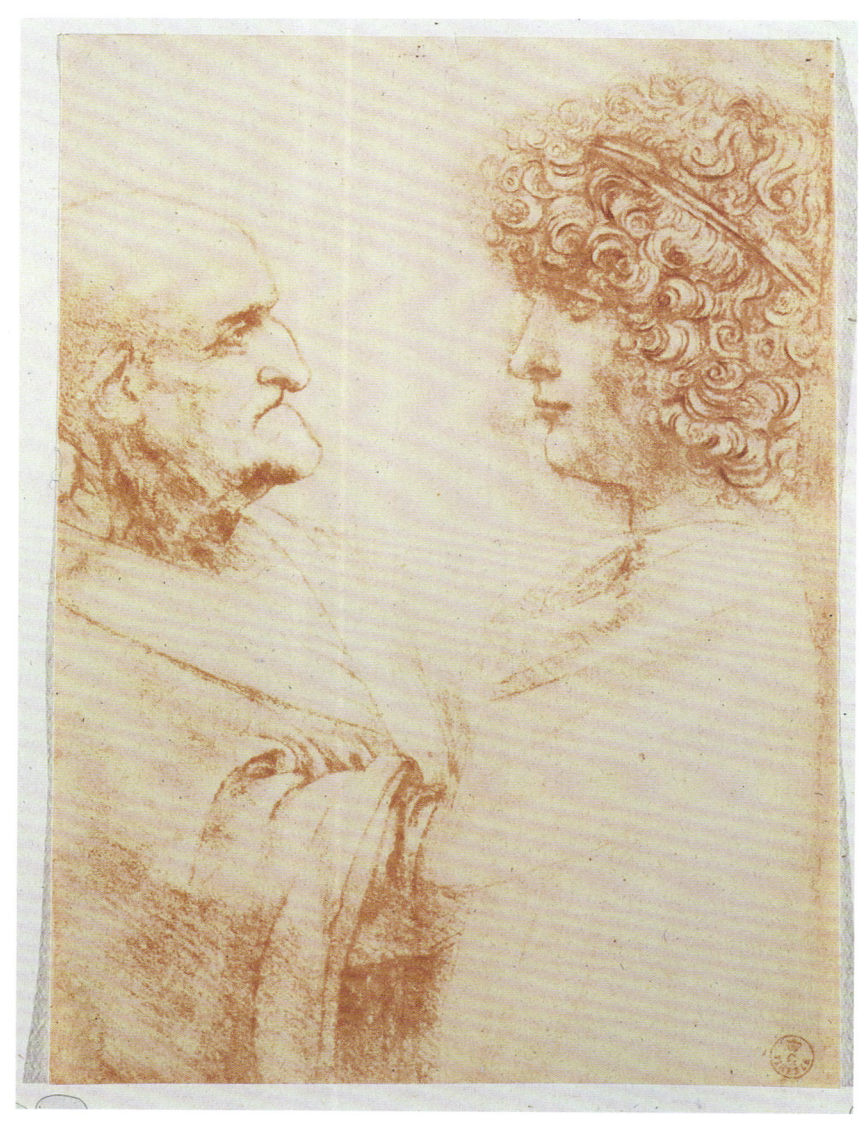

Two heads in profile
Deux têtes de profil
Zwei Köpfe im Profil
Dos cabezas de perfil
Due teste di profilo
Twee hoofden en profil

c. 1500, Red chalk on paper/Sanguine sur papier, Galleria degli Uffizi, Firenze

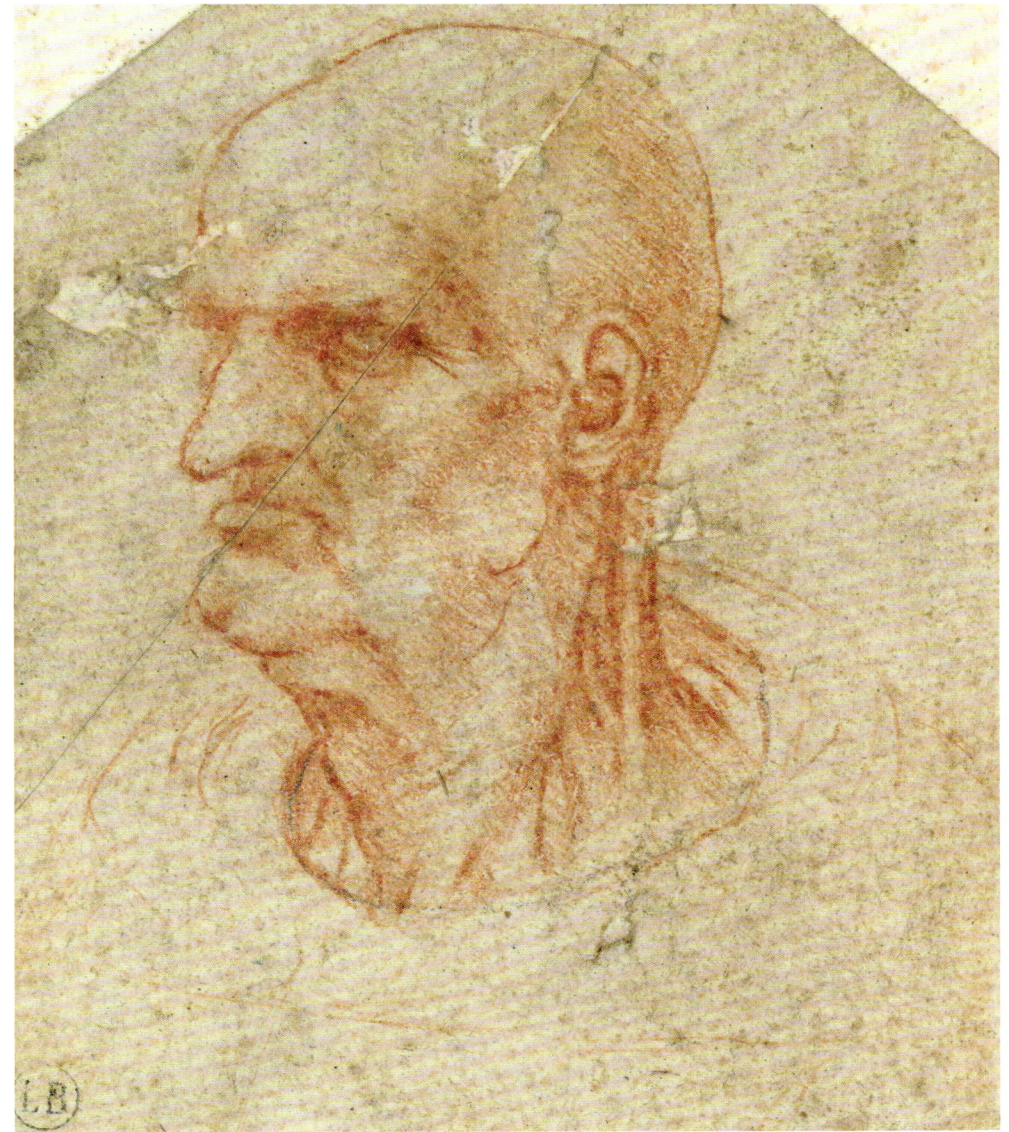

Head of beardless old man, in profile to the left

Tête de vieil homme sans barbe, de profil gauche

Kopf eines bartlosen alten Mannes, im Profil nach links

Cabeza de un hombre viejo sin barba, de perfil izquierdo

Testa di un anziano sbarbato, di profilo verso sinistra

Hoofd van een baardeloze man, linkerprofiel

Red chalk on paper/ Sanguine sur papier, 6,3 × 5,4 cm, Musée Bonnat, Bayonne

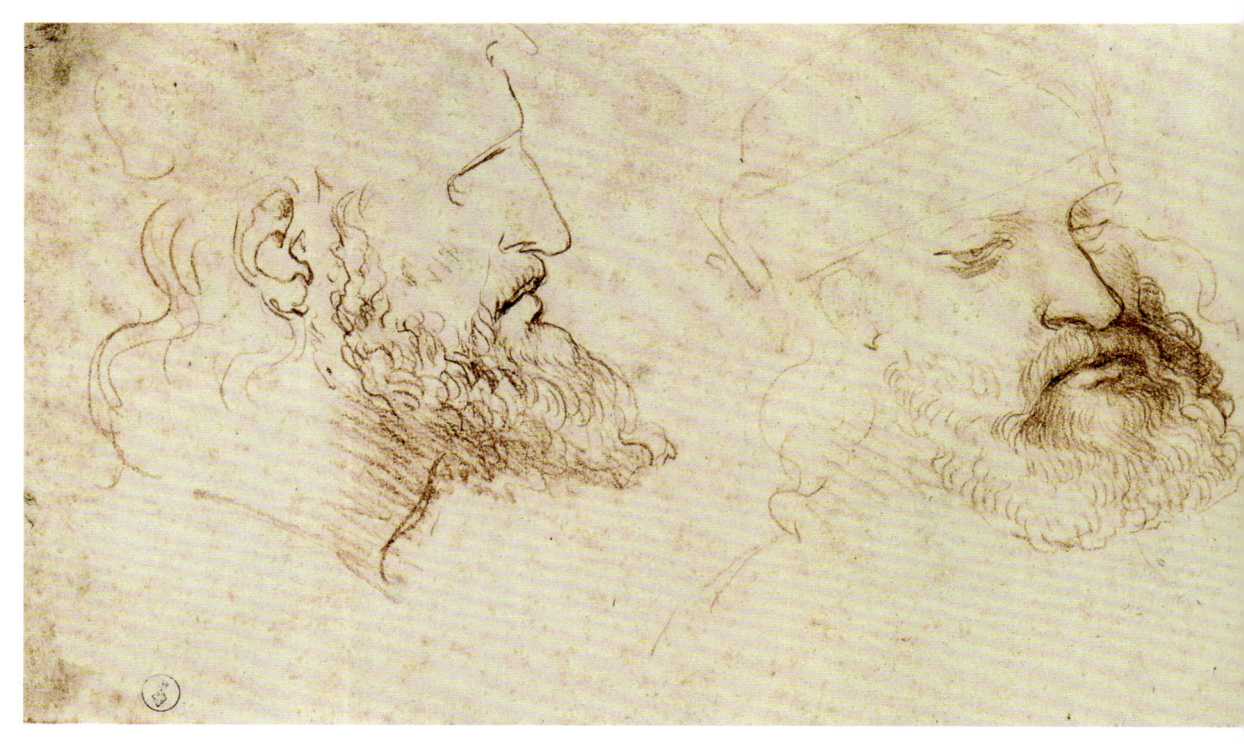

Study of a male head

Étude d'une tête masculine

Studie eines männlichen Kopfes

Estudio de una cabeza de hombre

Studio di una testa maschile

Studie van mannenhoofd

1502, Red chalk on paper/Sanguine sur papier, Biblioteca Reale, Torino

104

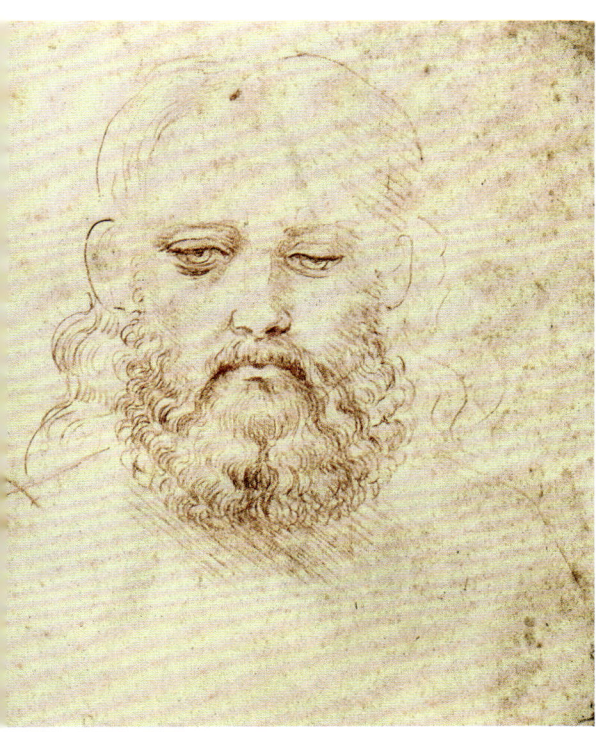

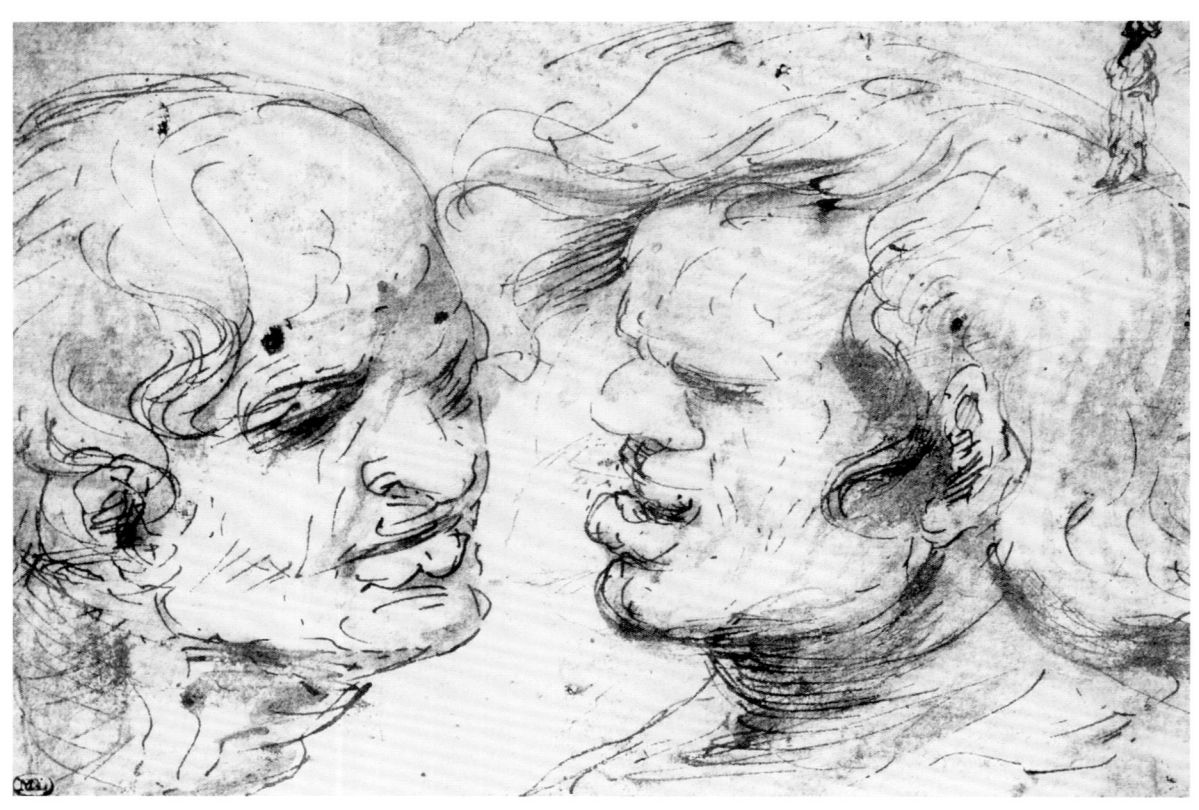

Two heads in profile
Deux têtes de profil
Zwei Köpfe im Profil
Dos cabezas de perfil
Due teste di profilo
Twee hoofden en profil

Pen and ink on paper/Plume et encre sur papier, Musée du Louvre, Paris

Studies for Nativity
Étude pour la Nativité
Studie der Geburt Christi
Estudio del nacimiento de Cristo
Studio della nascita di Cristo
Studie van de geboorte van Christus

Watercolor drawing/Aquarelle

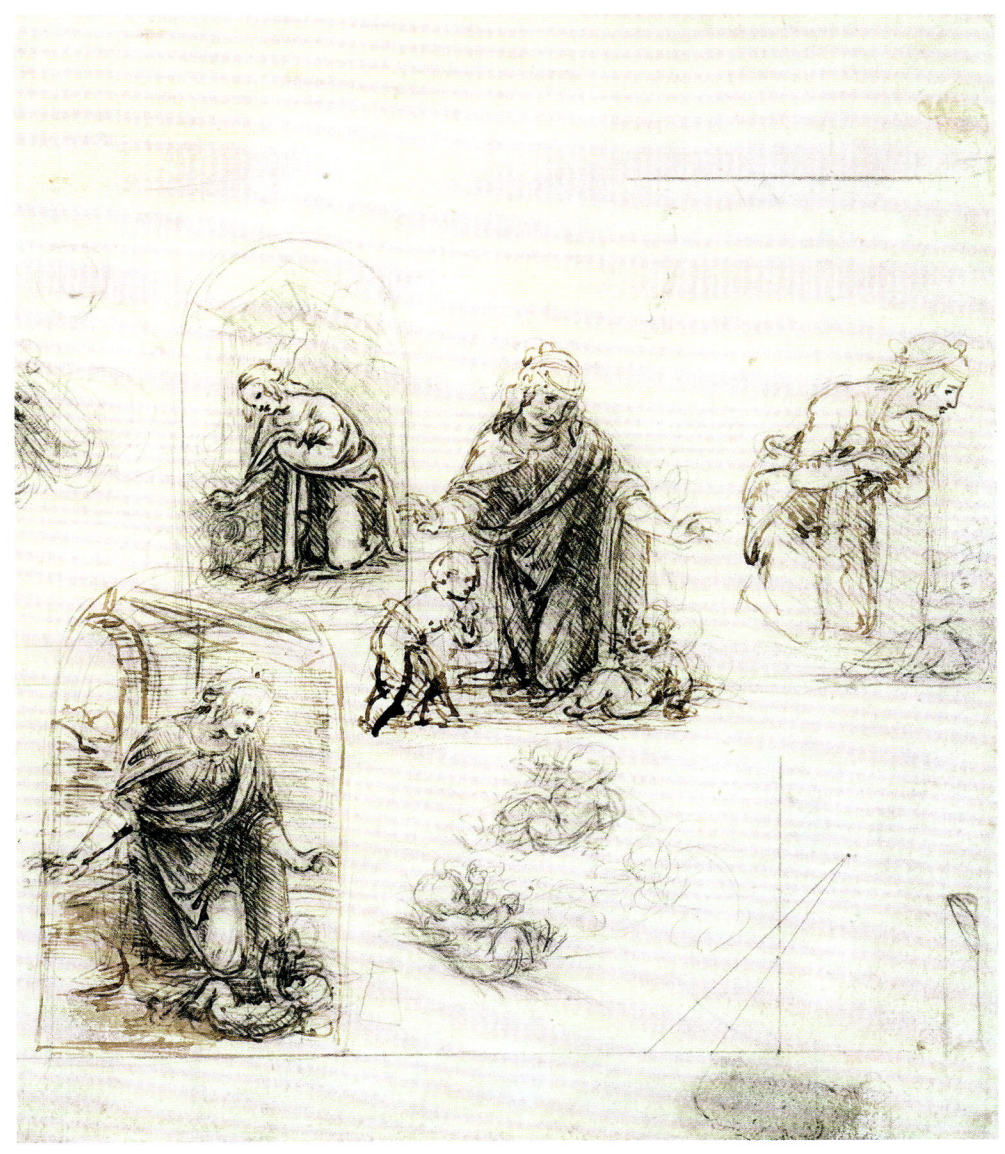

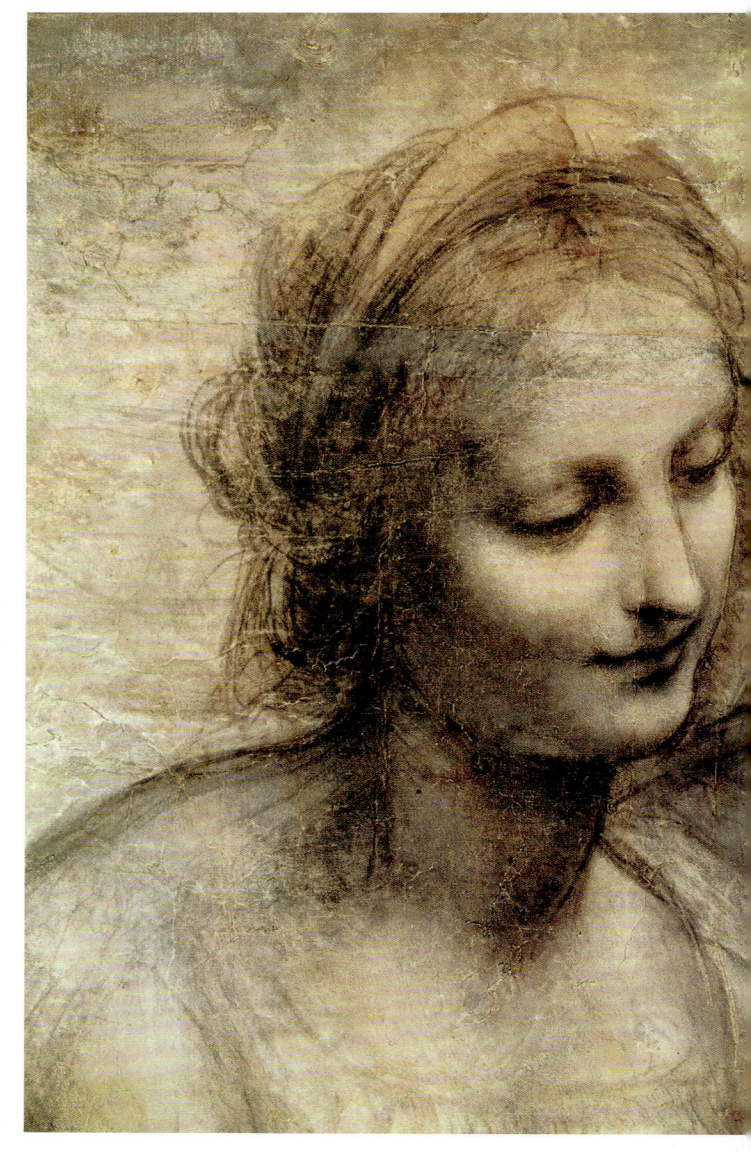

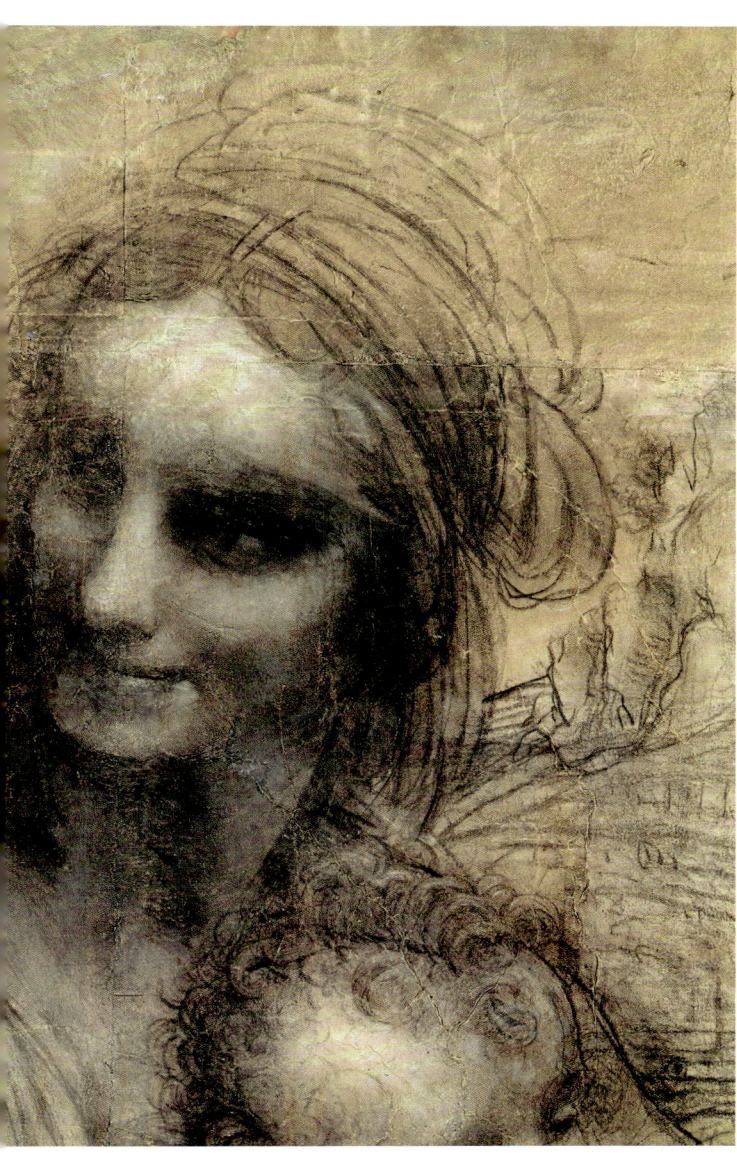

The Virgin and St. Anne, study
La Vierge, l'Enfant Jésus et sainte Anne, étude
Die hl. Anna selbdritt, Studie
Santa Ana trinitaria, estudio
Sant'Anna, la Vergine e il Bambino, studio
De Heilige Anna te Drieën, studie

c. 1499, Charcoal and white chalk on paper, mounted on canvas/Fusain et craie blanche sur papier, collé sur toile, National Gallery, London

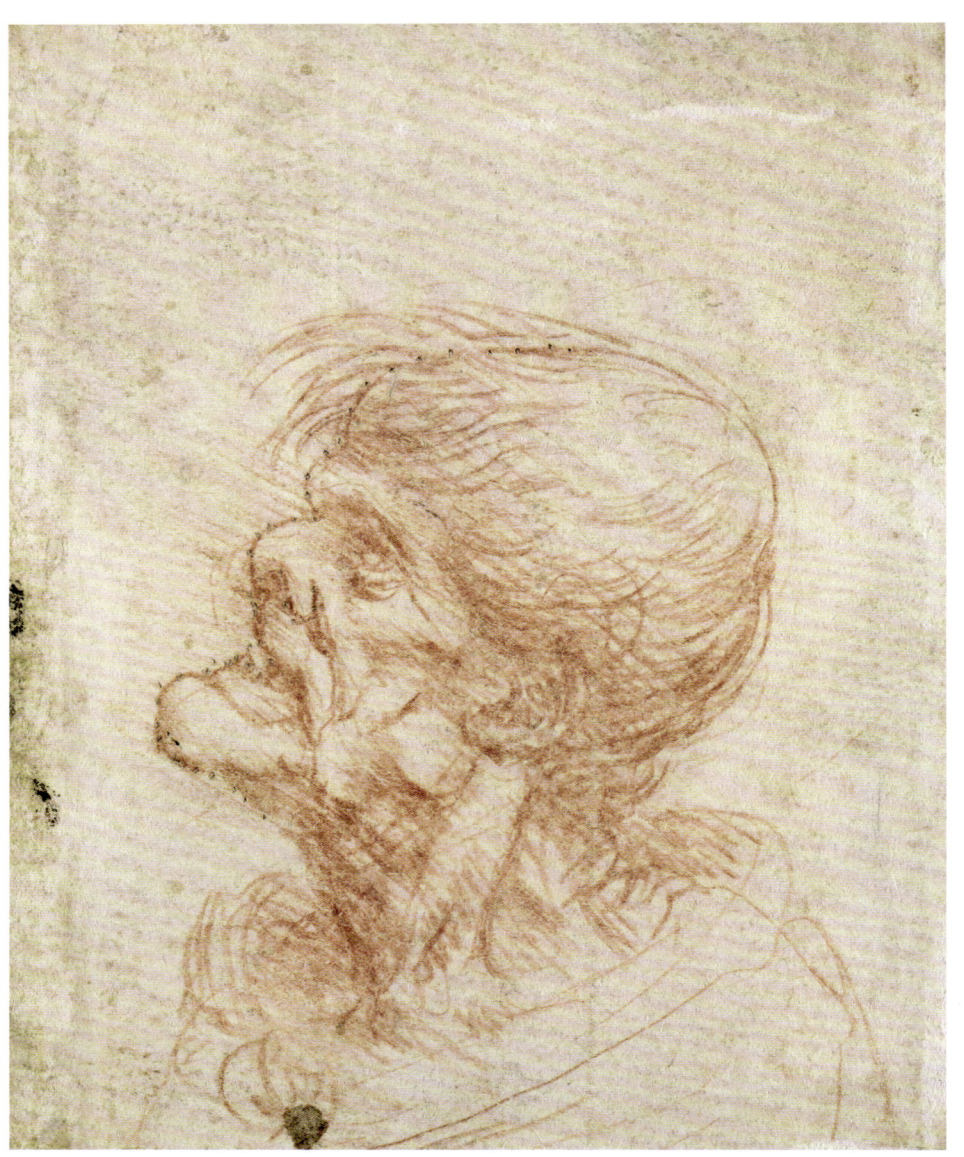

Caricature of an old man

*Caricature d'un
vieil homme*

*Karikatur eines
alten Mannes*

*Caricatura de un
hombre viejo*

Caricatura di un vecchio

Karikatuur van oude man

c. 1500–05, Red chalk on
paper/Sanguine sur papier,
9,8 × 8,2 cm, Kunsthalle,
Hamburg

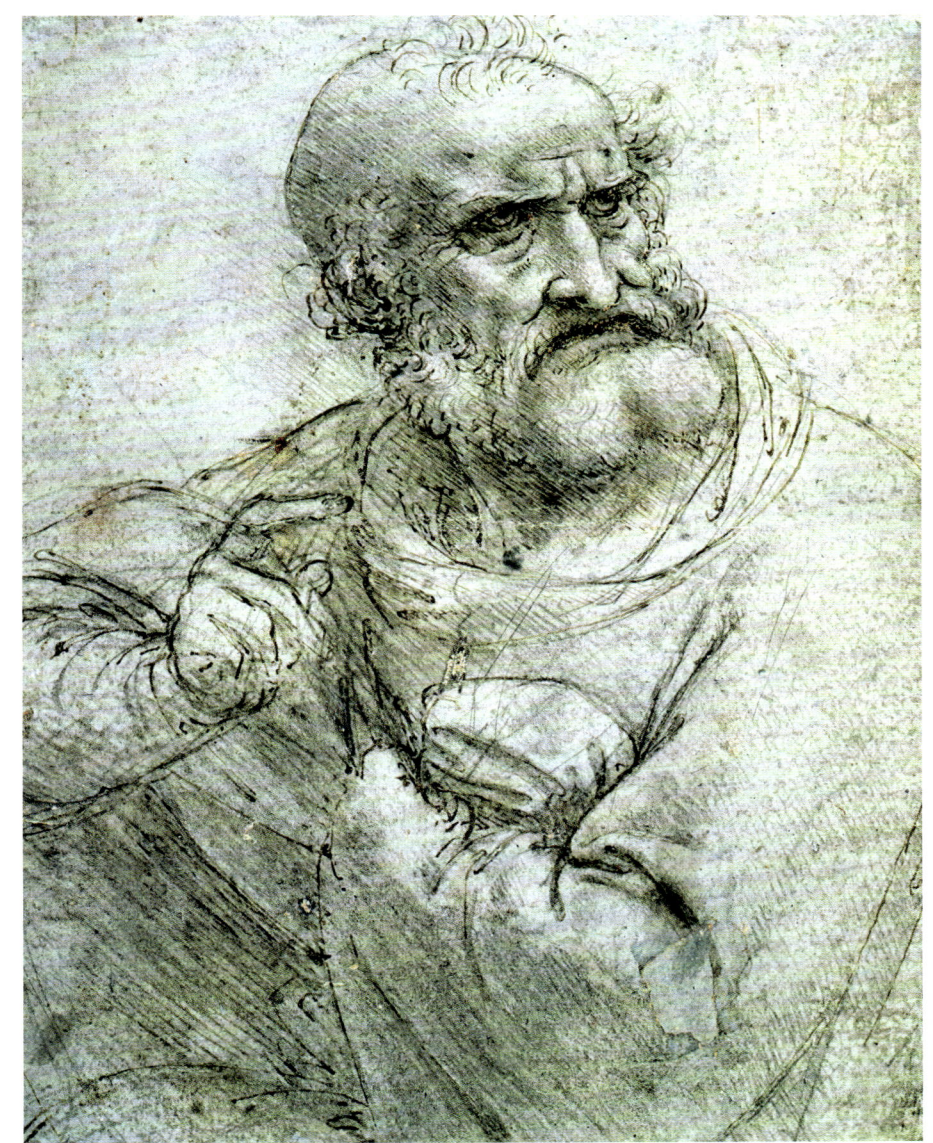

Study for *The Last Supper*

Étude pour un apôtre de *La Cène*

Das letzte Abendmahl, **Studie**

La Última Cena, **estudio**

L'Ultima Cena, **studio**

Het Laatste Avondmaal, **studie**

c. 1495, Pen and ink and metalpoint on paper/Plume, encre et pointe métallique sur papier, Graphische Sammlung Albertina, Wien

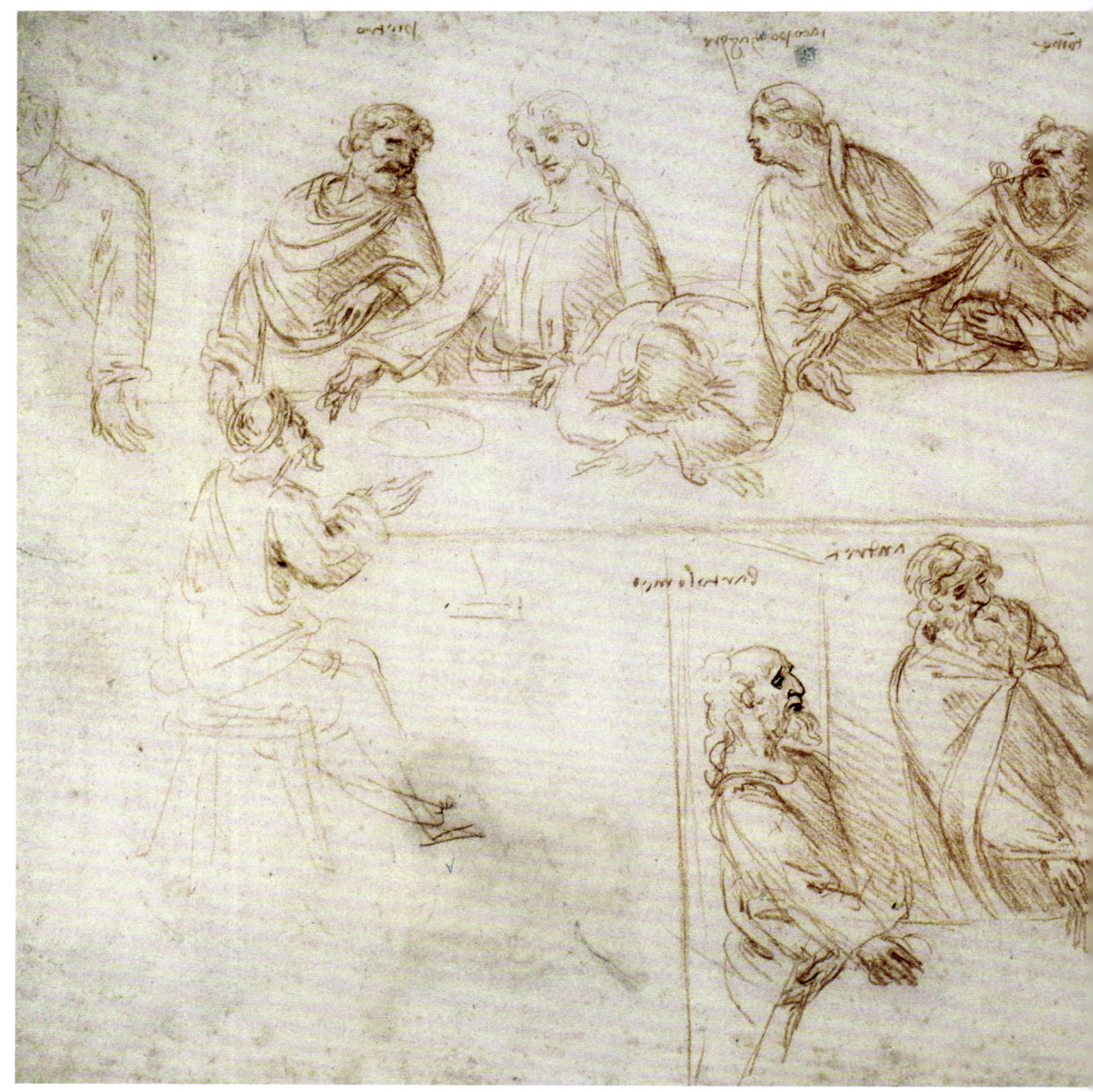

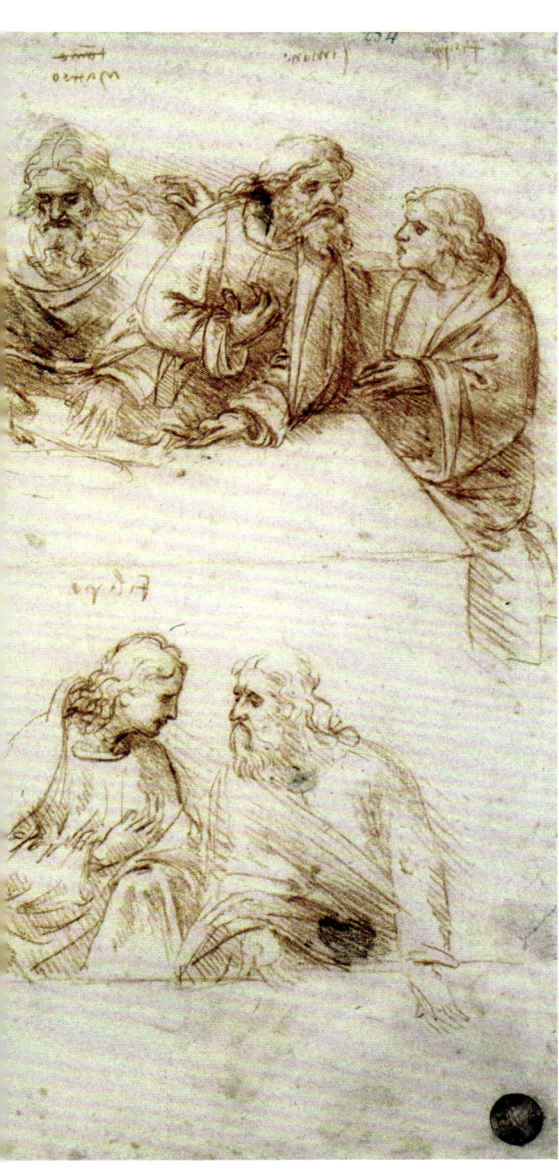

The Last Supper, preparatory drawing

La Cène, **esquisse préparatoire**

Das letzte Abendmahl, **Skizze**

La Última Cena, **esbozo**

L'Ultima Cena, **schizzo**

Het Laatste Avondmaal, **schets**

1495–97, Sepia ink on linen paper/Encre sépia sur papier de lin, Galleria dell' Accademia, Venezia

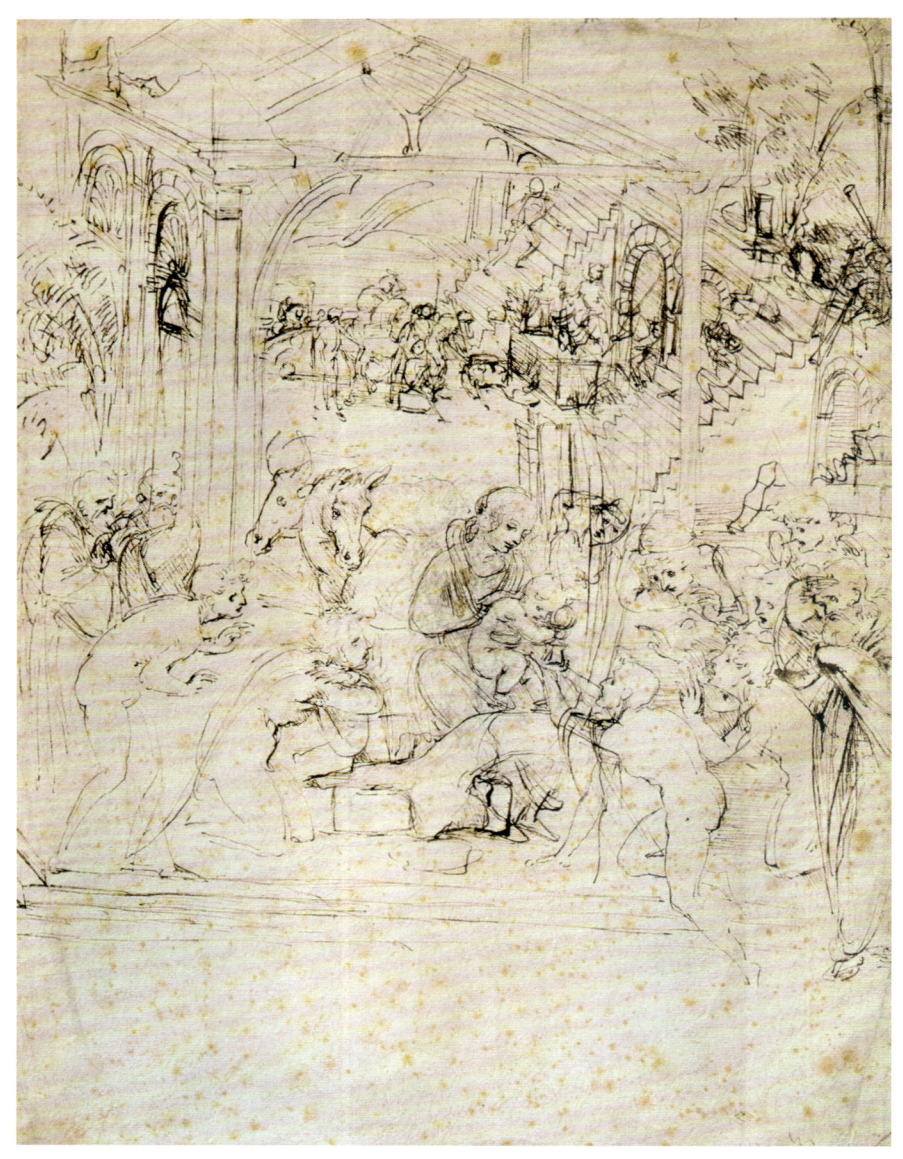

The Adoration of the Magi, composition sketch

L'Adoration des mages, étude de composition

Die Anbetung der Könige aus dem Morgenland, Kompositionsskizze

La adoración de los Reyes Magos, esbozo de composición

L'Adorazione dei Magi, schizzo per la composizione

De aanbidding door de Wijzen uit het Morgenland, compositieschets

1481, Pen and ink on paper/Plume et encre sur papier, Galleria degli Uffizi, Firenze

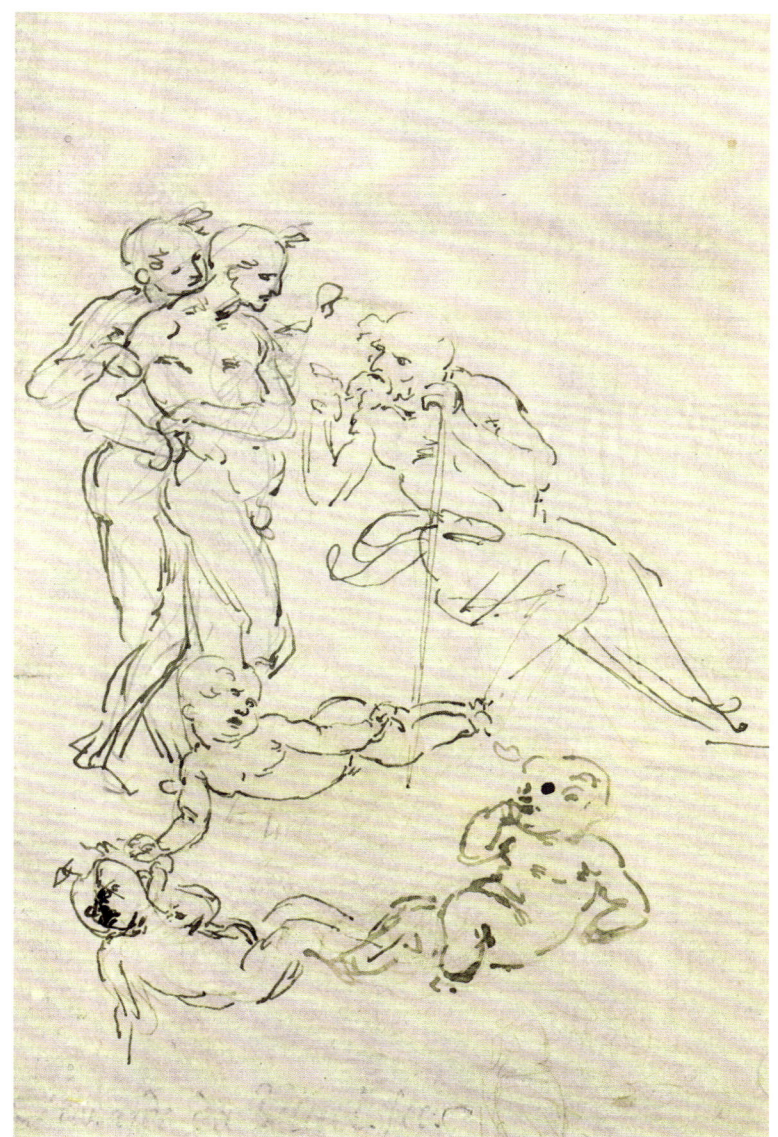

Figural study for the *Adoration of the Magi* (Joseph and two shepherds and sketches for the Christ Child)

L'Adoration des mages (Joseph et deux bergers, études pour l'Enfant Jésus)

Die Anbetung der Könige aus dem Morgenland (Joseph und zwei Schäfer und Skizzen des Jesuskindes), Figurenstudie

La adoración de los Reyes Magos (San José y dos pastorcillos y esbozos del niño Jesús), estudio de figuras

L'Adorazione dei Magi (Giuseppe, due pastori e schizzi di Gesù Bambino), studio di figure

De aanbidding door de Wijzen uit het Morgenland (Jozef en twee herders; schetsen van het Jezuskind, figurenstudie)

c. 1481, Pen and ink on paper/Plume et encre sur papier, Kunsthalle, Hamburg

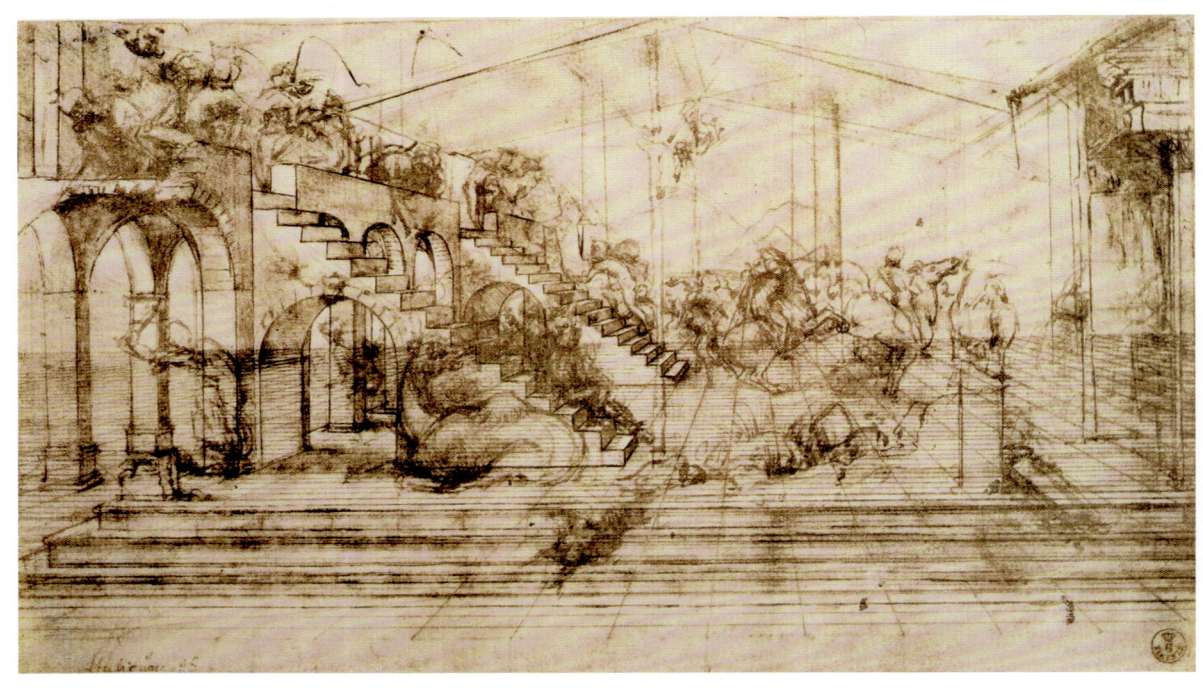

Perspective study for the background of *The Adoration of the Magi*

Étude de perspective pour l'arrière-plan de *L'Adoration des mages*

Perspektivische Studie für den Hintergrund der *Anbetung der Könige aus dem Morgenland*

Estudio de la perspectiva para el segundo plano de *La adoración de los Reyes Magos*

Studio prospettico per lo sfondo dell'*Adorazione dei Magi*

Perspectiefstudie voor de achtergrond van *De aanbidding van de Wijzen*

Pen and ink on paper/Plume et encre sur papier, Galleria degli Uffizi, Firenze

116

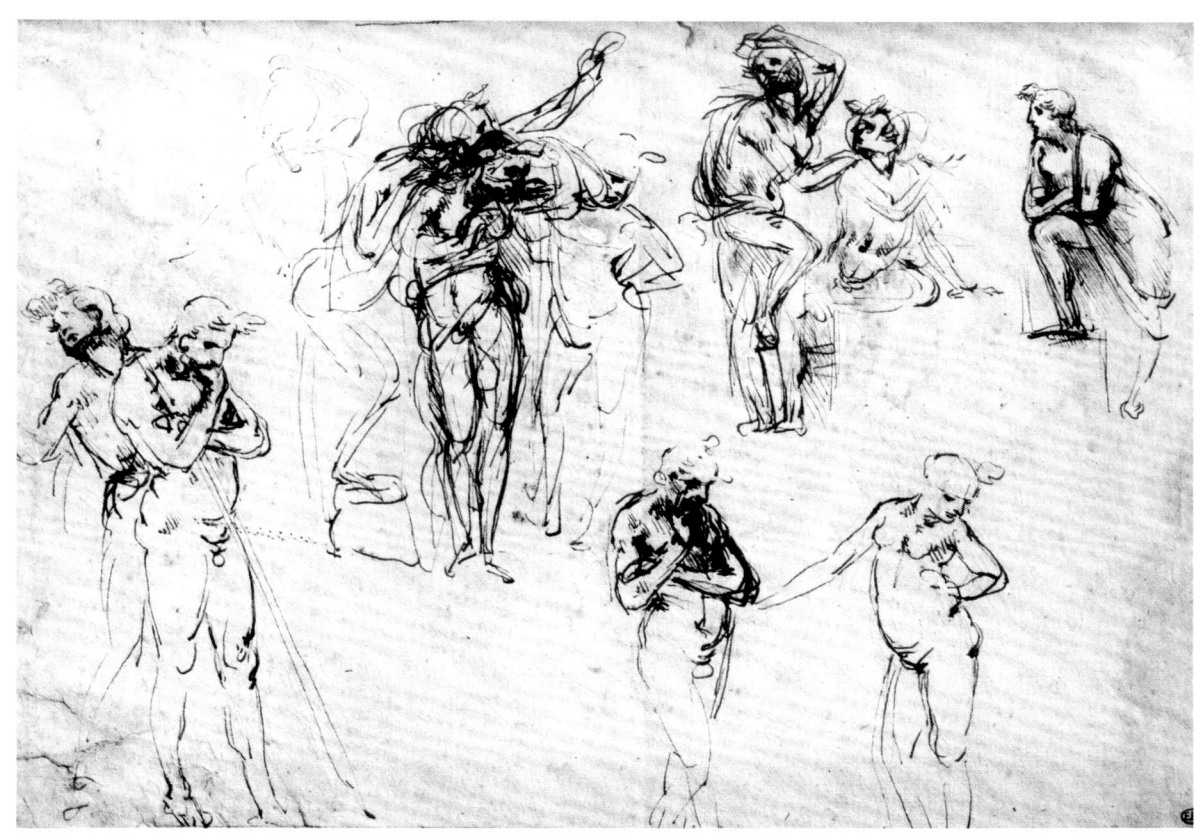

Study of nude men

Étude de nus masculins

Studie mit männlichen Akten

Estudio del desnudo masculino

Studio con nudi maschili

Studie met mannelijke naakten

Pen and ink on paper/Plume et encre sur papier, École Nationale Superieure des Beaux-Arts, Paris

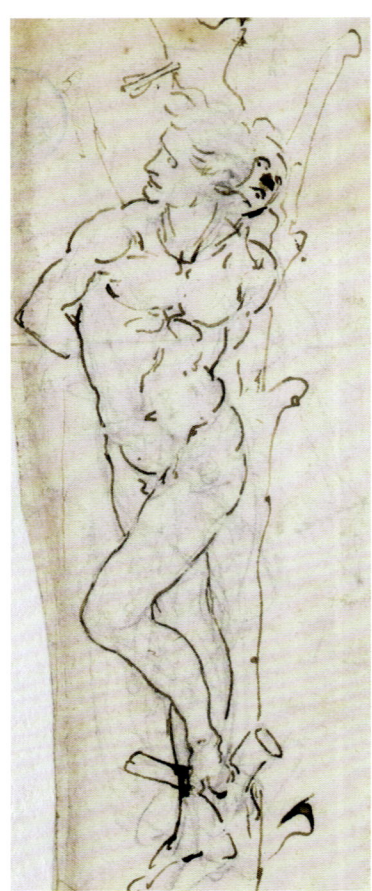

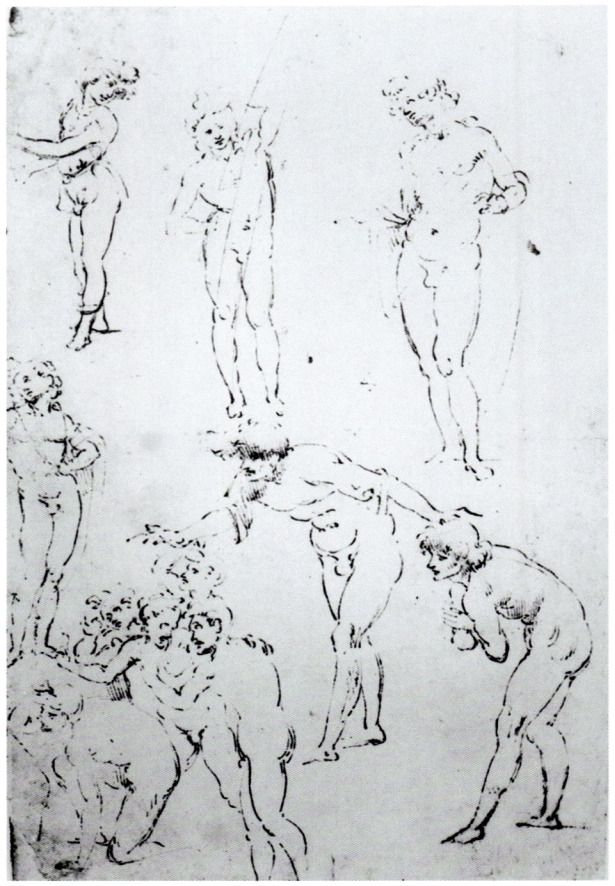

Study of St. Sebastian

Étude pour un saint Sébastien

Studie des hl. Sebastian

Estudio de San Sebastián

Studio di San Sebastiano

Studie van de Heilige Sebastiaan

1480–81, Pen and ink over pencil on paper/Plume et encre sur crayon, sur papier, 17,4 × 6,4 cm, Kunsthalle, Hamburg

Figural studies for *The Adoration of the Magi*

***L'Adoration des mages**, étude de personnages*

***Die Anbetung der Könige aus dem Morgenland**, Figurenstudie*

***La adoración de los Reyes Magos**, estudio de figuras*

***L'Adorazione dei Magi**, studio di figure*

***De aanbidding door de Wijzen uit het Morgenland**, figurenstudie*

c. 1481, Pen and ink on paper/Plume et encre sur papier, Wallraf-Richartz-Museum & Fondation Corboud, Köln

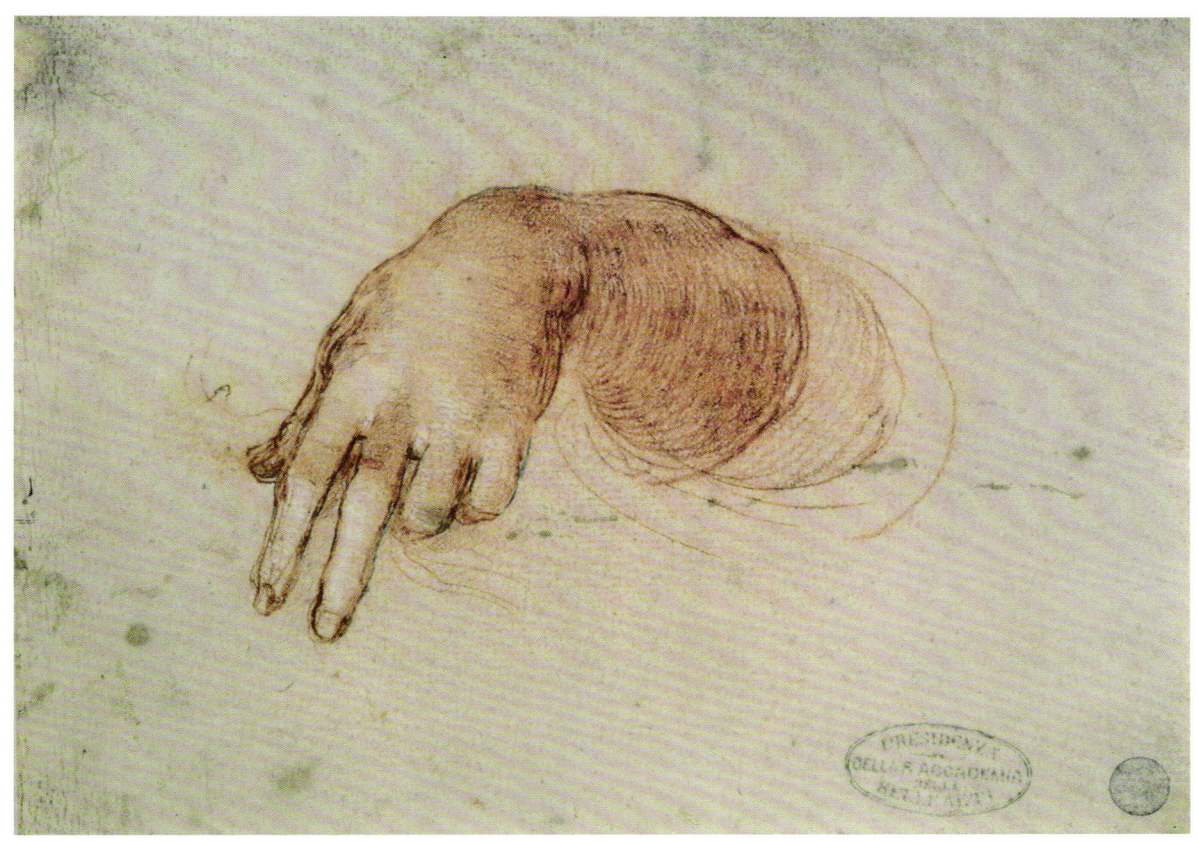

Study of a hand

Étude de main

Studie einer Hand

Estudio de una mano

Studio di una mano

Studie van hand

Red chalk on paper/Sanguine sur papier, Galleria dell' Accademia, Venezia

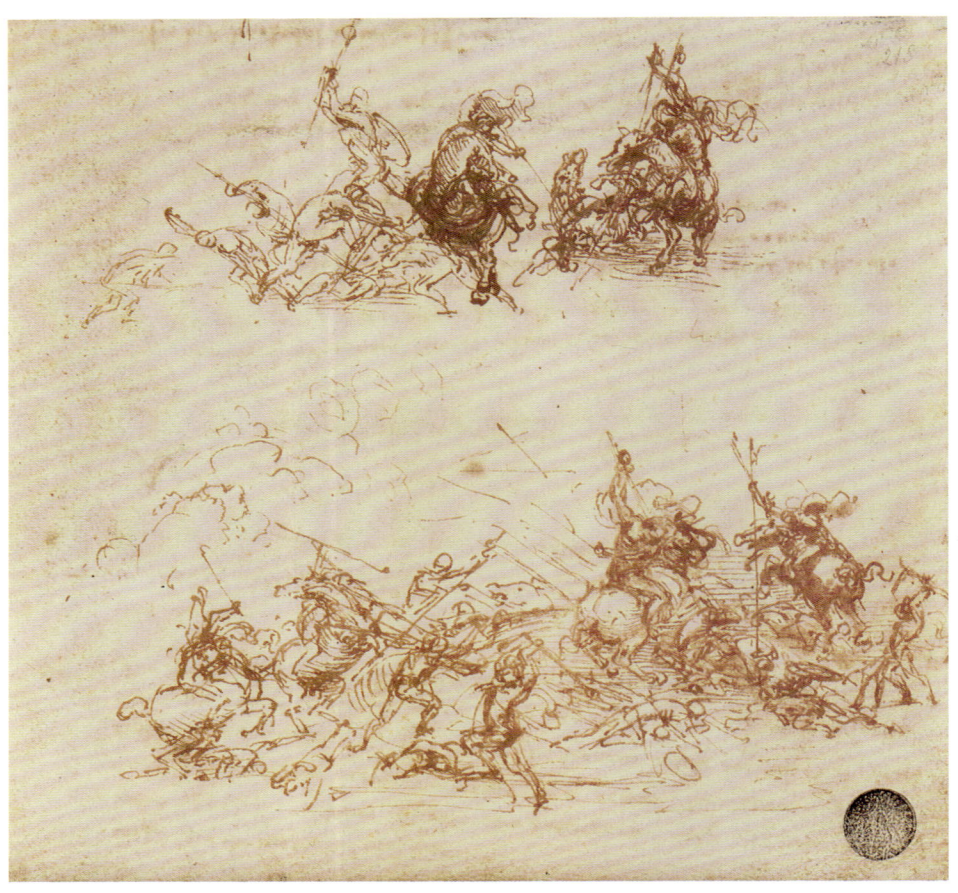

Study of horsemen in combat and foot soldiers

Étude de cavaliers et de fantassins combattants

Studie von Reitern im Kampf und Fußsoldaten

Estudio de jinetes en la batalla contra soldados de tierra

Studio di cavalieri in battaglia e fanti

Studie van ruiters in de strijd en voetsoldaten

1503, Pen and ink on paper/Plume et encre sur papier,
Galleria dell' Accademia, Venezia

Study of horsemen in combat and foot soldiers

Étude de cavaliers et de fantassins combattants

Studie von Reitern im Kampf und Fußsoldaten

Estudio de jinetes en la batalla contra soldados de tierra

Studio di cavalieri in battaglia e fanti

Studie van ruiters in de strijd en voetsoldaten

1503, Pen and ink on paper/
Plume et encre sur papier,
Galleria dell' Accademia,
Venezia

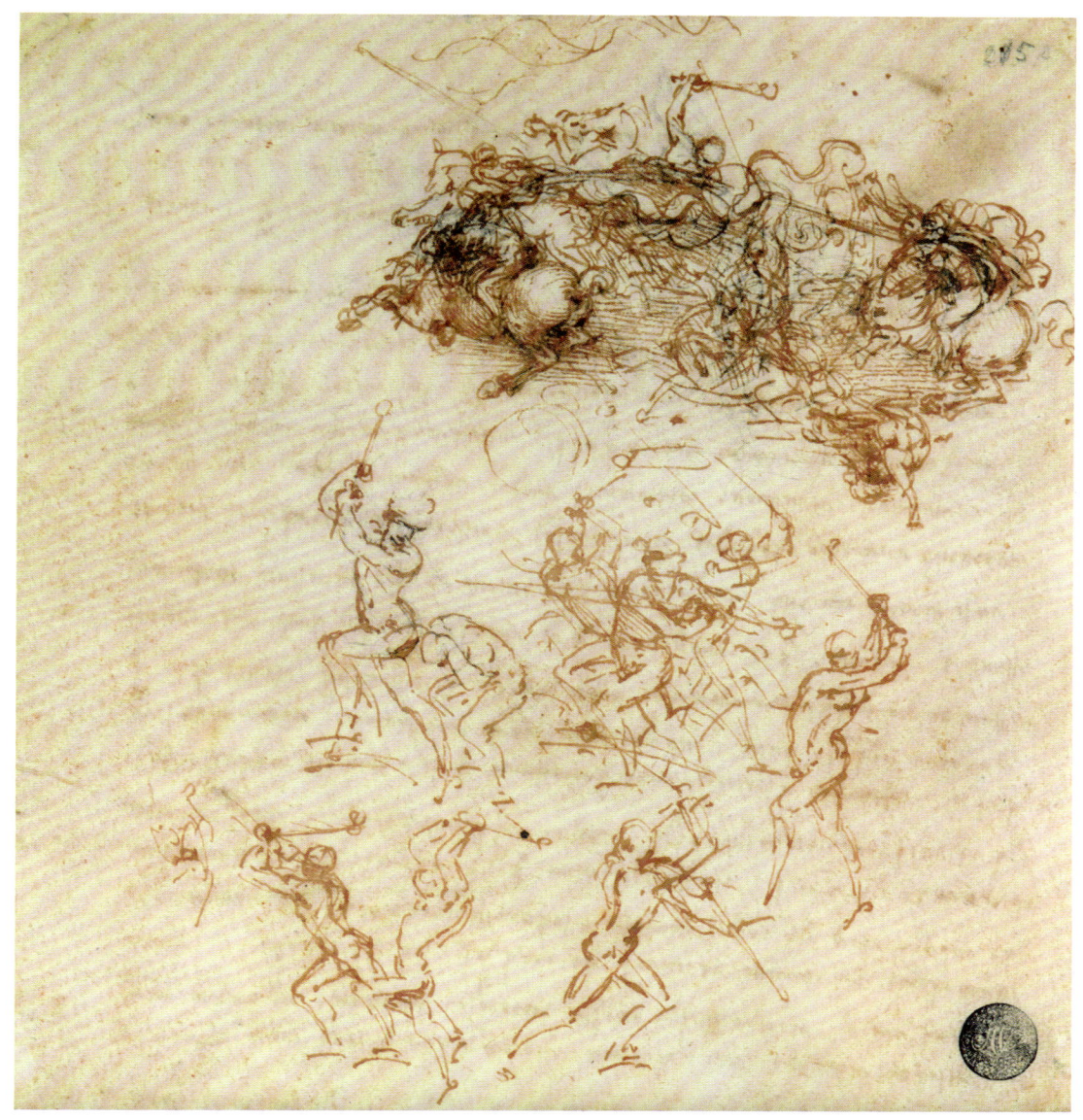

121

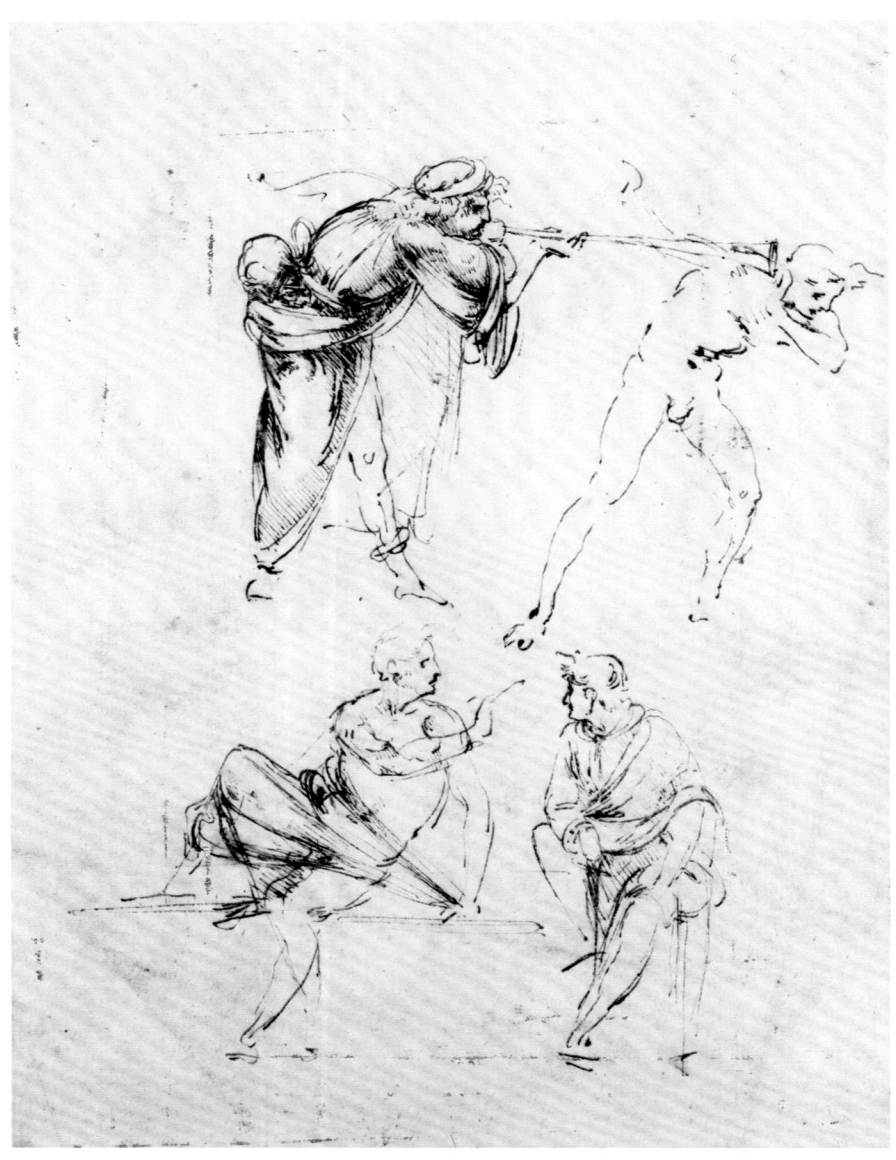

Study of a man blowing a trumpet in another's ear

Étude d'un homme qui joue de la trompette dans l'oreille d'un autre

Studie eines Mannes, der einem anderen die Trompete ins Ohr spielt

Estudio de un hombre, que toca la trompeta al oído de otro hombre

Studio di uomo che suona la tromba nelle orecchie di un altro

Studie van een man die een ander met een trompet in het oor toetert

c. 1480–82, Pen and ink on paper/ Plume et encre sur papier, British Museum, London

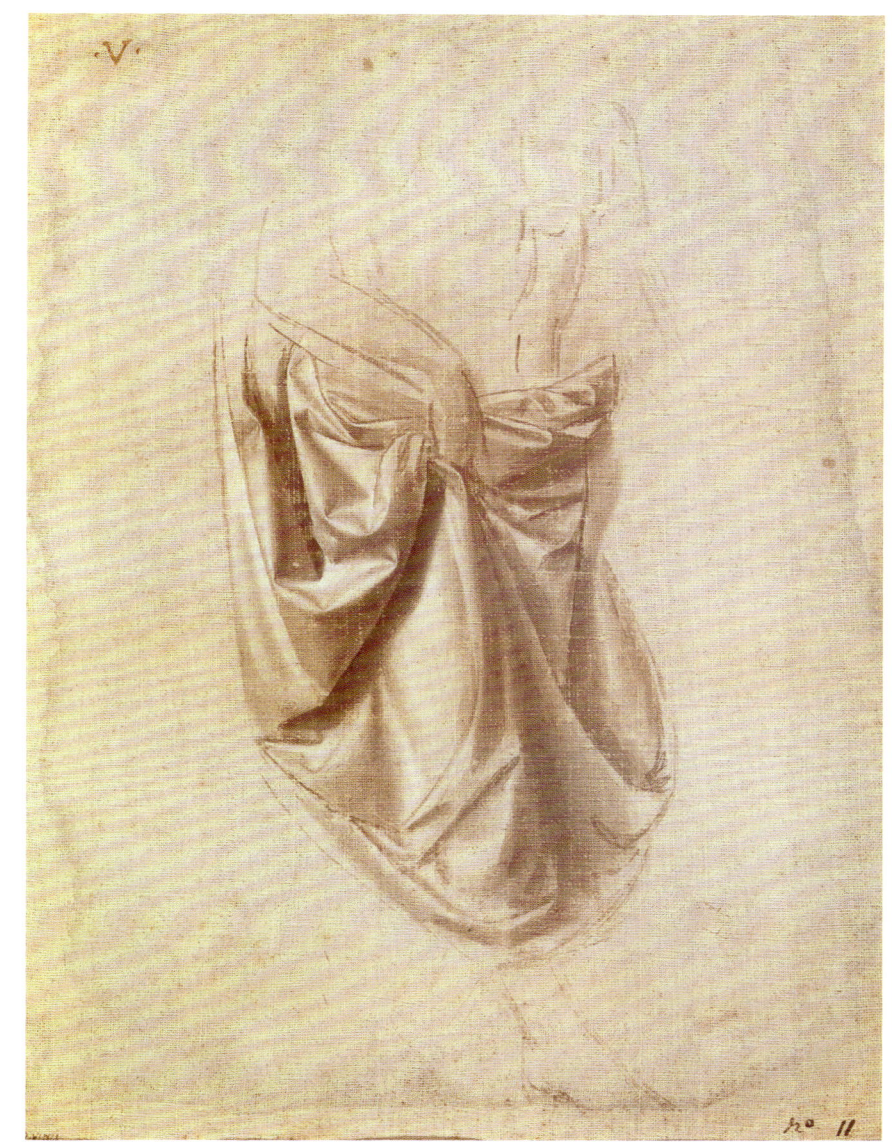

Drapery study

Étude d'habits

Gewandstudie

Estudio de la ropa

Studio di un drappeggio

Studie van een gewaad

Gouache on canvas/Gouache sur toile,
Musee des Beaux-Arts, Rennes

123

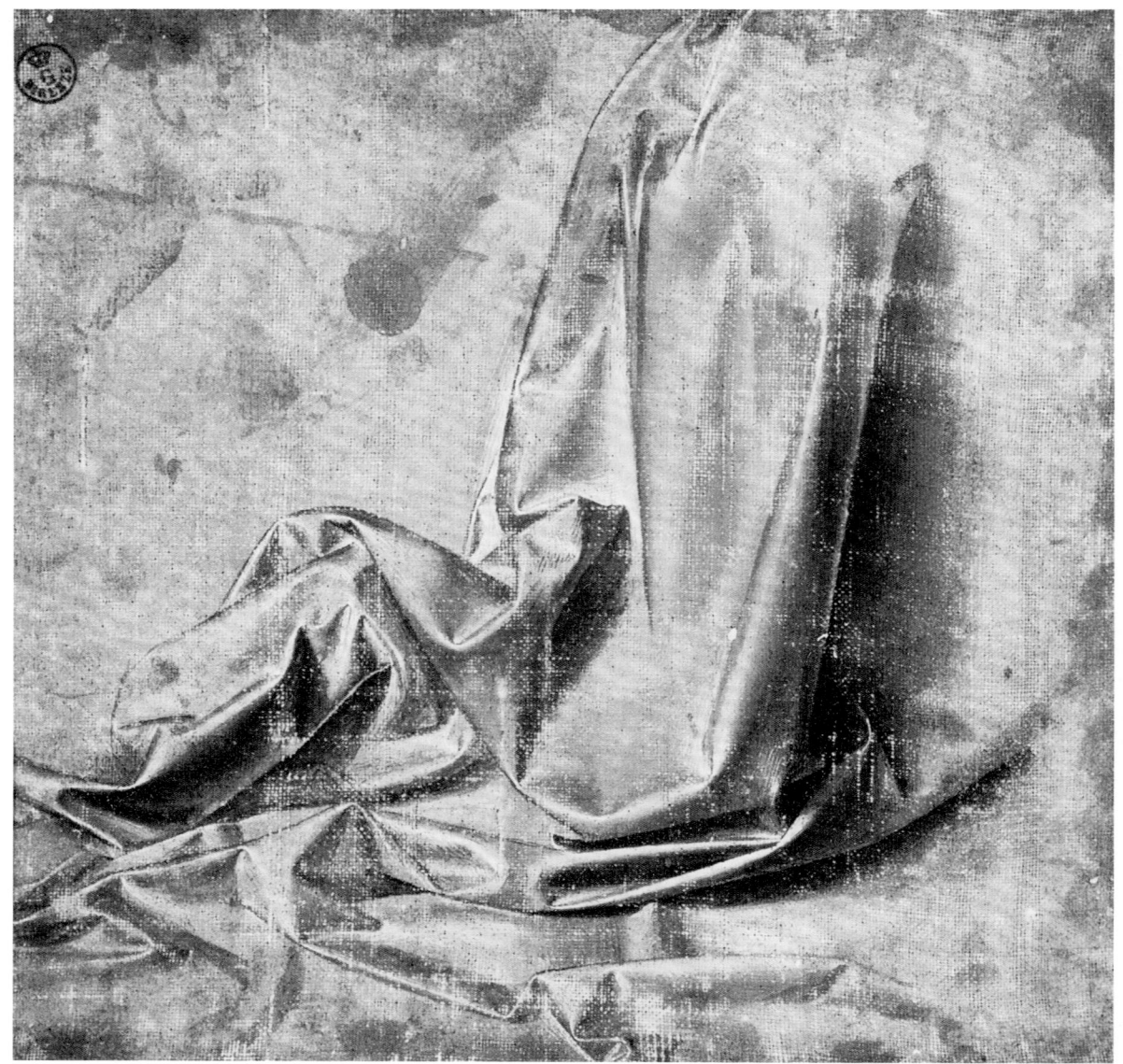

**Drapery study for a kneeling figure
in profil perdu to the right**

**Étude d'habits pour un personnage
agenouillé, en profil droit esquissé**

**Gewandstudie für eine kniende Figur
im verlorenen Profil nach rechts**

**Estudio de una figura de rodillas
del perfil derecho perdido**

**Studio del drappeggio di una figura
inginocchiata in profil perdu verso destra**

**Studie van een gewaad voor een knielende
figuur, verloren rechterprofiel**

*c. 1472–75, Brush and grey tempera with white
heightening on canvas/Pinceau et détrempe
brunâtre avec des rehauts de blanc, sur papier,
16,4 × 16,8 cm, Galleria degli Uffizi, Firenze*

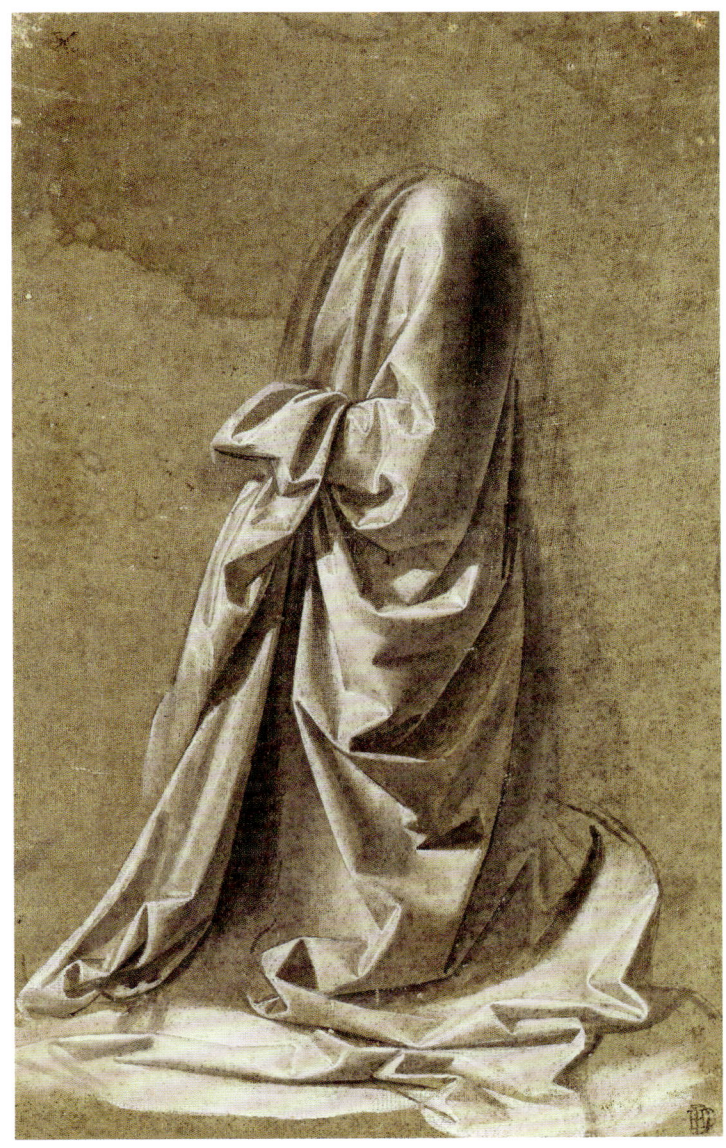

Drapery study for a kneeling figure

**Étude d'habits pour un
personnage agenouillé**

Gewandstudie für eine kniende Figur

Estudio de la ropa de una figura de rodilla

**Studio del drappeggio di una
figura inginocchiata**

**Studie van een gewaad voor
een knielende figuur**

*Brush and bownish-grey distemper with white
heightening on linen/Pinceau et détrempe
brunâtre avec des rehauts de blanc, sur papier,
28,8 × 18,1 cm, Private collection*

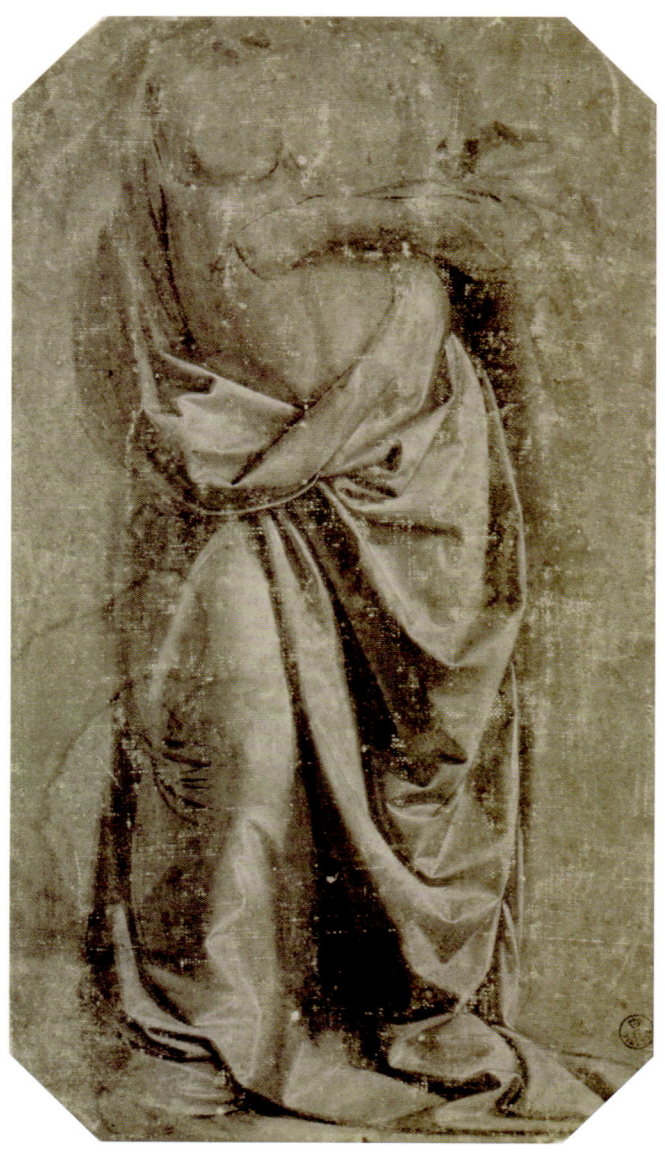

Drapery study for a standing figure seen from the front

Étude d'habits pour un personnage debout, en vue frontale

Gewandstudie für eine stehende Figur in Frontalansicht

**Estudio de la ropa de una figura de pie
desde una perspectiva frontal**

Studio del drappeggio di una figura in piedi vista di fronte

Studie van een gewaad voor een staande frontale figuur

*1478–80, Termpera and white heightening on paper/Détrempe et
rehauts de blanc sur papier, Galleria degli Uffizi, Firenze*

Drapery study for a seated figure

Étude d'habits pour un personnage assis

Gewandstudie einer sitzenden Figur

Estudio de la ropa de una figura sentada

Studio del drappeggio di una figura seduta

Studie van een gewaad voor een zittende figuur

*c. 1475–80, Oil on canvas/Huile sur toile,
26,6 × 23,3 cm, Musée du Louvre, Paris*

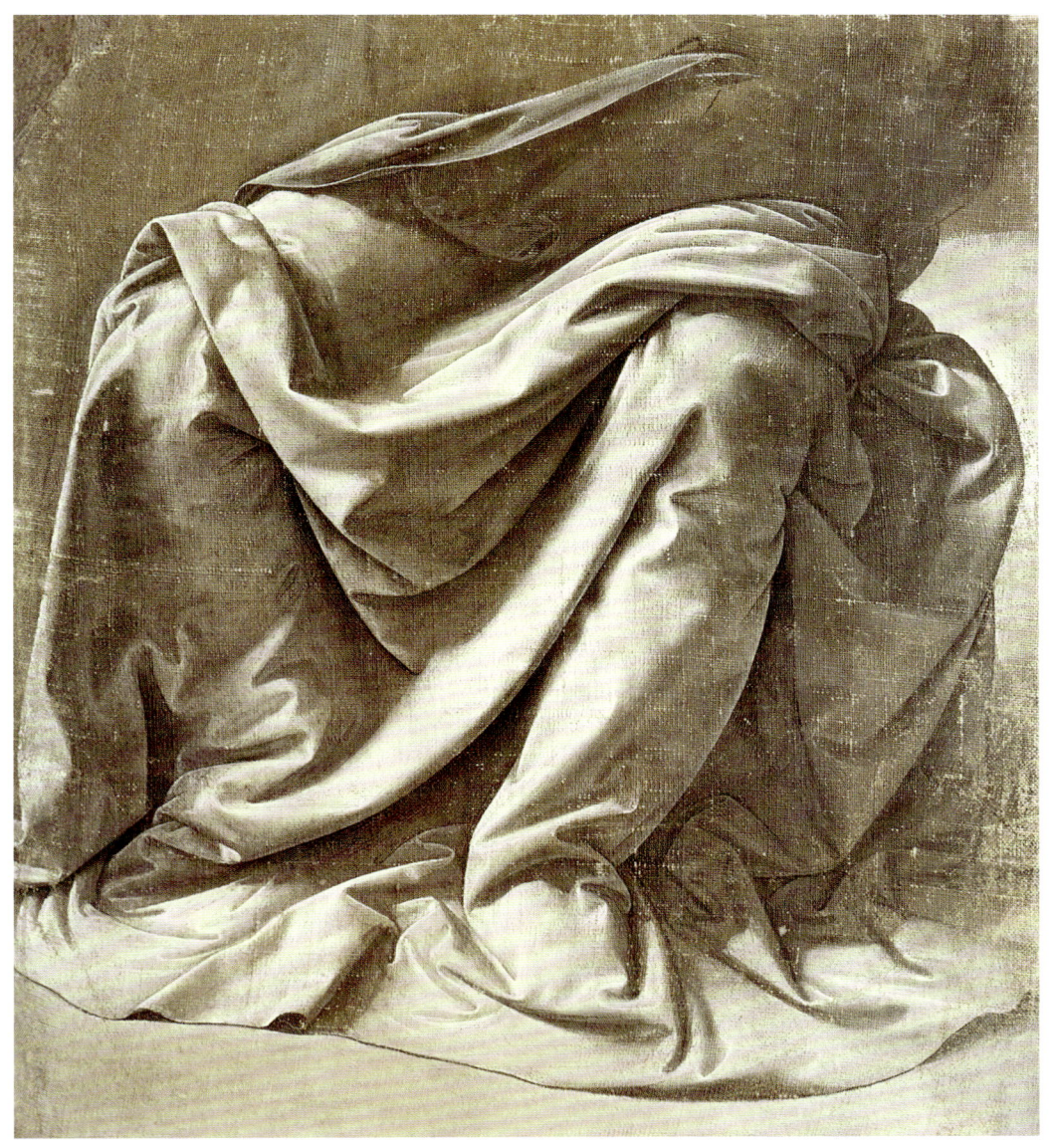

Natural science studies

Throughout almost his entire artistic life, Leonardo dealt with scientific problems, with astronomy and optics as well as with botany and anatomy. His approach was always empirical or observational; he did not think much of experiments.

Lacking formal education in both Latin and mathematics, Leonardo was not taken seriously by contemporary scholars, even though he taught himself Latin during his time in Milan and studied mathematics under Luca Pacioli.

The *Codex Leicester* provides the best overview of the almost limitless spectrum of his scientific interests.

L'étude des sciences de la nature

Durant presque toute sa vie d'artiste, Léonard s'est intéressé aux sciences naturelles, aux questions de l'astronomie et de l'optique tout comme ceux de la botanique et de l'anatomie. Si sa démarche était toujours empirique, peu de ses réalisations ont vu réellement le jour.

Sans éducation scolaire en latin ni en mathématique, Léonard n'était pas pris très au sérieux par les scientifiques de son temps – bien qu'il eût appris le latin lui-même pendant son séjour milanais et que le franciscain Luca Pacioli lui eût donné des leçons de mathématique.

Les soixante-douze pages du *Codex Leicester* offrent la meilleure vue d'ensemble du champ presque illimité de ses intérêts scientifiques.

Naturwissenschaftliche Studien

Fast sein gesamtes Künstlerleben hindurch beschäftigte sich Leonardo mit naturwissenschaftlichen Problemen, mit Astronomie und Optik ebenso wie mit Botanik und Anatomie. Sein Ansatz dabei war immer ein empirischer, von Experimenten hielt er offenkundig nicht viel.

Ohne formale Ausbildung weder in Latein noch in Mathematik, wurde Leonardo von zeitgenössischen Wissenschaftlern nicht recht ernst genommen, auch wenn er sich in seiner Mailänder Zeit selbst Latein beibringen sollte und bei Luca Pacioli Unterricht in Mathematik nahm.

Den besten Überblick über das schier unbegrenzte Spektrum seiner wissenschaftlichen Interessen bietet der *Codex Leicester*.

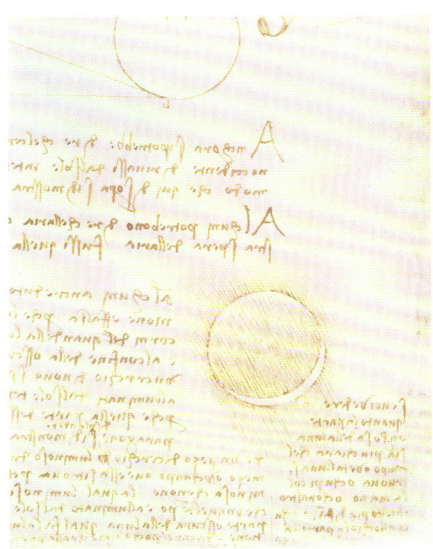

Codex Leicester

Detail showing the outer luminosity of the moon

Détail sur la « lumière cendrée » du clair de lune

Detail mit dem sogenannten „aschgrünen Mondschein"

Detalle con la denominada "luz de luna color ceniza verde"

Dettaglio con la cosiddetta "luce cinerea della luna"

Detail met de zogenaamde "asgroene maneschijn"

1508–12, Pen and ink on paper/Plume et encre sur papier, Private collection

Estudios científicos

Leonardo estudió durante casi toda su vida artística disciplinas científicas como la astronomía y la óptica, así como la botánica y la anatomía. Siempre se basó en un punto de partida empírico. Es notorio que no creía mucho en los experimentos.

Al no contar con estudios formales ni en latín, ni en matemáticas, los científicos de su época no lo tomaban realmente en serio. Por ello en su época de Milán intentaría aprender latín de forma autodidacta e iría a clases de matemáticas con Luca Pacioli.

El *Codex Leicester* ofrece una visión global del espectro casi ilimitado de sus intereses científicos.

Studi di scienze naturali

Per quasi tutta la sua vita artistica Leonardo si dedicò ai problemi di scienze naturali, di astronomia e ottica, oltre a botanica e anatomia. Essendo il suo approccio sempre di tipo empirico, é evidente che agli esperimenti non teneva molto.

Senza un'istruzione formale né in latino né in matematica, Leonardo non fu preso sul serio dagli scienziati suoi contemporanei, anche se durante il suo soggiorno a Milano imparò il latino da autodidatta e prese lezioni di matematica da Luca Pacioli.

La sintesi migliore della gamma pressoché illimitata dei suoi interessi scientifici è fornita dal *Codice Leicester*.

Natuurwetenschappelijke studies

Leonardo wijdde zich zijn gehele volwassen leven aan natuurwetenschappelijke kwesties, van de astronomie en de optica tot de botanica en de anatomie. Zijn uitgangspunt was daarbij altijd de empirische werkelijkheid, in plaats van theoretische experimenten.

Zonder formele opleiding in het Latijn en de wiskunde werd Leonardo door zijn academische tijdgenoten niet helemaal serieus genomen, ook al bracht hij zichzelf in zijn Milanese periode het Latijn bij en ging hij later in de leer bij de wiskundige Luca Pacioli.

Het beste overzicht van zijn schier eindeloze interesse in wetenschappelijke thema's biedt de *Codex Leicester*.

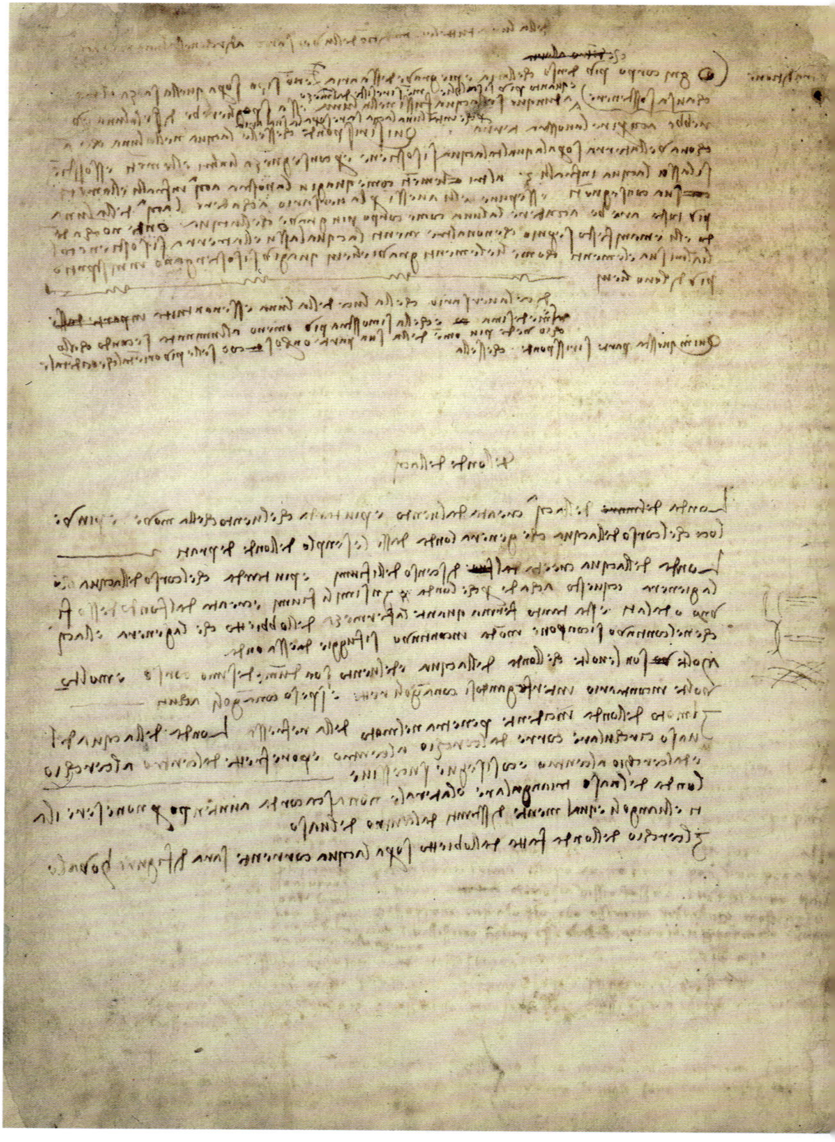

Codex Leicester

Studies of the illumination of the moon

Étude de clair de lune

Studien zum Mondlicht

Estudios de la luz de la luna

Studi della luce lunare

Studies van maneschijn

1508–12, Sepia ink on linen paper/Encre sépia sur papier de lin, Private collection

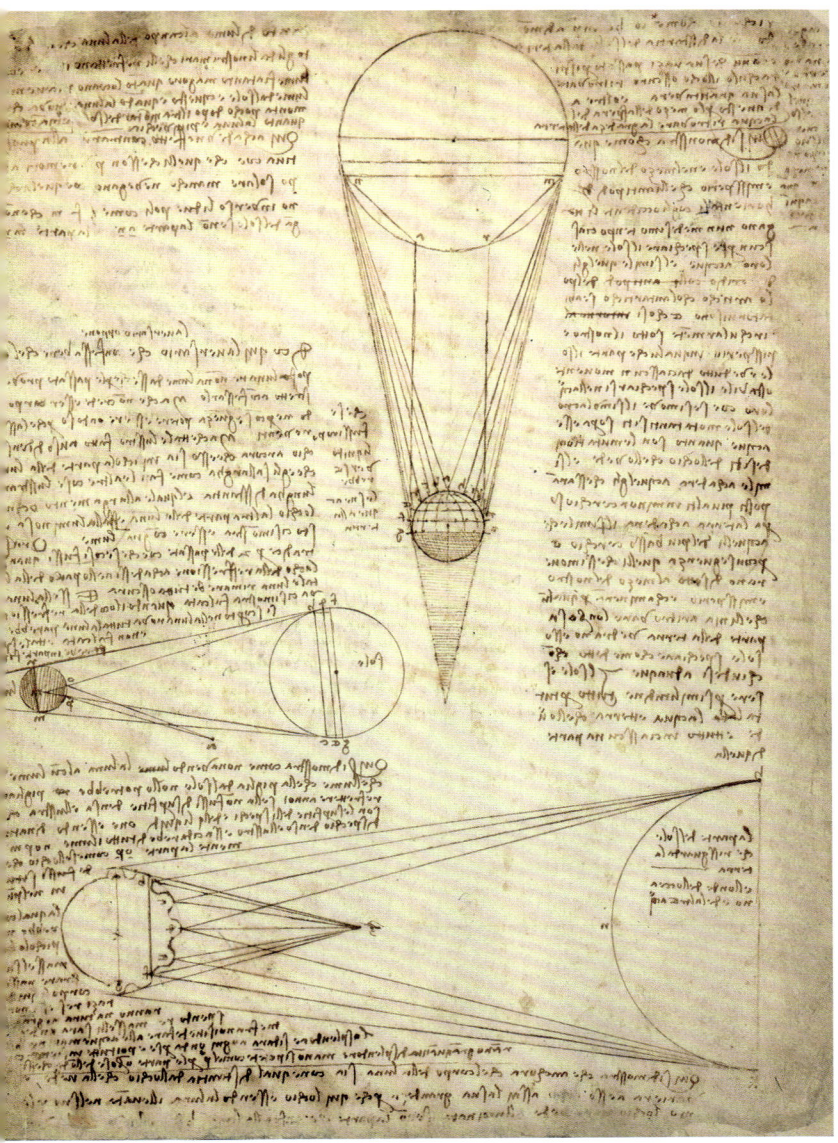

On this page of the *Codex Leicester,* Leonardo compares the brightness of the Sun with that of the Moon.

Sur cette page du *Codex Leicester,* Léonard compare la luminosité du Soleil avec celle de la Lune.

Auf dieser Seite des *Codex Leicester* behandelt Leonardo die Helligkeit der Sonne im Vergleich zu der des Mondes.

En esta página del *Códice Leicester* Leonardo trata el tema de la luminosidad del sol comparada con la de la luna.

In questa pagina del *Codice Leicester* Leonardo confronta la luminosità del sole con quella della luna.

Op deze bladzijde van de *Codex Leicester* behandelt Leonardo de helderheid van de zon in vergelijking tot die van de maan.

Codex Leicester

1508–12, Sepia ink on linen paper/Encre sépia sur papier de lin, Private collection

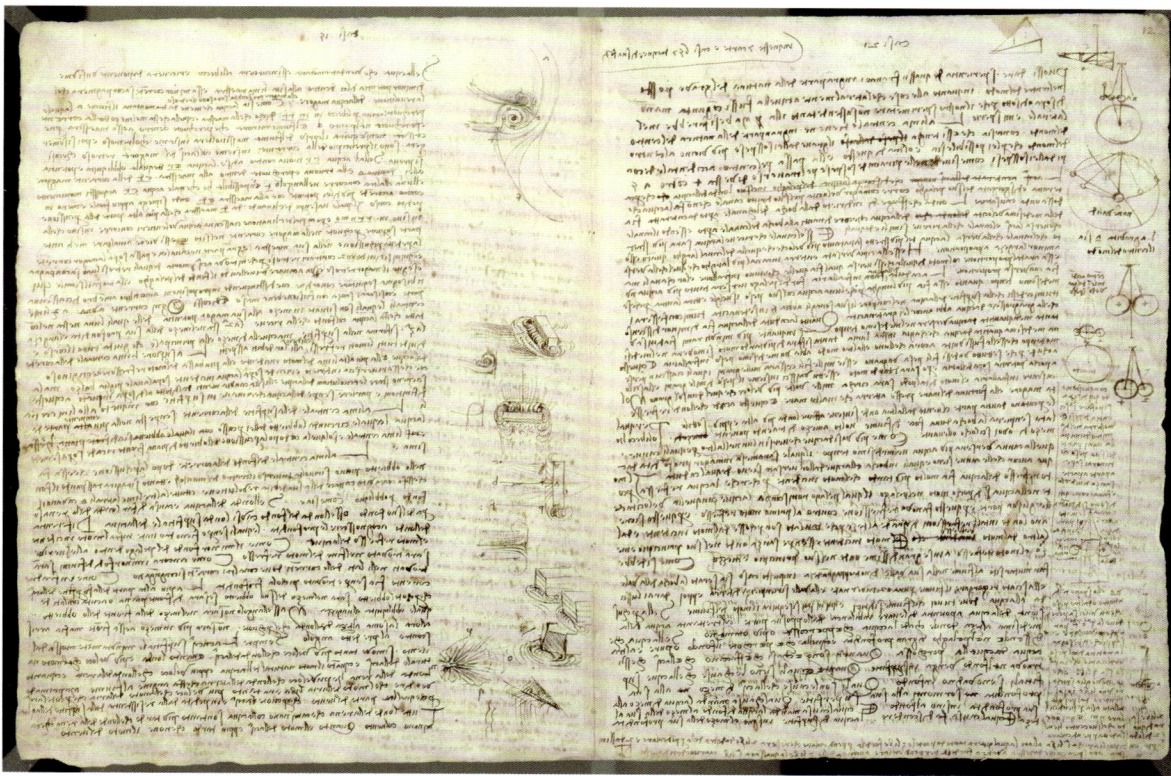

Codex Leicester

Scientific sketch

Croquis de sciences naturelles

Naturwissenschaftliche Skizze

Esbozo científico

Schizzo scientifico

Natuurwetenschappelijke schets

1508–12, Sepia ink on linen paper/Encre sépia sur papier de lin, Private collection

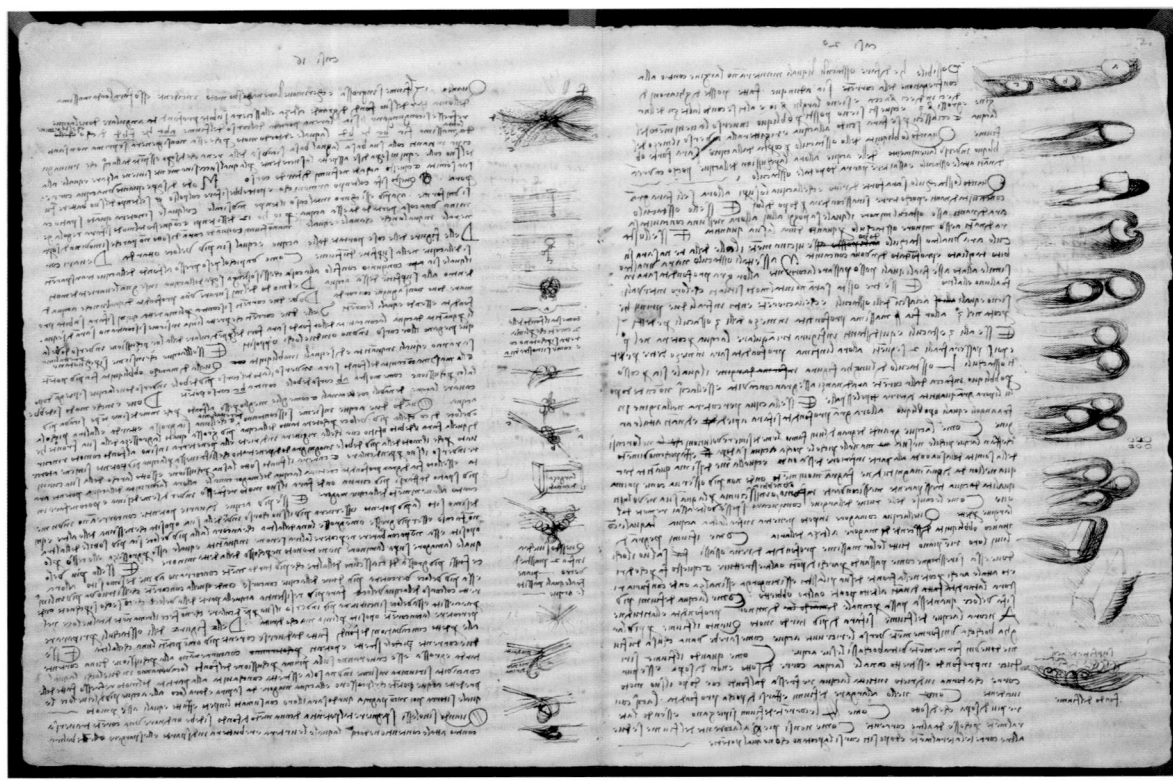

Codex Leicester

Scientific sketch

Croquis de sciences naturelles

Naturwissenschaftliche Skizze

Esbozo científico

Schizzo scientifico

Natuurwetenschappelijke schets

1508–12, Sepia ink on linen paper/Encre sépia sur papier de lin, Private collection

Codex Leicester
Scientific sketch
Croquis de sciences naturelles
Naturwissenschaftliche Skizze
Esbozo científico
Schizzo scientifico
Natuurwetenschappelijke schets

1508–12, Sepia ink on linen paper/Encre sépia sur papier de lin, Private collection

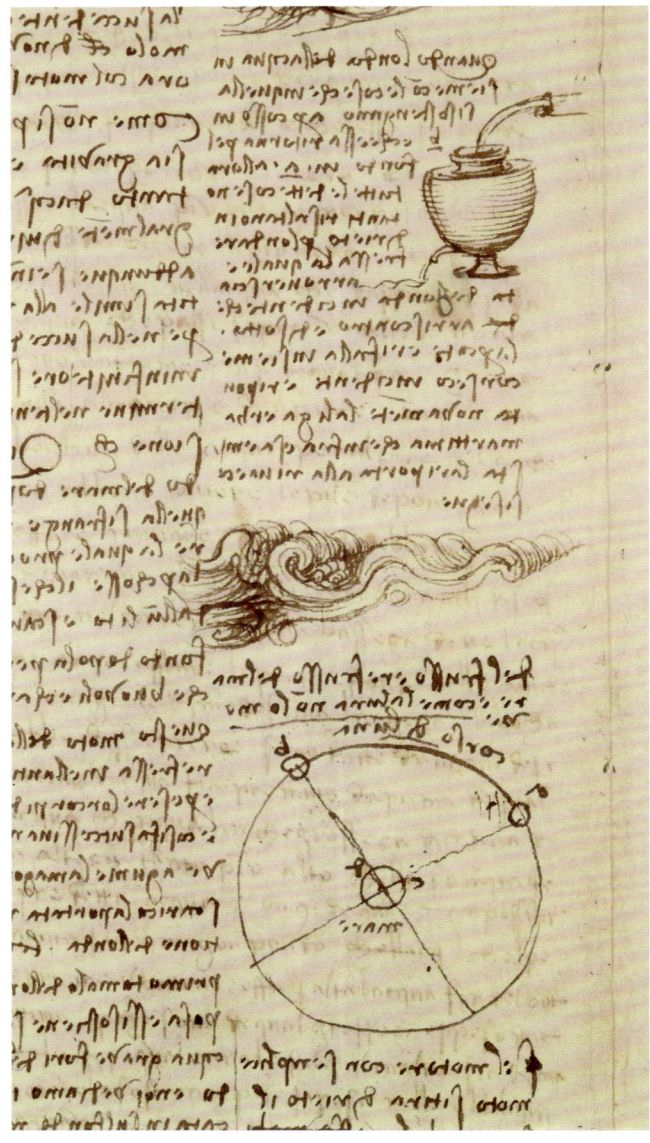

In the *Codex Leicester,* Leonardo devoted 18 pages to questions concerning the behaviour of water: currents, whirlpools, waves, channels—there was little that did not take his interest. On these pages, for example, he examines flow velocities and the methods used to measure these. Today's owner of the *Codex Leicester* is the billionaire Bill Gates, who acquired it in 1994 for more than 30 million dollars.

Dans le *Codex Leicester,* Léonard consacre dix-huit pages essentiellement au thème de l'eau : courants, tourbillons, vagues, canaux – peu de phénomènes ont échappé à son attention. Ces pages traite par exemple de la vitesse des courants et des méthodes pour la mesurer. L'actuel possesseur du *Codex Leicester* est le milliardaire américain Bill Gates qui l'a acheté en 1994 pour plus de 30 millions de dollars.

Im *Codex Leicester* widmet sich Leonardo auf 18 Blättern vor allem Fragen rund ums Thema Wasser: Strömungen, Strudel, Wellen, Kanäle – kaum etwas, für das er sich nicht interessiert hätte. Auf diesen Seiten geht es zum Beispiel um Strömungsgeschwindigkeiten und Methoden, diese zu messen. Der heutige Besitzer des *Codex Leicester* ist der Milliardär Bill Gates, der ihn im Jahr 1994 für mehr als 30 Millionen Dollar ersteigert hatte.

En el *Códice Leicester* Leonardo trata, en 18 folios, sobre todo cuestiones relacionadas con el agua: corrientes, remolinos, olas, canales –no hay prácticamente un tema por el que no se interesara-. Estes folios por ejemplo trata las velocidades de las corrientes y métodos para medirlas. El Códice Leicester es actualmente propiedad del multimillonario Bill Gates, que lo compró en subasta en 1994 por más de 30 millones de dólares.

Leonardo dedicò 18 fogli del *Codice Leicester* a tematiche legate all'acqua: correnti, vortici, onde, canali ecc.; argomenti per i quali non aveva mostrato prima interesse. Ad esempio, in questas paginas tratta la velocità delle correnti e i metodi per misurarla. L'attuale proprietario del Codice Leicester è il miliardario Bill Gates, che lo acquistò all'asta nel 1994 per oltre 30 milioni di dollari.

In de *Codex Leicester* wijdt Leonardo zich op achttien bladzijden vooral aan kwesties rondom het thema water: stromingen, draaikolken, golven, kanalen – weinig ontsnapte aan Leonardo's nieuwsgierigheid. Zo gaat het op deze bladzijden om stroomsnelheden en methoden om deze te meten. De huidige eigenaar van de *Codex Leicester* is de miljardair Bill Gates, die het werk op een veiling in 1994 voor ruim dertig miljoen dollar aankocht.

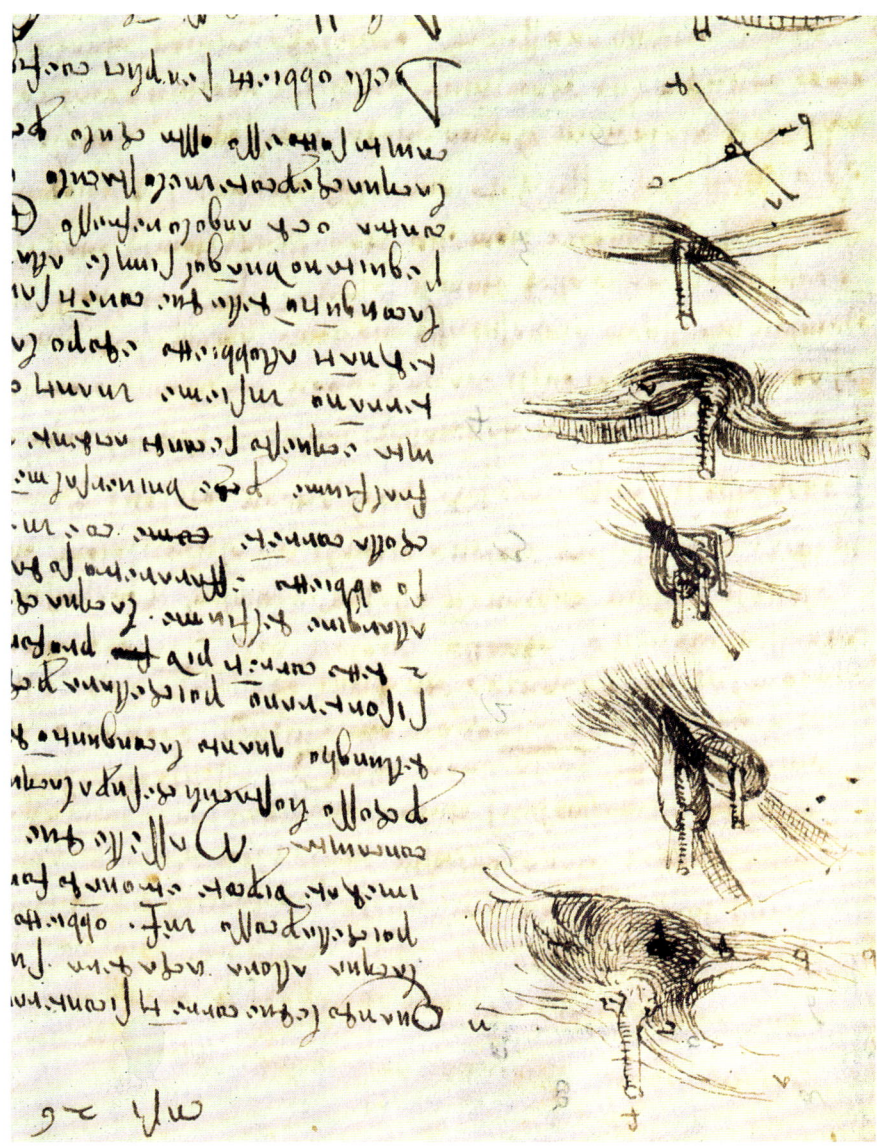

Codex Leicester
Scientific sketch
Croquis de sciences naturelles
Naturwissenschaftliche Skizze
Esbozo científico
Schizzo scientifico
Natuurwetenschappelijke schets

*1508–12, Sepia ink on linen paper/
Encre sépia sur papier de lin, Private
collection*

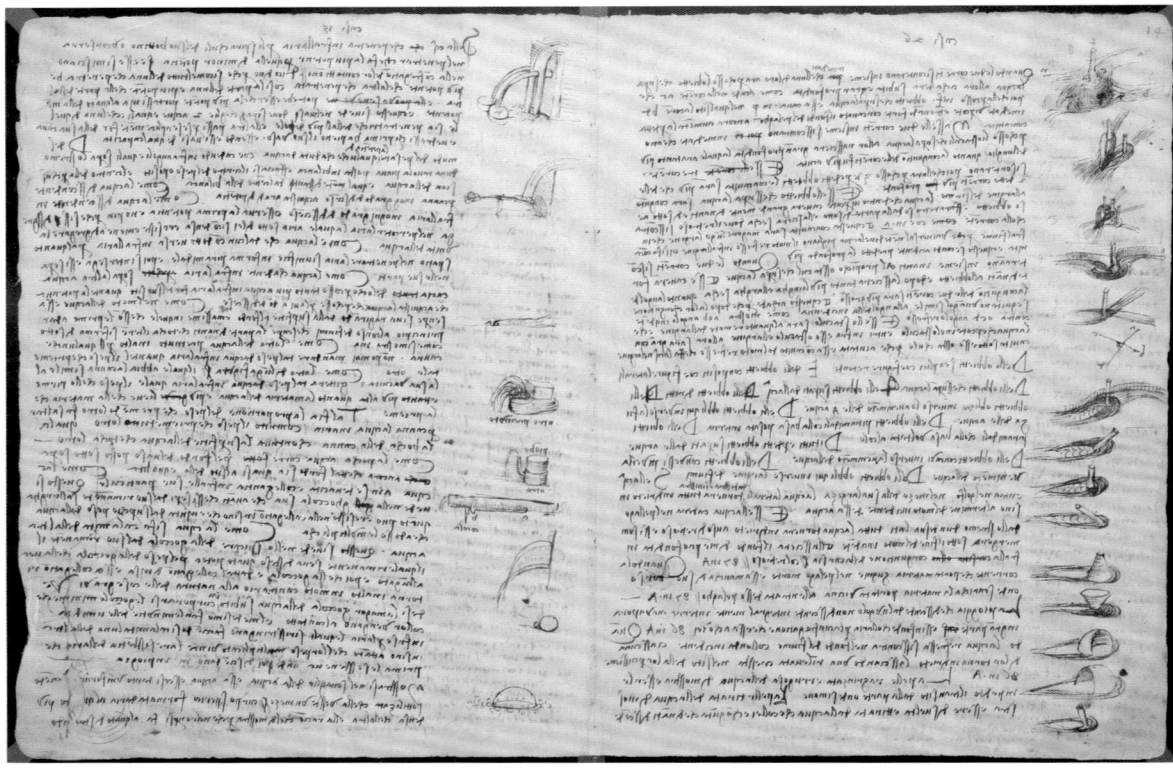

Codex Leicester

1508–12, Sepia ink on linen paper/Encre sépia sur papier de lin, Private collection

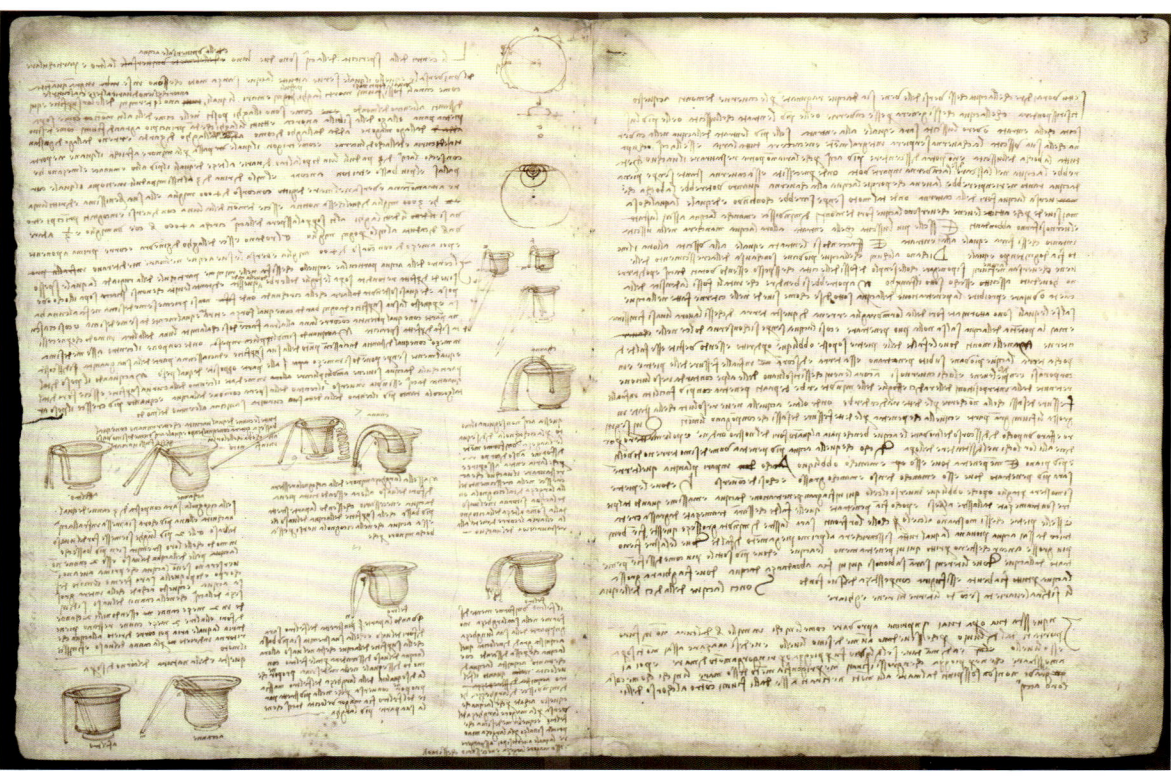

Codex Leicester

1508–12, Sepia ink on linen paper/Encre sépia sur papier de lin, Private collection

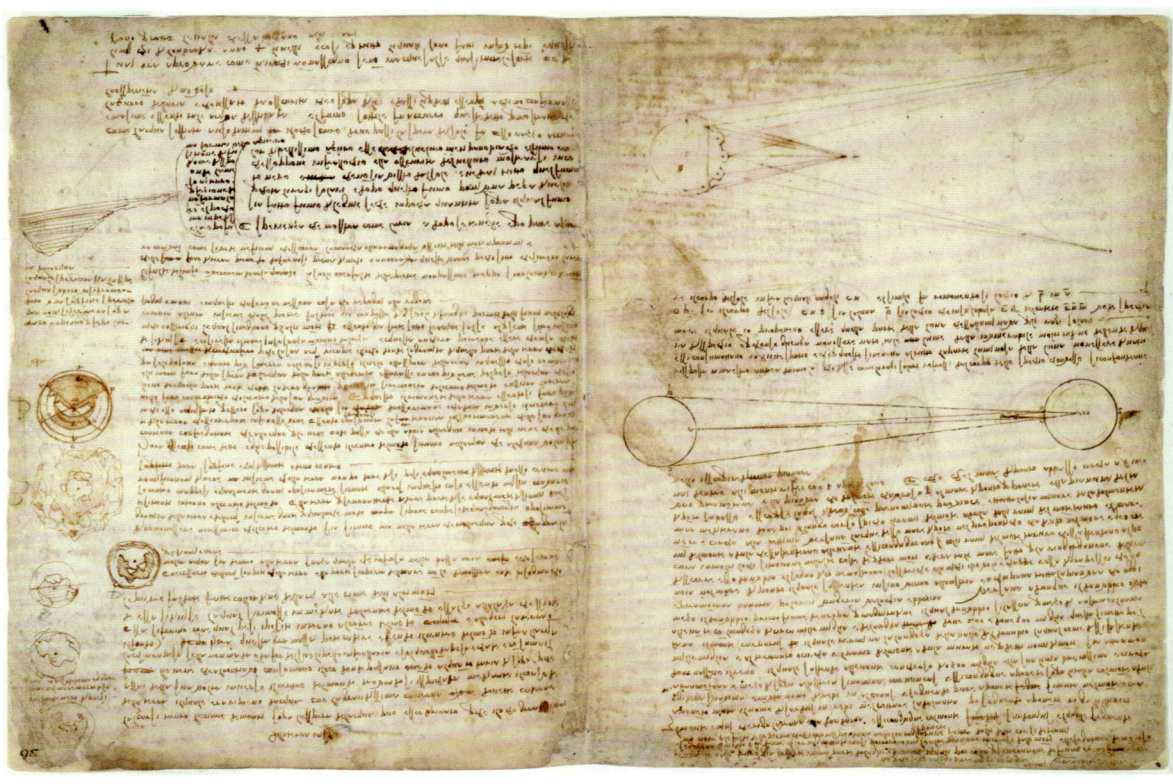

Codex Leicester

1508–12, Sepia ink on linen paper/Encre sépia sur papier de lin, Private collection

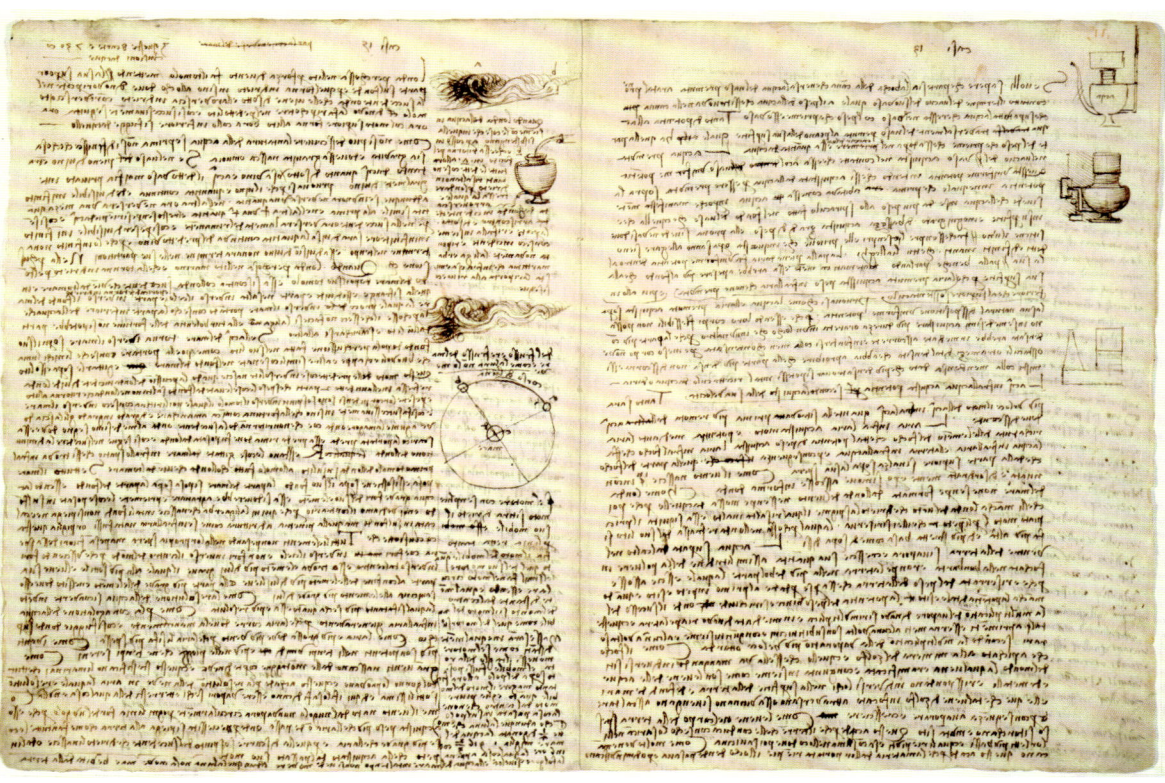

Codex Leicester

1508–12, Sepia ink on linen paper/Encre sépia sur papier de lin, Private collection

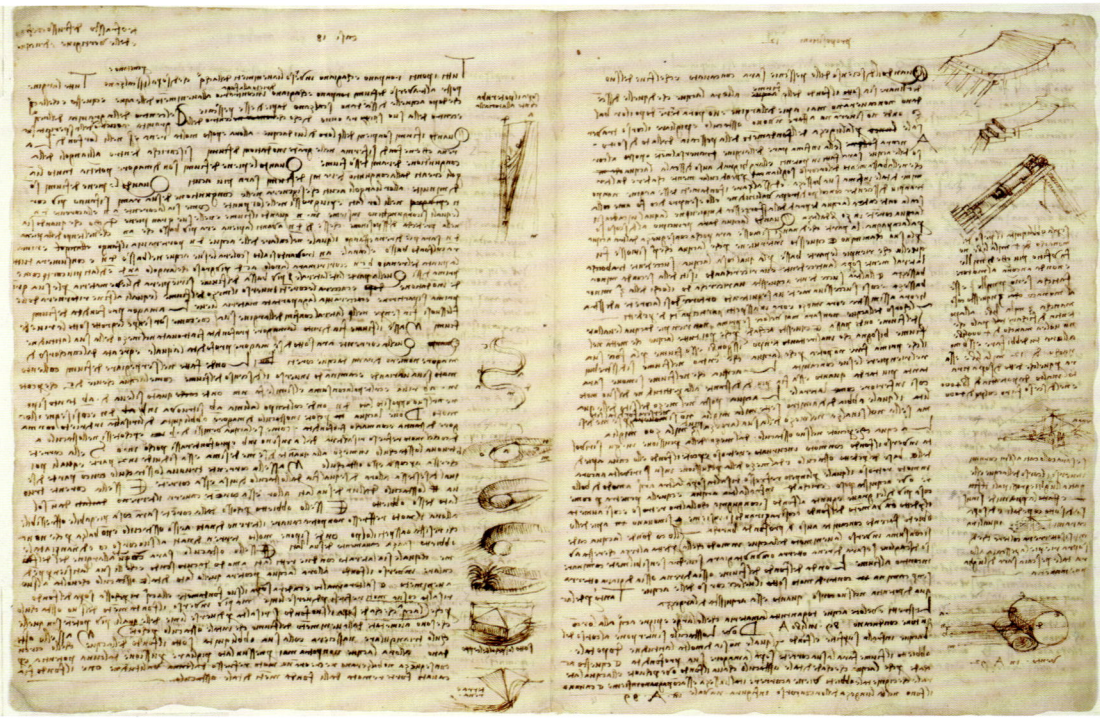

Codex Leicester

1508–12, Sepia ink on linen paper/Encre sépia sur papier de lin, Private collection

On the left side of this bookpage, Leonardo deals with the construction of bridges and weirs, discussing the effects of different geometric objects in the water.

Sur la page de livre de gauche, Léonard aborde les problèmes liés à la construction des ponts et des barrages, et expose les effets optiques de divers objets géométriques dans l'eau.

Auf der linken Buchseite befasst sich Leonardo mit Fragen des Baus von Brücken und Wehren und diskutiert die Effekte verschiedener geometrischer Objekte im Wasser.

En la página izquierda Leonardo trata cuestiones sobre la construcción de puentes y aliviaderos, y discute el efecto de diversos objetos geométricos en el agua.

Nella pagina del libro sinistra di questo foglio Leonardo tratta questioni relative alla costruzione di ponti e dighe e parla degli effetti di diversi oggetti geometrici nell'acqua.

Op de linkerpagina houdt Leonardo zich bezig met problemen rond de bouw van bruggen en sluizen en bespreekt de uitwerking van verschillende geometrische voorwerpen in stromend water.

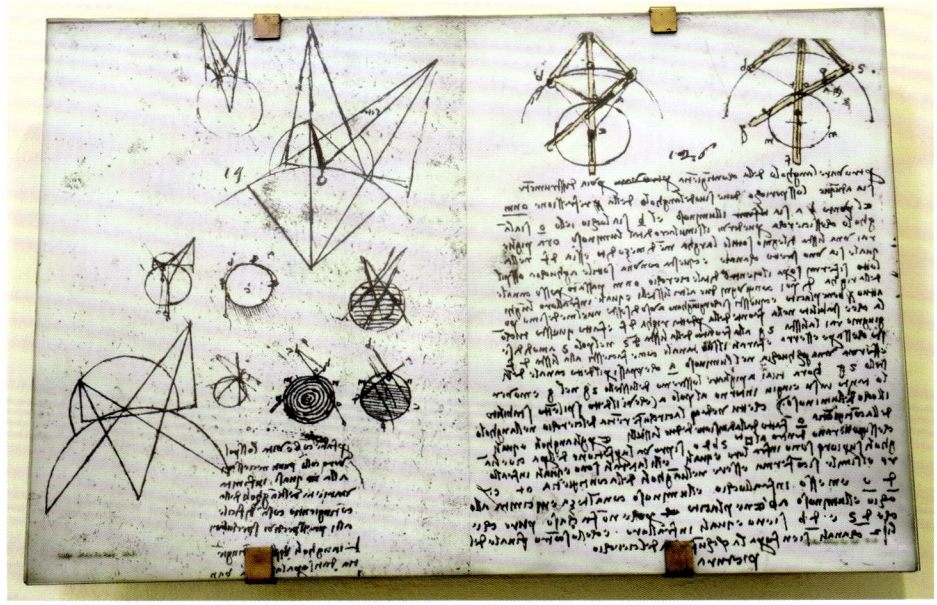

Codex Atlanticus

Alhazen's problem   **Alhazen'sches Problem**   **Il problema di Alhazen**

Le problème d'Alhazenschen   **El problema de Alhacén**   **Het 'probleem van Alhazen'**

Museo Nazionale della Scienza e della Tecnologia, Milano

Ibn al-Haytham (Alhazen) was a Muslim mathematician of either Persian or Arab origin, who lived around the year 1000 and is considered to be the founder of modern optics. The problem, described and solved by him, concerned a question already posed by Ptolemy regarding the reflection of light on reflecting surfaces.

Alhazen (965–1039), mathématicien d'origine arabe ou persane, est considéré comme le fondateur de l'optique moderne. La théorie à laquelle il a donné son nom porte sur un problème déjà soulevé par Ptolémée – celui de la réflexion de la lumière sur certaines surfaces.

Alhazen war ein muslimischer Mathematiker entweder persischer oder arabischer Herkunft, der um das Jahr 1000 lebte und als Begründer der modernen Optik gilt. Bei dem nach ihm benannten und gelösten Problem geht es um eine bereits von Ptomeläus aufgeworfene Frage, die mit der Reflexion des Lichtes an spiegelnden Oberflächen zu tun hat.

Alhacén fue un matemático musulmán de origen persa o árabe, que vivió hacia el año 1000, y que se considera el padre de la óptica moderna. En el problema nombrado y resuelto por él se trata una pregunta formulada ya por Ptolomeo, que tiene que ver con la reflexión de la luz sobre superficies especulares.

Alhazen fu un matematico musulmano di origine persiana o araba che visse intorno all'anno 1000 ed è considerato l'iniziatore dell'ottica moderna. Il problema da lui individuato e risolto è il modo in cui la luce si riflette su superfici riflettenti, una questione già sollevata in precedenza da Tolomeo.

Alhazen was een islamitische wiskundige van Perzische of Arabische afkomst die rond het jaar 1000 leefde en wordt beschouwd als de grondlegger van de moderne optica. Bij het naar hem vernoemde probleem draait het om een reeds door Ptomeleüs opgeworpen vraag met betrekking tot de reflectie van licht vanaf spiegelende oppervlakken.

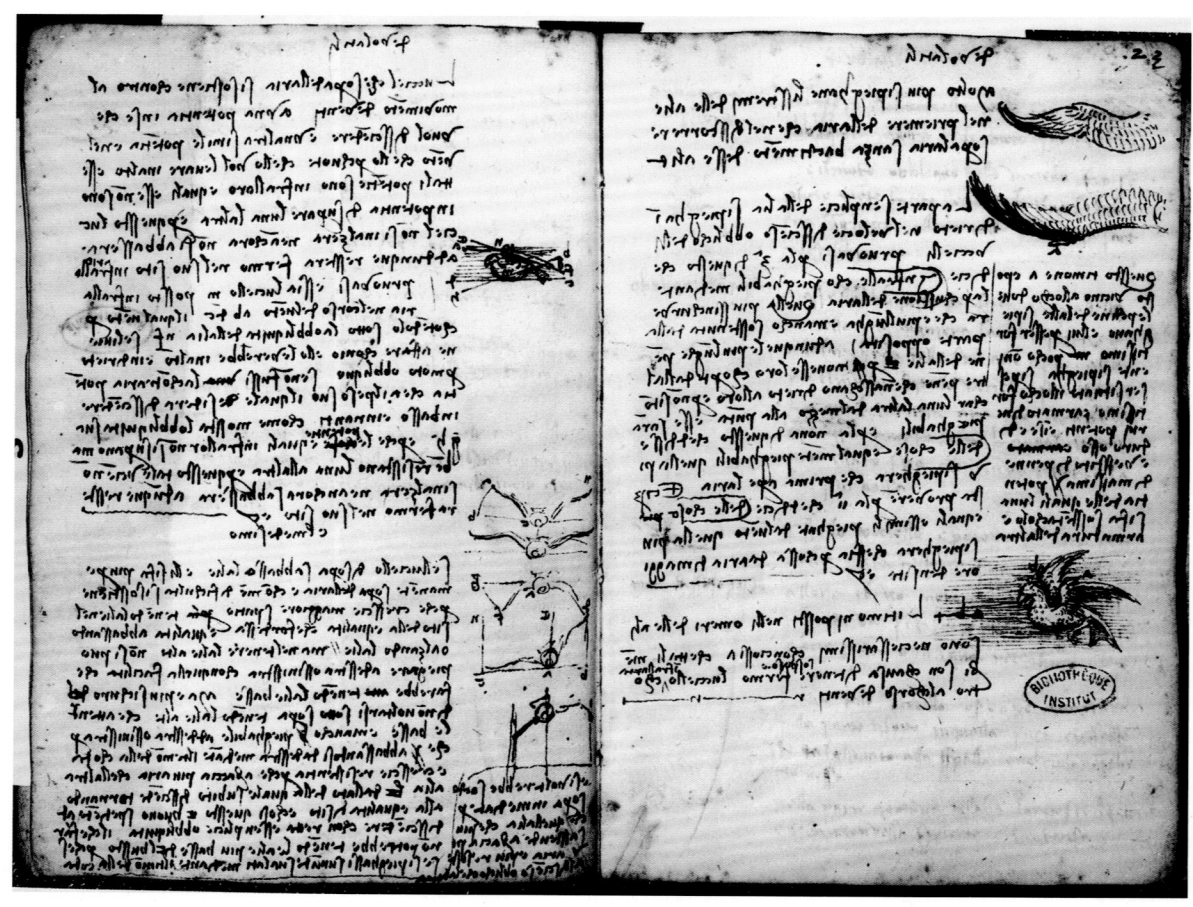

Sketch of two birds from the *Paris Manuscript E*

Croquis de deux oiseaux, tiré du *Manuscrit E de Paris*

Skizze zweier Vögel aus dem *Pariser Manuskript E*

Esbozo de dos pájaros del *manuscrito parisino E*

Schizzo di due uccelli dal *manoscritto parigino E*

Schets van twee vogels, uit het *Parijse Manuscript E*

1513/14, Pencil on paper/Crayon sur papier, Bibliothèque de l'Institut de France, Paris

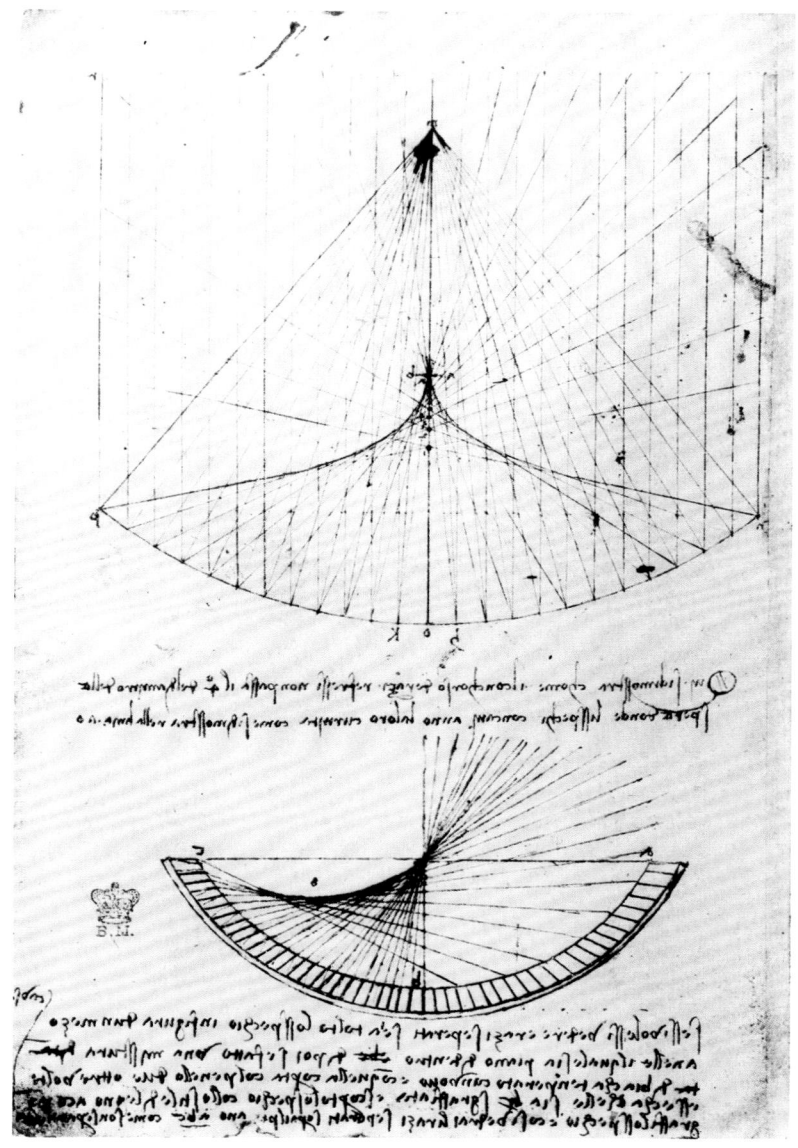

Codex Arundel

Studies of concave mirrors of constant and parabolic curvatures

Étude de miroirs concaves à courbure constante et parabolique

Studie von konkaven Spiegeln mit konstanter und parabelförmiger Krümmung

Estudio de espejos cóncavos con encorvaduras constantes y con forma de parábolas

Studio di specchi concavi con curvatura costante e parabolica

Studie van concave spiegels met constante en parabolische krommingen

c. 1490–1518, Pen and ink on paper/Plume et encre sur papier, British Library, London

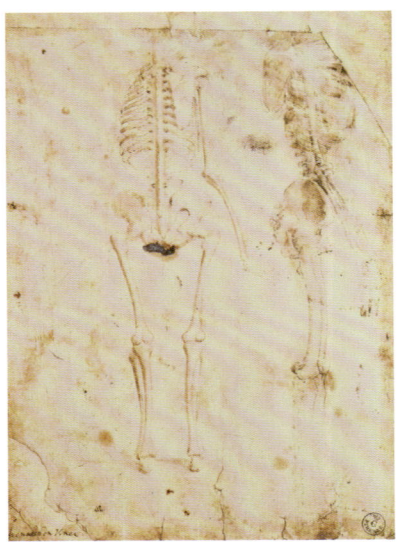

Two studies of a hanging skeleton
Deux études de squelette pendu
Zwei Studien eines hängenden Skeletts
Dos estudios de un esqueleto colgante
Due studi di uno scheletro appeso
Twee studies van een hangend skelet

Pen and ink with wash/Plume, lavis et encre de Chine,
Galleria degli Uffizi, Firenze

Anatomical studies

Already during his apprenticeship, Leonardo was encouraged by Verrocchio to intensively study human anatomy, as a basis of the painterly examination of the body. Various hospitals, first in Florence and then later also in Milan and Rome, provided him with corpses for dissection.

In more than 200 detailed drawings, Leonardo sketched practically all of the organs and muscles, and even offered the first representation of a foetus in the mother's body. Francesco Melzi, who had inherited many of Leonardo's works and was intending to publish this legacy, was overwhelmed and only a fraction of the notes and drawings appeared until long after Leonardo's death.

Les études d'anatomie

Verrocchio, déjà, avait mis son élève Léonard à l'étude intensive de l'anatomie, comme base indispensable de tout travail pictural sérieux sur le corps humain. Divers hôpitaux – d'abord à Florence, puis à Milan et même à Rome – fournissaient pour cela des cadavres à disséquer.

Dans ses plus de deux cents croquis détaillés, Léonard a pratiquement dessiné tous les organes et tous les muscles du corps ; il a même réalisé les premiers dessins (1510–1512) de fœtus encore dans le ventre de la mère. Francesco Melzi, élève et compagnon, puis héritier de Léonard sera chargé de la publication des écrits du Maître – mais il n'en paraîtra que des fragments, longtemps après la mort de celui-ci.

Anatomiestudien

Bereits Verrocchio hielt Leonardo während seiner Lehrzeit zu intensiven Studien der menschlichen Anatomie als Grundlage der malerischen Auseinandersetzung mit dem Körper an. Verschiedene Krankenhäuser, zuerst in Florenz, später auch in Mailand und Rom, stellten ihm Leichen zur Sektion zur Verfügung.

In seinen mehr als 200 detaillierten Zeichnungen skizzierte Leonardo praktisch alle Organe, Muskeln und schuf sogar die erste Darstellung eines Fötus im Mutterleib. Sein Erbe Francesco Melzi war mit der geplanten Publikation überfordert und nur ein Bruchteil der Aufzeichnungen sollte – lange nach Leonardos Tod – erscheinen.

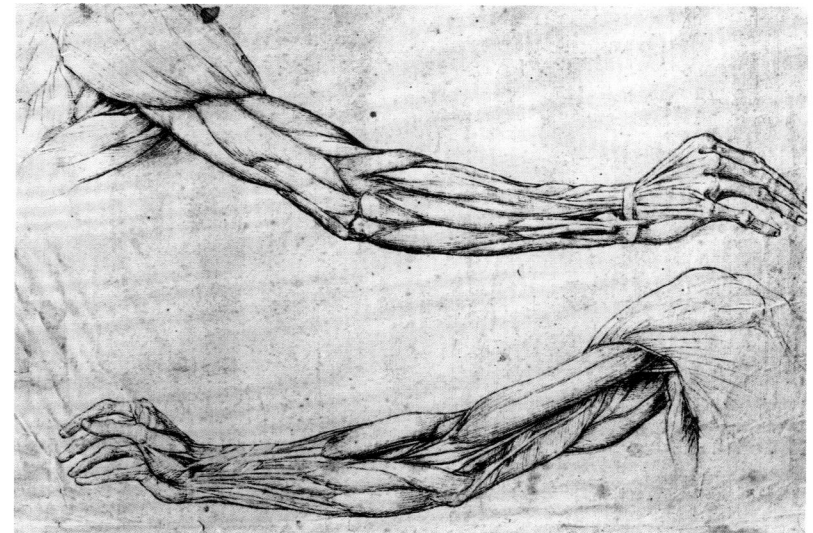

Estudios de anatomía

Verocchio fue el primero en pedirle a Leonardo, durante su periodo de aprendizaje, que se detuviera a estudiar la anatomía humana de forma intensiva para usarla como base de análisis pictórico del cuerpo humano. Varios hospitales, primero en Florencia, luego en Milán y en Roma, pondrían a su disposición cadáveres para ser diseccionados.

En sus más de 200 dibujos detallados, Leonardo esbozó prácticamente todos los órganos, músculos e incluso creó la primera representación de un feto en el vientre materno. Su sucesor Francesco Melzi, estaba desbordado a la hora de trabajar en la publicación de su obra póstuma, por lo que sólo una parte de las ilustraciones verían tras la muerte del artista la luz.

Studi di anatomia

Già il Verrocchio esortò Leonardo a compiere studi intensivi dell'anatomia umana durante il suo apprendistato, come base della discussione pittorica con il corpo. Diversi ospedali, prima a Firenze e in seguito anche a Milano e Roma, gli misero a disposizione dei cadaveri per l'autopsia.

Nei suoi oltre 200 disegni dettagliati, Leonardo schizzò praticamente tutti gli organi e i muscoli e creò persino la prima rappresentazione di un feto nel grembo materno. Il suo erede Francesco Melzi fu sopraffatto dalla pubblicazione prevista e solo una piccola parte dei disegni fu pubblicata, molto tempo dopo la morte di Leonardo.

Anatomiestudie

Het was Verrocchio die Leonardo in zijn leerperiode voorhield dat het intensieve onderzoek naar de anatomie tot de grondslagen van de uitbeelding van het lichaam behoorde. Ziekenhuizen in Florence, en later in Milaan en Rome, stelden Leonardo lichamen ter beschikking.

In ruim tweehonderd gedetailleerde tekeningen schetste Leonardo bijna alle belangrijke organen en spieren, en creëerde zelfs de eerste weergave van een foetus in het moederlichaam. Zijn erfgenaam Francesco Melzi kon de publicatie van zo veel tekeningen niet aan, waardoor slechts een fractie van dit werk – lang na de dood van Leonardo – zou verschijnen.

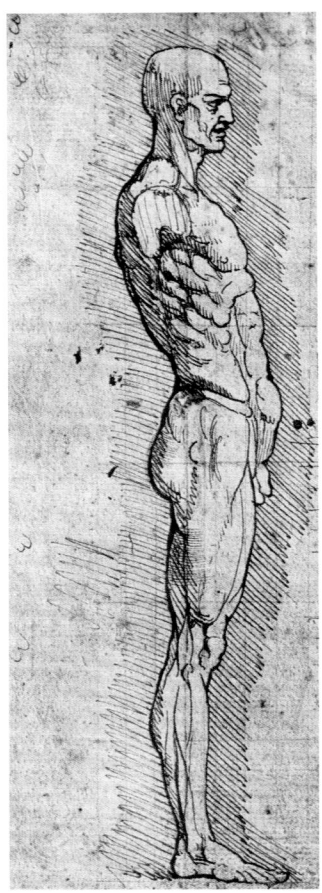

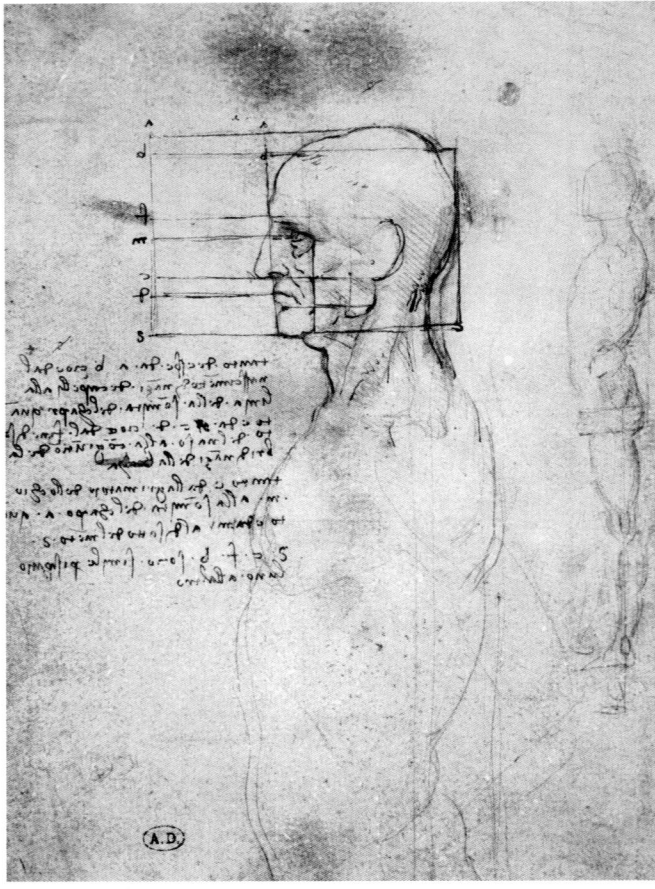

Anatomical study

Étude anatomique

Anatomische Studie

Estudio anatómico

Studio anatomico

Anatomische studie

Pen and ink on paper/Plume et encre sur papier,
Musée du Louvre, Paris

Head of an old man in profile

Tête d'un vieil homme, de profil

Kopf eines alten Mannes im Profil

Cabeza de un hombre mayor de perfil

Testa di un anziano di profilo

Hoofd van oude man en profil

Pen and ink on paper/Plume et encre sur papier,
Bibliothèque des Arts Décoratifs, Paris

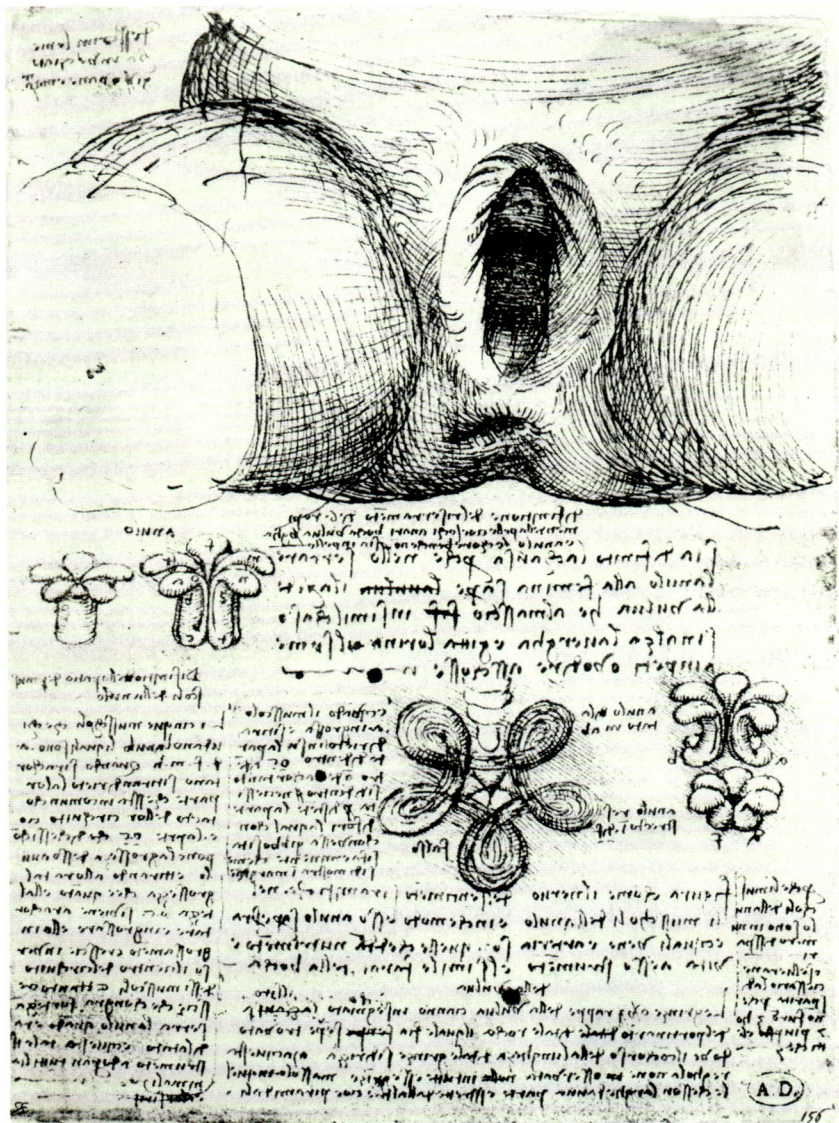

The female sexual organs
Les organes sexuels féminins
Die weiblichen Sexualorgane
Los órganos sexuales femeninos
Gli organi sessuali femminili
De vrouwelijke geslachtsorganen

Pen and ink on paper/Plume et encre sur papier, Bibliothèque des Arts Décoratifs, Paris

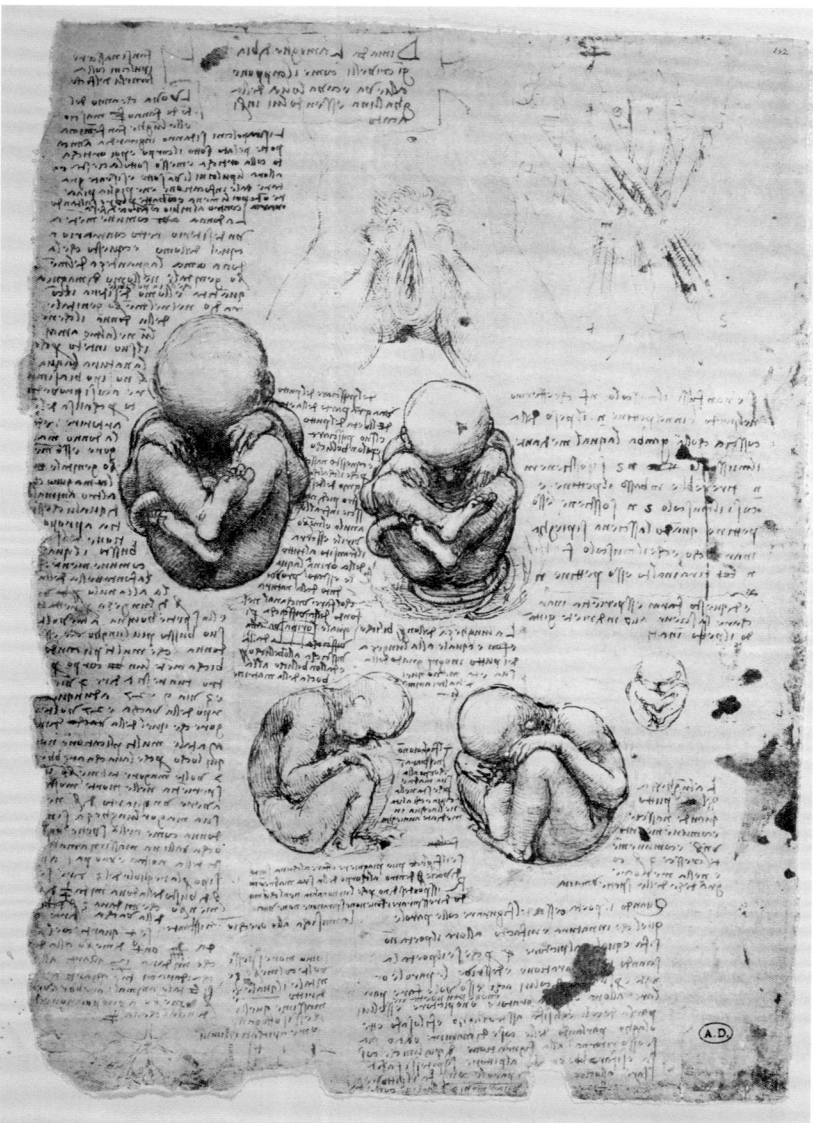

Five views of a foetus in the womb

Cinq vues d'un fœtus dans le ventre maternel

Fünf Ansichten eines Fötus im Mutterleib

Cinco vistas de un feto en el vientre materno

Cinque disegni di un feto nel grembo materno

Vijf schetsen van een foetus in het moederlichaam

Pen and ink on paper/Plume et encre sur papier, Bibliothèque des Arts Décoratifs, Paris

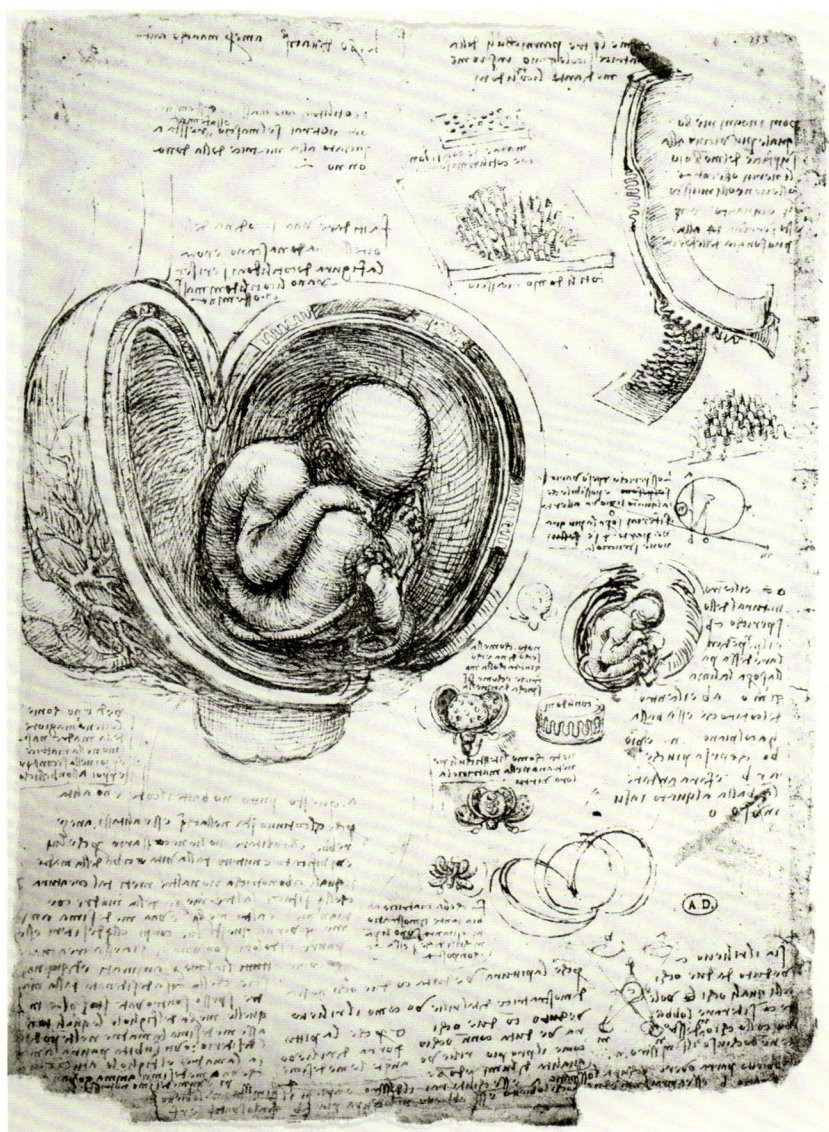

The human foetus in the womb

**Le fœtus humain dans
le ventre maternel**

Der menschliche Fötus im Mutterleib

El feto humano en el vientre materno

Il feto umano nel grembo materno

**Menselijke foetus in het
moederlichaam**

*Pen and ink on paper/Plume et encre sur
papier, Bibliothèque des Arts Décoratifs,
Paris*

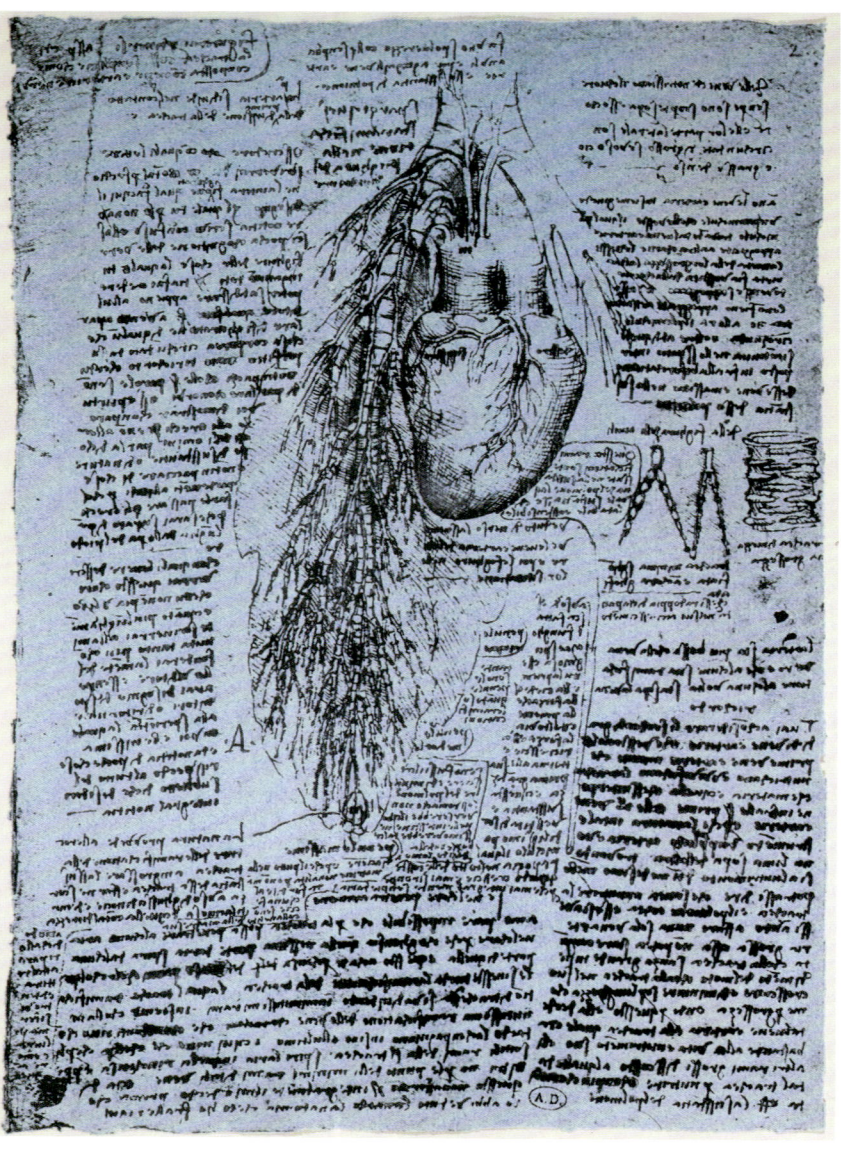

Codex Windsor

The heart and the bronchial arteries

Le cœur et les artères bronchiques

Das Herz und die Bronchialarterien

El corazón y las arterias bronquiales

Il cuore e le arterie bronchiali

Hart en longslagaders

Facsimile/fac-similé, Pen and ink on paper/Plume et encre sur papier, Bibliothèque des Arts Décoratifs, Paris

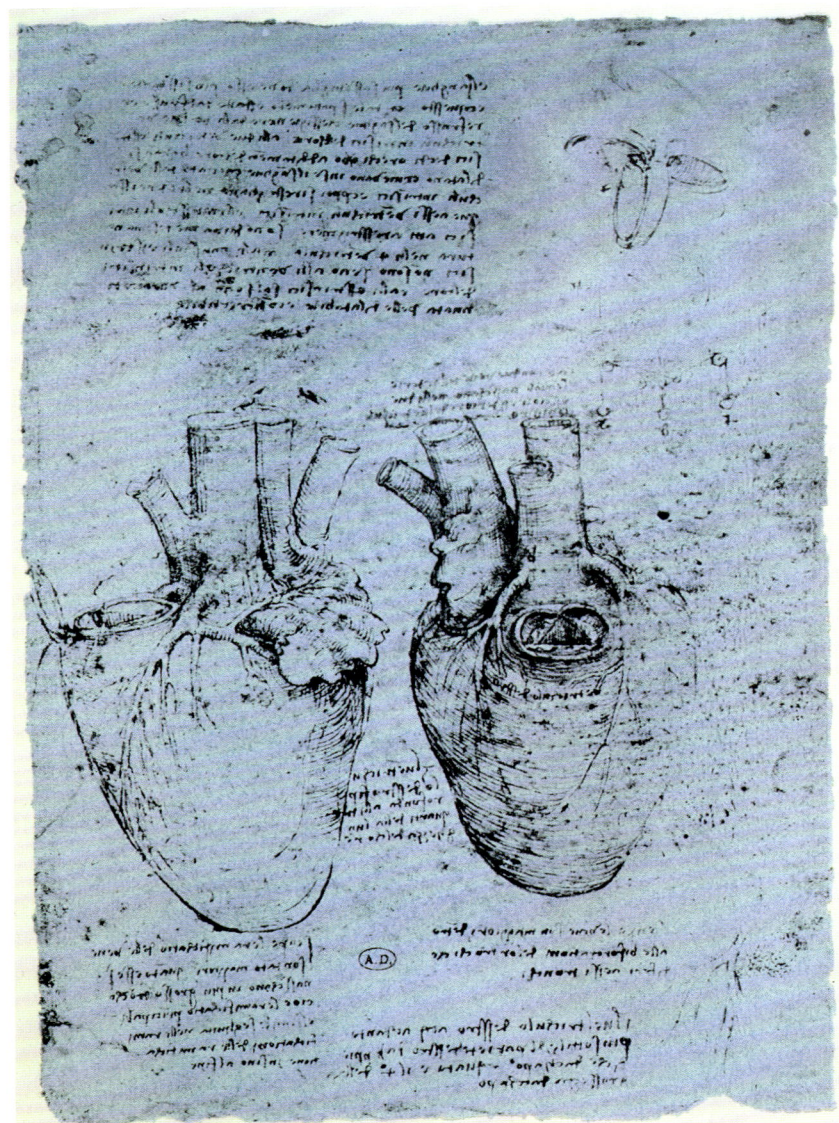

Codex Windsor
The heart
Le cœur
Das Herz
El corazón
Il cuore
Het hart

Facsimile/fac-similé, Pen and ink on paper/Plume et encre sur papier, Bibliothèque des Arts Décoratifs, Paris

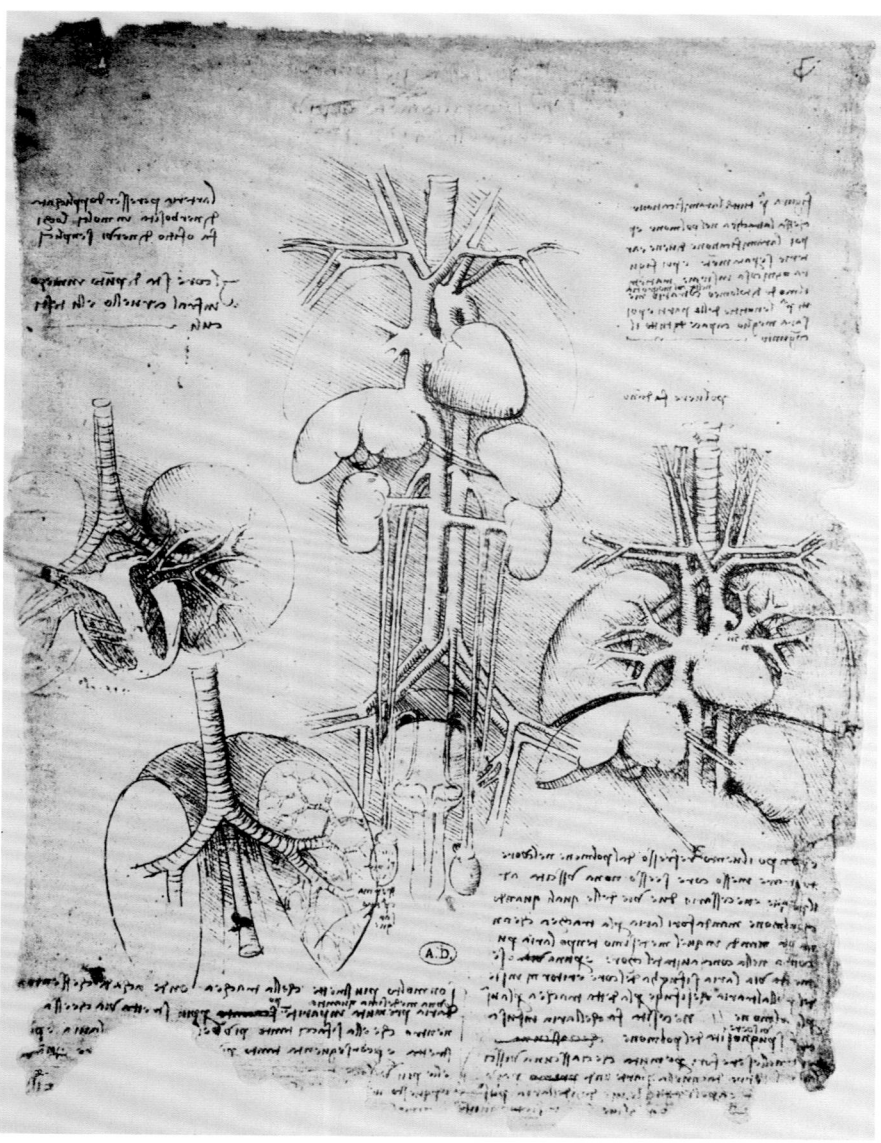

Codex Windsor

The heart and the circulation

**Le cœur et la circulation
sanguine**

Das Herz und der Blutkreislauf

**El corazón y la circulación
sanguínea**

**Il cuore e la circolazione
del sangue**

Hart en bloedsomloop

*Facsimile/fac-similé, Pen and ink on
paper/Plume et encre sur papier,
Bibliothèque des Arts Décoratifs,
Paris*

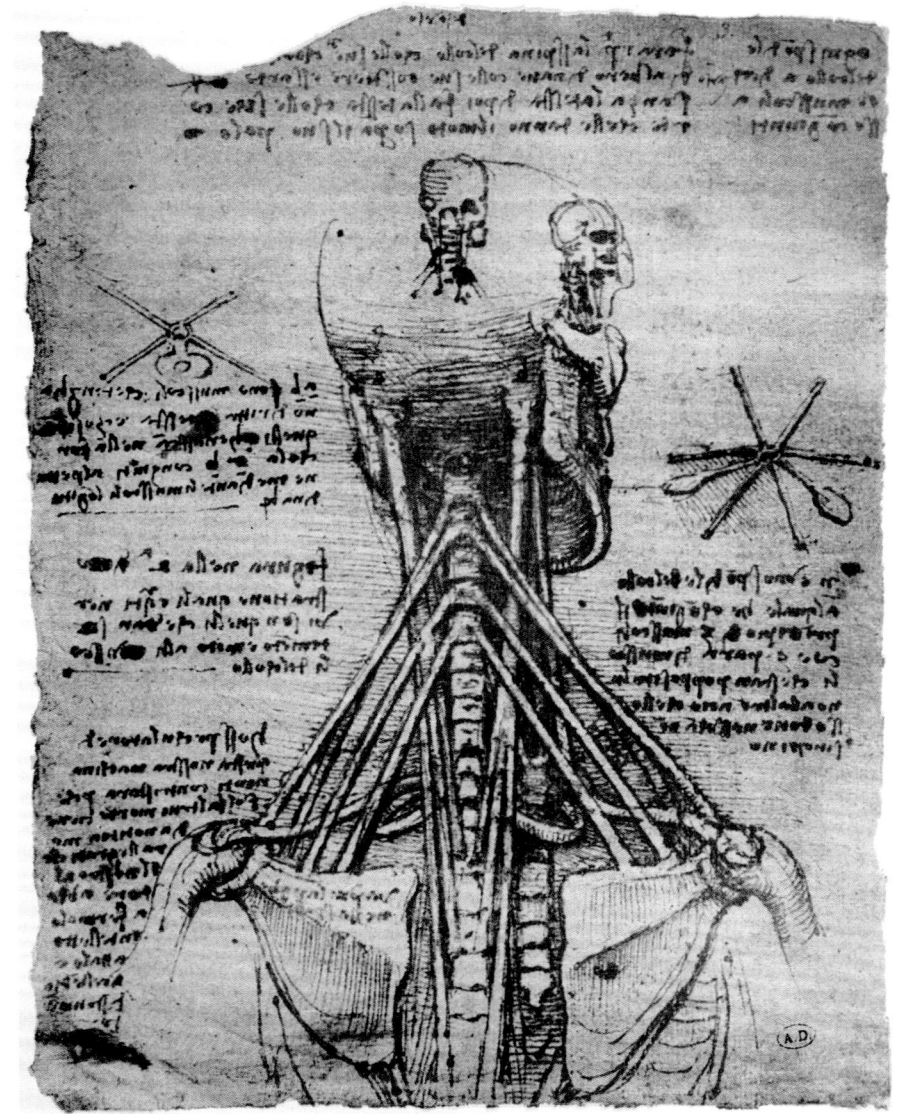

Codex Windsor

Bone structure of the human neck and shoulder

Structure osseuse du cou et des épaules humains

Knochenstruktur des menschlichen Nackens und der Schulter

Estructura ósea del cuello y de las espaldas humanas

Struttura ossea di nuca e spalle umani

Beenderstructuur van menselijke nek en schouder

Facsimile/fac-similé, Pen and ink on paper/Plume et encre sur papier, Bibliothèque des Arts Décoratifs, Paris

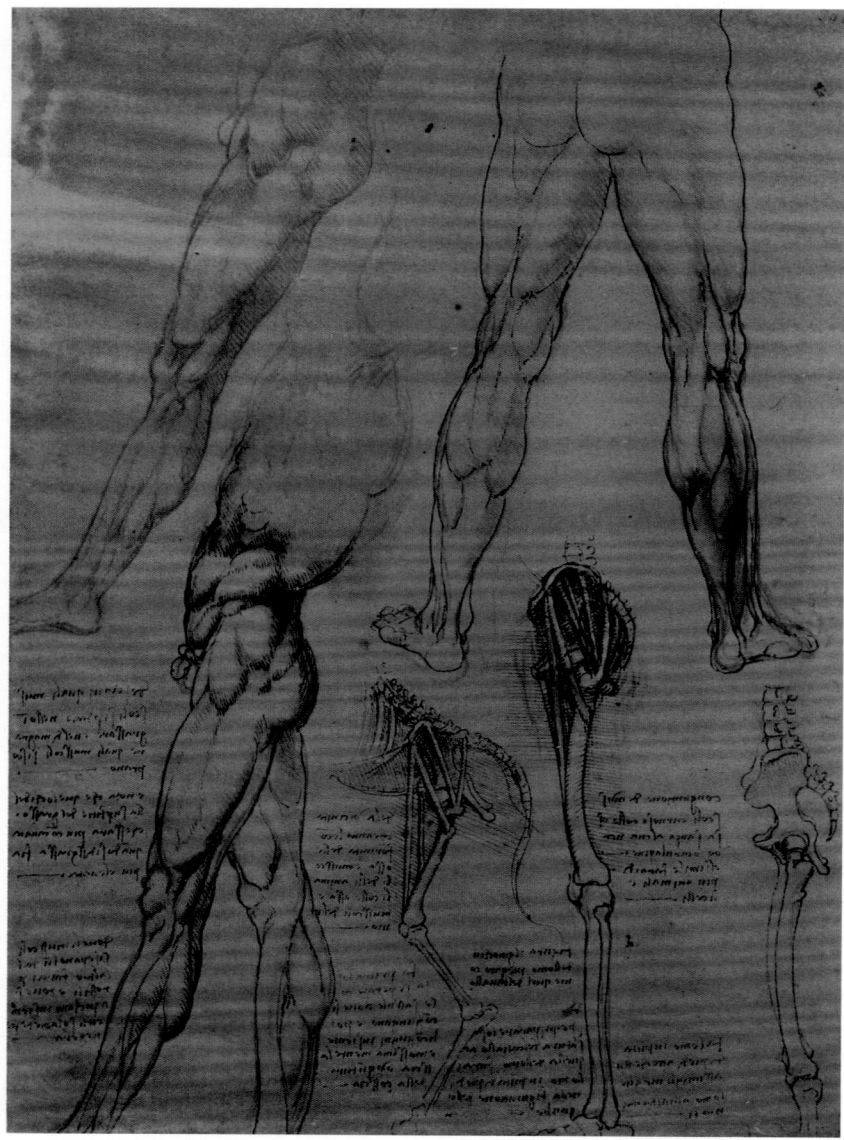

Codex Windsor

Page from the *Quaderni di Anatomia*

Page des *Quaderni di Anatomia*

Seite aus den *Quaderni di Anatomia*

Página de los *Quaderni di Anatomia*

Pagina dai *Quaderni di Anatomia*

Blad uit de *Quaderni di Anatomia*

Color lithograph/Lithographie en couleurs, Royal collection

Studies of the proportions of the face and eye

Étude des proportions du visage et de l'œil

Studien zu den Proportionen des Gesichts und des Auges

Estudio sobre las proporciones de la cara y del ojo

Studi delle proporzioni del viso e degli occhi

Studies voor de verhoudingen van gezicht en oog

1489/90, Pen and ink over metalpoint on paper/Plume et encre sur pointe métaliique, sur papier, Biblioteca Nazionale, Torino

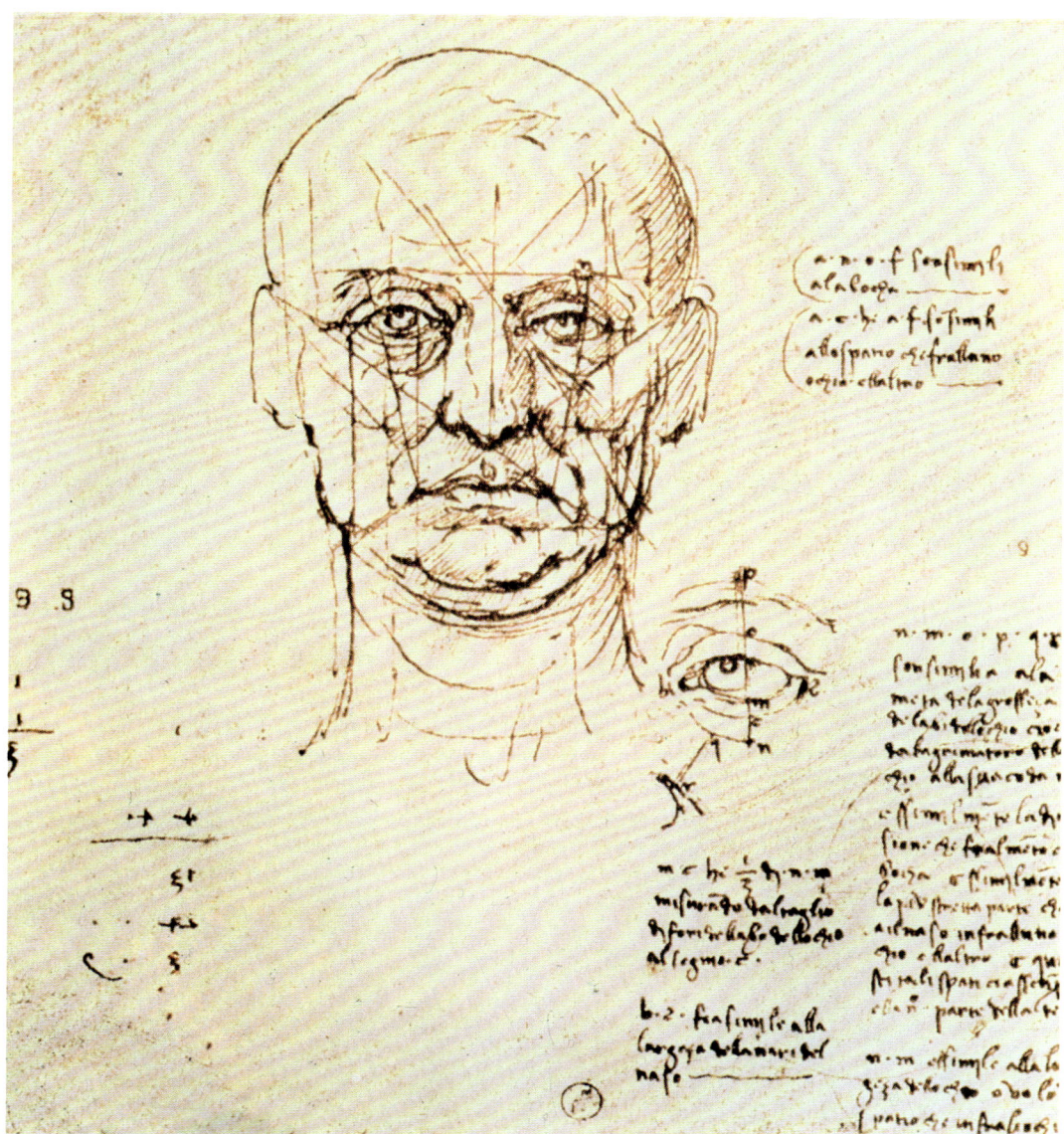

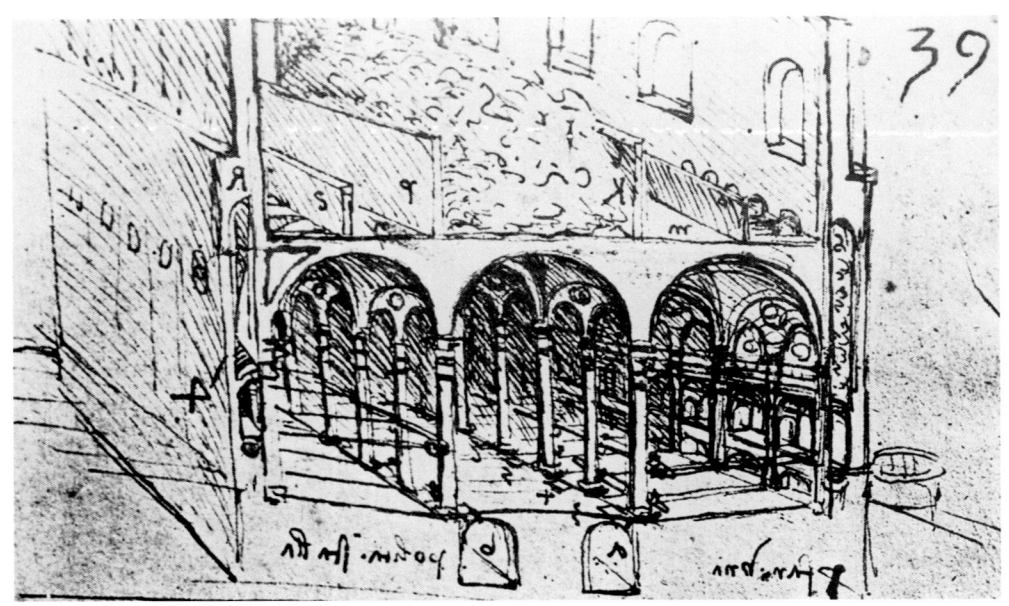

Architectural studies

Although he was interested in almost all architectonic questions of the time, and even considered writing a comprehensive architectural theory, today nothing is known of any plans which were actually implemented.

His interest in architecture was certainly reinforced by his acquaintance with some of the greatest contemporary master builders, Bramante in particular. His interests ranged from concrete questions, such as the use of different construction tools, to the design of individual building elements such as staircases and pillars and even encompassing the planning of an entire city.

Les études d'architecture

Bien que Léonard de Vinci se soit intéressé à presque tous les problèmes architecturaux de son temps (et qu'il ait même envisagé la rédaction d'une théorie générale de l'architecture), on ne connaît à ce jour rien de lui en fait de projets effectivement réalisés.

Son intérêt pour l'architecture fut assurément renforcé par ses accointances avec certains des plus grands architectes de son temps, en particulier avec Bramante. Ses sujets d'intérêt allaient de problèmes très concrets comme l'emploi de divers outillages pour la construction à la planification urbaine, en passant par la conception d'éléments architecturaux individuels tels que des colonnes ou des escaliers.

Architekturstudien

Obwohl er sich für fast alle damals aktuellen architektonischen Fragen interessierte (und sogar die Abfassung einer umfassenden Architekturtheorie ins Auge fasste), ist heute nichts bekannt von tatsächlich umgesetzten Planungen.

Verstärkt wurde sein Interesse für die Baukunst sicher von der Bekanntschaft mit einigen der größten zeitgenössischen Baumeistern, insbesondere mit Bramante. Dabei reichten seine Interessen von ganz konkreten Fragen wie der Nutzung unterschiedlicher Bauwerkzeuge über die Gestaltung einzelner Bauelemente wie Treppen und Säulen bis hin zur Stadtplanung.

Codex Atlanticus

Study for a fortress on a polygonal ground plan with a double moat

Étude d'une fortification à redans et double fossé

Studie einer Festung auf vieleckigem Grundriss und mit doppeltem Burggraben

Estudio de una fortaleza con vistas de una planta poligonal y con un foso doble

Studio di una fortezza su una pianta poligonale e con fossato doppio

Studie van een vesting met polygonaal grondplan en dubbele burgwal

1504–08, Facsimile/fac-similé, Pen and Indian ink on paper/Plume et encre de Chine sur papier, Private collection

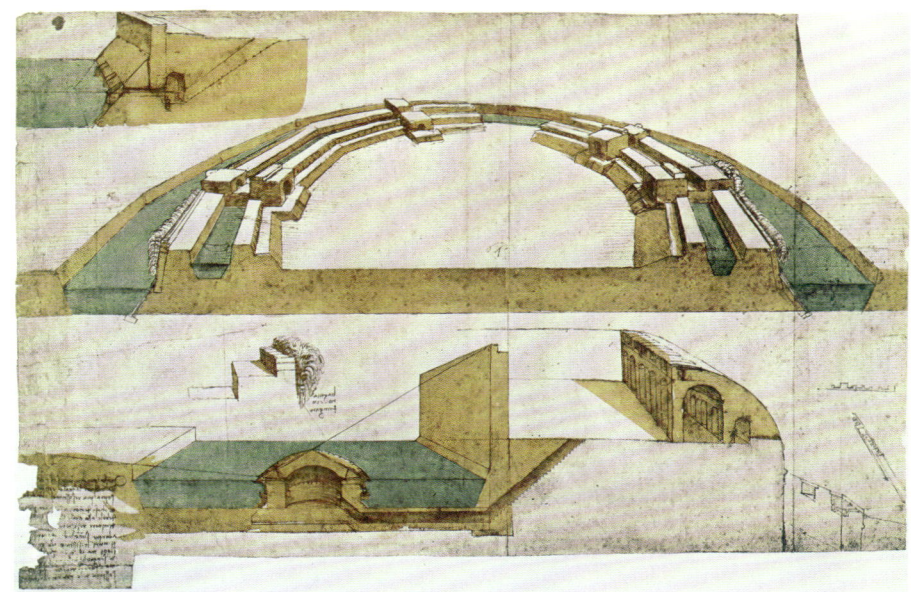

Estudios de arquitectura

Aunque se interesó por casi todas las preguntas arquitectónicas actuales de la época (e incluso llegó a considerar la redacción de una teoría de la arquitectura completa), hoy en día no tenemos conocimiento de planos que fueran realmente llevados a cabo.

Con toda seguridad contribuyó a aumentar su interés por la arquitectura su amistad con algunos de los constructores más importantes de la época, especialmente con Bramante. Estos intereses iban desde preguntas concretas como la utilidad de algunas herramientas de construcción pasando por el diseño de elementos constructivos como escaleras o columnas, hasta cuestiones de urbanismo.

Studi di architettura

Sebbene abbia trattato quasi tutte le questioni architettoniche attuali al suo tempo (e abbia pensato di redigere una teoria architettonica universale), ad oggi non se ne conoscono progetti reali.

Sicuramente il suo interesse per l'architettura fu rafforzato dalla conoscenza di alcuni dei più grandi architetti a lui contemporanei, in particolare Bramante. I suoi interessi spaziavano da questioni molto specifiche, come l'utilizzo di diversi strumenti di costruzione, fino alla pianificazione urbanistica, passando per la progettazione di singoli elementi, quali scale e colonne.

Architectuurstudie

Hoewel hij zich destijds voor bijna alle architectonische vraagstukken van zijn tijd interesseerde (en zelfs overwoog een alomvattende architectuur theoretische verhandeling te schrijven), wijst niets er tegenwoordig op dat hij dat voornemen ook heeft uitgevoerd.

Zijn interesse in de bouwkunst werd zeker ook vergroot door zijn contacten met enkele van de grootste architecten van zijn tijd, met name Bramante. Zijn nieuwsgierigheid liep uiteen van concrete kwesties als de toepassing van diverse bouwwerktuigen en de vormgeving van bouwelementen als trappen en zuilen tot de stadsplanning.

159

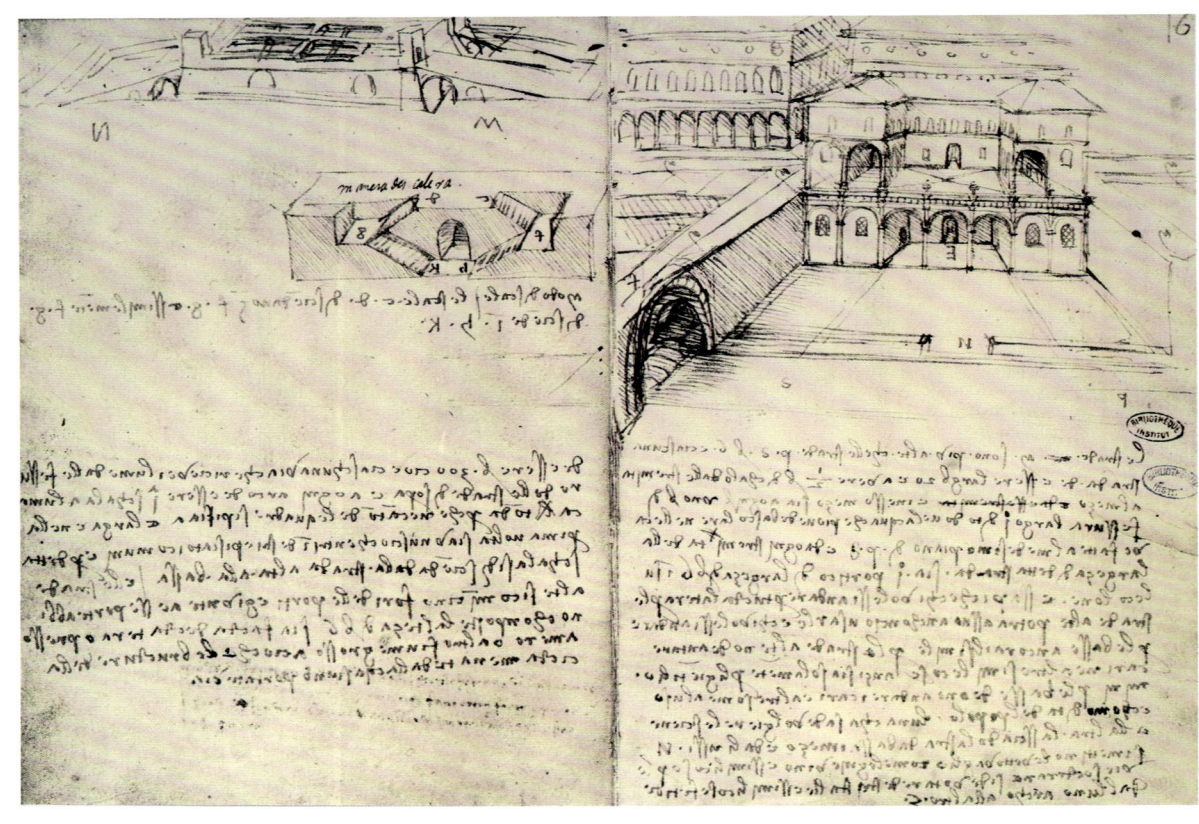

Steps and architectural sketch for an ideal city from *Paris Manuscript B*

Escalier et étude architecturale d'une ville idéale, tirés du *Manuscrit B de Paris*

Treppe und architektonische Studie einer idealen Stadt, aus dem *Pariser Manuskript B*

Escaleras y estudio arquitectónico de una ciudad ideal, del *manuscrito parisino B*

Scala e studio architettonico di una città ideale, dal *manoscritto parigino B*

Trap en architectonische studie van een ideale stad, uit het *Parijse Manuscript B*

1488–90, Pen and ink on paper/Plume et encre sur papier, Bibliothèque de l'Institut de France, Paris

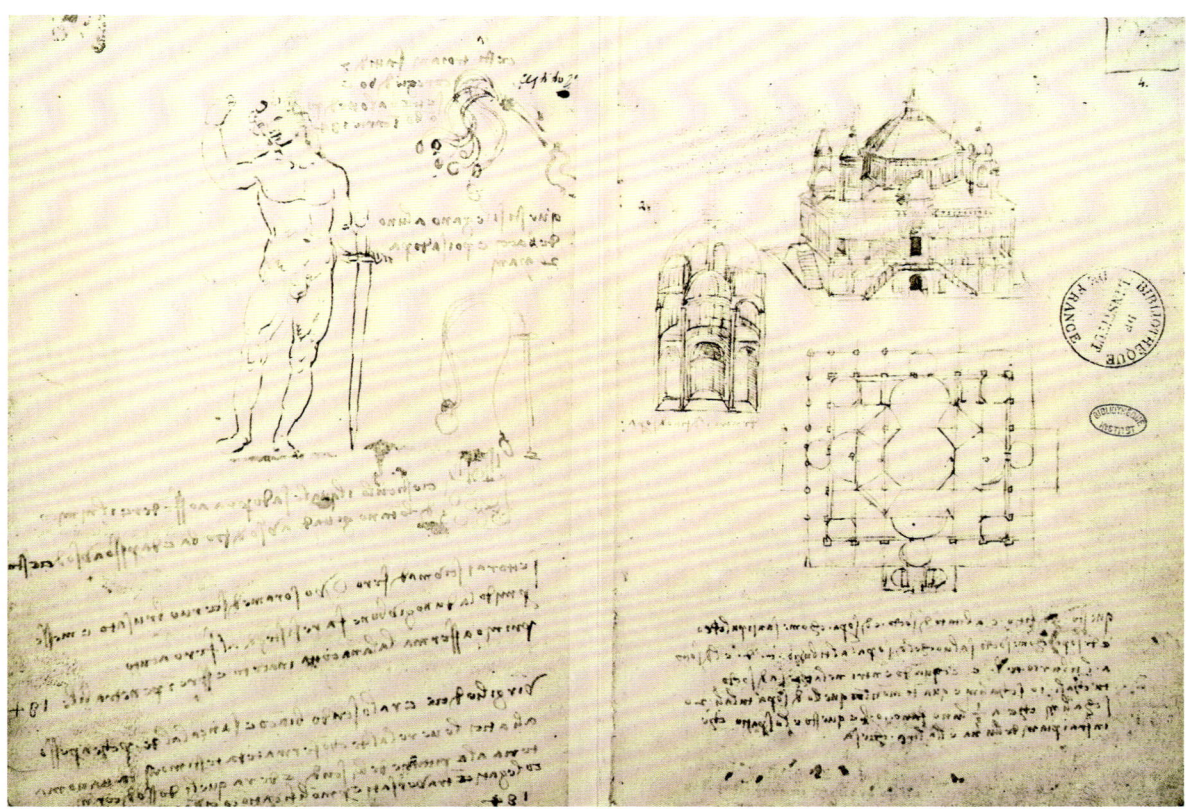

Codex Ashburnham

Sketch of a church similar to St. Sepolcro in Milan

Croquis d'une église semblable au San Sepolcro de Milan

Skizze einer Kirche, ähnlich San Sepolcro in Mailand

Esbozo de una iglesia, parecida al San Sepolcro de Milán

Schizzo di una chiesa, probabilmente San Sepolcro a Milano

Schets van een kerk, gelijkend op de San Sepolcro in Milaan

c. 1492, Pen and ink on paper/Plume et encre sur papier, Bibliothèque de l'Institut de France, Paris

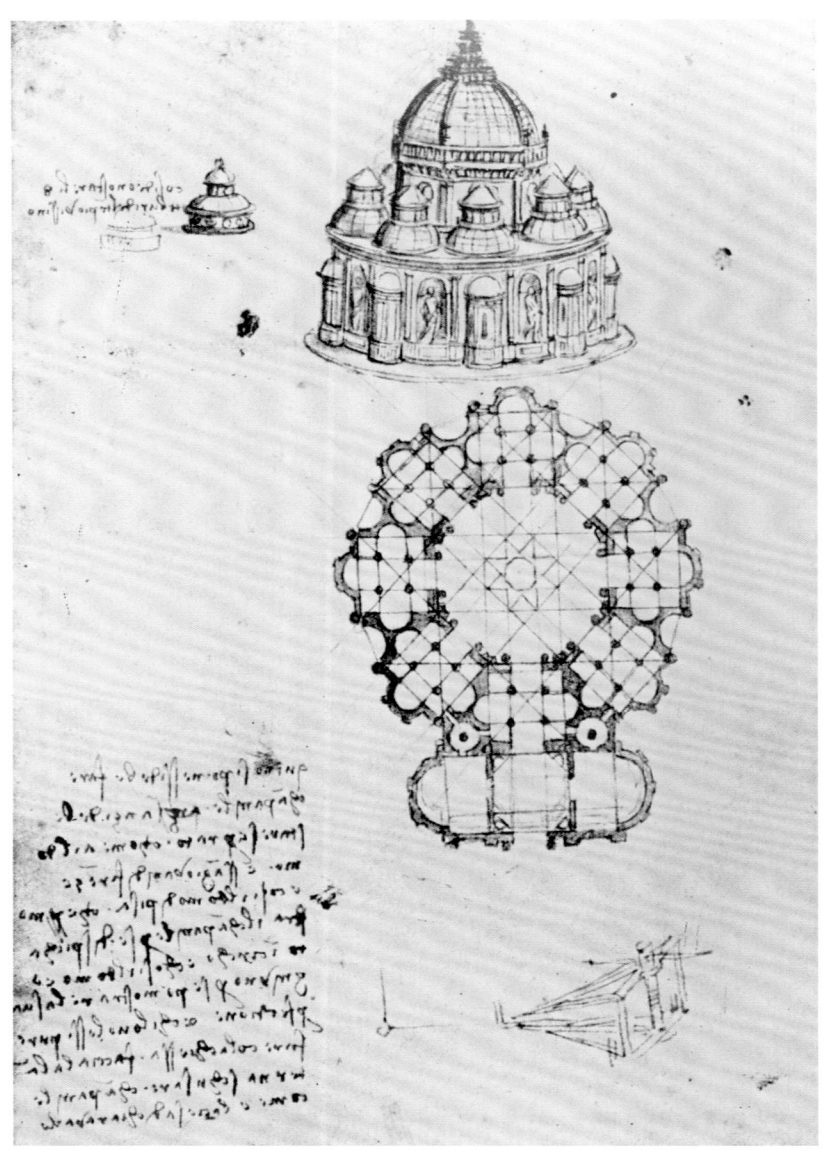

Codex Ashburnham

**Study of centralised church
and maritime engineering**

**Études d'une église à plan
central et de chantier naval**

**Studie einer Zentralkirche und
Schiffsmaschinenbau**

**Estudio de una iglesia central y de la
construcción de un motor naval**

**Studio di una chiesa a pianta
centrale e ingegneria marittima**

**Studie van sacrale rondbouw
en scheepmachine**

*c. 1488, Pen and ink on paper/Plume et encre
sur papier, Bibliothèque de l'Institut de France,
Paris*

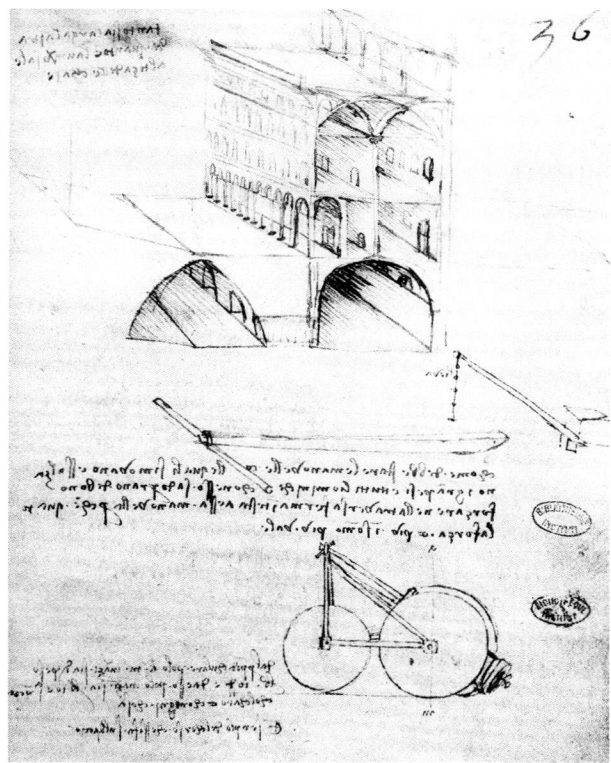

36

**Architectural studies on the development and
sections of buildings in city with raised streets**

**Études architecturales et parties de bâtiments,
dans une ville à rues surélevées**

**Architektonische Studien zur Entwicklung und Teilen
von Gebäuden in einer Stadt mit erhöhten Straßen**

**Estudios arquitectónicos sobre el desarrollo y partes
de edificios y una ciudad con calles elevadas**

**Studi architettonici per lo sviluppo e parti di
edifici in una città con strade rialzate**

**Architectonische voorstudies en bouwdelen
voor een stad met verhoogde straten**

*Pen and ink on paper/Plume et encre sur papier, Bibliothèque de l'Institut
de France, Paris*

One of the many charms that Leonardo's codices offer today is the fascinating variety of his ideas and inspirations, particularly evident here where an early design for a bicycle inhabits the same page as an architectural sketch.

Un des nombreux attraits offerts par la lecture des manuscrits de Léonard réside dans la multiplicité fascinante et toujours renouvelée de ses idées et de ses intuitions, particulièrement sensible quand se trouvent abordés sur une même page des sujets aussi divers que le projet d'un prototype de bicyclette et une esquisse d'architecture.

Einer der vielen Reize, die das Betrachten von Leonardos Codizes heute bereitet, liegt in der immer wieder faszinierenden Vielfalt seiner Ideen und Gedankenblitze, die sich besonders dann offenbart, wenn so verschiedene Dinge wie der Entwurf eines frühen Fahrrades auf der gleichen Seite Platz findet wie eine Architekturskizze.

Uno de los aspectos más atractivos que ofrece la contemplación de los códices de Leonardo, todavía hoy en día, es la siempre fascinante variedad de sus ideas e inspiraciones repentinas, que se manifiesta especialmente al combinarse temas tan diferentes como el diseño de una bicicleta primitiva en el mismo lugar que un boceto arquitectónico.

Una delle tante attraenti caratteristiche emerse dallo studio odierno dei codici di Leonardo è la sempre affascinante diversità delle sue idee e dei suoi pensieri, che si palesa soprattutto quando nella stessa pagina vengono affrontati argomenti estremamente differenti, come la progettazione di un'antica bicicletta e un disegno architettonico.

Een van de vele inzichten die het bestuderen van Leonardo's codexen opleveren, is de telkens weer verbluffende veelzijdigheid van zijn ideeën en invallen, zoals blijkt wanneer zulke verschillende zaken als een ontwerp voor een vroege fiets en architectuurstudies op één blad zijn te vinden.

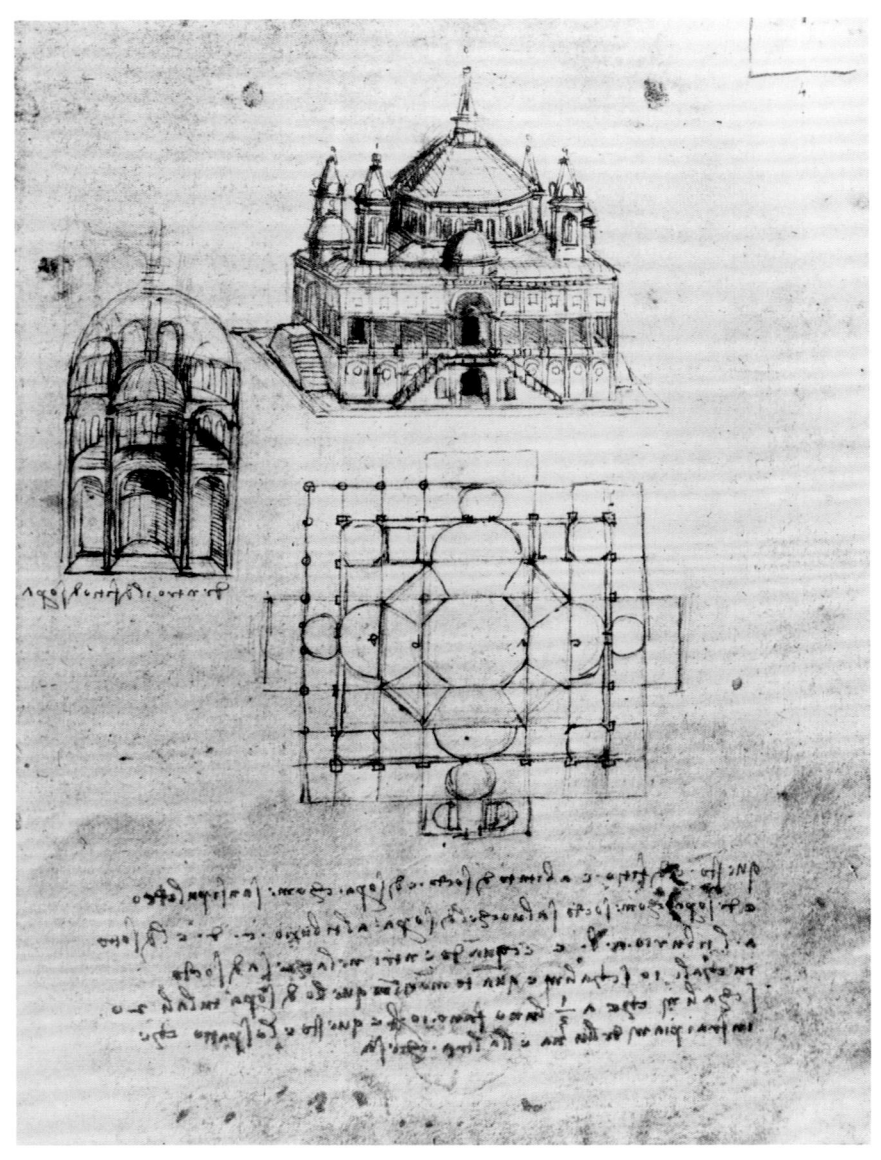

Design for a church

Projet d'église

Entwurf einer Kirche

Diseño de una iglesia

Schizzo di una chiesa

Ontwerp voor een kerk

Pen and ink on paper/Plume et encre
sur papier, Private collection

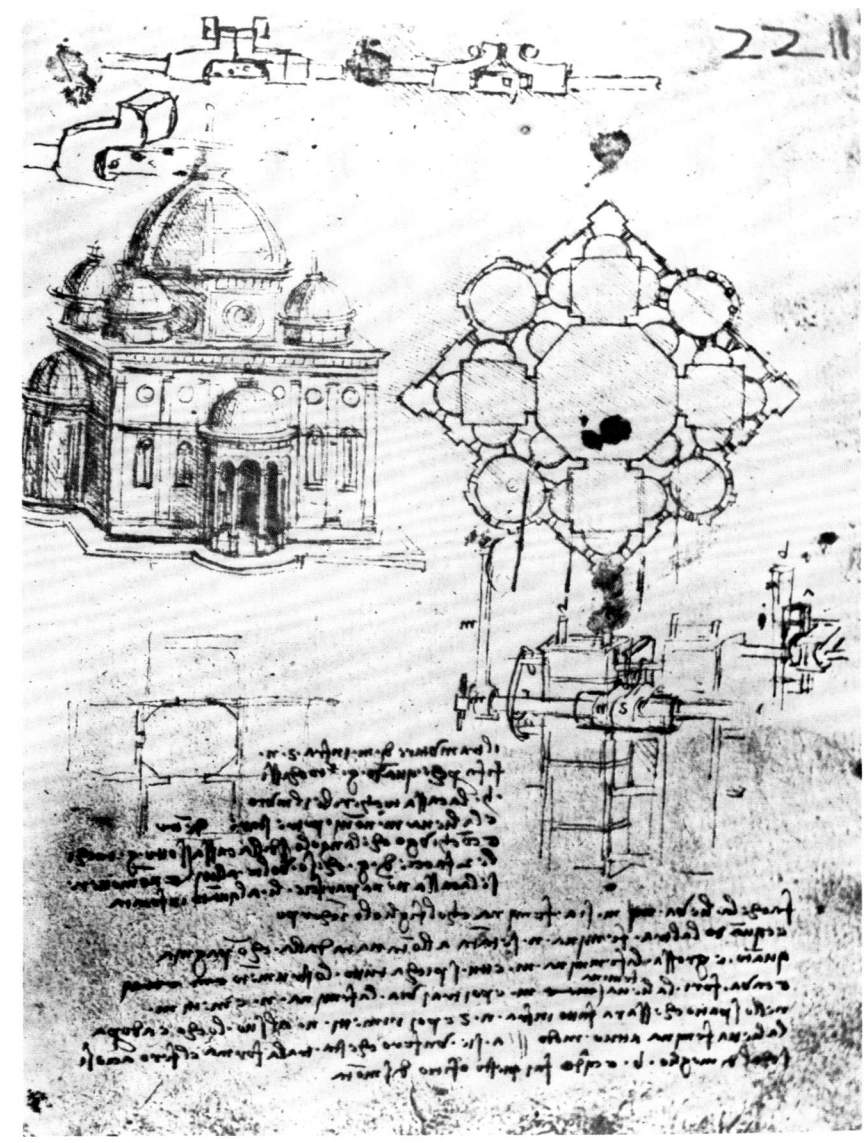

Design for a church

Projet d'église

Entwurf einer Kirche

Diseño de una iglesia

Schizzo di una chiesa

Ontwerp voor een kerk

Pen and ink on paper/Plume et encre sur papier, Private collection

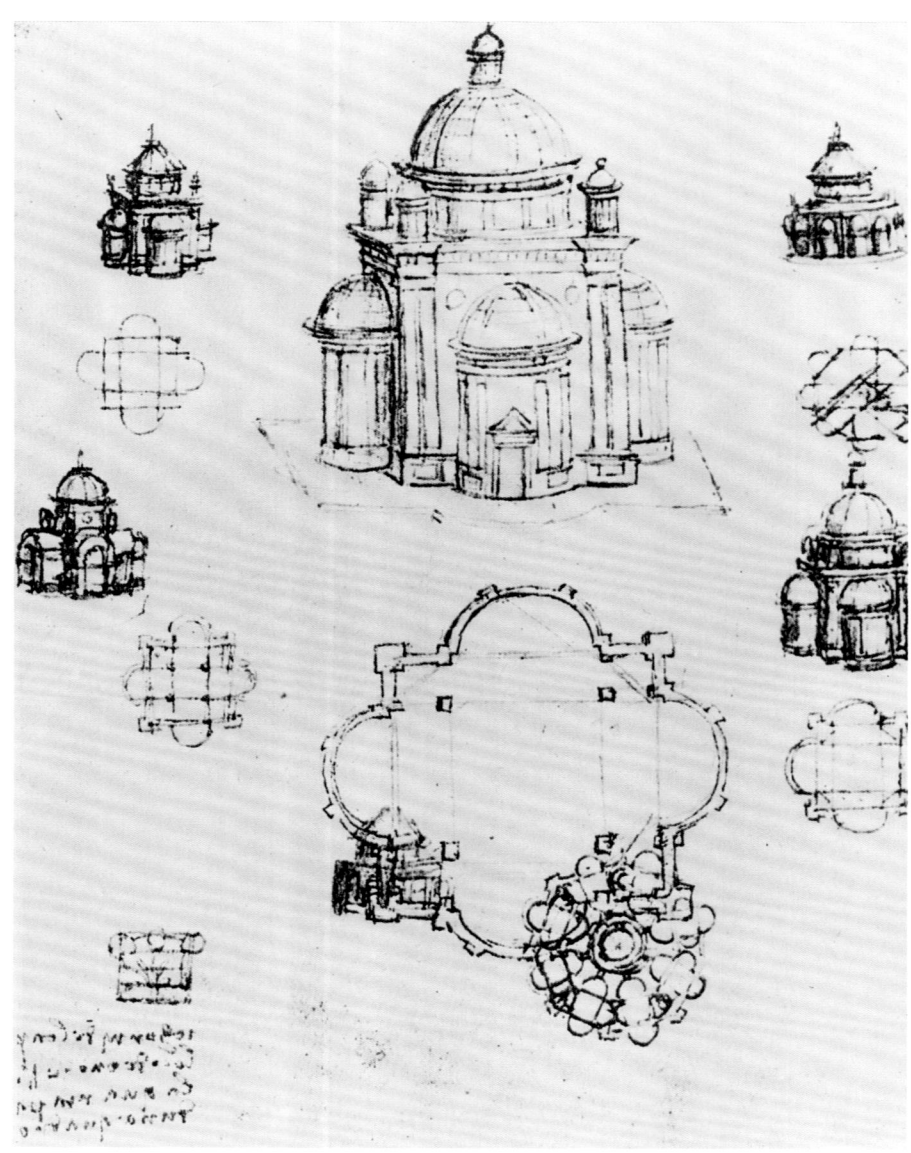

Codex Ashburnham

**Studies for a building
of a centralised plan**

**Études d'un bâtiment
à plan central**

**Studien eines Gebäudes
mit zentraler Ausrichtung**

**Estudios de un edificio
con orientación central**

**Studi di un edificio a
pianta centrale**

Studie van een rondbouw

*c. 1492, Pen and ink on paper/
Plume et encre sur papier,
Bibliothèque de l'Institut de
France, Paris*

Design for a palace and a park
Projet de palais avec un parc
Entwurf eines Palasts und eines Parks
Diseño de un palacio y de un parque
Schizzo di un palazzo e un parco
Ontwerp voor een paleis en een park

1517/18, Pen and ink on paper/Plume et encre
sur papier, Private collection

In 1516, Leonardo was commissioned by Francis I
of France to design a new capital city—sketches
of which are shown here. The project ran into
the sand and today Romorantin is a modest
provincial town on the Sologne, with fewer than
20,000 inhabitants.

En 1561, le roi de France François Iᵉʳ chargea
Léonard de concevoir les plans d'une nouvelle
capitale (ici, une des esquisses). Le projet fut
abandonné : Romorantin est aujourd'hui une
modeste ville provinciale de Sologne, avec moins
de 20 000 habitants.

1516 erhielt Leonardo vom französischen König
François I. den Auftrag zum Entwurf einer neuen
Hauptstadt – hier eine der Skizzen. Das Projekt
verlief im Sande, heute ist Romorantin an der
Sologne eine bescheidene Provinzstadt mit nicht
einmal 20 000 Einwohnern.

En 1516 Leonardo recibió del rey Francisco I de
Francia el encargo de diseñar una nueva capital
(aquí vemos uno de los bocetos). El proyecto
acabó fracasando y hoy en día Romorantin en
Sologne es una discreta ciudad provincial que no
llega a los 20 000 habitantes.

Nel 1516 Leonardo ricevette dal re francese
Francesco I l'incarico di progettare una nuova
capitale, di cui qui è possibile ammirare uno degli
schizzi. Il progetto, successivamente arenatosi,
corrisponde all'odierna Romorantin nella regione
Sologne, una modesta città di provincia con meno
di 20 000 abitanti.

In 1516 ontving Leonardo van de Franse koning
Frans I opdracht om een nieuwe hoofdstad
te ontwerpen, waarvan een van de schetsen
hier wordt getoond. Het project verzandde
en tegenwoordig is Romorantin aan de rivier
de Sologne een provincieplaats met amper
20 000 inwoners.

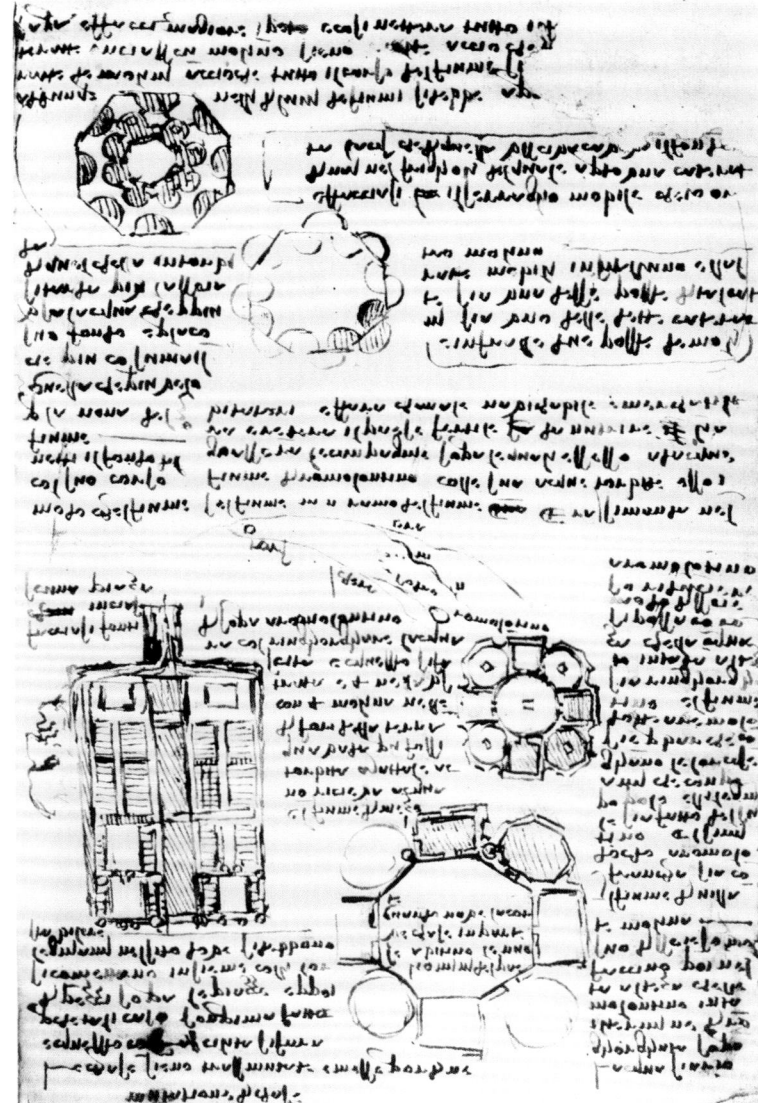

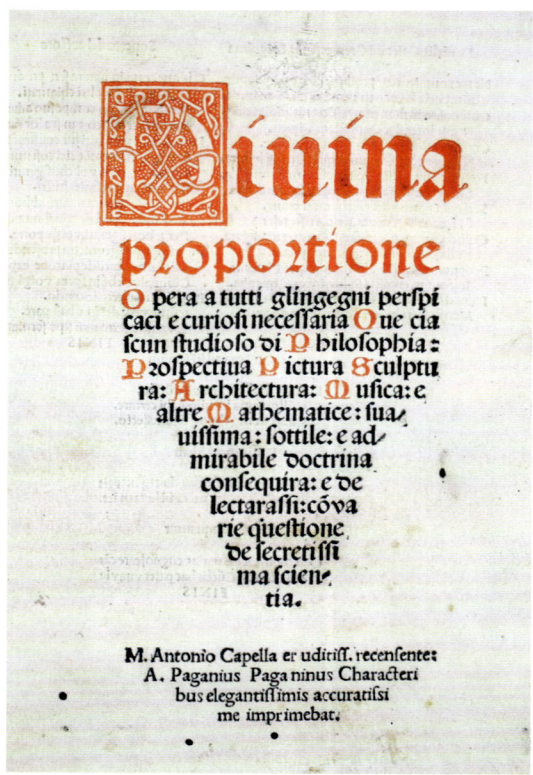

Leonardo's illustrations for Luca Pacioli's *De Divina Proportione*

The Franciscan monk Luca Pacioli, who was some years older than Leonardo, met him in Milan in 1497 and soon a friendship between them ensued. Known as the "father of the double-entry accounting system", Pacioli attracted Leonardo's attention mainly because of his mathematical abilities, which he had exhibited in 1494 in his enormously influential work *Summa de Arithmetica,*

Les illustrations par Léonard du traité *De Divina Proportione* de Luca Pacioli

Le moine franciscain Luca Pacioli – un peu plus âgé que Léonard – fait à Milan en 1497 la connaissance de celui-ci et noue bientôt avec lui de solides liens d'amitié. Connu pour être « l'inventeur de la comptabilité en partie double », Pacioli attire surtout Léonard par ses talents de mathématicien, qu'il a montrés en 1494 avec la publication d'une œuvre extrêmement importante, sa *Summa*

Leonardos Illustrationen zu Luca Paciolis *De Divina Proportione*

Der Franziskanermönch Luca Pacioli, wohl einige Jahre älter als Leonardo, lernte diesen 1497 in Mailand kennen und es entstand bald eine Freundschaft. Bekannt als „Vater der doppelten Buchführung" zog Pacioli Leonardo vor allem wegen seiner mathematischen Begabung in Bann, die er 1494 in seinem enorm einflussreichen Werk *Summa de Arithmetica, Geometria, Proportioni*

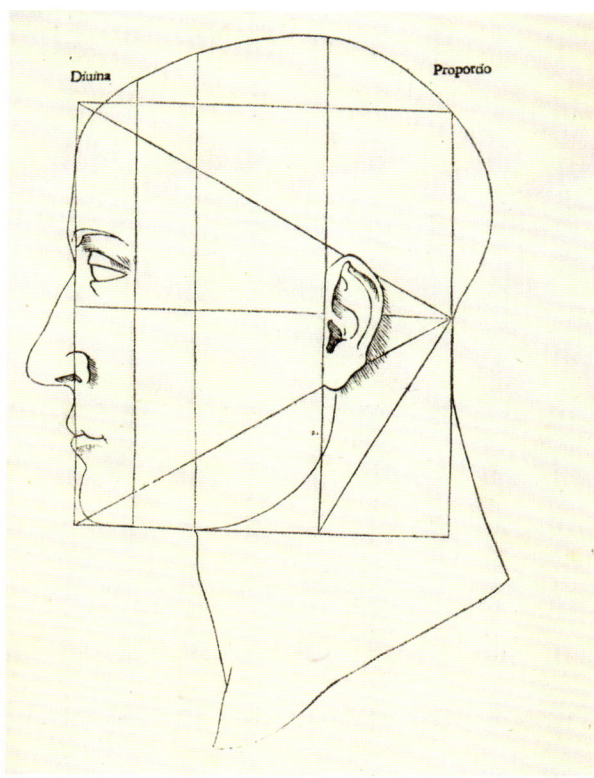

Las ilustraciones de Leonardo sobre *De Divina Proportione* de Luca Pacioli

El monje franciscano Fray Luca de Pacioli conoció a Leonardo, quién era algo más joven que él, en 1497 en Milán. Pronto se hicieron amigos. Conocido como "el padre del método contable de la partida doble" Pacioli llevó a Leonardo por su camino, sobre todo al reconocer sus grandes dotes para el pensamiento matemático, que había dejado patentes en 1494 en su obra *Summa de Arithmetica,*

Le illustrazioni di Leonardo per il *De Divina Proportione* di Luca Pacioli

Nel 1497 Leonardo conobbe a Milano il monaco francescano Luca Pacioli, di alcuni anni più vecchio, con il quale fece subito amicizia. Noto come "l'inventore della contabilità a partita doppia", Pacioli affascinò Leonardo soprattutto per il suo talento matematico, che aveva dimostrato nel 1494 nella sua autorevole opera *Summa de Arithmetica, Geometria, Proportioni et Proportionalità*. Già negli

Leonardo's illustraties bij Luca Pacioli's *De Divina Proportione*

Leonardo leerde de franciscaner monnik Luca Pacioli, die vermoedelijk enkele jaren ouder was dan hijzelf, in 1497 in Milaan kennen, waarna er al snel een goede vriendschap ontstond. Pacioli stond bekend als 'de vader van de dubbele boekhouding' en was voor Leonardo van grote waarde vanwege zijn wiskundige inzichten, die hij in 1494 in zijn invloedrijke *Summa de Arithmetica,*

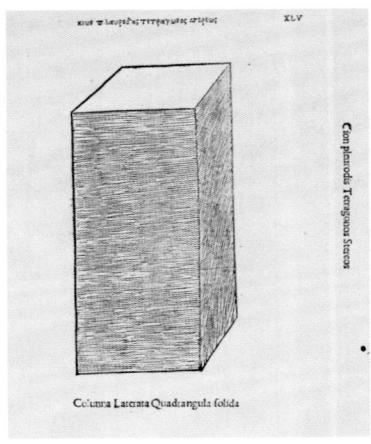
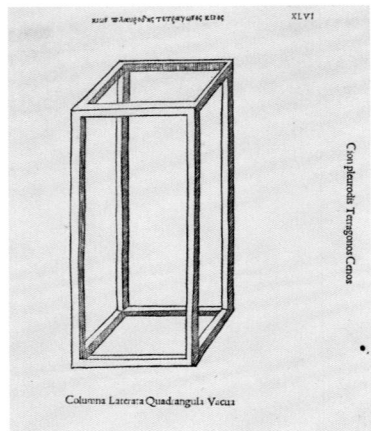
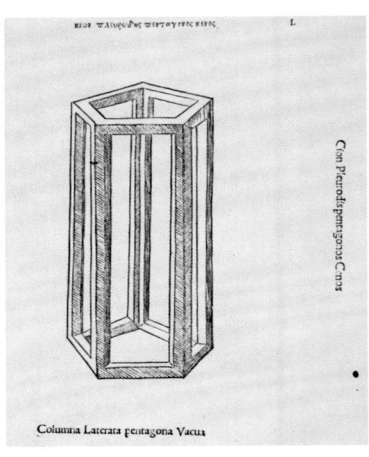

Geometria, Proportioni et Proportionalità. Pacioli had already worked as a professor at various Italian universities since the 1470s, before being invited to Milan by Ludovico Sforza.

The treatise on which Pacioli worked with Leonardo during the years following his arrival in Milan, during which time he shared accommodation with Leonardo and taught him mathematics, consisted of three parts. The first part deals with the Golden Section from a mathematical perspective and its application in art. In the second part, Pacioli considers Vitruvius's ideas on the use of mathematics in architecture, taking into account his views on the "human dimension", to which the architecture must be directed accordingly. The third part consists predominantly of a translation of some Latin texts of Piero della Francesca into Italian, which later

de Arithmetica, Geometria, Proportioni et Proportionalità. Depuis les années 1470 déjà, Pacioli avait travaillé comme professeur dans différentes universités italiennes, avant d'être appelé à Milan par Ludovic Sforza.

Le traité auquel le moine travaillait après son arrivée à Milan, en compagnie de Léonard avec qui il partageait la même résidence et à qui il enseignait les mathématiques, se composait de trois parties. La première étudie le Nombre d'or dans la perspective mathématique et de ses possibilités d'application dans l'art. Dans la deuxième partie, Pacioli traite des idées de Vitruve sur l'utilisation des mathématiques pour l'architecture et aborde aussi, ce faisant, ses considérations sur la « mesure humaine » qui doit être la référence absolue et la pierre de touche de l'architecture. La troisième partie est essentiellement une

et Proportionalità gezeigt hatte. Schon seit den 1470er-Jahren hatte Pacioli als Professor an verschiedenen italienischen Universitäten gearbeitet, bevor er von Ludovico Sforza nach Mailand geholt wurde.

Das Traktat, an dem Pacioli in den Jahren nach seiner Ankunft in Mailand gemeinsam mit Leonardo arbeitete, während er sich mit ihm eine Wohnung teilte und ihn in Mathematik unterrichtete, bestand aus drei Teilen. Der erste Teil beschäftigt sich mit dem Goldenen Schnitt aus mathematischer Perspektive und seinen Anwendungsmöglichkeiten in der Kunst. Im zweiten Teil behandelt Pacioli Vitruvs Ideen zur Nutzbarmachung der Mathematik für die Architektur und greift dabei auch dessen Ansichten zum „menschlichen Maß" auf, nach dem sich die Architektur zu richten habe. Den

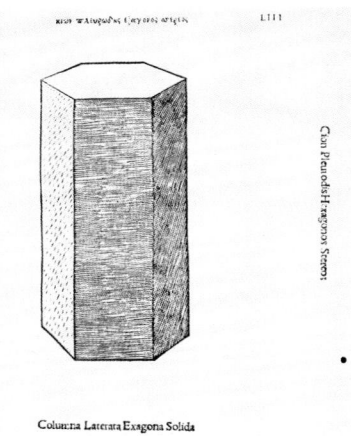

Columna Laterata Exagona Solida

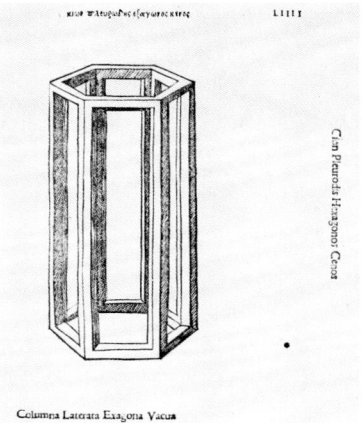

Columna Laterata Exagona Vacua

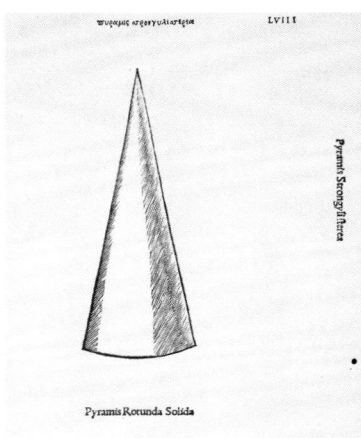

Pyramis Rotunda Solida

Geometria, Proportioni et Proportionalità de gran influencia. Desde los años 1470 Pacioli había trabajado como profesor en diversas universidades italianas, antes de que Ludovico Sforza lo llevará a Milán.

El tratado en el que Pacioli trabajaría conjuntamente con Leonardo, mientras compartían piso, tras su llegada a Milán se dividió en tres partes. La primera parte versaba sobre el número áureo desde la perspectiva matemática y sus posibilidades de aplicación en el arte. En la segunda parte, Pacioli analizaba las ideas de Vitruvio sobre la utilidad de las matemáticas en arquitectura, recurriendo para ello a su opinión sobre "las medidas humanas", según las que se debería regir la arquitectura. La tercera parte contiene sobre todo una traducción de algunas escrituras de textos de Piero della Francesca del latín al italiano, lo que posteriormente llevaría a Paciolo a

anni Settanta del 1400 Pacioli aveva lavorato come professore in diverse università italiane, prima di essere chiamato da Ludovico Sforza a Milano.

Il trattato al quale Pacioli lavorò con Leonardo negli anni della sua permanenza a Milano, mentre condivideva con lui un appartamento e lo istruiva in matematica, era composto da tre parti. La prima parte era dedicata al rapporto aureo da una prospettiva matematica e le sue possibilità di applicazione nell'arte. Nella seconda parte Pacioli tratta le idee di Vitruvio per l'utilizzazione della matematica in architettura e riprende anche quelle opinioni sulla "misura umana" alle quali si rivolge l'architettura. La terza parte è costituita prevalentemente da una traduzione in italiano di alcuni scritti in latino di Piero della Francesca, che in seguito portò a Pacioli un'accusa di plagio

Geometria, Proportioni et Proportionalità had samengevat. Al in de jaren veertig van de vijftiende eeuw had Pacioli als professor aan diverse Italiaanse universiteiten lesgegeven, waarna hij door Ludovico Sforza naar Milaan werd geroepen.

Na zijn aankomst in Milaan werkte Pacioli samen met Leonardo aan dit traktaat, terwijl hij met de kunstenaar een woning deelde en hem onderwees in de wiskunde. In het eerste deel van het traktaat gaat het over de gulden snede vanuit wiskundig perspectief en de toepassingen ervan in de kunsten. In het tweede deel behandelt Pacioli de ideeën van Vitruvius over toepasssingen van de wiskunde op de architectuur, waarbij hij ook ingaat op diens opvattingen over de 'menselijke maat' waarop alle architectuur zou moeten zijn gebaseerd. Het derde deel is een vertaling in het

171

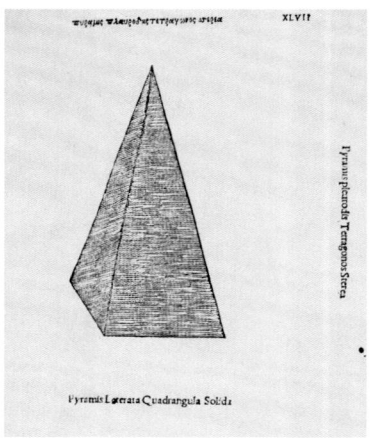

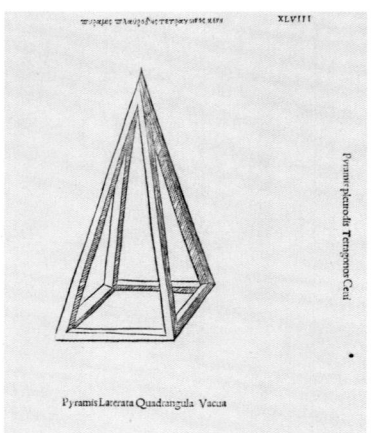

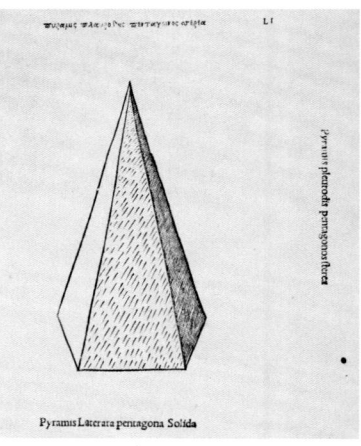

brought accusations of plagiarism against Pacioli, since he had not made it clear that it was the work of another.

Leonardo's contribution consisted mainly of illustrations reproduced in the appendix. These were subdivided into a sequence of 23 capital letters by Pacioli with a second series consisting of 56 woodcuts showing polyhedra, according to Leonardo's drawings, which may have originated in wooden models.

The year 1499 saw victory for the new French king, Louis XII, in the second Italian campaign, during which Milan fell to the French crown, forcing Leonardo and Pacioli to leave the city.

traduction en italien de quelques écrits (en latin) de Piero della Francesca – ce qui valut à Pacioli, plus tard, une accusation de plagiat, car il n'avait pas expressément signalé que c'était l'ouvrage d'un autre.

La contribution de Léonard réside avant tout dans l'appendice d'illustrations imprimées. Celles-ci se divisent à leur tour en une suite de 23 lettres majuscules de Pacioli et une seconde suite de 53 gravures sur bois représentant des polyèdres d'après des dessins de Léonard – peut-être exécutés eux-mêmes d'après des maquettes en bois.

En 1499, avec la victoire de Louis XII de France au cours de la deuxième campagne d'Italie, le duché de Milan échoit à la couronne française, ce qui contraint Vinci et Pacioli à quitter la ville.

dritten Teil bildet überwiegend eine Übersetzung einiger lateinischer Schriften Piero della Francescos ins Italienische, was Paciolo später einen Plagiatsvorwurf einbrachte, da er es nicht als Werk eines Anderen kenntlich gemacht hatte.

Leonardos Beitrag bestand vor allem in den im Appendix abgedruckten Illustrationen. Diese wiederum waren unterteilt in eine Abfolge von 23 Großbuchstaben und eine zweite Folge, bestehend aus 56 Holzschnitten von Polyedern nach Zeichnungen Leonardos, welche möglicherweise nach Holzmodellen entstanden waren.

1499, mit dem Sieg des neuen französischen Königs Ludwig XII. im zweiten italienischen Feldzug, fiel Mailand an die französische Krone, was Leonardo ebenso wie Pacioli dazu zwang, die Stadt zu verlassen.

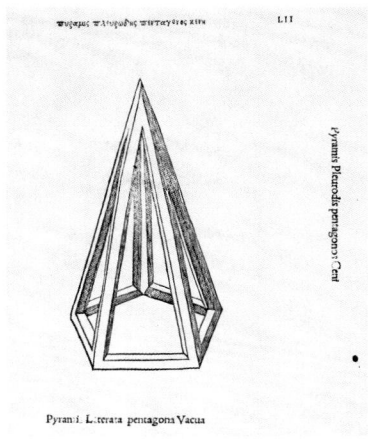

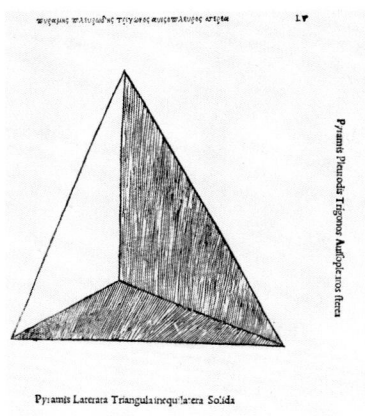

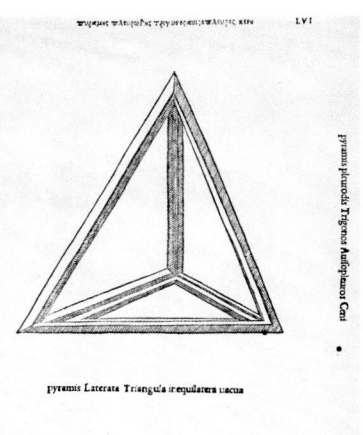

ser acusado de plagio, por no mencionar claramente que se trataba de la obra de otra persona.

Leonardo contribuyó sobre todo a las ilustraciones impresas en el apéndice. Éstas a su vez estaban divididas en una serie de 23 letras capitales y una segunda serie de 56 xilografías de poliedros llevadas a cabo según los dibujos de Leonardo, que probablemente se hubiesen gestado con modelos de madera.

En 1499 con la victoria del nuevo rey francés Luís XII durante la segunda campaña italiana, Milán calló bajo la corona francesa, lo que obligó tanto a Leonardo como a Pacioli a abandonar la ciudad.

perché non l'aveva riconosciuta come l'opera di un'altra persona.

Il contributo di Leonardo consiste soprattutto nelle illustrazioni pubblicate nell'appendice, che furono inoltre suddivise in una successione di 23 lettere maiuscole e una seconda serie composta da 56 xilografie di poliedri secondo i disegni di Leonardo, i quali probabilmente furono realizzati in base a modelli di legno.

Nel 1499, con la vittoria del nuovo re francese Luigi XII nella seconda campagna militare in Italia, Milano cadde sotto la corona francese, e Leonardo e Pacioli furono costretti ad abbandonare la città.

Italiaans van enkele Latijnse geschriften van Piero della Francesca, wat Paciolo op het verwijt kwam te staan dat hij plagiaat had gepleegd, aangezien hij niet had aangegeven dat dit werk door iemand anders was geschreven.

Leonardo's bijdrage aan het traktaat bestond vooral uit illustraties, die in een bijlage waren afgedrukt: deze waren onderverdeeld in een reeks van 23 grote kapitalen en een tweede reeks, bestaande uit 56 houtsneden van veelvlakken naar tekeningen van Leonardo, mogelijk op basis van houten modellen.

Met de zege in 1499 van de nieuwe Franse koning Lodewijk XII in de Tweede Italiaanse Oorlog viel Milaan aan de Franse kroon en moesten Leonardo en Pacioli de stad ontvluchten.

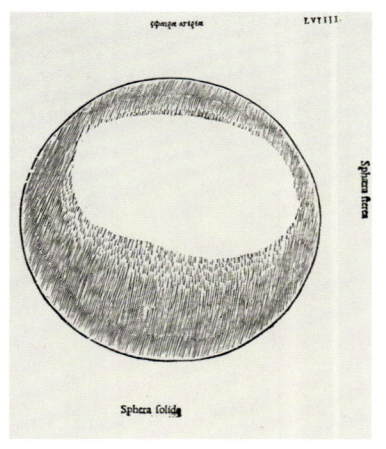

Sphera solida

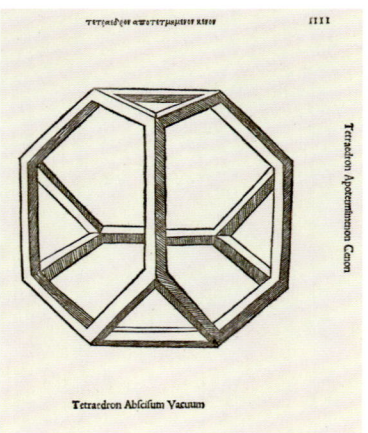

Tetraedron Abscisum Vacuum

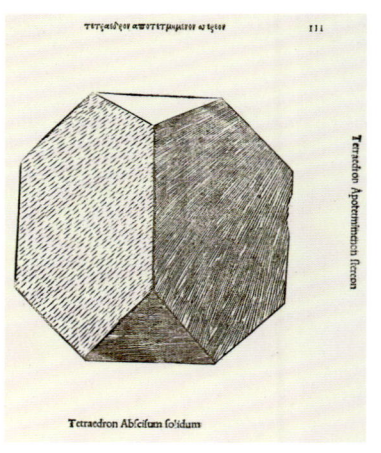

Tetraedron Abscisum solidum

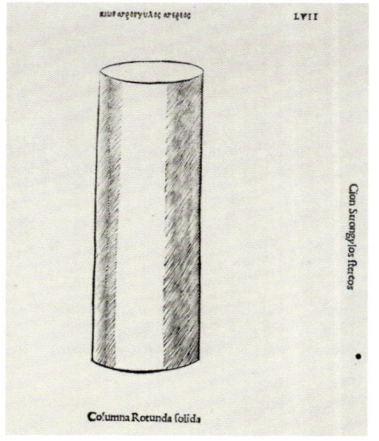

Columna Rotunda solida

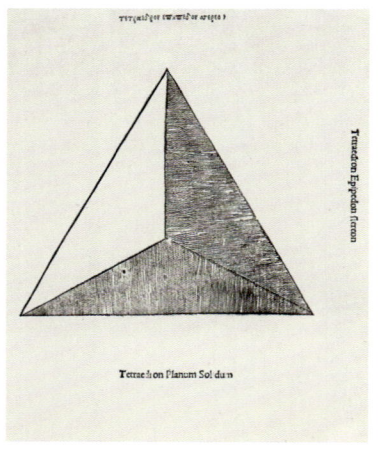

Tetraedron Planum Solidum

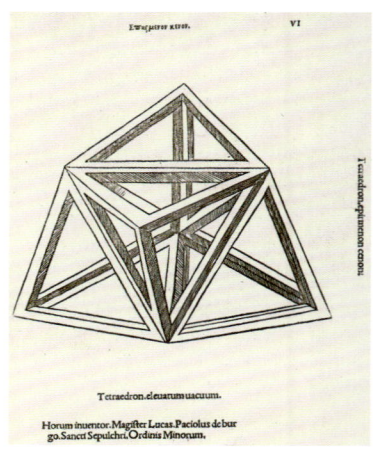

Tetraedron elevatum vacuum.

Horum inuentor. Magister Lucas. Paciolus de bur
go. Sancti Sepulchri. Ordinis Minorum.

Sphera ferrea

Tetraedron Apotetmimenon Cenon

Tetraedron Apotetmimenon stereon

Cion Strongylos stereos

Tetraedron Epipedon stereon

Τetraedron epianerion cenon.

174

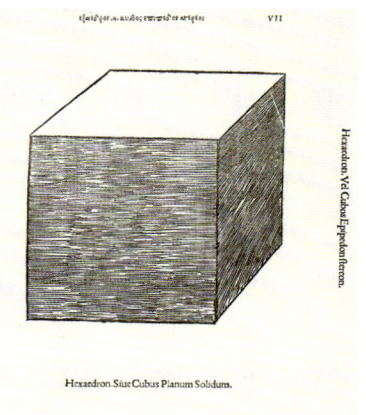

Hexaedron. Vel Cubus Expeditum stereon.

Hexaedron. Siue Cubus Planum Solidum.

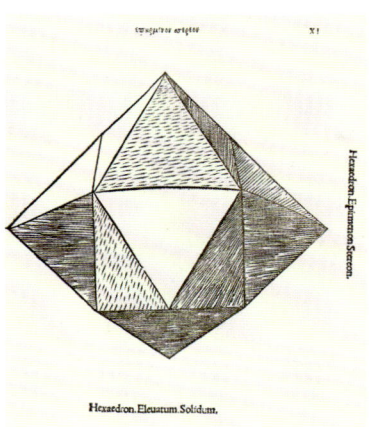

Hexaedron. Epiuncton Stereon.

Hexaedron. Eleuatum Solidum.

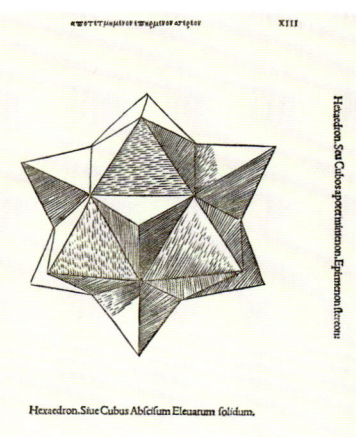

Hexaedron. Siue Cubus o potentminaton. Epiuncton stereon.

Hexaedron. Siue Cubus Abscisum Eleuatum solidum.

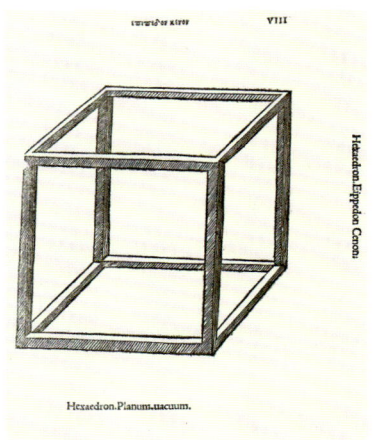

Hexaedron. Expeditum Cenon.

Hexaedron. Planum. uacuum.

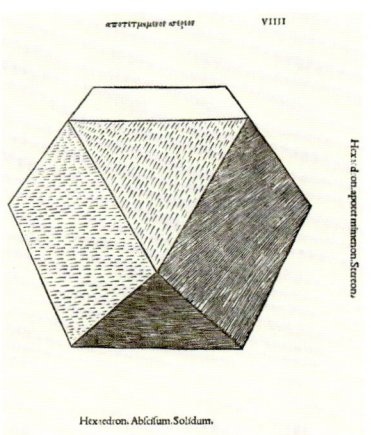

Hexaedron. o potentminaton. Stereon.

Hexaedron. Abscisum. Solidum.

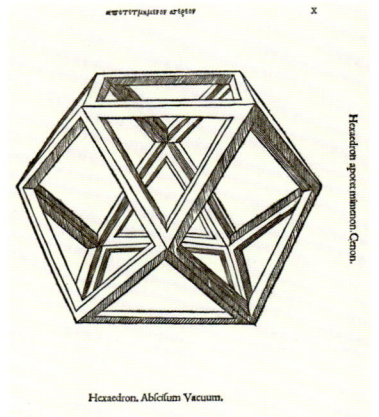

Hexaedron. apotetminaton. Cenon.

Hexaedron. Abscisum Vacuum.

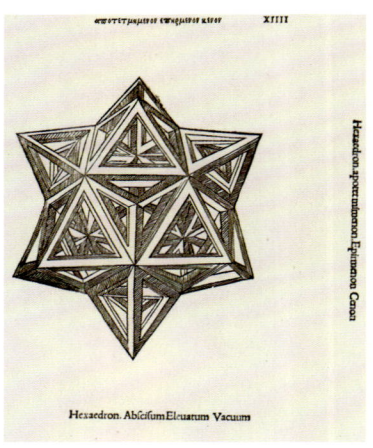

Hexaedron. Abscissum Eleuatum Vacuum

Hexaedron apocenitomon Epitameno Canon

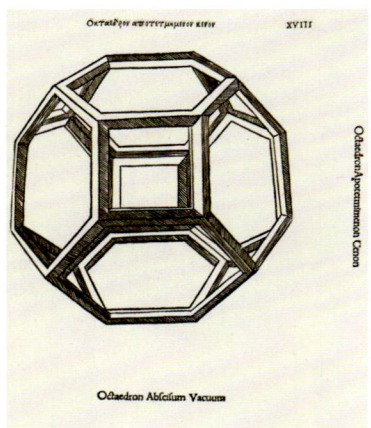

Octaedron Abscissum Vacuum

Octaedron Apocenitomon Canon

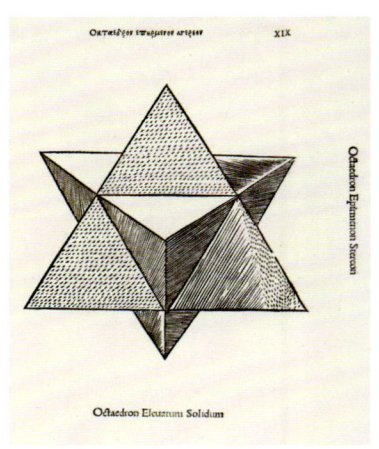

Octaedron Eleuatum Solidum

Octaedron Epitameno Stereon

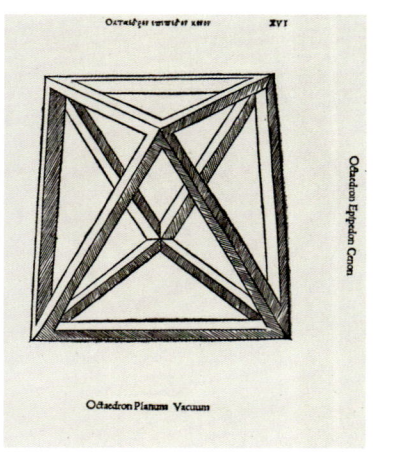

Octaedron Planum Vacuum

Octaedron Eppedon Canon

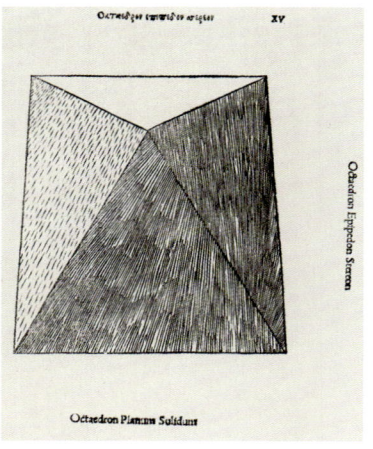

Octaedron Planum Solidum

Octaedron Eppedon Stereon

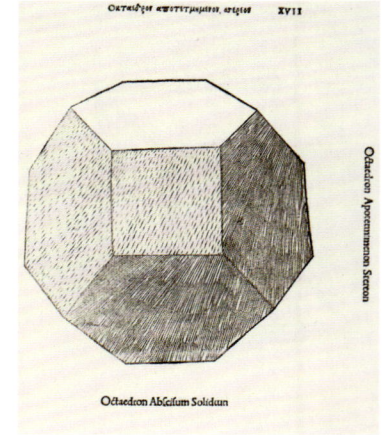

Octaedron Abscissum Solidum

Octaedron Apocenitomon Stereon

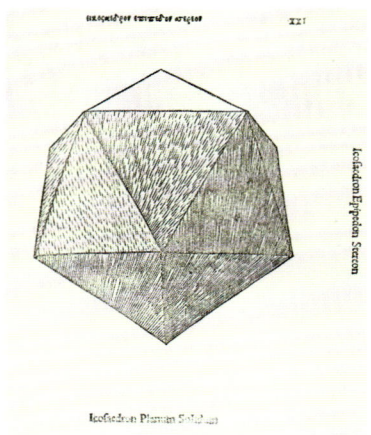

Icosaedron Planum Solidum

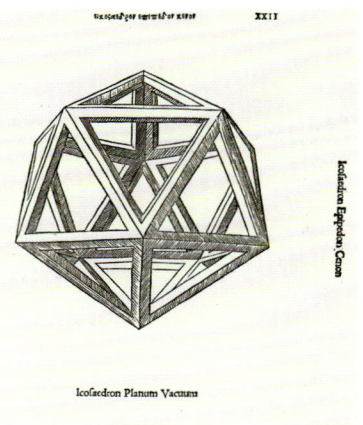

Icosaedron Planum Vacuum

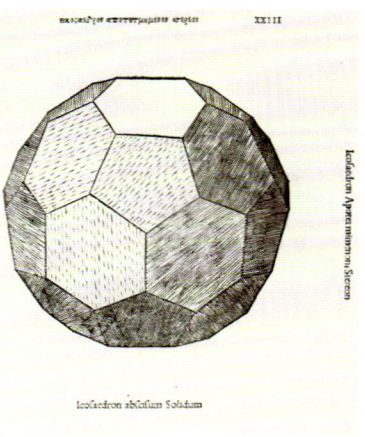

Icosaedron abscisum Solidum

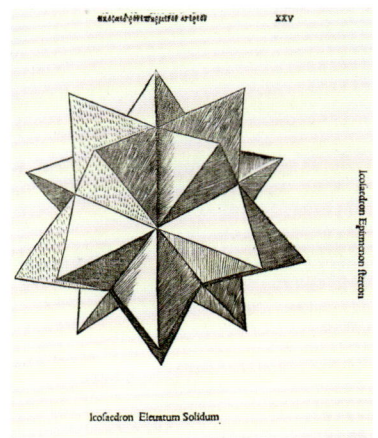

Icosaedron Eleuatum Solidum

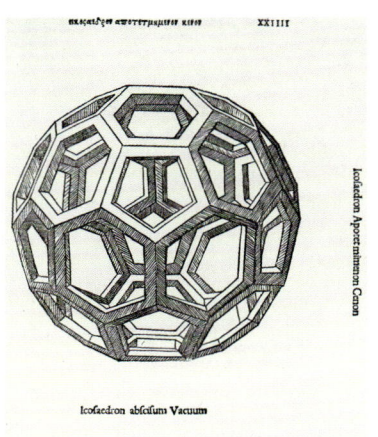

Icosaedron abscisum Vacuum

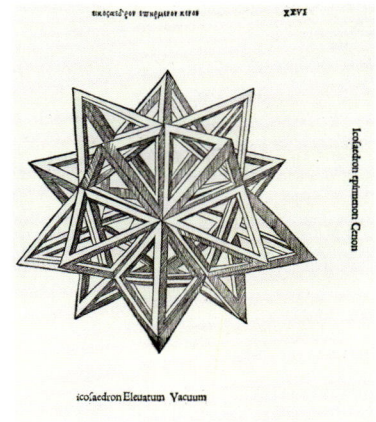

Icosaedron Eleuatum Vacuum

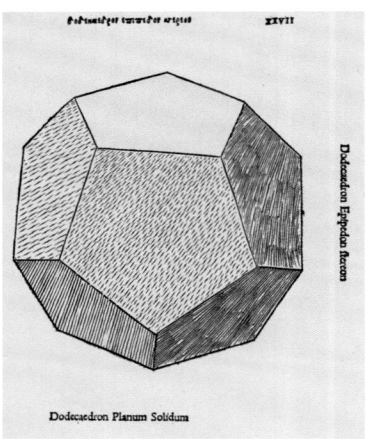

Dodecaedron Elipedon Planon

Dodecaedron Planum Solidum

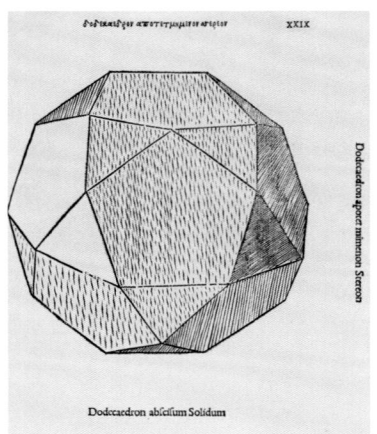

Dodecaedron apeci mixenon Sternon

Dodecaedron abscisfum Solidum

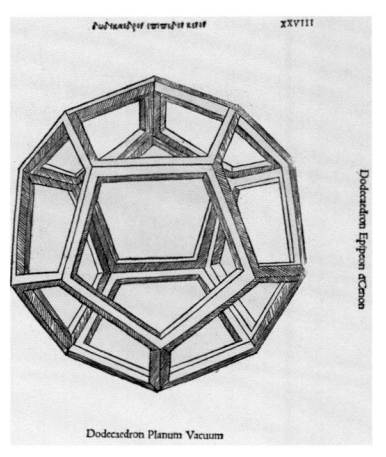

Dodecaedron Elipedon Cenon

Dodecaedron Planum Vacuum

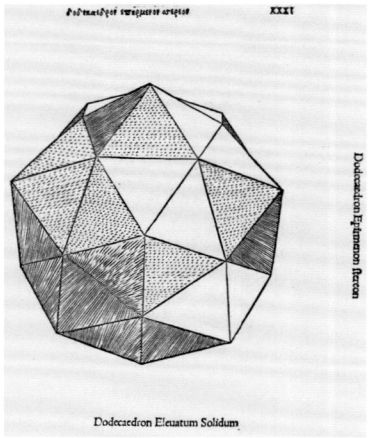

Dodecaedron Epistanon Sternon

Dodecaedron Eleuatum Solidum

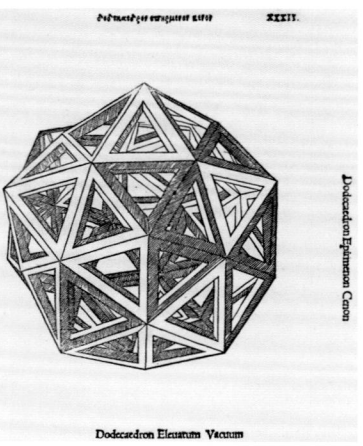

Dodecaedron Epistanon Cenon

Dodecaedron Eleuatum Vacuum

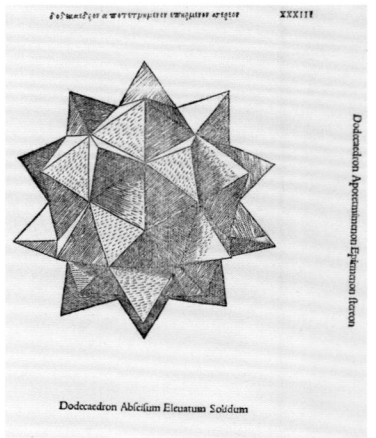

Dodecaedron Apecumixenon Epistanon Sternon

Dodecaedron Abscisfum Eleuatum Solidum

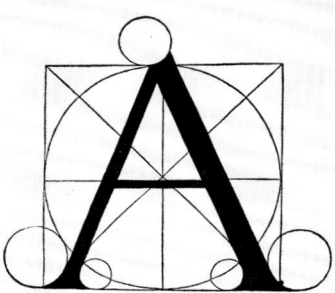

Questa letera A si caua del tondo e del suo quadro:la gãba da man drita uol esser grossa dele noue parti.una de la lterza. La gamba senistra uol esser la mita de la gãba grossa. La gamba de mezo uol esser la terza parte de la gamba grossa. La largheza de dita letera cadauna gamba per mezo de la crosiera.quella di mezo alquanto piu bassa, com meuedi qui per li diametri segnati.

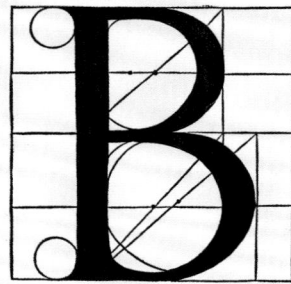

Questa letera.B. si compone de doi tõdi e quello desotto sie lo piu grando de li noue parti.una cioe uol esser li cinque nõi de la sua altera p diametro. E quella desopra uol esser li quatro noni medesimamente per diametro cõme qui desopra proportionatamēte negliochi te sa presente.

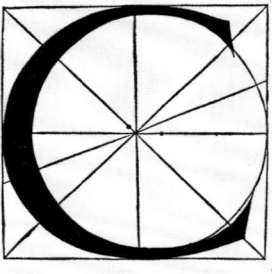

Questa letera .C.se caua del tondo e del suo quadro in grossandola la quarta parte de fore e ancora de dentro. La testa de sopra finesse sopra la croci del diametro e circonferentia. Quella de sotto passando la croci mezo nono a esso la costa del quadrato cõme apare in la figura e cause le comme uno. O.

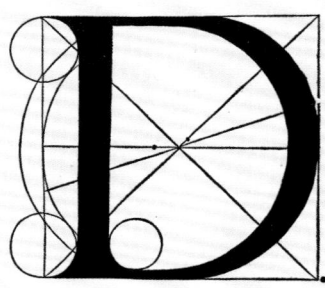

Questa letera. D. se caua del tondo e del quadro. La gamba derita uol esser de dentro le crosiere grossa de noue par ti.una il corpo se ingrossa cõmo de li altri tondi . La apicatura desopra uol esser grossa el terzo de la gamba grossa & quella de sotto el quarto ouer terzo.

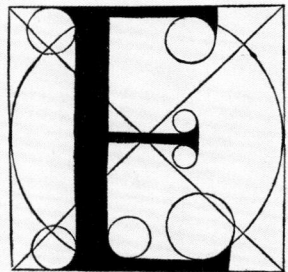

Questa lettera.E.se caua del tondo e del suo quadro . La gamba grossa uol esser de le noue parti.una . La gamba de sopra uol esser per la mita de la gamba grossa quella de sotto per simile . Quella de mezo per terza parte de la gãba grossa comme quella de mezo del . A. e la detta lettera uol esser larga meza del suo quadro & sic erit psectissima.

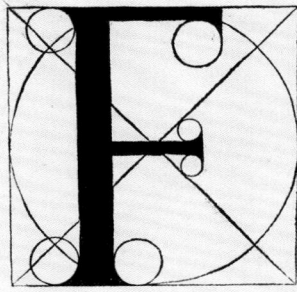

Questa littera .F.se forma a quel modo comela lfa .E. ne piu ne mãcho. excepto che .F. sie senza la terza gamba:come de nãci hauessi diffusamente alluoco de dicto .E. cum tutte sue proportioni. pero qui quello te basti .

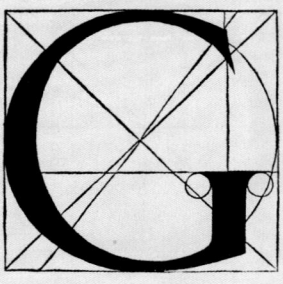

Questa lettera.G.se forma cõmel .C. del suo rondo e qua
dro. La gamba deritta de sotto uol esser alta un terzo del
suo quadro: e grossa de le noue parti luna de lalteza del
suo quadrato.

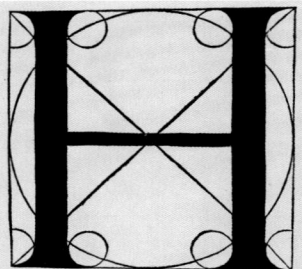

Questa lettera .H. se caua del tõdo e del suo quadro. le sue
gambe grosse se fanno per mezo le crosiere cioe doue se
intersecano li diametri del rondo e suo quadro. La grosse
za de ditte gambe uol esser de le noue parti una de lalteza
E quella de mezo se fa p mezeldiametro . la sua grosseza
uol esser la terza parte de la gamba grossa cõme trauer
so del. A.

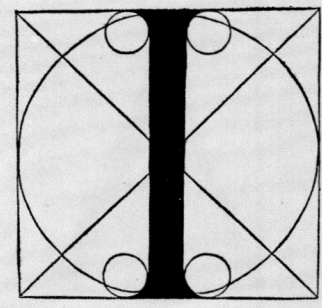

Questa lettera. I. se caua del tondo e del quadro la sua gro
seza uol esser de le noue parti luna che facil fia sua forma
tione fra laltre.

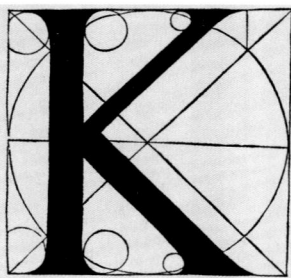

Questa lettera.K. se caua del rondo e del suo quadro tirã
do una linea per diametro del quadro i questa linea se fer
ma e termina le due gambe per mezo la gamba grossa. La
gamba de sotto uol esser grossa comme laltre gambe una
parte de le noue. Quella de sopra la mita de la grossa cõ
me la sinistra del. A. Quella de sotto uol esser longa fin ala
crociera ouer di fora. Quella de sopra dentro la crociera:

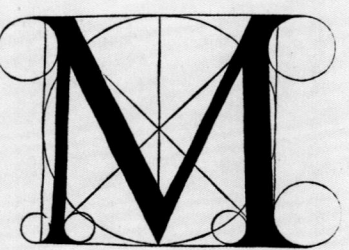

Questa lettera .M. se caua del tondo e del suo quadro le
gambe suttili uogliõo esser per mezo de le grosse comme
la sinistra del. A. le extreme gambe uogiano esser al quan
to dentro al quadro le medie fra quelle e le intersecationi
de li diametri lor grosseze . grosse e sutili se referiscano a
quele del. A. cõme di sopra in figura aperto poi compren
dere.

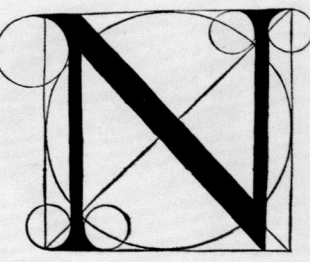

Questa lettera .N. se caua del suo rondo & etiam quadro
La prima gamba uol esser fora de la intersecatiõe de li dia
metri La trauersa de mezo uol esser grossa de le noue par
ti luna presa diametraliter. La terza gamba uol esser fora
de la crociera. Prima gamba & Vltima uogliõo esser gros
se la mita de la gamba grossa cioe d'una resta.

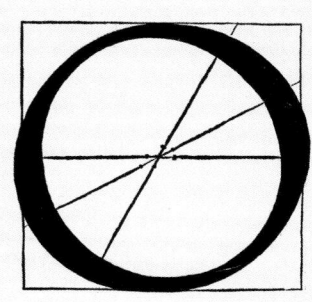

Questo .O. e perfectissimo.

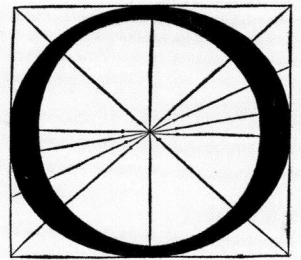

Questa lettera .O. se caua del rondo e del suo quadro se diuide in quatro parti cioe in croce per mezo le quatro li nee el corpo suo uol esser grosso de le noue parti luna el corpo suo de sopra uol esser p mezo del suo grosso. Le sue pance una uol pender in su laltra in giu el surile del corpo uol esser per la terza parte de la sua pacia. E per che de li sui sonno doi opinioni po dinanze re no posto un altro a mio piacere perfectissimo e tu prendi qual te pare e di loro for marai el .Q. comme disotto intenderai a suo luoco.

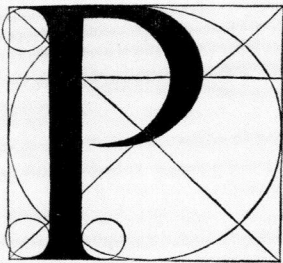

Questa lettera .P. si caua del rondo e del suo quadro. La sua gamba grossa uol esser de le noue parti luna la forma del tondo uol esser grande comme quela del .B. da basso e la sua grosseza de la pancia uol esser tanto quanto la gã ba grossa e si uol principiar ditta lettera da le crociere del tondo grande cioe da le intersecationi de li d amenti & sic erit perfectissima

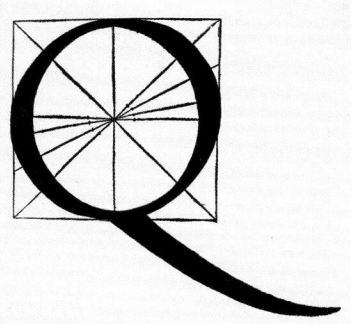

Questa lettera .Q. comme disopra dissi se caua del .O. terminãdo sua gamba tre teste de sua alterza sotto el qdrato cioe de le ni ue parti de le sue teste e le noue parti de le sue teste de le noue parti e le parti dretto del suo quadrato ouero diametro del suo rõdo cõ me qui appare proportionata guidando le pance grosse Te e sue suri li opposite a pũcto comme del .O. suo ditto E la sua giba uol esser longa noue teste cioe quanto el suo quadrato arelargu o. e la fine uol esser alta la pontha in su un nono de lalterza se cuando la curuita de la penna cõ la digradatione de la sua grossezza.

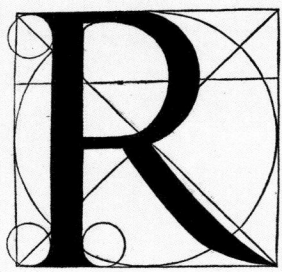

Questa lettera .R. se caua de la lettera .B. el suo rondo sie de sotto dal centro una meza gamba. Tutta questa lettera uol esser detro de le croci excepto la gãba storta uol uscir for de le croci fin al fin del quadro. Dicta gãba storta uol esser grossa de le noue parti luna terminata sursã in põta nel lã gulo del quadro a modo de curuelinee ut hic in exẽ plo patet.

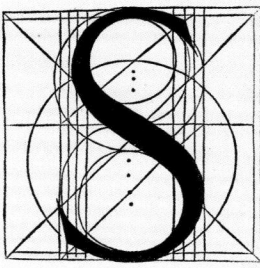

Questa lettera .S. se caua de octo tondi & questa sie la sua Ragione ut hic in exemplo apparet li quali per le sue pa a lelle trouãdo lor centri trouerai quelli de sotto esserma giori de li de sopra un terzo del nono del suo quadro. La pancia de mezo uol esser grossa el nono aponto de lalte za. Le suri in un terzo de la grosseza terminando le teste cõ sua gratia.

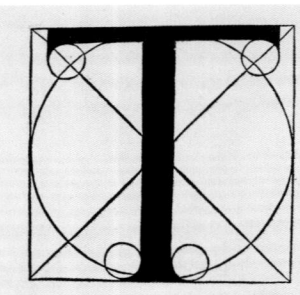

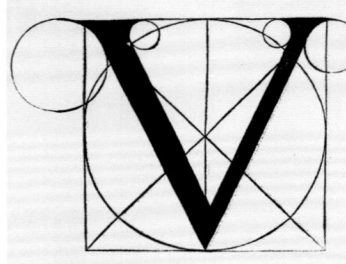

Questa lettera, T. se caua del suo quadro e tondo. La gam
ba grossa uol essere poncto comme del. I so decto.   Quel
la trauersa uol esser grossa per la mita de la grossa comme
quelle disopra al. E. & F. e uol terminare mezza testa per
lato da le coste del suo quadro e sia ala uista gratilima.

Questa lettera. V. se caua del suo quadro tutto intero. La
gamba senistra uol esser grossa el nono del suo quadro
sa diameraliter cóme la dextra del. A e trauersa di. N. la
dextra la mita de la grossa pur diameetraliter presa cóme
la senistra del. A e termina ponetto nela basa del quadro
in fin del diametro del tondo.

182

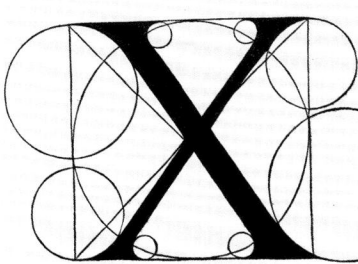

Questa lettera.X. uol tutto el suo quadro incrociádo sue
gambe nella intersecatione de li diametri.E luna uol esser
grossa la nona parte de laltezza.Laltra la mita prese dia /
metraliter terminando sue gambe com debita gratia secó
do la forza de li tondi piccoli.

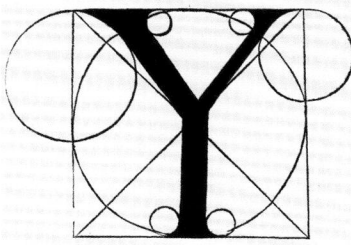

Questa letera.Y.uol tutto el quadro.le gambe dextra e si
nistra uogliano esser grosse côme la proportione de quelle
del.V.saluo che le terminano a ponchto in su la interseca /
tione de li diametri.e da inde in giu se cira tor côiunctione
ala basa del quadrato .grossa el nono del qdrato le reste
de sopra finescano suli so rondi côme uedi.

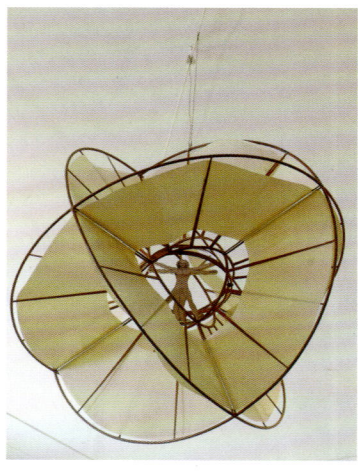

Reconstruction of da Vinci's flying sphere
Reconstitution d'un projet de sphère volante
Rekonstruktion von Leonardos fliegender Kugel
Reconstrucción de la esfera voladora de Leonardo
Ricostruzione della sfera volante di Leonardo
Reconstructie van Leonardo's vliegende kogel

Museo Leonardiano, Vinci

Leonardo as an inventor

Most of the writings and designs on mechanics, architecture and engineering come from Leonardo's time at the Milan court. However, it does not seem too far-fetched to search for the roots of his inventiveness earlier, with his constant curiosity towards nature in general, and with humans and animals in particular. If there is a common motivation shared by many of his inventions, it is the search for a meaningful connection between human power and the force of nature. A second possible source of inspiration may be that Leonardo had witnessed the construction work on Florence Cathedral, with the various items of equipment necessary for the undertaking awakening in him a strong interest in technology and mechanics.

This applies in particular to the imaginative devices and apparatus which owed thanks to the age-old human dream of flying. Leonardo developed

Léonard l'inventeur

La plupart des écrits et des projets de Léonard concernant la mécanique, l'architecture et l'ingénierie datent du temps passé à la cour de Milan. Toutefois, il n'est pas inconcevable de rechercher antérieurement les racines de son génie inventif – dans son intérêt constant pour la nature en général et pour les organismes vivants en particulier, qu'ils soient humains ou animaux. Car s'il existe une motivation commune à beaucoup de ses découvertes, c'est bien la quête incessante d'une relation raisonnée entre la force de l'Homme et la puissance de la Nature. La deuxième source d'inspiration, suppose-t-on, pourrait avoir été que Léonard devait participer aux travaux de la cathédrale de Florence, de sorte que les différents matériels indispensables à ce chantier ont dû éveiller chez lui un très fort intérêt pour la technique et la mécanique.

Leonardo als Erfinder

Die meisten Schriften und Entwürfe zur Mechanik, zur Architektur und zum Ingenieurswesen stammen aus Leonardos Zeit am Mailänder Hof. Dennoch erscheint es nicht zu weit hergeholt, die Wurzeln für seine Erfindungskunst bereits früher zu suchen, in seiner steten Beschäftigung mit der Natur im Allgemeinen und mit den menschlichen wie tierischen Lebewesen im Besonderen. Denn wenn es eine gemeinsame Motivation in vielen seiner Erfindungen gibt, so ist es die Suche nach einer sinnvollen Verbindung zwischen menschlicher Kraft und der Kraft der Natur. Die zweite Inspirationsquelle, so vermutet man, könnte gewesen sein, dass Leonardo noch die Bauarbeiten am Dom von Florenz miterleben durfte, wobei die verschiedenen dafür notwendigen Gerätschaften bei ihm ein starkes Interesse an Technik und Mechanik ausgelöst haben sollen.

Model of a water wheel
Maquette d'une roue hydraulique
Modell eines Wasserrads
Modelo de una rueda hidráulica
Modello di una ruota idraulica
Model van een waterrad

Wood/Bois, Museo Leonardiano, Vinci

Leonardo como inventor

La mayoría de las escrituras y bocetos sobre mecánica, arquitectura e ingeniería proceden de la época de Leonardo en la Corte de Milán. No parece que nos remontemos demasiado en el tiempo, si buscamos los orígenes de su capacidad de invención desde sus inicios como artista, en su continuo análisis de la naturaleza, en particular de los seres humanos y animales. Pues si es que existe un denominador común en aquello que motivó la mayoría de sus inventos, es la búsqueda de una conexión entre la fuerza del ser humano y la fuerza de la naturaleza. Su segunda fuente de inspiración, según lo que se especula, podría haber sido que Leonardo haya podido vivir los trabajos de construcción del Domo de Florencia en primera persona. Con ello el uso de los diferentes artilugios necesarios para su construcción despertaría en él un gran interés por la técnica y la mecánica.

Leonardo come inventore

La maggioranza degli scritti e disegni di meccanica, architettura e ingegneria provengono dal periodo che Leonardo trascorse alla corte milanese. Tuttavia non sembra troppo inverosimile ricercare le radici della sua arte dell'invenzione già prima, cioè nel suo studio costante della natura in generale e degli esseri viventi umani e animali in particolare. Se esiste una motivazione comune in molte delle sue invenzioni, questa è la ricerca di un legame ragionevole tra la potenza umana e la forza della natura. La seconda fonte di ispirazione si presume che possa essere il fatto che Leonardo abbia assistito ai lavori di costruzione del Duomo di Firenze, e le varie attrezzature necessarie per tale impresa devono avere suscitato in lui un forte interesse per la tecnica e la meccanica.

Questo vale in modo particolare per i congegni e gli attrezzi ricchi di inventiva a cui si deve il sogno umano di volare.

Leonardo als uitvinder

De meeste van Leonardo's geschriften en ontwerpen met betrekking tot de mechanica, architectuur en vestingbouw stammen uit zijn tijd aan het Milanese hof. Maar het is waarschijnlijk dat de oorsprong van deze uitvindersspassie verder in het verleden ligt, in zijn voortdurende aandacht voor de natuur en met name voor het dierlijke en menselijk leven. Als we één duidelijke interesse kunnen aanwijzen die aan al zijn uitvindingen ten grondslag ligt, dan is het zijn zoektocht naar een zinvol verband tussen de krachten van de mens en die van de natuur. Een andere inspiratiebron was mogelijk het feit dat Leonardo de bouwwerkzaamheden aan de Florentijnse dom heeft meegemaakt, waarbij de verschillende kranen en andere werktuigen die daarvoor benodigd waren, bij hem een grote interesse voor techniek en mechanica moeten hebben opgewekt.

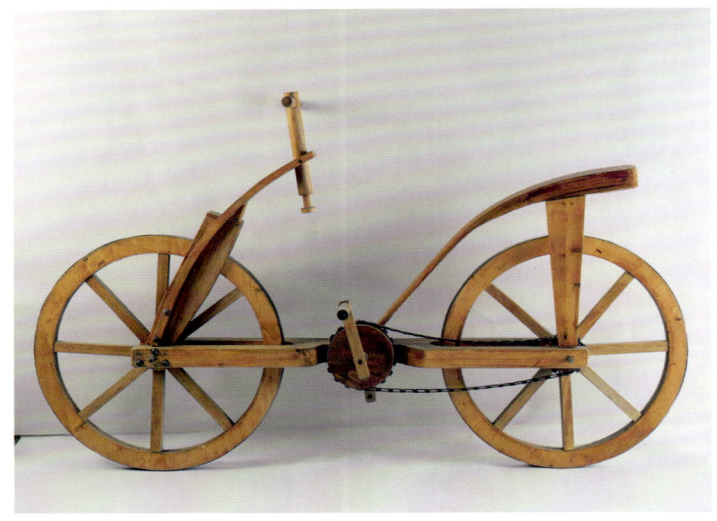

not only a parachute, but also aids to flight inspired by the wings of birds. In addition, he designed several devices which no longer relied solely on human muscle power, such as an aircraft whose propulsion drive is reminiscent of that of a modern helicopter, as well as a glider.

More mundane, but at least as useful, were his designs for different mechanical devices, such as spinning and weaving machines, or apparatuses for grinding needles and files.

If we consider the heartfelt and reverent paintings which we now associate with Leonardo, it may surprise us as to how much imagination and inventiveness he invested in military engineering. While this may seem to contradict our picture of the sensitive artist, one must, however, refer to the political background and the structure of Italy during the Renaissance times, with

Cela vaut en particulier pour les appareils et outillages si ingénieux attachés au vieux rêve humain de voler. Léonard développa ainsi non seulement un prototype de parachute, mais aussi des ailes artificielles. Il imagina en outre plusieurs dispositifs ne reposant plus sur la force musculaire humaine : par exemple un engin volant qui évoque ante litteram le système d'un hélicoptère moderne, ou encore un planeur. Plus prosaïques mais au moins aussi utiles, ses projets pour des outillages mécaniques domestiques – métier à filer, métier à tisser, appareils pour affûter limes et aiguilles – sont tout aussi remarquables.

Quand on songe aux peintures si profondément senties et religieuses attachées au nom de Léonard, on pourrait être surpris devant les trésors d'imagination et d'inventivité déployés

Dies gilt insbesondere für die erfindungsreichen Vorrichtungen und Geräte, die sich dem menschlichen Traum vom Fliegen verdanken. Leonardo entwickelte nicht nur einen Fallschirm, sondern auch Vogelflügeln nachempfundene Flughilfen. Darüber hinaus aber entwickelte er mehrere Geräte, die nicht mehr nur auf die menschliche Muskelkraft vertrauen, so etwa ein Fluggerät, dessen Luftschrauben-Antrieb sehr an einen modernen Hubschrauber erinnert sowie ein Gleitflugzeug.

Profaner, aber mindestens genauso nützlich, sind seine Entwürfe für unterschiedliche mechanische Geräte wie Spinn- und Webmaschinen oder Apparate zum Schleifen von Nadeln und Feilen.

Hält man sich die so tief empfundenen und andachtsvollen Gemälde vor Augen, die wir heute mit Leonardo

Model of a car driven by springs
Maquette d'une voiture mue par des ressorts
Modell eines von Federn angetriebenen Wagens
Modelo de un carro propulsado por resortes
Modello di un carro azionato da molle
Model van een door een veer aangedreven wagen

Wood/Bois, Museo Leonardiano, Vinci

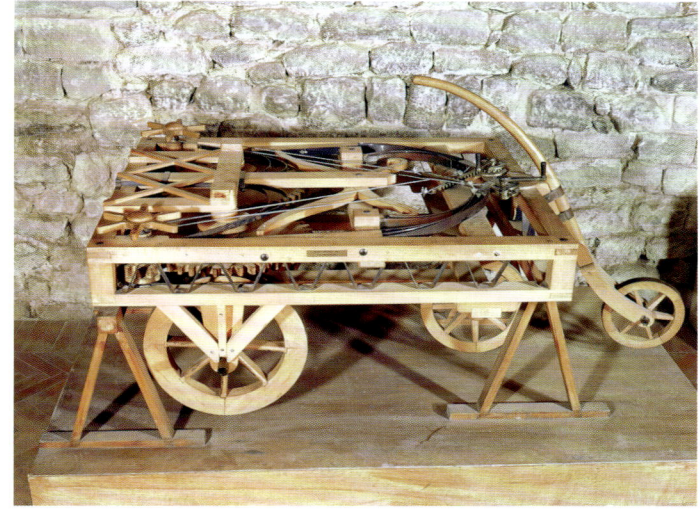

Su interés es sobre todo trasladable a los ingeniosos dispositivos y aparatos que se crearon para cumplir con el sueño de volar del ser humano. Leonardo no sólo desarrolló un paracaídas, sino que también diseñó unas alas de pájaro pensadas como una ayuda para alzarse al vuelo. Además también desarrolló varios artefactos, que no se basan en la fuerza motriz del ser humano, como por ejemplo un artefacto para volar, cuya propulsión por medio de una hélice recuerda a un helicóptero moderno, así como también un ala delta.

Más profanos, pero como mínimo tan útiles, son sus diseños para varios artilugios mecánicos de diversa utilidad, como las máquinas de hilar y tejer o los aparatos para afilar las agujas y limas.

Cuando evocamos a nuestra memoria las emotivas pinturas que hoy en día relacionamos con Leonardo, puede

Leonardo progettò non soltanto un paracadute, ma anche delle macchine per volare che si ispirano alle ali di uccello. Inoltre sviluppò diversi apparecchi che non si basavano più soltanto sulla forza muscolare umana, come ad esempio una macchina volante il cui azionamento ad elica ricorda molto un moderno elicottero o un aliante.

Profani, ma altrettanto utili, sono i suoi disegni di differenti attrezzi meccanici come filatrici e telai o apparecchi per affilare aghi e lime.

Se si considerano i dipinti così ricchi di sentimento e devozione che oggi si collegano a Leonardo, ci si può anche sorprendere di quanta fantasia e ricchezza di inventiva egli investì anche nell'ingegneria militare, il che sembra contraddire la nostra immagine dell'artista sensibile. Se però si pensa al quadro politico, quindi il periodo di

Dit geldt vooral voor Leonardo's vernuftige ontwerpen en apparaten waarmee hij de droom van de menselijke vlucht najoeg. Hij ontwikkelde niet alleen de parachute maar ook klapwiekvleugels om mensen als vogels te laten vliegen. Daarnaast ontwierp hij meerdere apparaten die niet afhankelijk waren van menselijke spierkracht, zoals een zweefvliegtuig en een vliegmachine met luchtschroef, die aan de moderne helikopter doet denken.

Alledaagser maar niet minder nuttig waren zijn ontwerpen voor verschillende contrapties, waaronder mechanische spinnenwielen en weefgetouwen en apparaten voor het scherpen en slijpen van naalden en vijlen.

Als we stilstaan bij de dromerige en intense schilderijen waarmee wij Leonardo tegenwoordig associëren, zal het misschien verrassen hoeveel

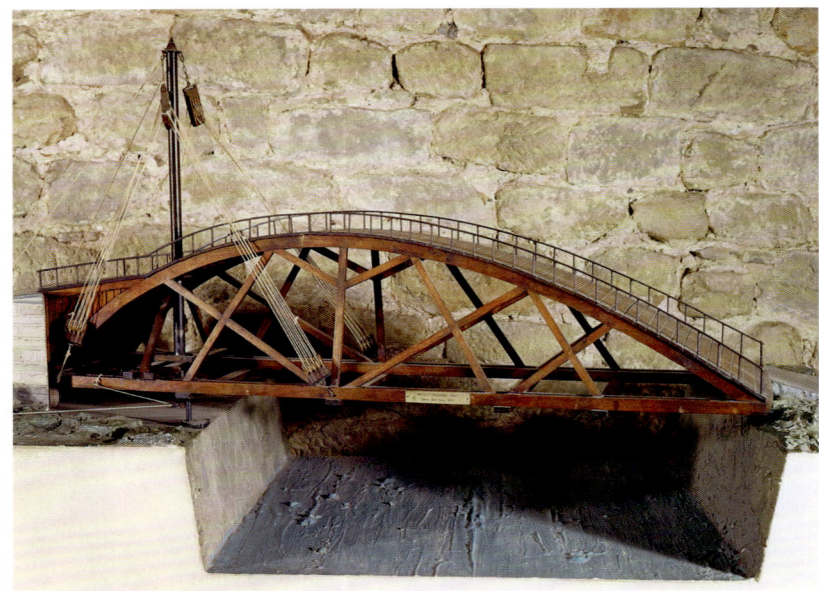

its continually warring micro-states. It is clear that a polymath such as Leonardo would also serve the warlords when in financial difficulties.

Only a few of his designs were realised during his lifetime, but more than a few —albeit centuries later—have proved their functionality.

par l'artiste dans l'ingénierie militaire – en contradiction avec notre vision de son raffinement, de son humanisme et de sa foi. Mais il suffit de penser au contexte politique dans l'Italie de la Renaissance, avec cette multitude de principautés belliqueuses toujours prêtes à guerroyer entre elles, pour comprendre que même un génie universel comme Léonard se soit mis au service des seigneurs de la guerre quand il avait besoin d'argent…

Seuls quelques-uns de ces projets ont été réalisés de son temps, mais fort peu se sont révélés fiables et efficaces ; il en va de même pour ceux qui ont été réalisés bien des siècles plus tard.

verbinden, so mag es überraschen, wie viel Fantasie und Erfindungsreichtum er auch in militärische Ingenieurskunst investierte, erscheint uns diese doch unserem Bild vom feinsinnigen Künstler zu widersprechen. Denkt man jedoch an den politischen Hintergrund, also die Umbruchzeit der Renaissance und die Struktur Italiens in dieser Zeit mit seinen sich ständig bekriegenden Kleinstterritorien, wird erklärlich, dass auch ein Universalgenie wie Leonardo sich den Kriegsherren andiente, wenn er in Geldnot war.

Nur einige seiner Entwürfe wurden bereits zu seiner Zeit realisiert, doch haben sich nicht wenige – wenn auch Jahrhunderte später – als funktionstüchtig erwiesen.

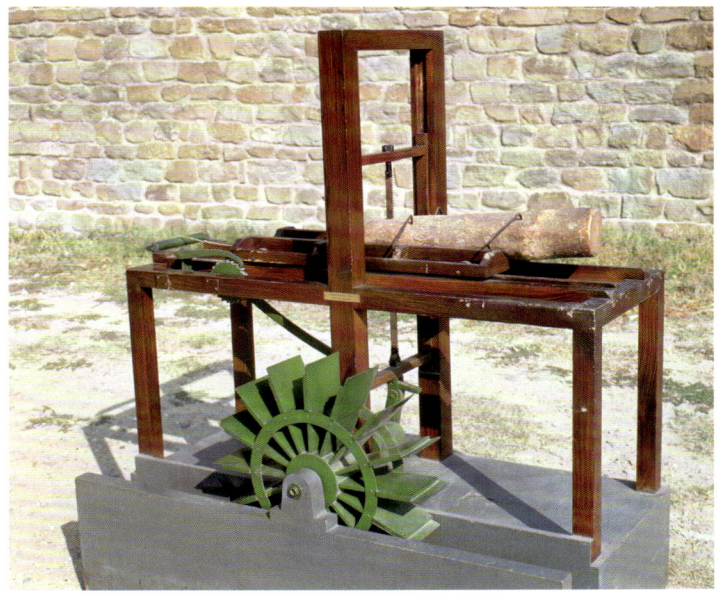

Model of a hydraulic saw
Maquette d'une scie hydraulique
Modell einer hydraulischen Säge
Modelo de una sierra hidráulica
Modello di una sega idraulica
Model van een hydraulische zaag

Wood/Bois, Museo Leonardiano, Vinci

parecer sorprendente lo fantasioso e ingenioso que también fue en el arte de la ingeniería militar, aunque parezca contradecir la imagen de artista sensible que tenemos de él. No obstante, si pensamos en el trasfondo político de la época, es decir, los radicales cambios durante el renacimiento y en la estructura de Italia, con sus pequeños territorios, constantemente en guerra, es de entender, que incluso un genio universal como Leonardo, sirviese a los señores de la guerra, cuando necesitaba dinero.

Sólo algunos de sus proyectos se convertirían en objetos reales, aunque no pocos de ellos llegarían a funcionar, tal como se demostraría siglos más tarde.

radicale cambiamento del Rinascimento e la struttura dell'Italia a quell'epoca, con i suoi piccoli stati costantemente in guerra, si comprende perché anche un genio universale come Leonardo si offrisse ai signori della guerra quando aveva bisogno di denaro.

Solo alcuni dei suoi progetti furono realizzati già nella sua epoca, tuttavia non pochi hanno dimostrato la loro funzionalità, anche se secoli dopo.

fantasie en vindingrijkheid hij ook in het ontwerpen van geniewerktuigen en vestingen investeerde en hoezeer hij daarmee ons beeld van de fijnzinnige kunstenaar lijkt te weerspreken. Maar als we denken aan de politieke achtergronden van de roerige Renaissance en aan de elkaar bitter bestrijdende Italiaanse stadstaten, wordt duidelijk dat zelfs een *uomo universale* als Leonardo zich bij krijgsheren meldde als hij in financiële nood verkeerde.

Slechts enkele van Leonardo's ontwerpen werden in zijn eigen tijd uitgevoerd, maar van veel andere uitvindingen werd eeuwen later bewezen dat ze uitvoerbaar en bruikbaar waren.

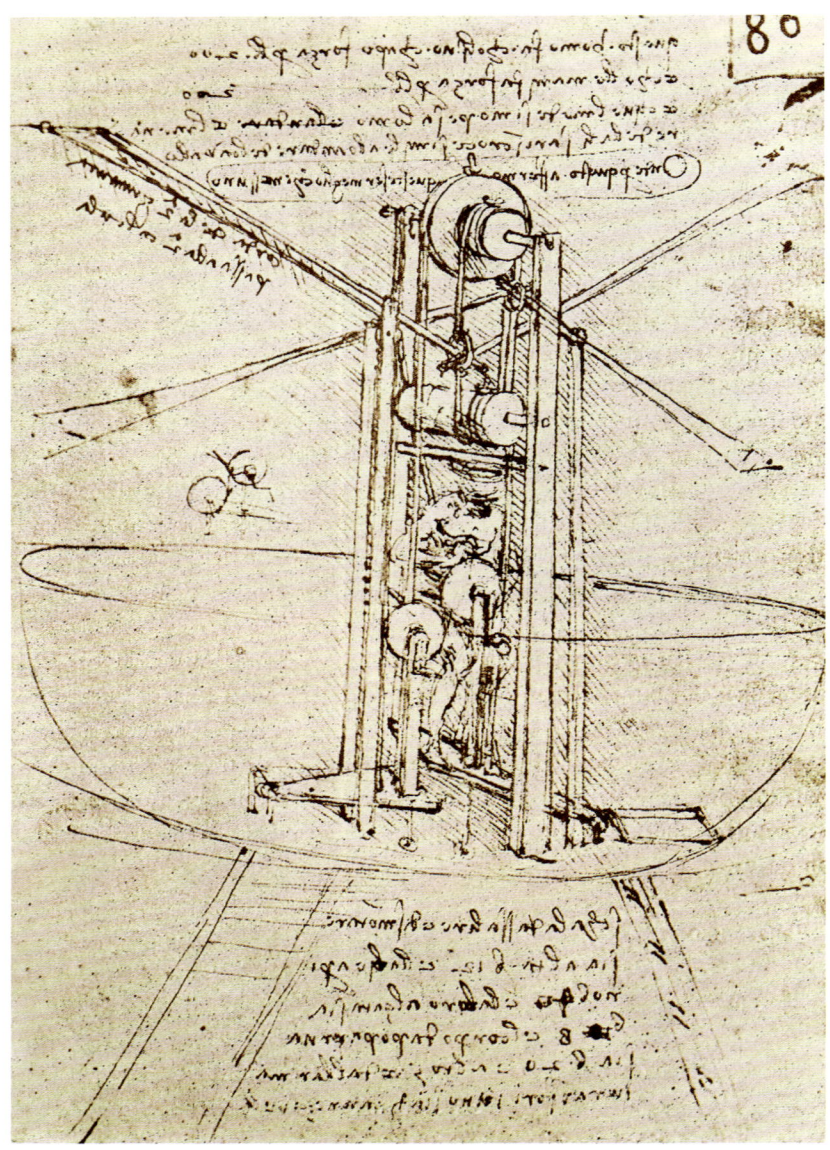

Sketch of vertically standing bird's-winged flying machine from *Paris Manuscript B*

Croquis d'une machine volante verticale, tiré du *Manuscrit B de Paris*

Skizze einer senkrecht stehenden Flugmaschine, aus dem *Pariser Manuskript B*

Esbozo de un dispositivo de vuelo en vertical, del *manuscrito parisino B*

Schizzo di una macchina volante in posizione verticale, dal *manoscritto parigino B*

Schets van een verticaal staande vliegmachine, uit het *Parijse Manuscript B*

1488–90, Pen and ink on paper/Plume et encre sur papier, 23,2 × 16,5 cm, Bibliothèque de l'Institut de France, Paris

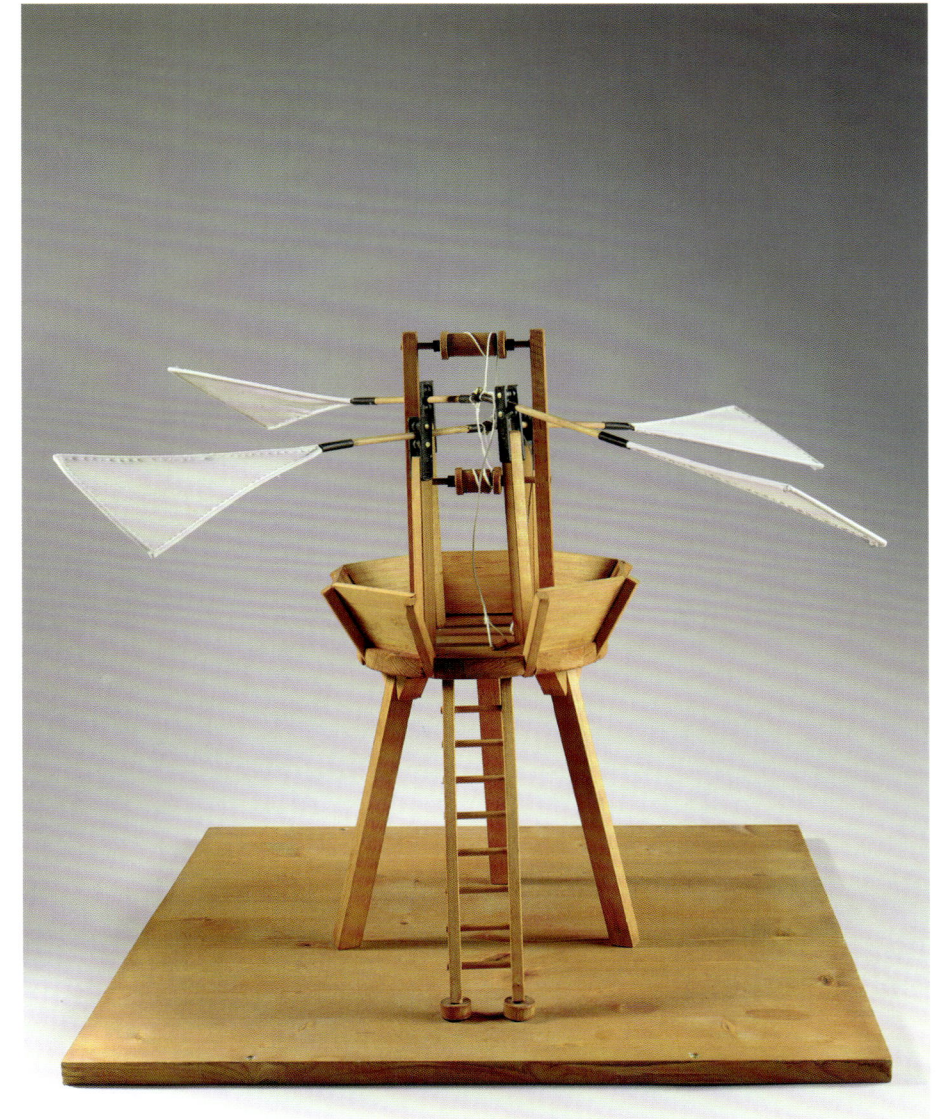

Model reconstruction of da Vinci's design for a vertical ornithopter

Reconstitution du projet d'un ornithoptère vertical

Rekonstruktion von Leonardos Entwurf eines senkrechten Ornithopters

Reconstrucción del diseño del ornitóptero de Leonardo en vertical

Ricostruzione del disegno di Leonardo di un ornitottero verticale

Reconstructie van Leonardo's ontwerp voor een verticale ornitopter

Wood, cloth and string/ Bois, étoffe et corde, Private collection

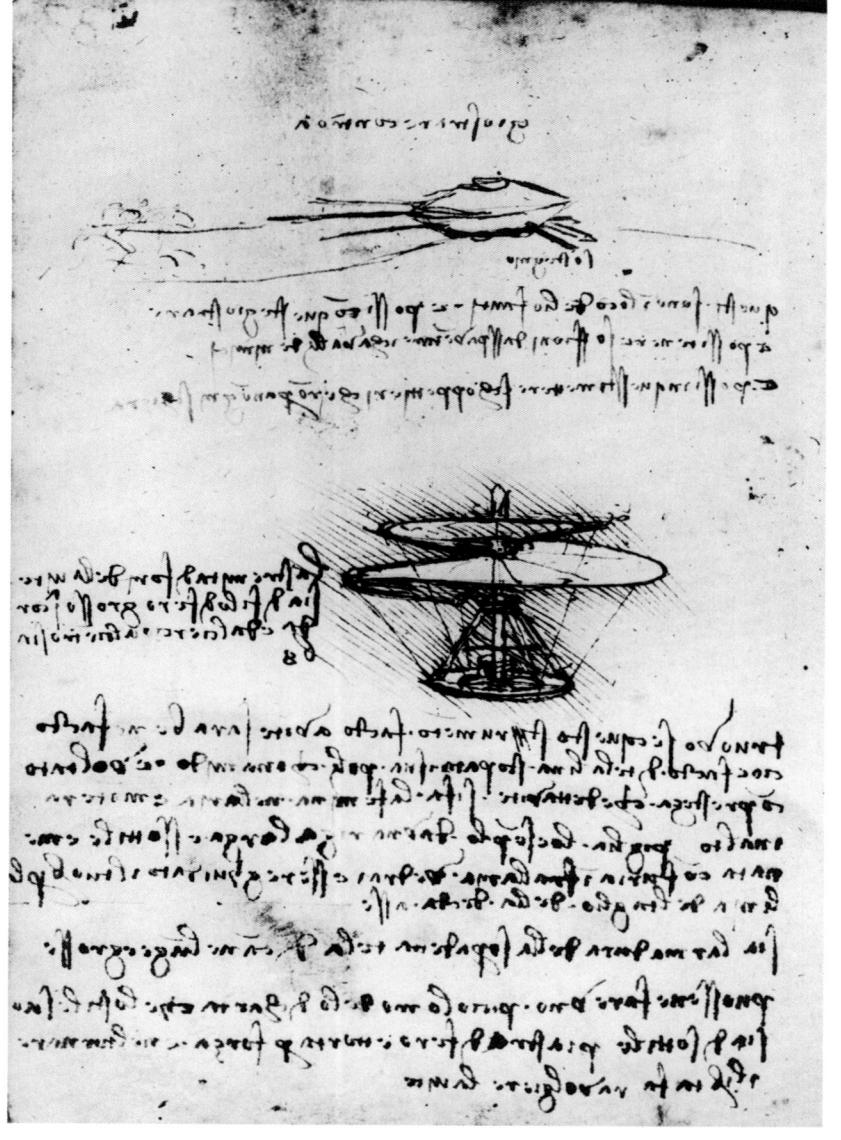

Page of text and sketches for a flying machine from *Paris Manuscript B*

Page de texte avec croquis d'une machine volante, tirée du *Manuscrit B de Paris*

Textseite mit Skizzen zu einer Flugmaschine, aus dem *Pariser Manuskript B*

Página de texto con esbozos de un dispositivo de vuelo, del *manuscrito parisino B*

Pagina di testo con schizzi di una macchina volante, dal *manoscritto parigino B*

Tekstblad met schetsen voor een vliegmachine, uit het *Parijse Manuscript B*

1488–90, Pen and ink on paper/Plume et encre sur papier, Bibliothèque de l'Institut de France, Paris

Reconstruction of da Vinci's design for an aerial screw *from Manuscript B*

Reconstitution d'un projet de vis aérienne, tiré du *Manuscrit B de Paris*

Rekonstruktion von Leonardos Entwurf einer Luftschraube, aus dem *Pariser Manuskript B*

Reconstrucción del diseño de una hélice voladora de Leonardo, del *manuscrito parisino B*

Ricostruzione del disegno di Leonardo di una vite aerea, dal *manoscritto parigino B*

Reconstructie van Leonardo's ontwerp voor een vliegschroef, uit het *Parijse Manuscript B*

Wood, cloth and string/Bois, étoffe et corde, Private collection

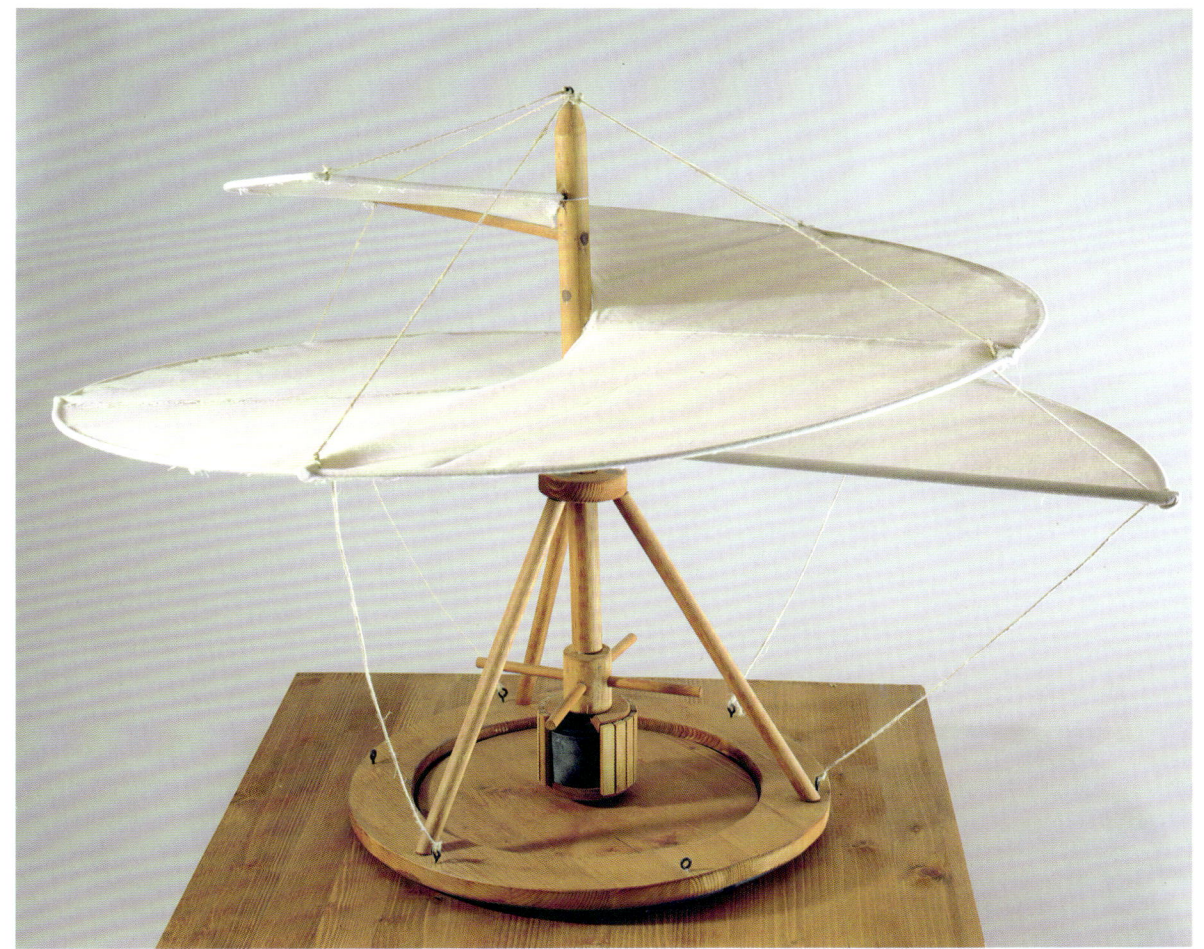

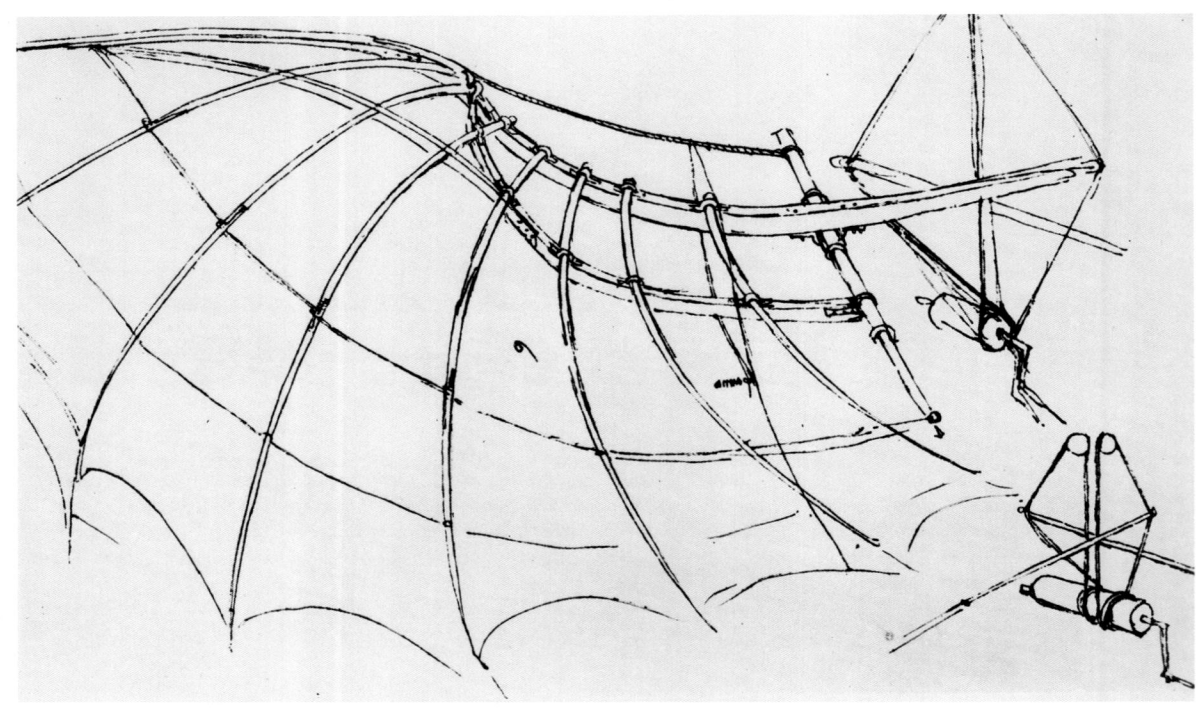

Detail of a mechanical wing from *Paris Manuscript B*

Détail d'une aile mécanique, tiré du *Manuscrit B de Paris*

Detail eines mechanischen Flügels, aus dem *Pariser Manuskript B*

Detalle de un ala mecánica, del *manuscrito parisino B*

Dettaglio di un'ala meccanica, dal *manoscritto parigino B*

Detail van een mechanische vleugel, uit het *Parijse Manuscript B*

1488/89, Pen and ink on paper/Plume et encre sur papier, Bibliothèque de l'Institut de France, Paris

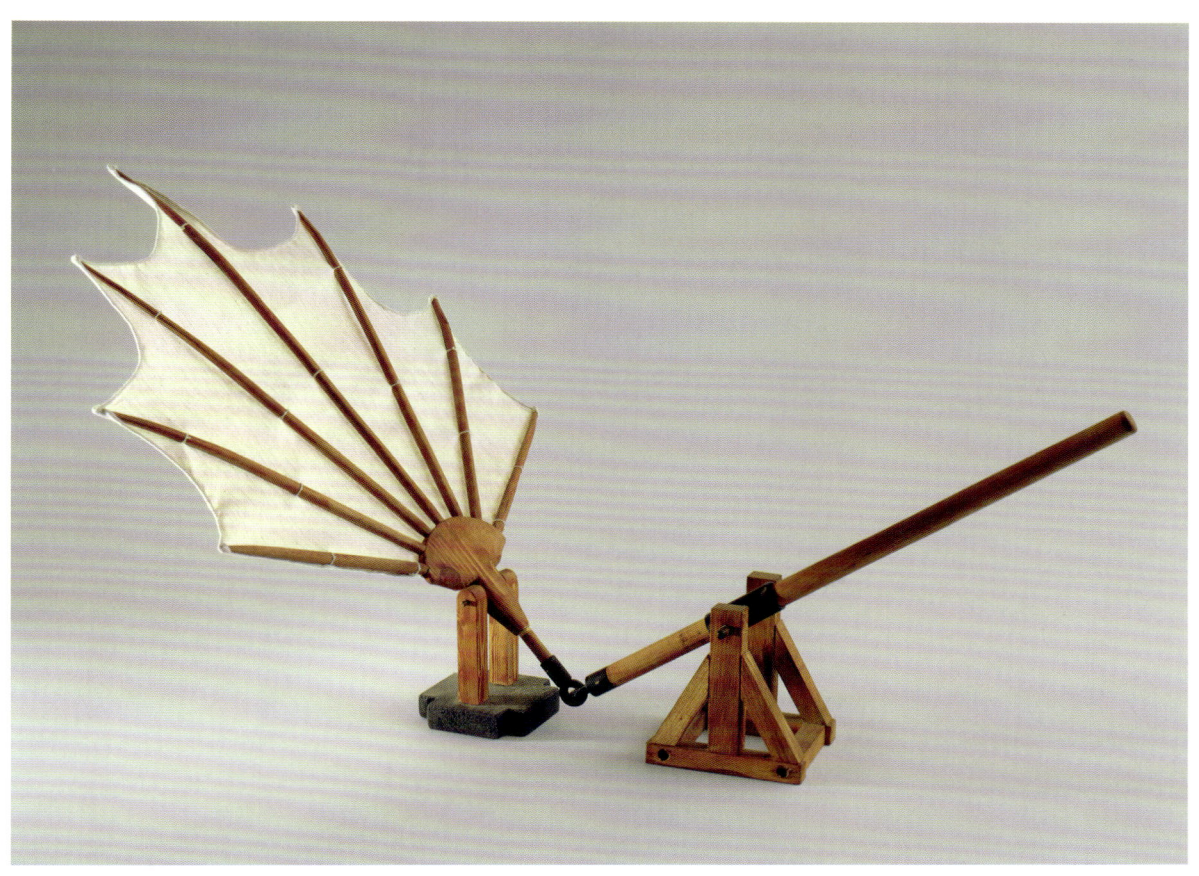

Model reconstruction of da Vinci's design for a beating wing

Reconstitution du projet d'une aile battante

Rekonstruktion von Leonardos Entwurf eines schlagenden Flügels

Reconstrucción del diseño de un ala batiente de Leonardo

Ricostruzione del disegno di Leonardo di un'ala battente

Reconstructie van Leonardo's ontwerp voor een wiekslagvleugel

Wood and cloth/Bois et étoffe, Private collection

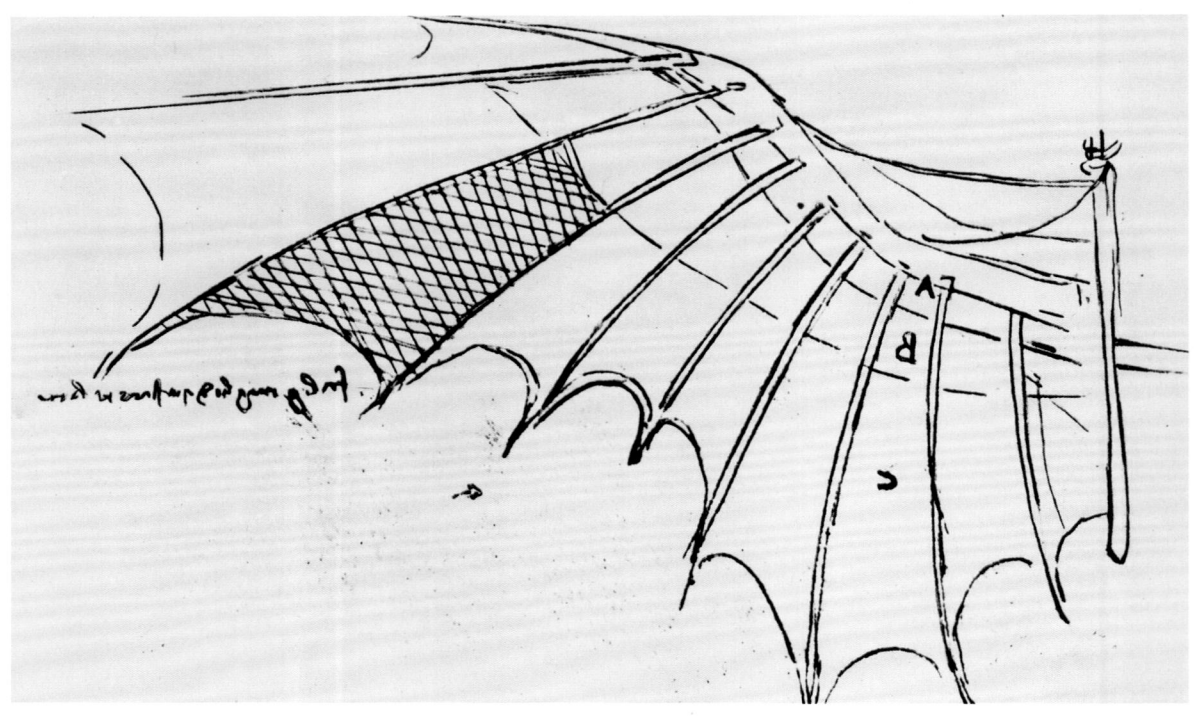

Detail of a mechanical wing from *Paris Manuscript B*

Détail d'une aile mécanique, tiré du *Manuscrit B de Paris*

Detail eines mechanischen Flügels, aus dem *Pariser Manuskript B*

Detalle de un ala mecánica, del *manuscrito parisino B*

Dettaglio di un'ala meccanica, dal *manoscritto parigino B*

Detail van een mechanische vleugel, uit het *Parijse Manuscript B*

1488/89, Pen and ink on paper/Plume et encre sur papier, Bibliothèque de l'Institut de France, Paris

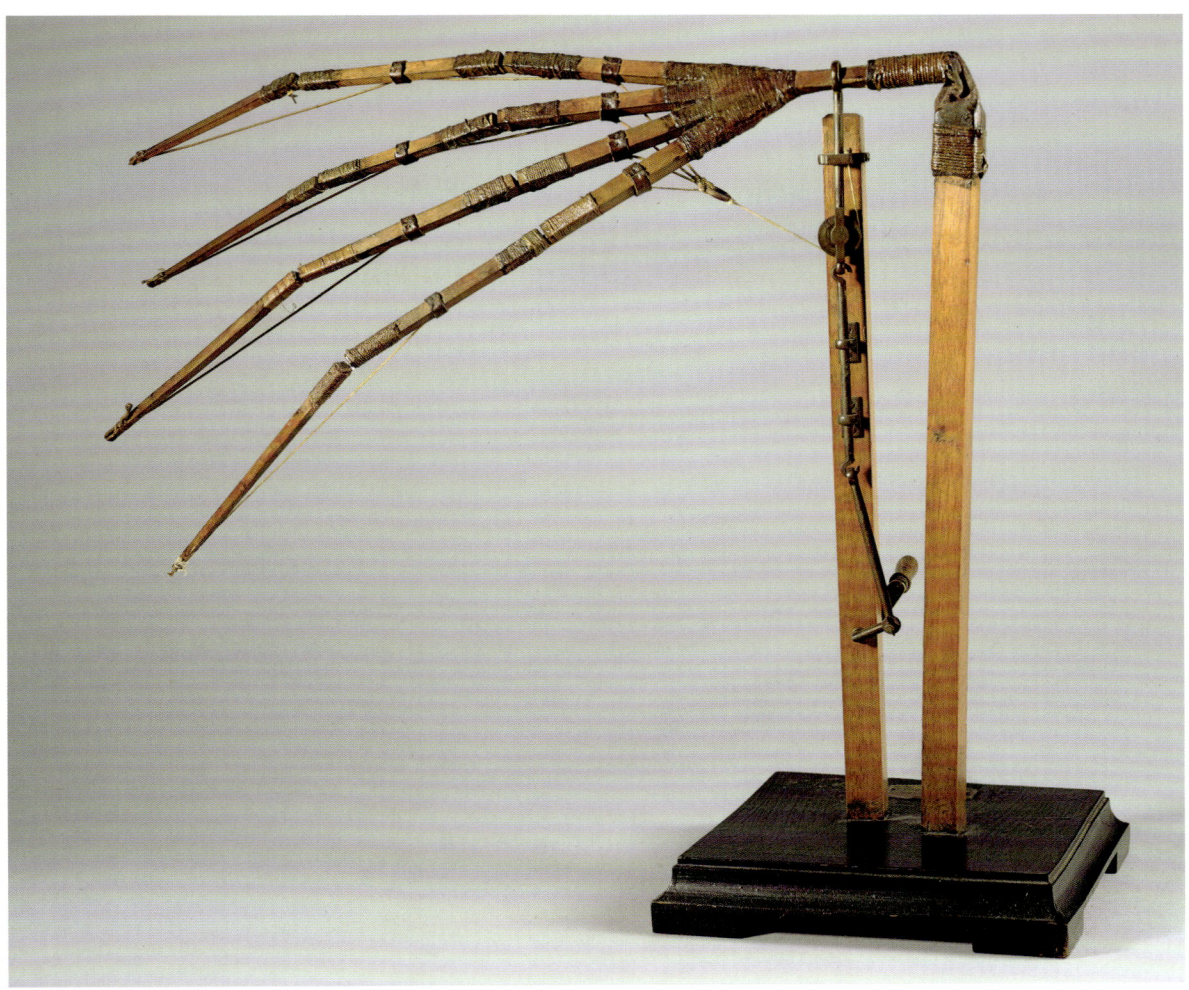

Model reconstruction of da Vinci's design for an articulated wing

Reconstitution d'un projet d'aile articulées

Rekonstruktion von Leonardos Entwurf eines gegliederten Flügels

Reconstrucción del diseño de un ala estructurada de Leonardo

Ricostruzione del disegno di Leonardo di un'ala articolata

Reconstructie van Leonardo's ontwerp voor een gesegmenteerde vleugel

Wood and metal/Bois et métal, Museo Leonardiano, Vinci

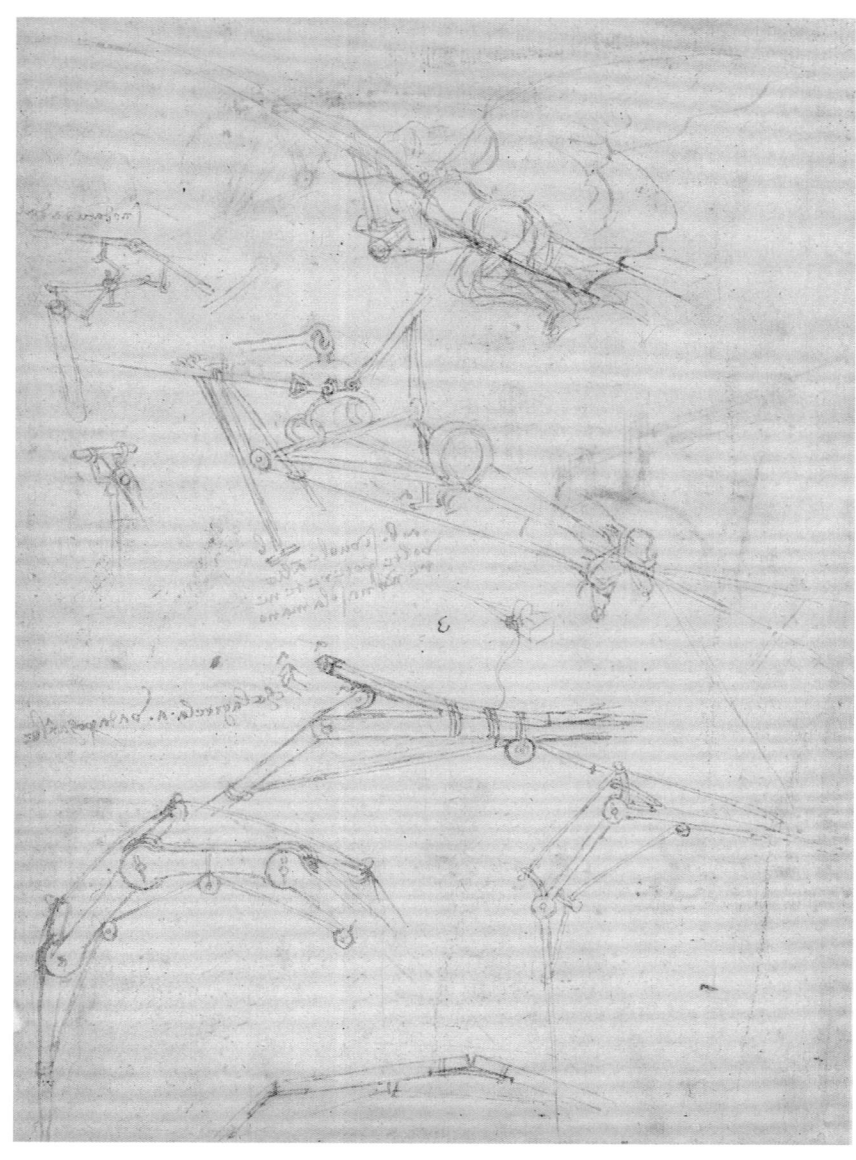

Codex Atlanticus
Flying machine
Machine volante
Flugmaschine
Dispositivo de vuelo
Macchina volante
Vliegmachine

Pen and ink on paper/Plume et encre sur papier, Biblioteca Ambrosiana, Milano

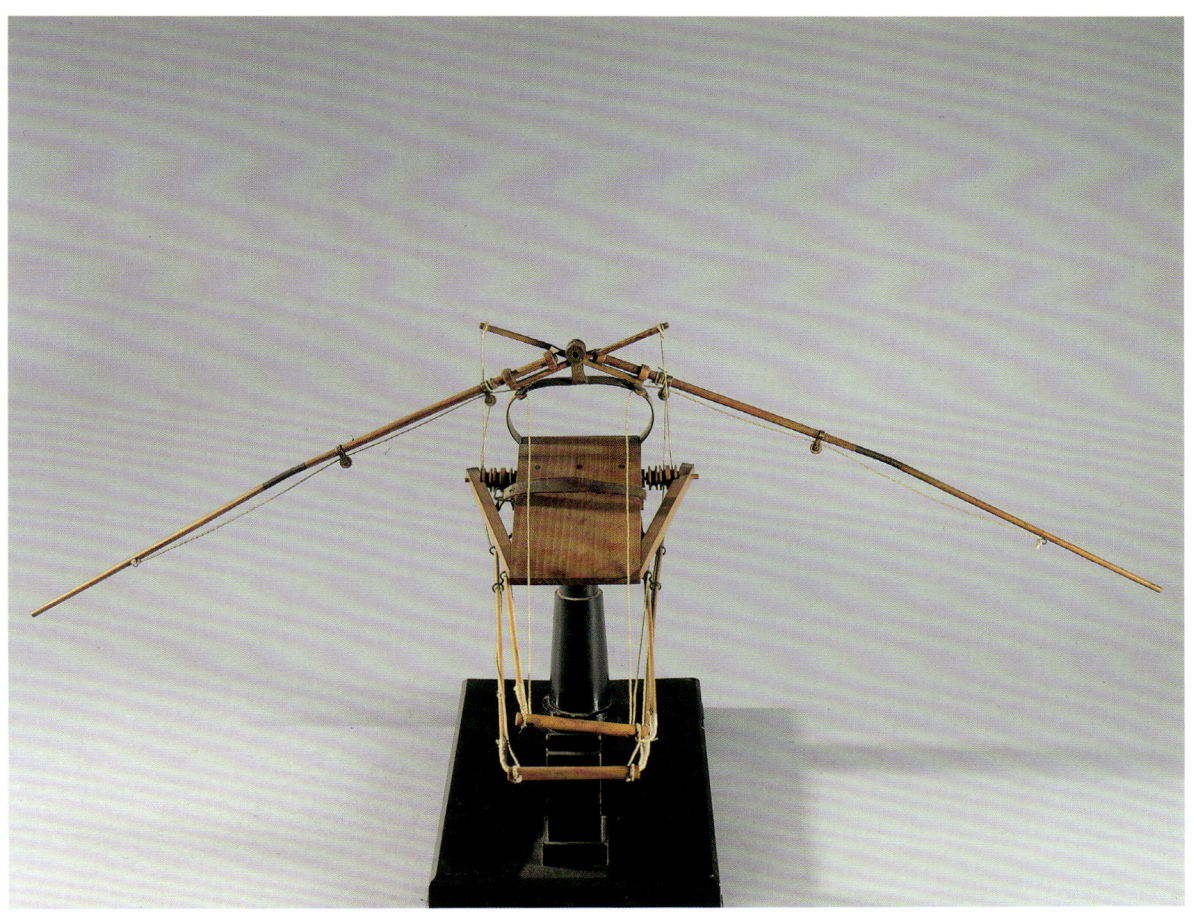

Reconstruction of da Vinci's design for a flying machine from *Paris Manuscript B*

Reconstitution du projet d'une machine volante, tiré du *Manuscrit B de Paris*

Rekonstruktion von Leonardos Entwurf einer Flugmaschine, aus dem *Pariser Manuskript B*

Reconstrucción del diseño de un dispositivo de vuelo de Leonardo, del *manuscrito parisino B*

Ricostruzione del disegno di Leonardo di una macchina volante, dal *manoscritto parigino B*

Reconstructie van Leonardo's ontwerp voor een vliegmachine, uit het *Parijse Manuscript B*

Wood, leather and string/Bois, cuir et corde, Museo Leonardiano, Vinci

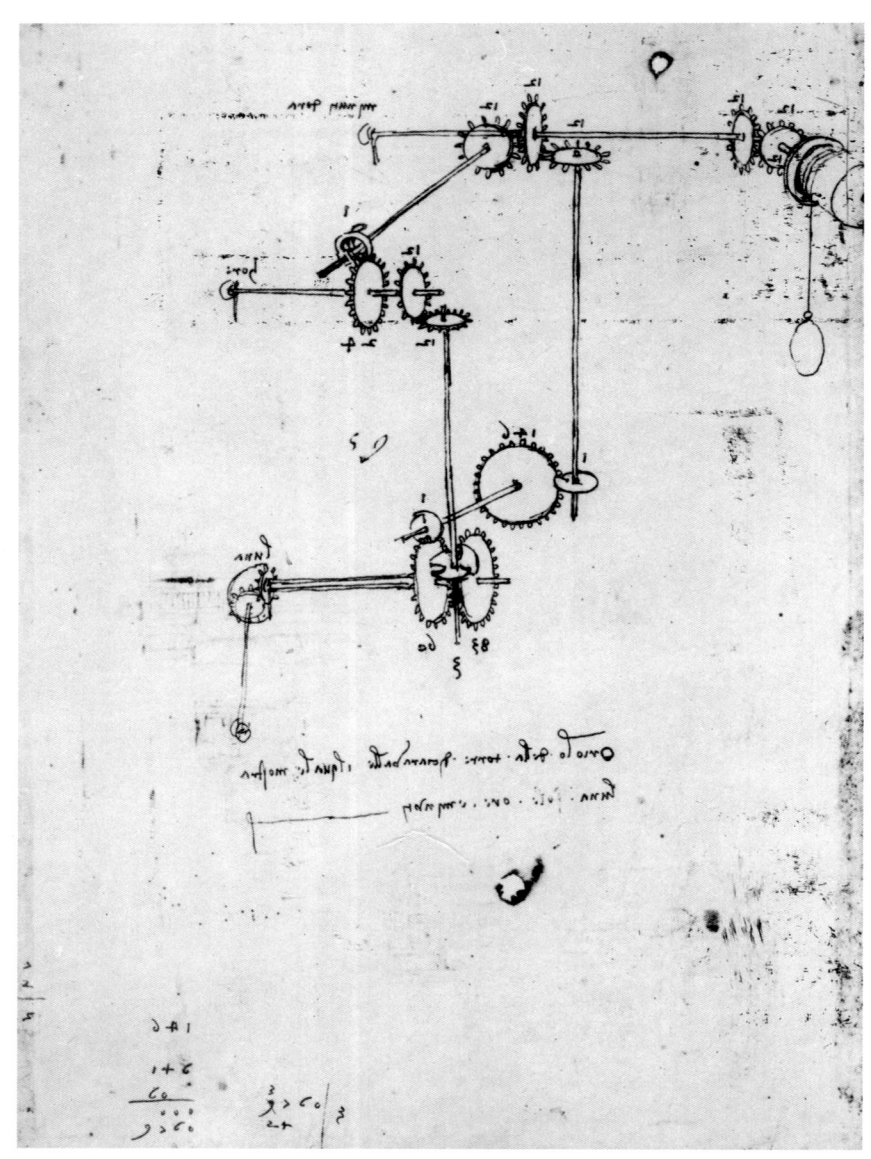

Machine designs

Projets de machines

Maschinenentwürfe

Diseños de máquinas

Disegni di macchinari

Ontwerpen voor machines

Pen and ink on paper/Plume et encre sur papier, Private collection

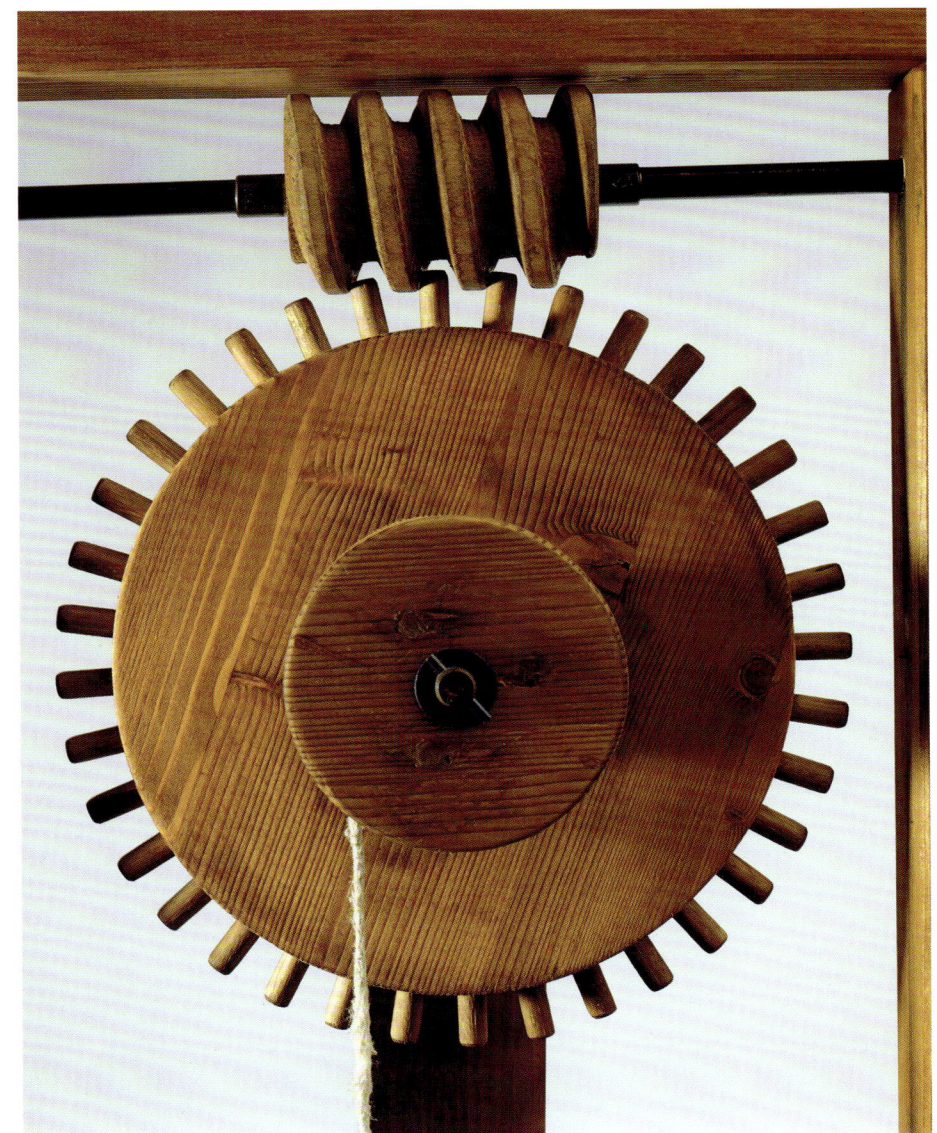

Model reconstruction of a helicoid mechanism

Reconstitution d'un mécanisme hélicoïdal

Rekonstruktion eines helikoiden Mechanismus

Reconstrucción de un mecanismo helicoidal

Ricostruzione di un meccanismo elicoidale

Reconstructie van een schroefmechanisme

Wood, metal and string/ Bois, métal et corde, Private collection

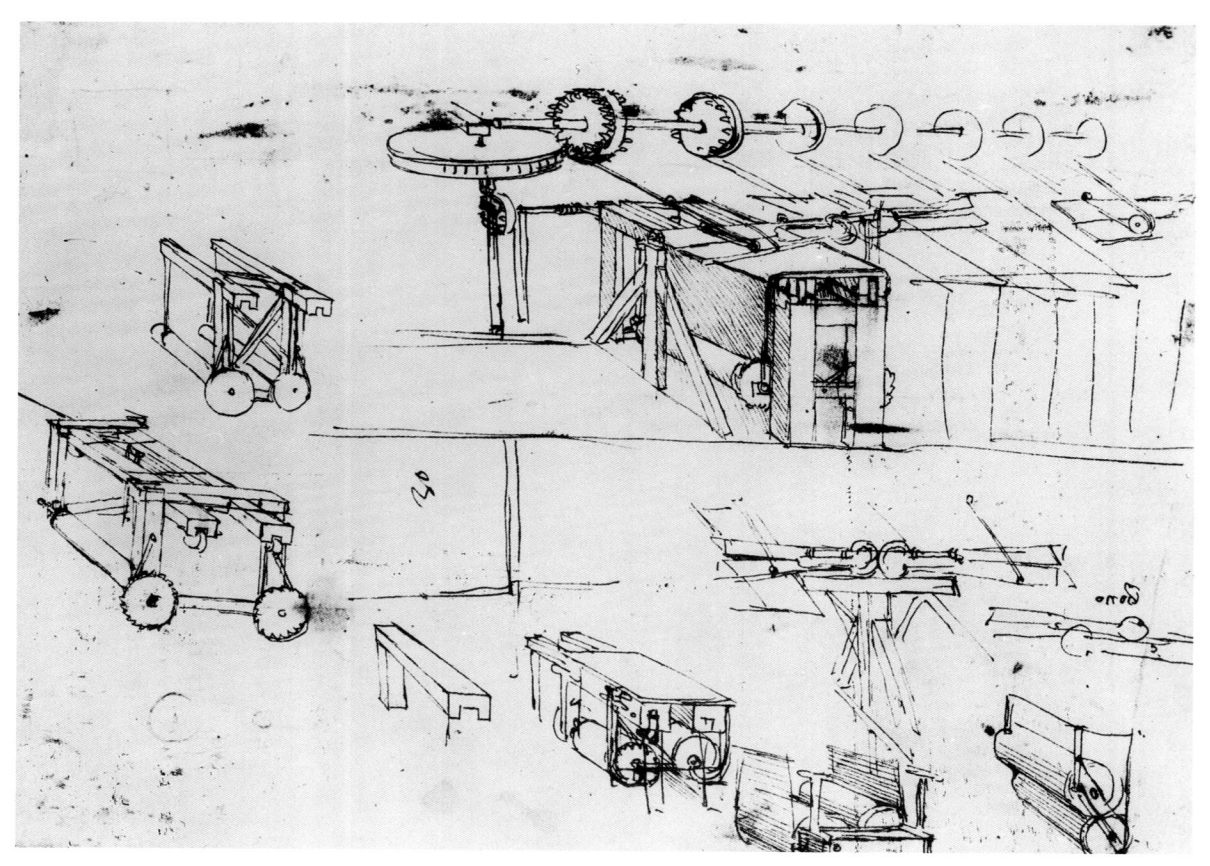

Machine designs

Projets de machines

Maschinenentwürfe

Diseños de máquinas

Disegni di macchinari

Ontwerpen voor machines

Pen and ink on paper/Plume et encre sur papier, Private collection

202

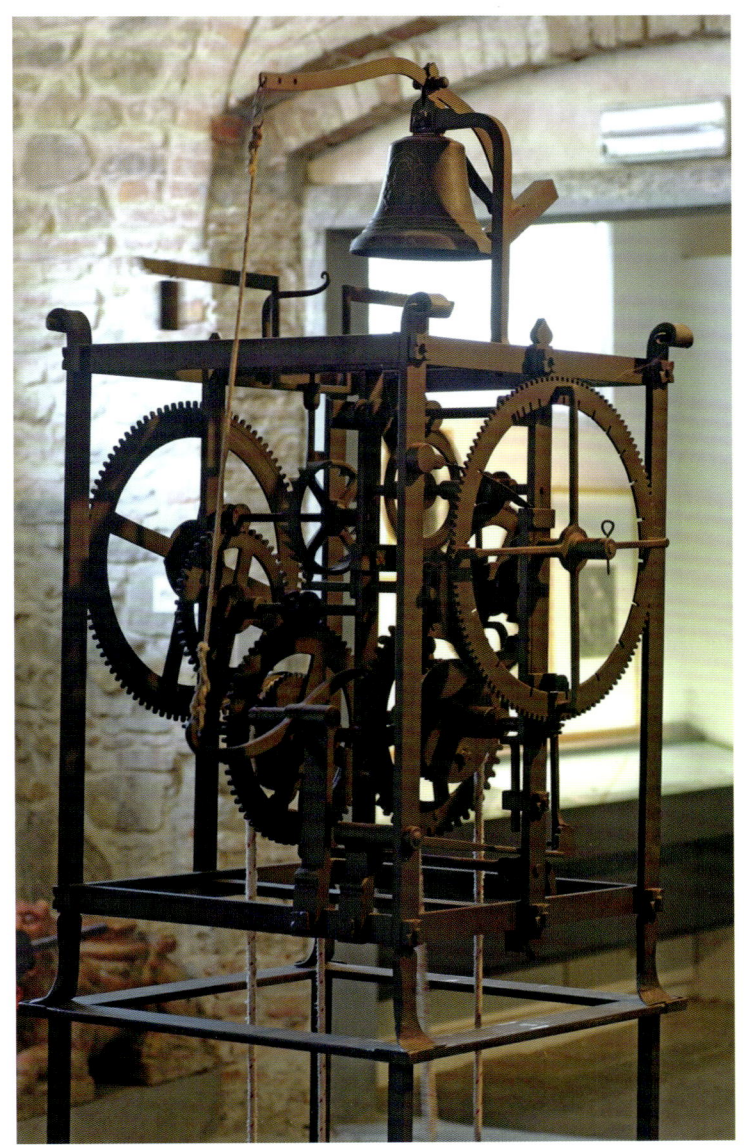

Reconstruction of a mechanical clock
Reconstitution d'une montre mécanique
Rekonstruktion einer mechanischen Uhr
Reconstrucción de un reloj mecánico
Ricostruzione di un orologio meccanico
Reconstructie van een mechanische klok

Wood/Bois, Museo Leonardiano, Vinci

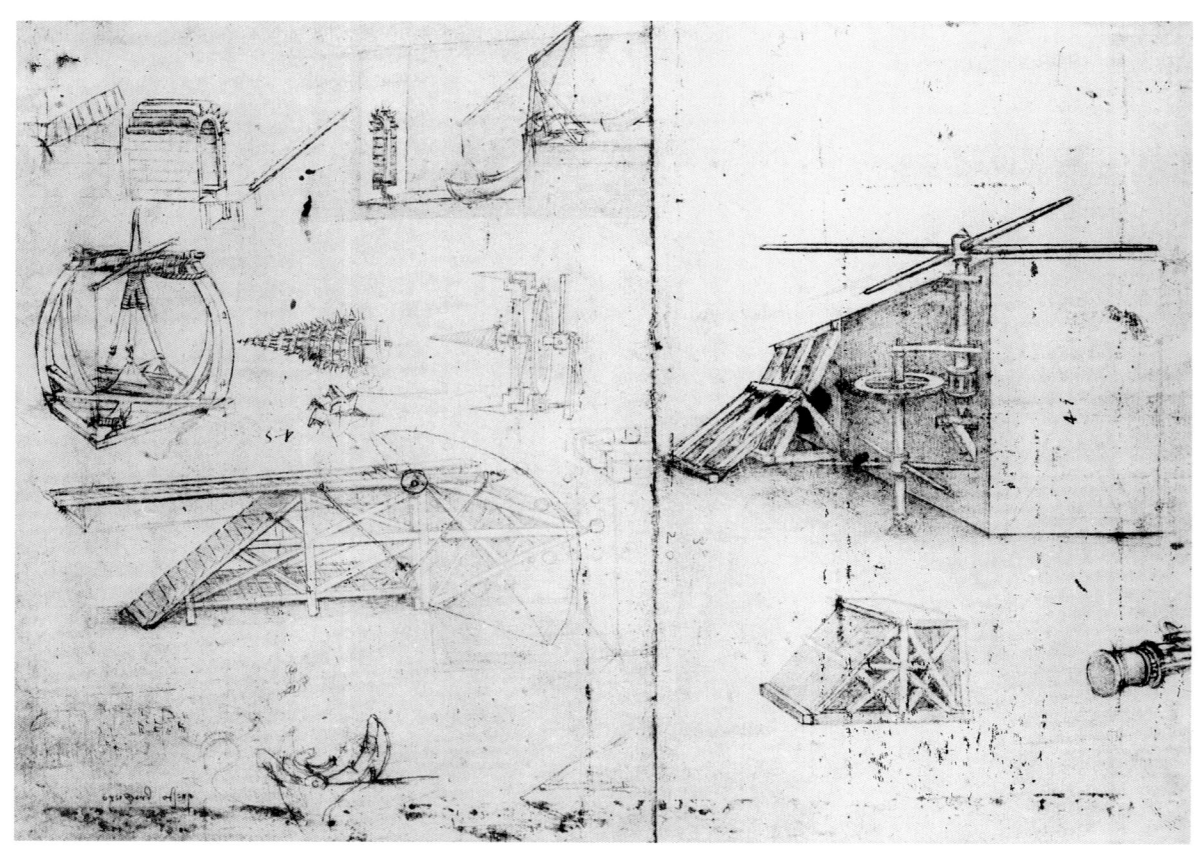

Machine designs

Projets de machines

Maschinenentwürfe

Diseños de máquinas

Disegni di macchinari

Ontwerpen voor machines

Pen and ink on paper/Plume et encre sur papier, Private collection

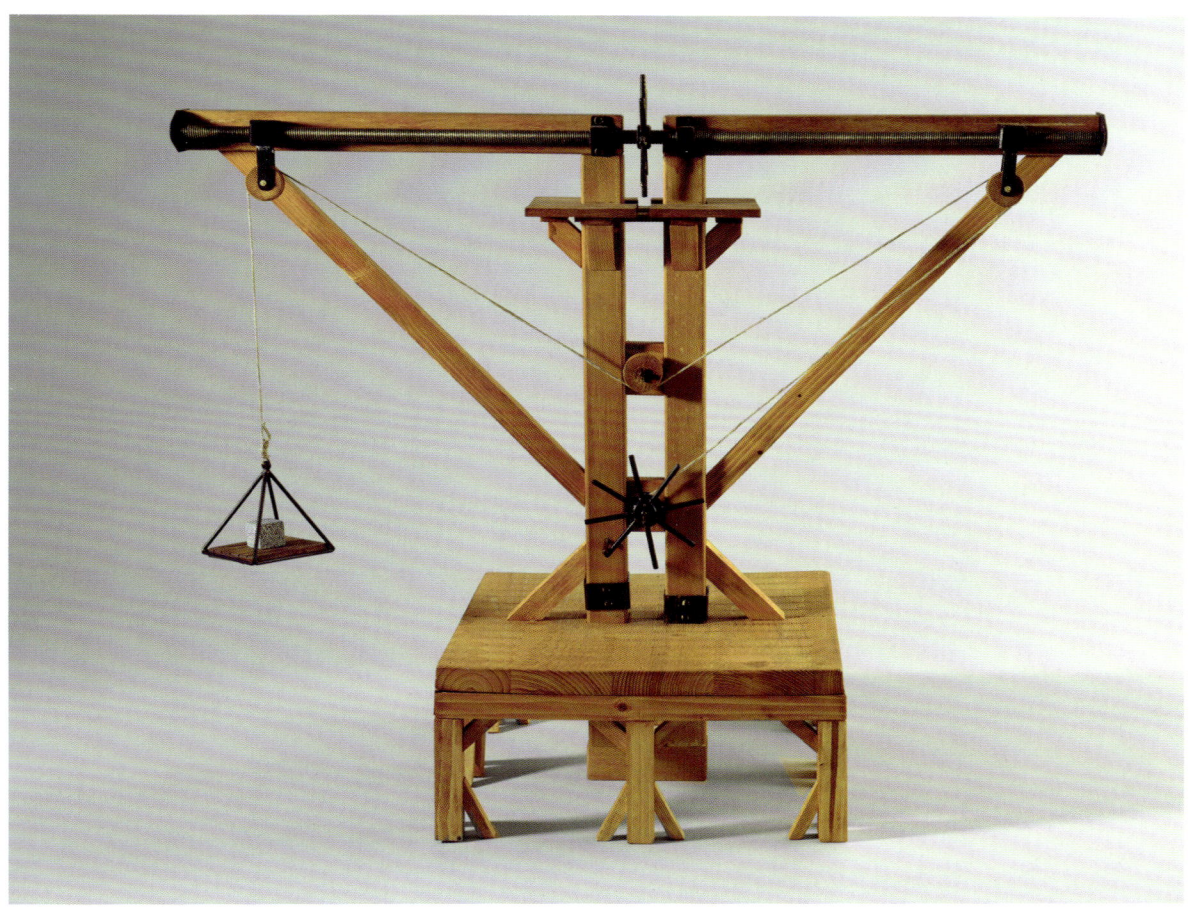

Model reconstruction of a double-winch crane

Reconstitution d'une grue pivotante à double action

Rekonstruktion eines Krans mit doppelter Winde

Reconstrucción de una grúa con doble cabestrante

Ricostruzione di una gru a doppio braccio

Reconstructie van een kraan met dubbele windas

Wood, metal and string/Bois, métal et corde, Private collection

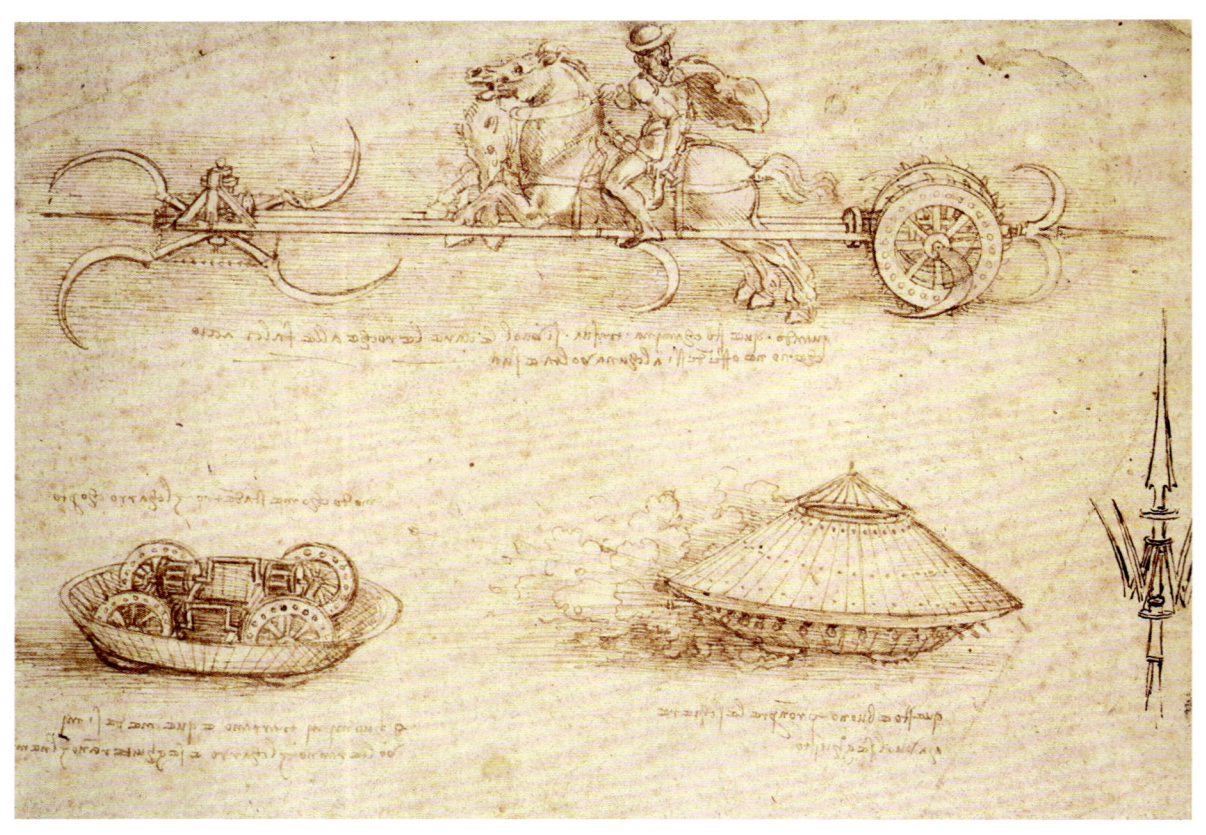

Studies of war machines

Études de machines de guerre

Studien von Kriegsmaschinen

Estudios de máquinas de guerra

Studi di macchine da guerra

Studies van oorlogsmachines

Sanguine on paper/Sanguine sur papier

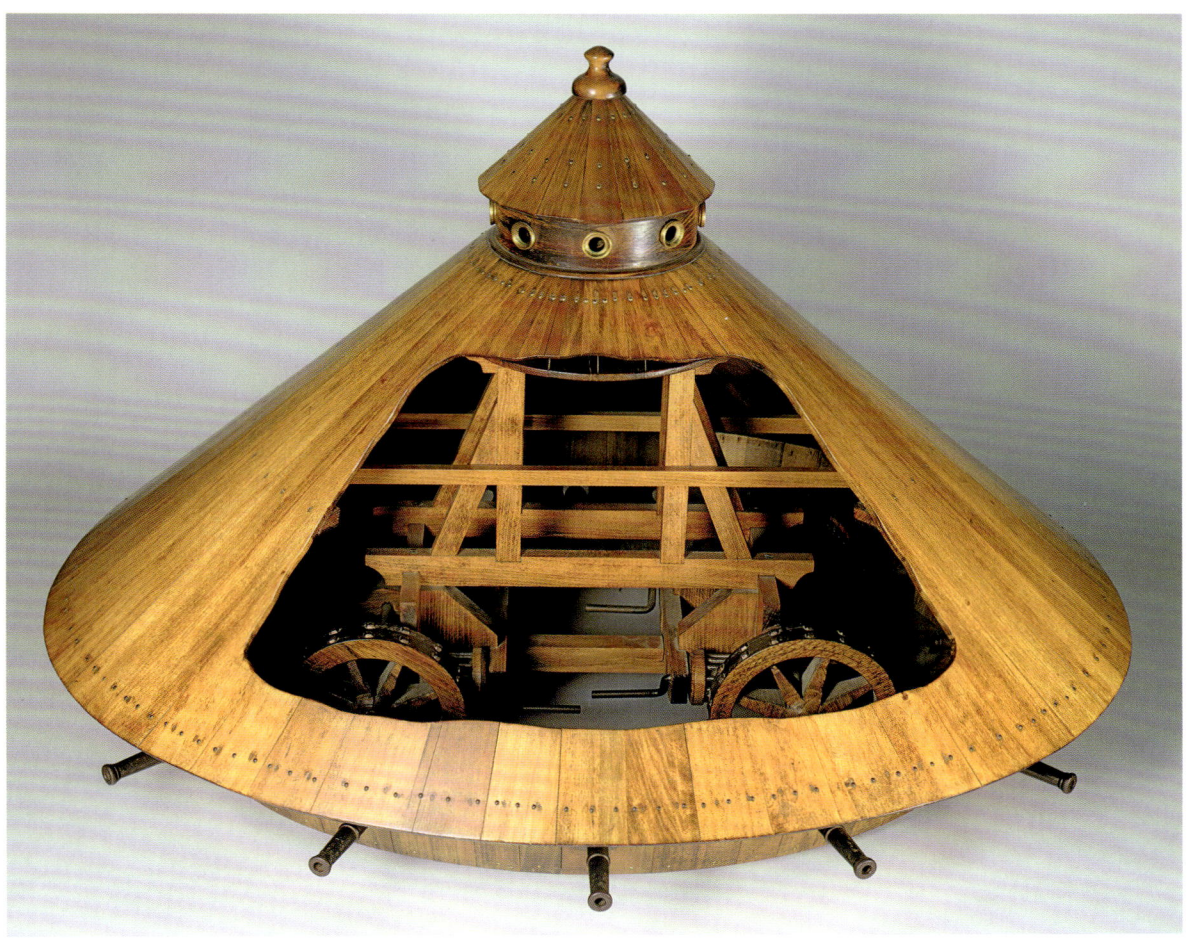

Model reconstruction of da Vinci's design for a tank

Reconstitution d'un projet de véhicule blindé

Rekonstruktion von Leonardos Entwurf eines Panzerfahrzeugs

Reconstrucción del diseño de un vehículo acorazado de Leonardo

Ricostruzione del disegno di Leonardo di un carro armato

Reconstructie van Leonardo's ontwerp voor een pantservoertuig

Wood and metal/Bois et métal, Museo Leonardiano, Vinci

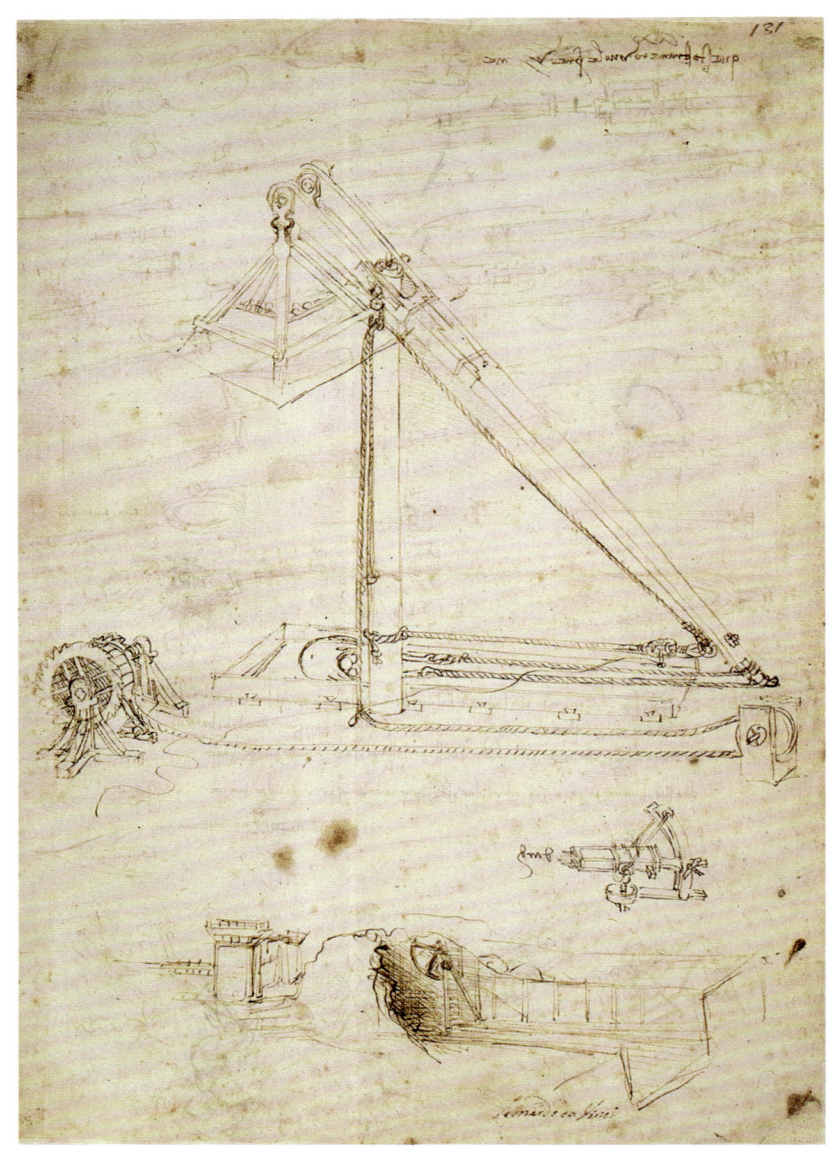

War machine

Machine de guerre

Kriegsmaschine

Máquina de guerra

Macchina da guerra

Oorlogsmachine

Pencil on paper/Crayon sur papier, Galleria dell' Accademia, Venezia

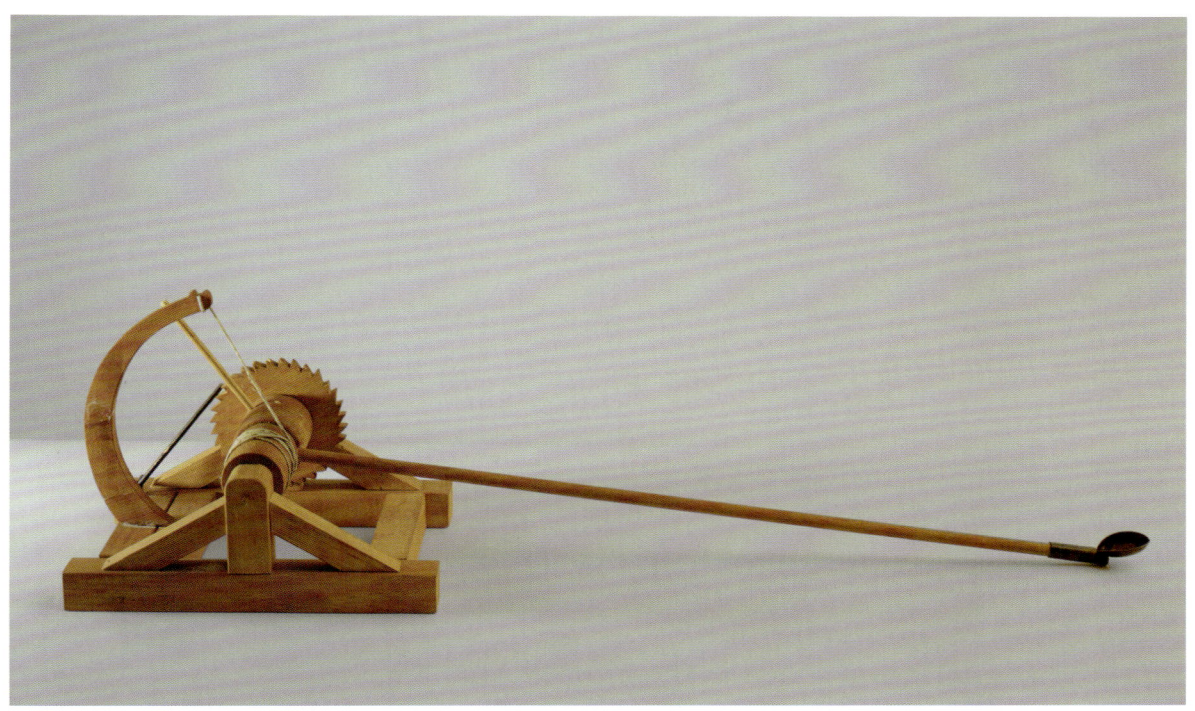

Model reconstruction of da Vinci's design for a catapult

Reconstitution d'un projet de catapulte

Rekonstruktion von Leonardos Entwurf eines Katapults

Reconstrucción del diseño de una catapulta de Leonardo

Ricostruzione del disegno di Leonardo di una catapulta

Reconstructie van Leonardo's ontwerp voor een katapult

Wood, metal and string/Bois, métal et corde, Private collection

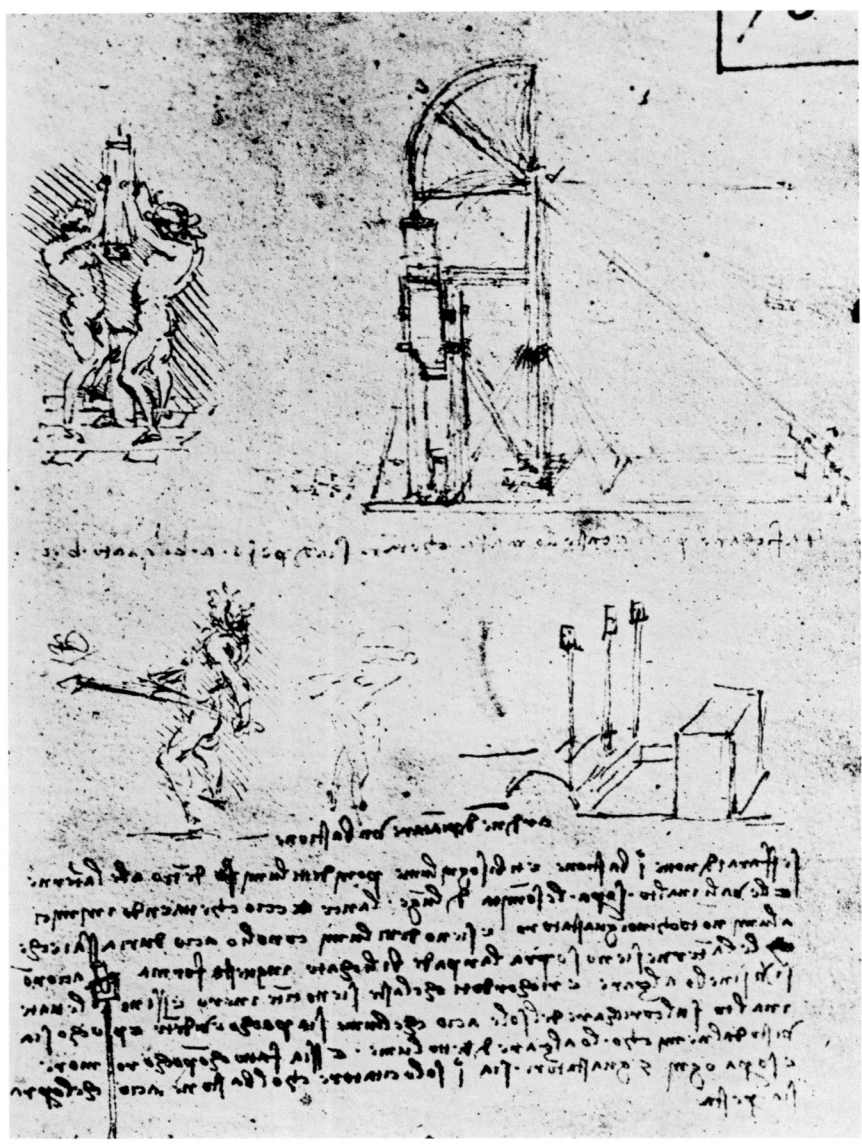

Suggestions on how to
construct a bastion at night
from *Paris Manuscript B*

Suggestions pour la construction
nocturne d'une forteresse,
tirées du *Manuscrit B de Paris*

Vorschläge zum Bau einer
Festung in der Nacht, aus
dem *Pariser Manuskript B*

Propuesta para la construcción
de una fortificación durante la
noche, del *manuscrito parisino B*

Proposte per la costruzione di
una fortezza durante la notte,
dal *manoscritto parigino B*

Voorstellen voor de nachtelijke
bouw van een vesting, uit
het *Parijse Manuscript B*

*1488–90, Pen and ink on paper/Plume
et encre sur papier, Bibliothèque de
l'Institut de France, Paris*

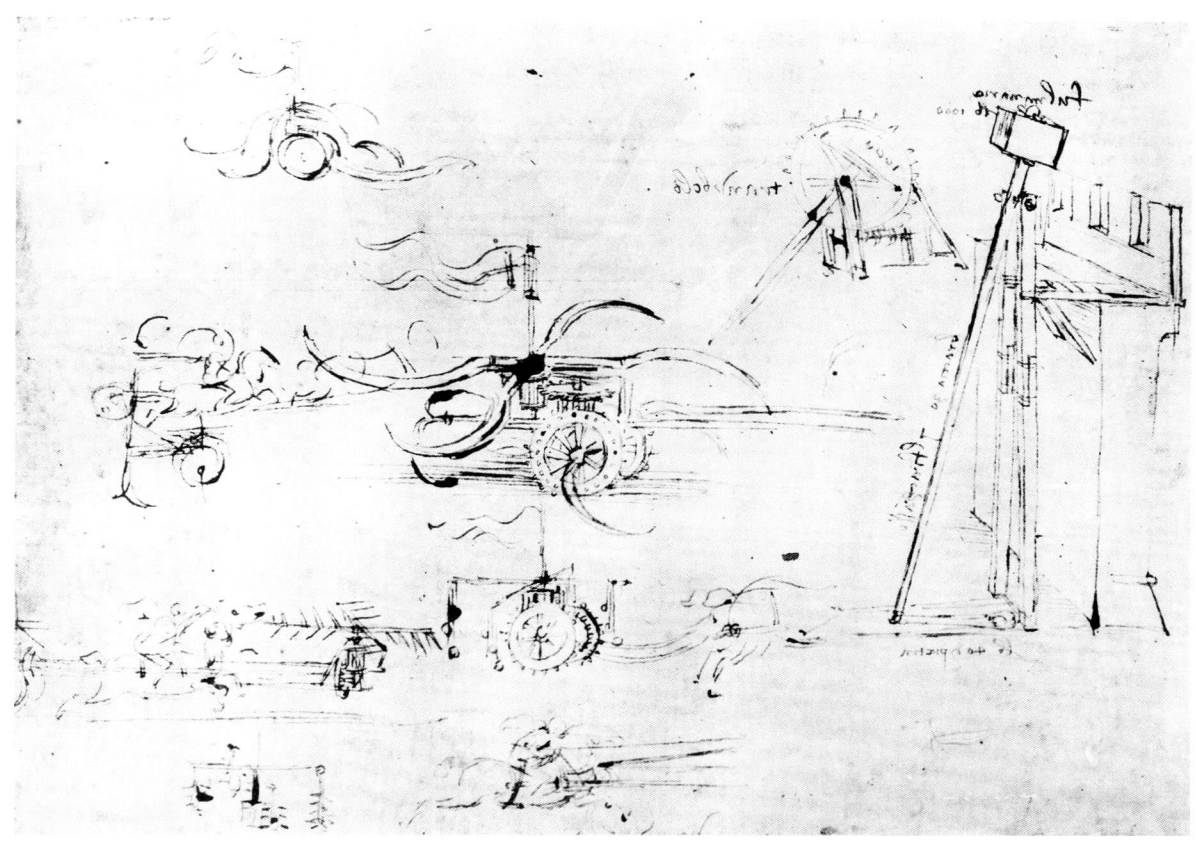

Weaponry designs

Projets de matériels de guerre

Entwürfe für Kriegsgerät

Diseños para artilugios de guerra

Disegni per armamenti

Ontwerpen voor oorlogstuig

Pen and ink on paper/Plume et encre sur papier, Private collection

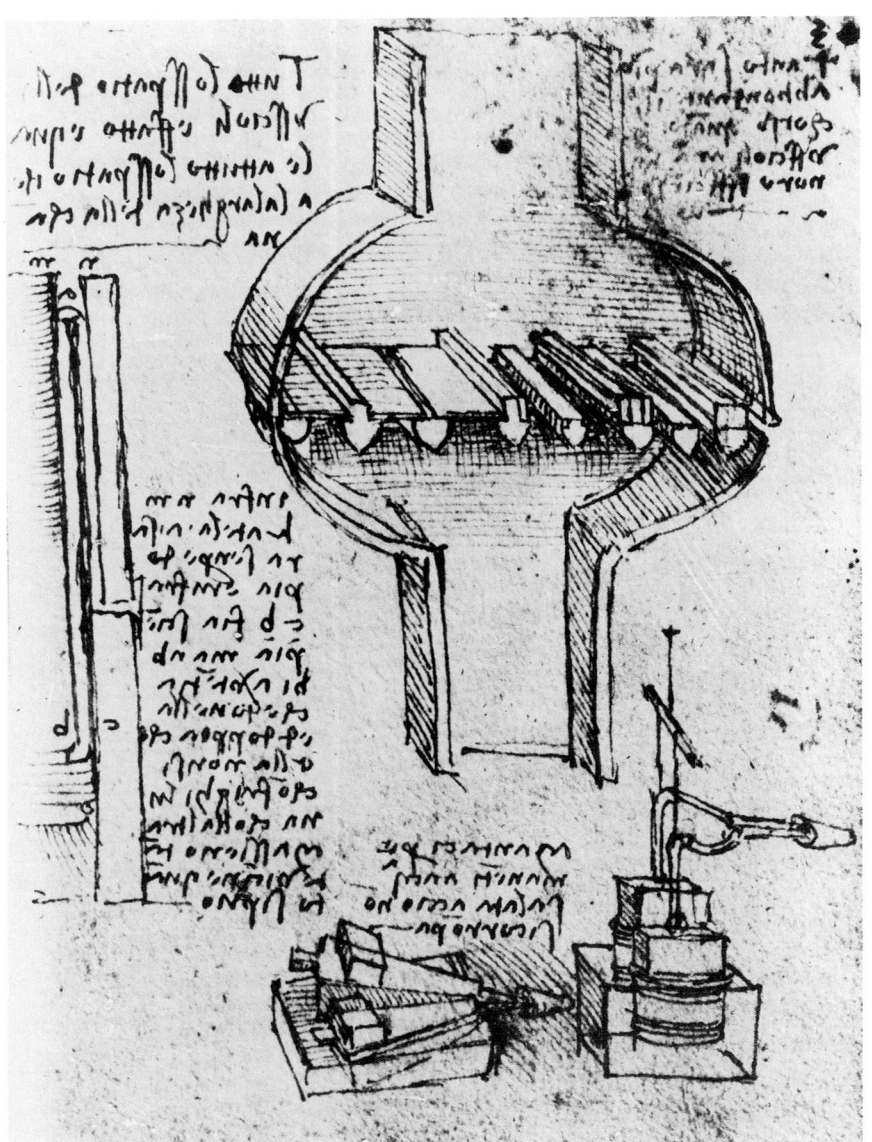

Fol. 34 r from *Manuscript E*

Folio 34 (recto) du
Manuscrit E de Paris

Seite 34 r. aus dem
Pariser Manuskript E

Página 34 del *manuscrito parisino E*

Pagina 34 dal *manoscritto
parigino E*

Pagina 34 recto uit het
Parijse Manuscript E

*1513/14, Pen and ink on paper/Plume
et encre sur papier, Bibliothèque de
l'Institut de France, Paris*

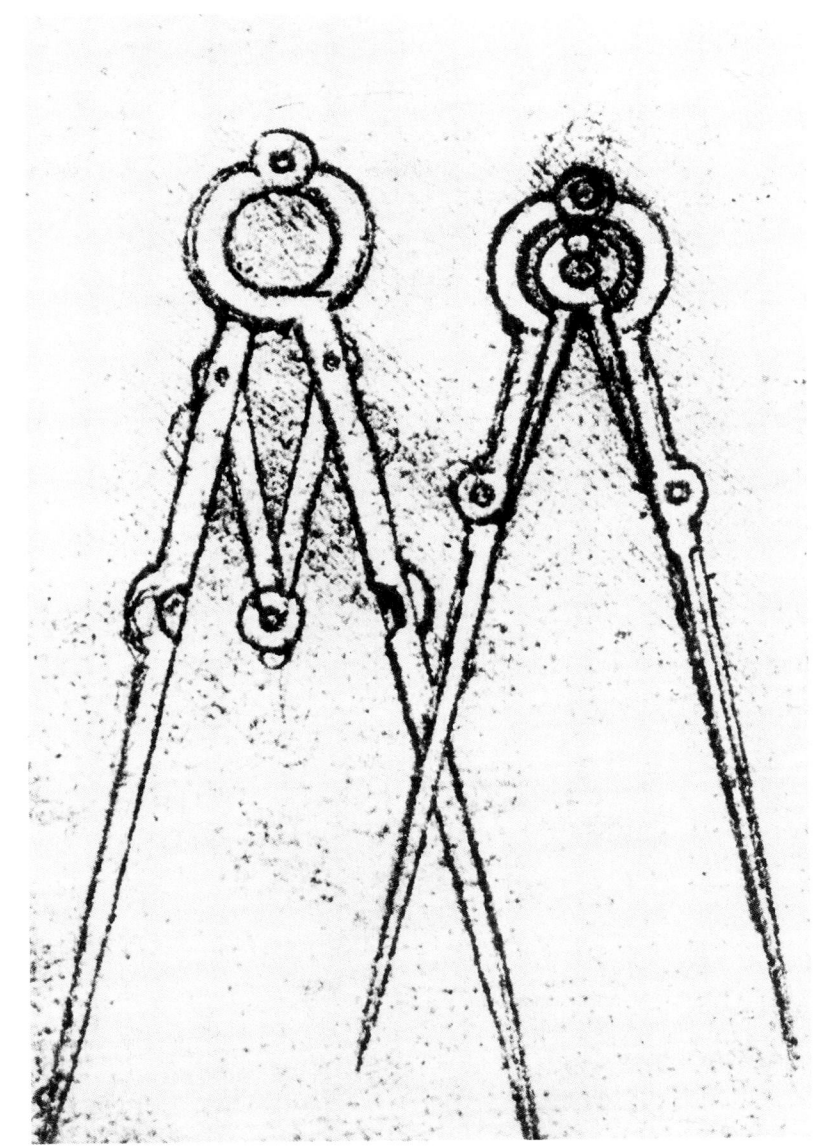

Two types of adjustable-opening compasses
Deux types de boussole réglable
Zwei Typen eines justierbaren Zirkels
Dos tipos de brújula ajustables
Due tipi di bussola regolabile
Twee soorten instelbare kompassen

*1493/94, Pen and ink on paper/Plume et encre sur
papier, Bibliothèque de l'Institut de France, Paris*

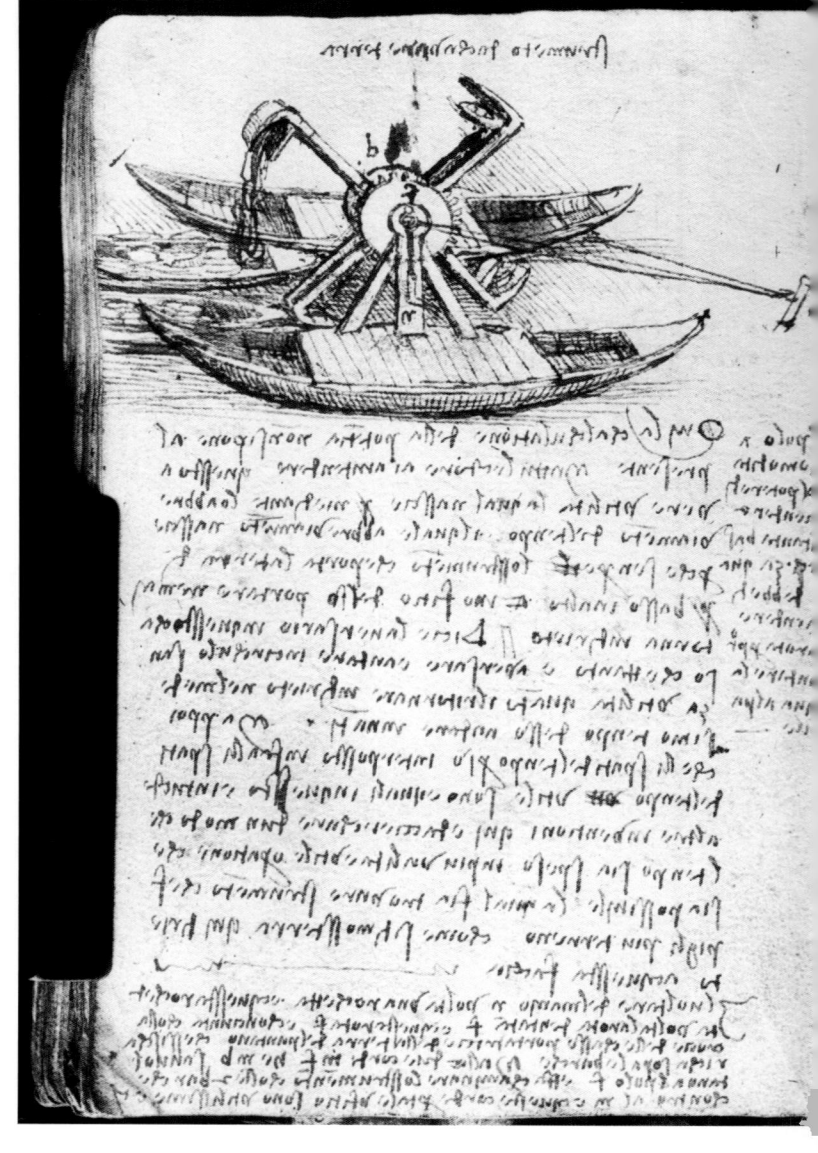

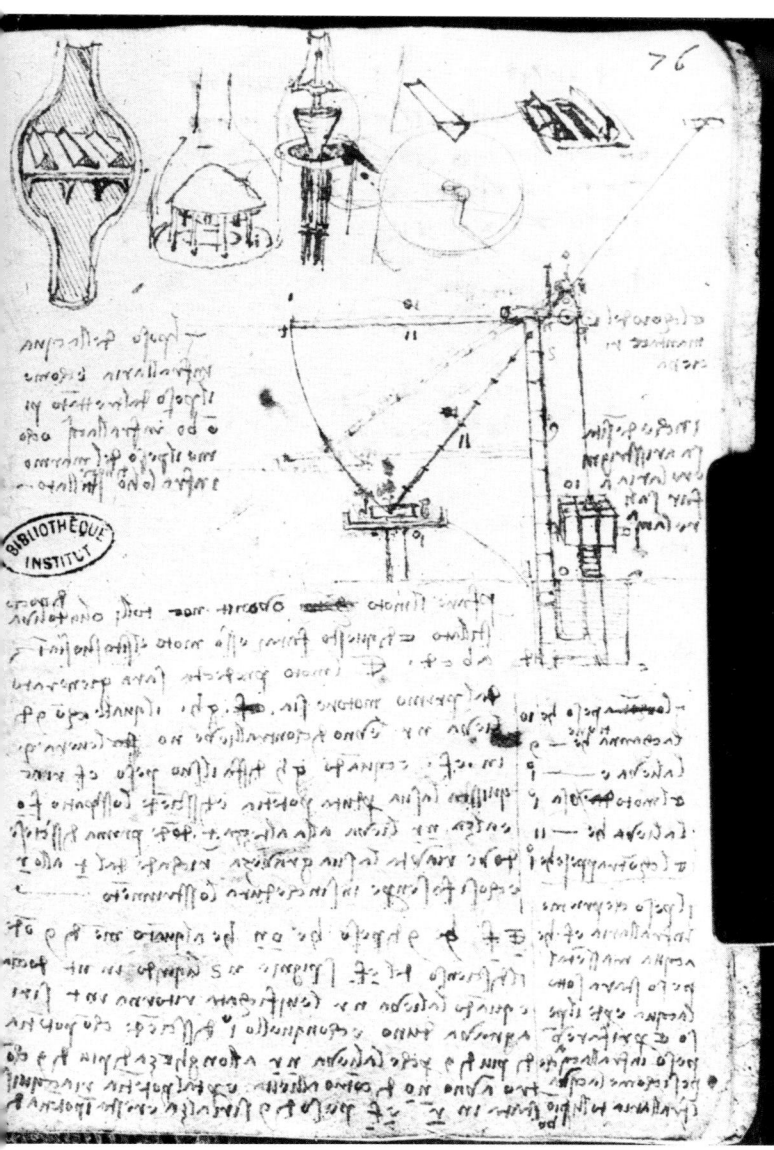

Design for a dredger and various hydraulic
machines from *Paris Manuscript E*

Projets d'un excavateur et de divers engins
hydrauliques, tirés du *Manuscrit E de Paris*

Entwurf eines Schaufelbaggers und
verschiedener hydraulischer Geräte,
aus dem *Pariser Manuskript E*

Diseño de una draga excavadora y de diversos
aparatos hidráulicos, del *manuscrito parisino E*

Disegno di una draga e diverse macchine
idrauliche, dal *manoscritto parigino E*

Ontwerp voor een emmerbaggermolen
en verschillende hydraulische apparaten,
uit het *Parijse Manuscript E*

*1513/14, Pen and ink on paper/Plume et encre sur
papier, Bibliothèque de l'Institut de France, Paris*

215

Recommended Literature

Kenneth Clark, *Leonardo da Vinci. An Account of His Development as an Artist,* Cambridge 1952

Martin Kemp, *Leonardo,* Oxford, 2005

Shana Priwer/Cynthia Phillips, *The Everything Da Vinci Book: Explore the Life and Times of the Ultimate Renaissance Man,* Cincinnati, OH 2006

Littérature recommandée

Lucia Aquino (dir.), *Léonard de Vinci,* Paris, 2005

Daniel Arasse, *Léonard de Vinci,* Paris, 2011

Sophie Chauveau, *Léonard de Vinci,* Paris, 2008

Kenneth Clark, *Léonard de Vinci,* Paris, 2005

Francesca Debolini, *Léonard de Vinci,* Paris, 2000

Jean-Claude Frère, *Léonard de Vinci,* Paris, 2001

Charles Nicholl, *Léonard de Vinci,* Paris, 2006

Frank Zöllner, *Léonard de Vinci (1452–1519) : Tout l'œuvre peint et graphique,* Cologne, 2005

Literaturempfehlungen

Daniel Arasse, *Leonardo da Vinci und seine Welt,* Bayreuth 1982

Kenneth Clark, *Leonardo da Vinci,* Hamburg 1969

Francesca Debolini, *Leonardo da Vinci,* Köln 1999

Alessandra Fregolent, *Leonardo. Das Universalgenie,* Berlin 2003

Jean-Claude Frère, *Leonardo da Vinci,* Frechen 2001

Martin Kemp, *Leonardo,* München 2005

Charles Nicholl, *Leonardo da Vinci. Die Biographie,* Frankfurt/M. 2009

Frank Zöllner, *Leonardo,* Köln 2005